This lucid and wide-ranging survey is the first study in English to identify a distinctive urban phase in the history of the early modern crowd.

Through close analysis of the behavior of protestors and authorities in more than fifteen seventeenth-century cities, Professor Beik explores a full spectrum of urban dissidence, from spontaneous individual actions to factional conflicts, princely parties and major popular uprisings, culminating in the dramatic Ormée movement in Bordeaux. The "culture of retribution" was a form of popular politics with roots in the religious wars and implications for future democratic movements. Community-based crowds stoned and pillaged not only intrusive tax collectors but even their own magistrates, whom they viewed as civic traitors. The authorities, torn between royal dictates and the imperatives of local governance, were unable to respond effectively because of flawed local power structures. By exploring in depth this interaction of crowds and authorities, the author makes a centrally important contribution to the study of absolute monarchy, urban power structures, contentious movements, and popular culture.

Urban protest in seventeenth-century France

The place des Terreaux and the hôtel de ville of Lyon in the seventeenth century, by R. Pigout. This building was completed in 1655 and modified by Mansart in 1674. Although it postdates the principal disturbances of the 1630s, the picture captures some of the bustle of Lyon's central square.

Urban protest in seventeenth-century France

The culture of retribution

William Beik

Associate Professor of History, Emory University

CAMBRIDGE
UNIVERSITY PRESS

Published by the Press Syndicate of the University of Cambridge
The Pitt Building, Trumpington Street, Cambridge CB2 1RP
40 West 20th Street, New York, NY 10011-4211, USA
10 Stamford Road, Oakleigh, Melbourne 3166, Australia

First published 1997

Printed in Great Britain at the University Press, Cambridge

A catalogue record for this book is available from the British Library

Library of Congress cataloguing in publication data

Beik, William, 1941–
    Urban protest in seventeenth-century France : the culture of
retribution / William Beik.
      p.   cm.
    Includes bibliographical references.
    ISBN 0-521-57308-4 (hc). – ISBN 0-521-57585-0 (pbk).
    1. France–History–Louis XIV, 1643–1715–Religious aspects.
2. Huguenots–France–History–17th century. 3. Protest movements –
France–History–17th century. I. Title.
DC126.B45   1997
944′ .033–dc20   96-2951
                                                        CIP

ISBN 0 521 57308 4 hardback
ISBN 0 521 57585 0 paperback

For Millie

Contents

Illustrations

Tables

Acknowledgments

This project has taken many years and incurred many obligations. It was developed during a fruitful semester spent as Fellow of the Shelby Cullom Davis Center at Princeton in the autumn of 1974. It was generously supported by the people of the United States through a Younger Humanist Fellowship from the National Endowment for the Humanities in 1974–5 and a Summer Stipend from the same source in 1986, and by Grants-in-Aid from the American Council of Learned Societies in 1974 and 1984, Summer Grants from Northern Illinois University in 1984, 1985, and 1988, a Research Grant from the American Philosophical Society in 1987, and sabbatical leaves of absence from Northern Illinois University (1977, 1987) and Emory University (1993).

The late Nancy Roelker was constant in her support and Charles Tilly, who seemed to have preceded me in every archive, was helpful beyond all call of duty. Robert Descimon was generous with his expertise and an invitation to the EHESS. Christian Jouhaud shared his knowledge of seventeenth-century Bordeaux. Yves-Marie Bercé was extremely gracious despite our differences of perspective. I am indebted to the courteous staffs of a great many departmental and municipal archives, and especially to Monsieur Avisseau, Conservateur des Archives Municipales de Bordeaux, to Jean Burias, Directeur, and Lucille Bourrachot, archiviste, in the Archives de Lot-et-Garonne, and to Jean-Marc Roger, Directeur des Archives de l'Aube. Julius Ruff advised me on life in Bordeaux and John Hurt did the same for Rennes; Gregory Hanlon introduced me to the bastides of the Agenais.

I am also grateful for suggestions or encouragement from Perry Anderson, Robert Brenner, Carl Kauffman, Eric Kauffman, Jean Nicolas, Christiane Passevent, Larry Portis, Richard Price, the History Department at UCLA, the History Department and the Graduate School at Northern Illinois University, and the James Vann Seminar at Emory University. The manuscript was greatly improved by the careful readings of David Hunt, Jamie Melton, and David Paradis. Colleagues have been especially supportive. At Northern Illinois these included Thomas

Blomquist, Ralph Bowen, C. H. George, Meg George, Pierre Gravel, Stephen Kern, Carroll Moody, Otto Olsen, Marvin Rosen, and Jack Weiner; at Emory, Thomas Burns, Margot Finn, Russell Major, Judith Miller, Jonathan Prude, James Roark, Sharon Strocchia, and Steve White. Amy Enright spent many hours on the bibliography. Richard Fisher, who invented the title, was an exemplary editor. The anonymous reader for Cambridge University Press pointed out some important corrections. I am also grateful to the editors of *Social History* for permission to reprint sections of my article "The Culture of Protest in Seventeenth-Century French Towns," 15 (1990), 1–23, and to the editors of *French Historical Studies* for permission to reprint part of my article "Urban Factions and the Social Order during the Minority of Louis XIV," 15 (1987), 36–67. The entire project is dedicated to Millie Beik in memory of Winston, an old dog who had his own style of retribution.

Urban protest

Protest was a distinctive feature of life in seventeenth-century French cities.[1] It took a variety of forms ranging from isolated grumblings to clandestine threats, gatherings of angry citizens, harassment of targeted scapegoats, rock throwing, pillaging, seizures of public places, armed forays through the streets, expulsions of purported traitors, sometimes mutilations or murders. Such activity was not experienced every day, but it was frequent enough to represent an ubiquitous danger in the minds of authorities who knew full well that small incidents lay on one end of a spectrum leading to full-scale insurrection. In this sense genuinely popular protest constituted a significant aspect of the everyday political landscape. Its place in urban life was further complicated by the fact that not all protest was genuinely popular in origin. Some public demonstrations were actually factional quarrels generated by elites. Thus the overlapping of people attacking authorities and factions fighting other factions formed a complex pattern which calls for close examination.

Each case comes to us as a story involving a confrontation. When many such stories are read in succession, a picture begins to emerge of the possibilities and limits of popular politics in an urban setting under absolutism. Public disturbances expressed relationships. They were dialogues about power: how it was held, how it could be challenged, how it ought to be used. These dialogues were especially important in the seventeenth century because social equilibrium was built upon the ritual interaction between the symbolic authority of magistrates and the collective pride of popular groups. Each confrontation thus tells us something

---

[1] The most intelligent surveys of this phenomenon are Robin Briggs, "Popular Revolt in its Social Context," in *Communities of Belief: Cultural and Social Tension in Early Modern France* (Oxford, 1989), pp. 106–77; and Christian Jouhaud, "Révoltes et contestations d'ancien régime," in André Burguière and Jacques Revel (eds.), *L'état et les conflits* [vol. III of *Histoire de la France*] (Paris, 1990), pp. 21–99. The Soviet book that inaugurated the study of French popular protest was Boris Porchnev, Les *soulèvements populaires en France de 1623 à 1648* (Paris, 1963). The counterattack by Roland Mousnier and some of the subsequent discussion are well presented in P. J. Coveney (ed.), *France in Crisis 1629–1675* (Totowa, NJ, 1977).

about the boundaries of community solidarity and the nature of community conflict. Studied as a body of experience, these incidents chart the limits of practical authority and the possibility of rebellion, the prospects for popular-elite collaboration and the possibility of class conflict.

Argenteuil, 1644

But the stories have to be reconstructed from one-sided narratives filled with repetitive situations and stereotyped judgments.[2] Here is one example. On 29 July 1644 Hierosme Regnard, a Parisian process-server, was sent on a mission to the town of Argenteuil some ten miles north of the capital.[3] His task was to enforce payments owed for the *greffe des notaires*, a royal office attributing special fees to notaries that had been created by the king in 1640 as a money-raising expedient. Large numbers of these *greffes* had been authorized on paper and the right to peddle them or collect their fees had been sold to cartels of financiers who subcontracted out these rights in each district of France. Regnard's task was thus to make tangible to the people of Argenteuil the effects of a deal struck between the state and its financial backers by collecting fees they owed. Although just a process-server, he was powerfully connected. He carried in his sack a variety of papers relating to the affairs of important tax farmers, agents of royal ministers, and local people, including a roll of sums totalling 1,200 livres to be collected for another tax, the *amortissement*. Thus although his superiors are not identified in the documents, he was a functionary doing legal work for Parisians of some importance.

Regnard set out with two sergeants, Hemard de Hedin from the bailliage of Fort Levêque and Jean de Foy from Paris. They worked vigorously for two days in Argenteuil, issuing warrants to some eighty residents and sequestering many items of property. These men must have been highly visible in their judicial regalia as they rapped on doors and read lengthy legal pronouncements to each offender. Some residents barred their entry or made threatening remarks, but they still accumulated a considerable body of confiscated property which they left in the custody

---

[2] On interpreting popular discourse, see Natalie Zemon Davis, *Fiction in the Archives: Pardon Tales and their Tellers in Sixteenth-Century France* (Stanford, 1987); Arlette Farge, *Subversive Words: Public Opinion in Eighteenth-Century France*, tr. Rosemary Harris (University Park, PA, 1994); Clay Ramsay, *The Ideology of the Great Fear: the Soissonnais in 1789* (Baltimore, 1992), pp. 123–55.
[3] BN Ms. fr. 18432, fol. 3: procès-verbal 1 August 1644. Argenteuil was a substantial town with a population of 1,020 hearths in 1709, according to Jacques Dupâquier, *Statistiques démographiques du bassin parisien 1636–1720* (Paris, 1977), p. 415.

Figure 1 France in the seventeenth century: provinces and towns.

of neighbors, pending sale at auction. Much of it was deposited with the local innkeeper, Pierre Gentil, whose establishment also served as a base of operations. Satisfied with a job well done, the three were settling in for the night when they were accosted at the door of the inn by Denis Pernet and several other unidentified local men. "You bloody extortionists [*bougres de maltôtiers*]," growled Pernet, "you've been having a fine time these last two days but tomorrow . . . you will be nicely awakened and thrown in the river, even if I have to ring the tocsin myself." Night was falling and it was too late to return to Paris.

Sure enough, Regnard and his assistants awoke to trouble. Before they could pay their bill, two messengers from the community barged in and addressed them ceremoniously as if the drama that was to follow required a formal prologue. "Mordieu, bloody extortionists," they cursed, "your bodies are about to be degraded: here come more than five hundred persons to cut you to pieces." Then a large crowd came pouring out of the church. The innkeeper and his wife, fearing that their building would be burned down, urged Regnard to escape out the back, but it was too late. The house and garden filled with men shouting "Kill! Kill!" or "Drag him to the river!" while Regnard and his assistants barricaded themselves in their room. Even as Regnard attempted to reason with his assailants through the locked door, he could hear the sound of their axes smashing it down while another contingent chopped a hole in the wall and a third started tearing up the beams in the attic overhead. Rushing to the window, Regnard saw "4,000" angry citizens massed in the street, some pelting his window with rocks, others looking for fire to burn down the building.[4] Then the besiegers poured in and started pummeling the three victims with clubs. Finding the large sack in which Regnard carried his legal documents, the pillagers threw it out the window to the people below, who tore up the papers and scattered them about, saying "Here is the sack of the *maltôte*: it must be burned with the extortionists [*maltôtiers*] who own it."

Both sergeants were dragged down the stairs and out into the street by their hair. Hedin fell to his knees, pleading for mercy: "Messieurs, save my life, please forgive me, I will pray to the Lord for you, I promise I will never return here"; but the crowd shouted "Drag him! Drag him! Throw him in the river: at least that will teach others not to come to this place with the maltôte!" He was rescued when a group of soldiers lodging nearby took pity on him. Foy was similarly dragged and beaten until he broke away from his captors and darted into a pastry shop where the master pastrycook and his apprentices tried to hold the door shut while he escaped out the back. He was recaptured and knocked down; then he pretended he was dead and escaped into some vines when the crowd wasn't looking. After hiding out until midnight, he staggered out of town and hitched a ride back to Paris on a merchant's cart.

Meanwhile back in his room, Regnard was being manhandled by the ringleaders of the attack, who tore his clothes, demanded his money and weapons, and reminded him sanctimoniously of the purpose of their visit: "Didn't we promise you yesterday evening that you wouldn't want to live?" Their dialogue, as reported by Regnard, has a ring of folklore about it:

[4] A crowd of 4,000 would have approximated the entire population of Argenteuil.

REGNARD My dear brothers, I beg you to save my life. I assure you that I am a man
who can serve you just as easily as I can retaliate against you for the "pleasure" you have given me in this situation.

ASSAILANTS You bugger, you're pretty brazen and insolent to come to this *pays*
and collect for the *notifications*. Don't you know that they will never be paid
and whoever comes here will be killed?

REGNARD Brothers, if it hadn't been me who came here it would have been
someone else. But I promise you I will never come back.

ASSAILANTS Don't you know that you're never going to leave this *pays*, because
twelve of the richest men from here promised us ten pistoles to drag you into
the water, you and your companions. But if you want to give us [the money],
we'll leave you here.

Regnard's captors then took his 55 livres, he claimed, along with swords,
sheets, handkerchiefs, hats, and Hedin's coat, and left.

As soon as they were gone Regnard climbed out a window with the help
of the women of the house who urged, "My poor man, save yourself, they
are coming back and this time they'll kill you." He mounted a ladder to a
neighbor's attic and hid for several hours while the angry crowd returned.
Then he made his way through vineyards to a neighboring village, while
off in the distance he heard a large crowd searching for him in a nearby
mill. In the end, all three agents made it back to Paris, where they drew up
their reports and the two sergeants were examined by a surgeon, who
found them "badly beaten."

What can this story, insignificant in itself, tell us? Regnard was an
unimportant agent who had to assert a modicum of authority against
inhabitants of an insignificant place who didn't want to obey. People did
not always resist in this way. If they had, government under absolutism
would have been impossible. In fact, we would not even know about
Regnard if his report had not been filed in the papers of Pierre Séguier,
chancellor of France. Thus on the one hand the case was unusual enough
to warrant the attention of the royal government, but on the other there
were probably many other Argenteuils that never produced this fortuitous documentation.

In a different way, however, as a piece of a larger picture, Argenteuil is
important. Regnard's account gives us a rare insider's view of an experience that happened to a great many authority figures – messengers,
judges, tax collectors, magistrates, intendants, hoarders of grain. He was
treated to a performance that was classic in its simplicity, that resonated
with the expression of popular values and tactics. The real confrontation
was between a complex of social and financial special interests protected
under the mantle of royal legitimacy and a group of townspeople indignant to the point of rage at the actions of an interloper. The protestors'
responses were also characteristic. The formal warnings and curses, the

siege of the inn, the ritual of dragging victims through the streets and dumping them in the river, the attempt to purge the community of an outsider who at the same time was to serve as an example so that "nobody would come to this place with the maltôte," the destruction of legal papers – all these were elements repeated in thousands of other independent situations.

Violence was real and significant, but also limited. People in French communities did sometimes pillage, dismember, and murder persons who directly represented the interests of the powerful, and this was a reality faced by every agent, one which we struggle to understand. At the same time the action was improvised and collective and governed by complex unwritten constraints. We sense in Regnard's account a combination of forces. There was a circle of instigators – leading citizens who, if the account is truthful, promised bounties to less fortunate neighbors to intimidate the invaders. But the movement was broader and more spontaneous than an arranged assassination. There was real popular mobilization: a growing indignation after two days of observed offenses, a meeting in the church, a crowd of sympathetic demonstrators who shouted, surrounded, attacked, and pursued without much evident organization. But there was also support for Regnard from citizens who received sequestered goods, issued sympathetic warnings, and helped the offenders to escape. The community was in no sense unanimous. Not everyone joined the lynching party, whether because of fear, indifference, or vested interest. The unspoken restraint is the most interesting aspect of the affair. Despite the intense hatred expressed by the crowd and the clear intent to do harm, the actual confrontation was anti-climactic. The angry citizens seemed disorganized and reticent about going all the way, and the victims escaped with only cuts and bruises.

Why did a potential lynch mob end up administering nothing more than a stern warning, and why did the three process-servers not end up at the bottom of a well like some of their compatriots? The answer can only be found by studying other instances which extend the evidence of possible actions and outcomes. Comparison makes it possible to delineate a spectrum of options and to construct a typology of the culture of protest despite the limited evidence in any given instance.

Approaching urban protest

There are many ways to study popular protest, and my approach is based on a particular set of choices that should be made clear from the outset. This is a study of "culture" in the sense that every confrontation entailed repetitive forms of behavior. In the clash between the two or more sides we see a range of gestures, tactics, slogans, and beliefs that had meaning for the participants because they were drawn from a repertory of similar actions undertaken in parallel circumstances. It is by pondering and comparing those responses that I attempt to understand how people mobilized, how they conceptualized their actions, and what their interaction tells us about governance and class relationships in the city. Since all information derives from the reports of the authorities, it is necessary to delineate their position very carefully, as I do in chapters 4 and 5. But my primary concern is to bring the people of French cities onto the stage and give them their due, without condescension but also without romanticization, as important participants in this very human drama.

Historians have used many approaches in studying revolts, all of them valuable. The first, which might be called conjunctural analysis, focuses on the incidence of revolt as a way of determining its nature. By plotting the frequency or the geographical distribution of disturbances, one can find correlations to factors such as grain prices, tax levels, wars, or the chronology of state development. One can also plot the time of day, the time of year, and the site within the city as indicators of the patterns of disturbance in relation to cycles of work, cycles of festivity, residential patterns, and so forth. This technique, used extensively by Yves-Marie Bercé and René Pillorget, is frequently invoked also by synthesizers who seek to find meaning in the pattern of revolt over time.[5]

The second approach, especially associated with Bercé and the many who adopt his conclusions, classifies crowds in terms of their objectives: religious purification, opposition to taxes, regulation of prices, reassertion of community values, protest against soldiers.[6] Its merit is the ability to classify and simplify; its limitation is that it separates crowds into distinct compartments, obscuring aspects that were common to several kinds of riots and losing sight of crowd methods and underlying beliefs. A variation is the attempt by historical sociologists like Charles Tilly to link the purposes of crowds to broad changes like the rise of the state or the rise of

[5] Yves-Marie Bercé, *History of Peasant Revolts: the Social Origins of Rebellion in Early Modern France*, tr. Amanda Whitmore (Ithaca, NY, 1990), which is an abridgment of *Histoire des Croquants: étude des soulèvements populaires au XVIIe siècle dans le sud-ouest de la France*, 2 vols. (Geneva, 1974); René Pillorget, *Les mouvements insurrectionnels de Provence entre 1596 et 1715* (Paris, 1975). Of course most authors use more than one approach.
[6] In Bercé, *History of Peasant Revolts*, pp. 169–243, this typology is explicit. For the dissemination of such ideas, see Pierre Goubert, *The French Peasantry in the Seventeenth Century*, tr. Ian Patterson (Cambridge, 1986), pp. 205–19. On types of riots, see Natalie Zemon Davis, "The Rites of Violence," in *Society and Culture in Early Modern France* (Stanford, 1975), pp. 152–87; Cynthia A. Bouton, *The Flour War: Gender, Class and Community in Late Ancien Regime French Society* (University Park, PA, 1993); François Hincker, *Les français devant l'impôt sous l'ancien régime* (Paris, 1971).

capitalism by tracing a historical transition from one type of crowd to another and seeing the forms taken by crowd action as a reflection of the changes taking place in society.[7]

The third approach is to analyze the sociology of the participants. Who were the rioters, where did they live, what were their occupations, their income levels, their titles, their citizenship status, their links of family and patronage, their common membership in organizations? This technique, closely associated with George Rudé and utilized by many practitioners, requires better evidence than most seventeenth-century archives can provide, and raises methodological problems. Historians are increasingly wary of systems of social stratification because the "boxes" they put people in are arbitrary, and there is not always a connection between an individual's label and his or her social identity.[8]

The fourth approach, crowd psychology, views the group of demonstrators as an organism with an irrational life of its own that transcended the independent will of the participants, or drew them into patterns of behavior that they would not have chosen as individuals. When treated in the manner of Gustave Le Bon and his modern successors, this approach has very little relevance for early modern crowds.[9] But when the group of demonstrators is analyzed anthropologically in terms of the meaning of their collective attitudes towards violence, ritual, and belief, in the manner of Natalie Davis or Robert Muchembled, the process is much more fruitful, though still subject to methodological challenge.[10] It then merges into a fifth, more ideological approach which measures crowds against an ideal form of consciousness or sees them as manifestations of a particular set of social relationships. Here we have on the one hand Roland Mousnier and his "society of orders" and on the other the "class

[7] The classic example is Charles Tilly, *The Contentious French: Four Centuries of Popular Struggle* (Cambridge, MA, 1986); another is Emmanuel Le Roy Ladurie, "Révoltes et contestations rurales en France de 1675 à 1788," *Annales ESC* 29 (1974), 6–22.

[8] George Rudé, *The Crowd in the French Revolution* (Oxford, 1959) and many other works. A sophisticated analysis of the sociology of a single community is Emmanuel Le Roy Ladurie, *Carnival in Romans*, tr. Mary Feeney (New York, 1979).

[9] On the Le Bon tradition, see Serge Moscovici, *The Age of the Crowd: a Historical Treatise on Crowd Psychology* (Cambridge, 1985). For a critique, see Anthony Oberschall, *Social Conflict and Social Movements* (Englewood Cliffs, NJ, 1973); Clark McPhail, *The Myth of the Madding Crowd* (New York, 1991). A recent sociological synthesis is Sidney Tarrow, *Power in Movement: Social Movements, Collective Action and Politics* (Cambridge, 1994).

[10] Natalie Zemon Davis, "The Reasons of Misrule," in *Society and Culture*, pp. 97–123; Robert Muchembled, *La violence au village: sociétés et mentalités dans la France moderne, 16e-18e siècle* (Paris, 1989); Le Roy Ladurie, *Carnival in Romans*, pp. 289–324; Steven G. Reinhardt, *Justice in the Sarladais 1770–1790* (Baton Rouge, LA, 1991); Denis Crouzet, *Les guerriers de Dieu: la violence au temps des troubles de religion (vers 1525–vers 1610)*, 2 vols. (Seyssel, 1990).

conflict" of Boris Porchnev or the more nuanced and "cultur
analysis of E. P. Thompson and his many admirers.[11]

My approach borrows from all of these methods but privileges certain
elements and downplays others. By focusing on behavior during revolts
and thus on the cultural interaction between protesters and authorities, I
highlight forms of social solidarity and conflict in the context of the functioning of the political process. I concentrate on urban revolts because of
their intrinsic interest. Peasant movements lasted for weeks or months,
mobilized large numbers of communities, and generated regional assemblies with broad sets of demands. As a result they have made a greater
impression on historians.[12] By contrast urban disturbances tend to seem
like colorful diversions with no long-term significance except in the
aggregate. They appear episodic, attack only selected targets, and last for
brief periods of time. Nevertheless urban revolts provide a rich window
on urban society. They challenged resident political authorities directly
and stirred up issues of political rivalry, civic loyalty, and class consciousness. In the narrow streets of the city it was common for many constituencies – guild masters, militia companies, neighborhood leaders, priests,
local judges, women, children, the poor, municipal magistrates, sovereign
court judges, intendants, governors – to confront one another face to face
and also to interact. These multiple layers of authorities were unique to
the city, as were the tribunals, grain depots, hôtels de ville, townhouses,
and shops that were often targeted. I have drawn no artificial line between
urban and rural; nor have I hesitated to use evidence from smaller places
when it seemed appropriate, as I have just done with Argenteuil. But this
book is about town life, not peasant armies.

Another choice involves coverage. I set out initially to locate a wide
range of well-documented cases without following any rigorous principle
of selection. It was more important to find well-documented cases which
provided narratives from several perspectives than it was to achieve an
ideal chronological or geographical balance. I ended up doing research in
about twenty provincial cities and adding scattered materials from other
places as well. I did not tackle Paris, where the sources are extremely dispersed and the situation in the capital was arguably unique. My time

[11] E. P. Thompson, "The Moral Economy of the English Crowd in the Eighteenth
Century," *Past and Present* 50 (Feb. 1971), 76–136; reproduced with a new commentary in
Customs in Common: Studies in Traditional Popular Culture (New York, 1993); for Mousnier
and Porchnev see note 1, along with Roland Mousnier, *Peasant Uprisings in France, Russia
and China*, tr. Brian Pearce (New York, 1970) and Madeleine Foisil, *La révolte des Nu-
Pieds et les révoltes normandes de 1639* (Paris, 1970).
[12] For example, J. H. M. Salmon, "Peasant Revolt in Vivarais, 1575–1580," *French Historical
Studies* 11 (1979), 1–28; Bercé, *Les Croquants*; Mousnier, *Peasant Uprisings*; Yvon Garlan
and Claude Nières (eds.), *Les révoltes bretonnes de 1675* (Paris, 1975).

period, ranging from the 1590s to the end of the reign of Louis XIV, was also informally chosen. It represents an era in the history of power structures, but probably not a distinct phase in the history of popular culture.

Once in the archives, I searched as widely as possible. I explored municipal council records, often for many years on either side of the crucial events. I looked as far as possible into the parallel sessions of law courts, the correspondence of governmental agents, memoirs of eyewitnesses, criminal proceedings, and anything else that looked promising. Thus I used all the main sources that describe who did what and how the authorities responded. However, my coverage was not exhaustive. After the richest lodes of material had been mined, there were still notarial archives, tax records, and parish registers, any of which could have yielded additional facts about the material background of individual participants, their family relations, and their connections to one another. I did not explore these sources systematically. A specialist studying one city or one revolt can always glean additional insights from such material, but the student of the culture of popular protest rapidly faces diminishing returns.

In work of this kind the construction of "what happened" becomes critical, and establishing an informed narrative is half the battle. The evidence is always contradictory because the eyewitness narrators had their own axes to grind and because they were not very precise about matters that seemed of no importance to them such as where the crowd went first, what they said when, and who fired what weapon. But such details can be crucial to understanding the significance of a confrontation. The analyst has to decide which version to believe concerning each individual aspect by evaluating each reporter's consistency, degree of detail, source of knowledge and motivation and by factoring in a developing personal sense of the way such incidents unfolded. It is perfectly possible for good historians to disagree on these judgments of detail, and the choices they make are inevitably influenced by their priorities.

When we turn to secondary accounts, the problem is even more acute. Many of the revolts I discuss have been written up before, but careful examination demonstrates that such narratives, even the best of them, contain chronological condensations and interpretive choices that obscure essential clues. For this reason I followed a policy of going directly to the sources of each major disturbance studied, leaving out even famous cases if I could only approach them through secondary writings.[13] The accounts that follow represent a scrupulous reconstruction of what I

---

[13] Thus I do not discuss the Nu-Pieds of Normandy (1639) despite the importance of this revolt.

believe to be the most plausible sequence of events in each case, based on long pondering of all the evidence. This is not to say that they are necessarily "correct" or that some other version might not be equally plausible.

A perfect illustration of the problem of interpretation is the *procès-verbal*, one of the principal sources of documentation about popular protest. This standard category of legal report – for example the one Regnard drew up about Argenteuil – was a blow by blow description designed to justify the conduct of the narrator, to incriminate those who had committed illegal acts, or to certify that certain legal steps had been taken. These documents give us invaluable details: the narrator got the news in such and such a place at such and such at time, proceeded to the scene, found people saying and doing certain things, issued commands, got responses, and so forth. But they are myopic. The reporter records only what he personally experienced and only what he considered relevant to his legal purpose. He always omits the broader context, writing of the event as if it had come out of nowhere: "I was sleeping in my bed when a crowd of angry women suddenly pounded on the door." And he fails to present the other side of the story. Regnard does not tell us that there had been prior trouble in Argenteuil, although documents accompanying his report suggest that this was the case, and he fails to report any valid reasons the residents might have had for their actions.[14] If we had *their* procès-verbal, it would probably detail insults uttered by Regnard, illicit seizures, and procedural irregularities, and it would minimize the violence, making it look as if the villagers had simply been defending their rights against outrageous provocations. When both accounts do exist there is no way to tell which side was telling the truth. Procès-verbaux can provide precious information about social interaction, such as what the crowd was saying and doing, provided we look for details that the reporter took for granted and collect as much parallel and contradictory testimony as possible. In this way we can learn quite a bit about how crowds typically acted without necessarily ever knowing for sure what "really happened" in a given instance.

The data for this study is thus a collection of carefully read instances of popular protest, ranging from the most spontaneous incident to the most complex political struggle. Analyzing this evidence entails a considerable amount of interpretive intuition. Intentions have to be derived from descriptions of action. Small clues seen in gestures, slogans, the direction of a crowd, or a sequence of events have to be taken as indicators of motivation. In the absence of personal testimony from popular

[14] The documentation makes it clear that there had been earlier problems in Argenteuil in April.

demonstrators, *how* they did what they did becomes very important. It also becomes necessary to transfer insights from one situation to another on the assumption that collective action had continuities between different times and places. What we learn about the process of guarding the ramparts, the way a crowd denounced its enemies, or how a posted denunciation was displayed *in one city* is applied *in another city*. Seen in this way, the various uprisings become themes with variations. What we cannot know about one event is supplied by another, and gradually they form a composite picture of all the possibilities.

Is it valid to treat urban revolts this way, as a single body of experience? When I started to expand outward from my earlier work in Languedoc to other provinces, I wondered whether there were regional traditions of revolt that might invalidate such transference. I soon concluded that while there were local variations, the similarities far outweighed the differences, whether one was in Artois, the Ile de France, or Provence. Crowds acted in parallel fashion because their towns had similar features and authority structures, their populations led similar sorts of lives, and they shared a wider culture which had common forms of thought and behavior.

In the chapters that follow I endeavor to explore the way protesters and authorities interacted. I proceed from the most simple form of protest, a momentary flareup of anger, to increasingly complex kinds of organization and communication. I do not proceed chronologically, and I jump from place to place, linking together incidents that are distant in time and space but close to each other in form, even when this process causes the history of particular localities to become fractured. For example, I discuss the Bordeaux revolt of 1675 in the chapter before the Bordeaux revolt of 1648–52 because the latter was more sophisticated than the former.

In addition to this increasing complexity, I also try to delineate different forms of elite–popular interaction. This is a complex subject that requires careful distinctions. It is relatively easy to identify small popular outbursts that were completely spontaneous and coups that were entirely managed "from above." But most episodes involved mixed motives on all sides, and there was no simple "above" and "below." The "people" consisted not of an undifferentiated mass but of overlapping sub-communities of individuals with many kinds of personal linkages. The "elite" were more clearly distinguishable as the limited circle of families possessing influence over public issues; but they too were divided into magistrates holding office through the city hall, officers holding office through royal appointment, military commanders with noble pedigrees who held governorships and army positions, and local clan leaders who might dominate client systems without holding official positions.

There were classic popular uprisings in which the majority of the community turned against their own elites who, in turn, fought tooth and nail to defend their hegemony. There were other cases where the magistrates were trapped into enforcing measures that they really disliked and that compromised them with their own populations. There were cases where factions of leaders took arms against each other, drawing popular supporters along with them. And there were cases where local groups became tied to outside parties following princely leaders. The following chapters explore each of these possibilities. All of them involve relationships between upper-class authorities and protesting common people, but the nature of the relationship varies in different kinds of situations, as does the degree of popular spontaneity and the intensity of the threat to the social order. I argue that these distinctions are important and can be derived from the protest behavior itself. But my real focus is on the protesters: what they wanted, how they tried to get it, and to what extent they were able to influence a system of power that was designed to exclude them.

The setting and the people

The cities were crowded, exciting places. Each had a distinctive topography that influenced the style of its revolts, but all had certain features in common.[15] Most important was the wall that separated the urban unit from the surrounding faubourgs and countryside. Punctuated by gates leading outward in various directions, the wall was a liminal boundary devoted to contradictory purposes. On the one hand gates were official checkpoints for authorities monitoring those entering the city and for tax farmers collecting duties on merchandise. On the other they were familiar passageways where popular sentinels could watch for the arrival of dreaded government messengers and persons wanted for rebellion could escape out into the countryside. The massive portals were guarded with varying degrees of nonchalance by gatekeepers. They were shut at night and during disturbances to contain the trouble or to keep out reinforcements from the surrounding villages. But despite the special keys jealously guarded by principal magistrates, gates were always vulnerable to infiltration, and fear of nocturnal treason if someone let in the enemy was invariably a powerful mover of public opinion in times of trouble. The

[15] The best general works on early modern French cities are Bernard Chevalier, *Les bonnes villes de France du XIVe au XVIe siècle* (Paris, 1982); Jean-Pierre Leguay, *La rue au Moyen Age* (Rennes, 1984); Emmanuel Le Roy Ladurie (ed.), *La ville classique* [vol. III of Georges Duby (ed.), *Histoire de la France urbaine*] (Paris, 1981); Philip Benedict (ed.), *Cities and Social Change in Early Modern France* (London, 1989).

ramparts provided platforms from which to observe the surrounding countryside as well as settings for promenades and surreptitious meetings. They were patrolled at night by militia companies which might introduce an element of order or disorder, depending on circumstances. Outside the walls open ditches served as playing fields for rival gangs of youths or as meeting places and garbage dumps.

Most towns had several poles of authority. First there was the *hôtel de ville*, focal point of civic pride, from which the échevins and their committees of notables governed the city. This was usually an older, historic building steeped in tradition in which could be found a jumble of meeting rooms, courts, archives, and prisons, and which frequently had a belfry from which a symbolic tocsin could be rung in times of danger. The hôtel de ville was treated like a fortress, but it was usually poorly supplied and badly defended. In front of it might be some sort of open space where crowds could mass, but such squares were usually quite small in the seventeenth century. Leading up to the central square were the main "avenues" down which protesters might storm and across which insurgents frequently built barricades. But before the great urbanization projects begun under Louis XIV these too were cramped and narrow. Other municipal spaces included market squares where diverse crowds of people were frequently assembled, churches, which served a variety of purposes, and cemeteries. Ecclesiastical establishments could be havens of calm where gardens, cloisters, and outbuildings clustered behind sheltering walls and where the religious might sympathize with subversive views or, more often, harbor spies and organize gestures to pacify unruly populations. The *hôtels* of the great were likewise places where the elite could gather and discuss strategies, although their meetings were never unobserved by the people in the street.

Another likely pole of attraction was the seat of the chief royal court, whether a senéchaussée, présidial or parlement. Like the hôtel de ville, this consisted of a building, a body of judges, and a collection of supporting personnel. Such jurisdictions usually had their prisons right in their main buildings. These were thus readily accessible and usually badly guarded. The cathedral with adjacent bishop's palace could be another authority center. In cities of some importance these various centers were often dispersed, representing rival points of reference for official processions, or conversely for protesting crowds.

Streets were winding and narrow, in the older and denser quarters lined with houses of several stories, sometimes with overhanging roofs. Their courtyards and back alleys, as well as their aerial proximity, provided a maze of passageways through which threatened officials or pursued rebels could escape "over the roofs" or "through the rear entrance" or "into the

Figure 2 Street in Amiens near the church of Saint Sulpice, as sketched in 1854 by Aimé or Louis Duthoit. This nineteenth-century view captures the ambiance of a popular neighborhood not unlike those in seventeenth-century cities.

cemetery next door." The popular quarters were teeming with workshops on the ground floors, their projects spilling out into streets and court-yards. These streets were second nature to the people who used them: they knew shortcuts and escape routes and they were cognizant of the location of grain stores and the houses of prominent citizens, sometimes even to the extent of knowing where particular individuals had gone at a given moment. When important strangers came to town it was known what inn they were staying at; and word always got out – sometimes accurately, sometimes not – concerning who they were and what they were doing. Citizens were also well informed concerning what business was transacted in which buildings, what ships were in the harbor, which mes-sengers had recently arrived from Paris and which officials were rumored to be planning unpopular measures.

The city was divided into parishes whose identity centered around the parish church. However, individual streets or neighborhoods could also have their identities. Rich and poor quarters were not sharply differenti-ated because craftsmen and servants lived near their work and accommodations of various degrees of comfort existed side by side.

Figure 3 The city of Bordeaux in 1685.

Nevertheless, most cities had older, denser merchant quarters, often located near ports or gates, and newer, more fashionable quarters where space permitted the construction of larger hôtels suitable for nobles and high officers. There were usually also popular quarters that were significantly poorer than the rest of the city.

All French towns were small enough to walk from any point within the walls to any other point within an hour. However, there were few thoroughfares, and negotiating the maze of winding passageways could slow one's progress much more than today's tourist might imagine, especially if it was necessary to go from one extremity to the other by passing through the middle. Crowds could cause a ruckus in one location without adjacent neighborhoods, shielded by side streets and cul de sacs, being aware of it.

Bordeaux is a case in point.[16] Lying north and south along the west side of the Garonne river, which had no bridges, the city was separated from its river "port" by walls. At its northern extremity sat a royal fortress, the Château Trompette, which housed the royal garrisons used to dominate the city. Sheltered in the shadow of this fortress was the elegant "Chapeau Rouge" quarter, center of the townhouses of parlementaires. This affluent neighborhood extended southeastward into the older merchant quarters that paralleled the port, then was separated from the newer popular quarters to the south by a transitional zone of "moats" and open spaces representing the exterior of an obsolete thirteenth-century line of ramparts. South of this zone lay the teeming popular parishes of Saint Michel and Sainte Croix, while over on the southwest corner just opposite another old pile, the Château du Hâ, was the parish of Sainte Eulalie. Jean-Pierre Poussou has evoked the atmosphere of popular quarters like Saint Michel, divided between "the commercial fever of the merchants' counting tables . . . and the racket produced by the workbenches in the rue de la Carpenteyre or the forges in the rue des Faures, where carpenters, barrelmakers, and ironsmiths worked on the armaments for ships." There in myriad shops "tools and materials accumulate in the 'chamber' of the artisan . . . Many families may share the same well, the same courtyard, the same entranceway . . . Space is always limited and the tortuous street outside requires close neighborly relations." In the more open areas near the medieval ramparts, "the ditches are cluttered . . . with coopers' lumber and resins; at Saint Eloi by the carts and cattle of the people from the Landes who are heading for the nearby marketplace." Farther west, the quieter quarter of Sainte Eulalie, "still largely rural with its population of vinegrowers, nevertheless includes . . . tanners washing their skins in the waters of the moat. On the Peugue stream which limits the quarter to the northwest, riverbank houses plunge their piles into the stream that receives all the refuse from the neighborhood."[17]

These three artisanal parishes were forever threatening and subversive. Again and again in the seventeenth century their crowds stormed down the narrow thoroughfares leading to the Chapeau Rouge end of town, or

[16] For references, see chapter 6 where the Bordeaux revolt of 1635 is discussed.
[17] Charles Higounet (ed.), *Histoire de Bordeaux* (Toulouse, 1980), pp. 214–15.

built barricades across these same streets if there was a counterattack. And as fate would have it, their chief targets, the magistrates, were perched in a vulnerable position *between* the two contrasting ends of the city. The hôtel de ville was on the thirteenth-century line of ramparts, adjacent to the chapel of Saint Eloi and the gate tower holding the Great Bell. Several blocks northeast, not far from the turbulent central market, sat "l'Ombrière," the ramshackle medieval pile that served as Palais de Justice for the Parlement. Both buildings lay in the line of march from Saint Michel to Chapeau Rouge, and either one could easily be invested by angry demonstrators. The palais was invaded at least six times by popular crowds during the seventeenth century, and the hôtel de ville about as often.

Who were "the people" who protested so vociferously in seventeenth-century cities? They were a very heterogeneous group, subdivided into small overlapping units – households, shops, trades, streets, neighborhoods, parishes – with which they identified closely. Grouped in this way, they did not easily join together in large cross-city movements, making all the more remarkable those occasions when such movements did occur. More usual were protests ignited when a particular constituency came in contact with a perceived abuse: the trades affected by a tax, the persons present at a market where prices were too high, the bystanders who encountered a detested "hoarder" at a tense moment, the people on a particular street who organized to stop the troops of a governor. Such movements were capable of expanding as rumors spread and agitators organized meetings, but they still developed along paths which followed channels of personal contact or geographical proximity.

There were also class divisions based on broadly clashing interests. The circle of individuals who held decision-making power over the lives of the majority of the population was very small. Most municipal decisions were made by a handful of échevins, whose functions are described in chapter 4. They were advised by a wider circle of councillors from leading families, along with the top royal judges, the bishop, a military governor, or a royal intendant. This ruling circle shared an interest in protecting property and maintaining social deference, cultivating congenial relations with the royal court and the power brokers in the external society, and keeping the general working population functioning effectively. But despite these common objectives the authorities were always split among themselves by conflicts of jurisdiction, owing to rivalries among the representatives of the municipality, the church, the royal officers, and the direct agents of the crown. Nevertheless there was a class line defined by power between these "dominant" power brokers and the rest of the "dominated" – between the few and the many – that was deeply felt on both sides. There was also an economic split between the somewhat larger group that was materially secure and the vulnerable majority, with the former confident that their basic needs for food and shelter would be assured, while the latter were immediately affected by any breakdown in the system of supply and employment or any adjustment in the structure of taxes and fees. These social fault lines – between powerful and powerless and between well-off and insecure – tended to come to the surface during crises and to serve as the motivating force for further extension of the conflict, but even then people's primary allegiances derived from their more immediate attachment to trades, households, and shops.

It is not easy to break down urban social structures for analytical purposes because the records kept by authorities reflected assumptions different from ours about how society was constituted. Thus tax rolls omitted the privileged rich and the clergy as well as the masses of the poor; and head counts proceeded by household, making it difficult to account for women, children, servants, apprentices, and other subordinate members of the household. In a few cases historians' reconstructions of tax series have made it possible to get a profile of the populations of certain cities. Using James Farr's estimates I created the rough figures displayed in Table 1. These are based on Farr's estimate for the size of the total population.[18] The figures for Aix, developed by Jean Paul Coste and Jacqueline Carrière, are somewhat more satisfying because they derive from the capitation survey of 1695 which encompassed almost everybody.[19] Here we can better distinguish between servants, manual laborers, and the poor, although we still cannot disentangle the subordinate members of households from the trades or professions of their household heads.

Given these anomalies, it is surprising how closely the percentages correspond in the two cities. We see some 4 percent clerics; 2 percent persons claiming noble, tax-exempt status, including some of the parlementaires and royal officers; 17 percent male heads of household with established occupational titles; 8 to 10 percent manual laborers, engaging

---

[18] Based on estimates by James R. Farr in *Hands of Honor: Artisans and their World in Dijon, 1550–1650* (Ithaca, NY, 1988), pp. 271–4 and the figures for the tax of 1643 in his, "Consumers, Commerce and the Craftsmen of Dijon," in Benedict, *Cities and Social Change*, pp. 139, 169–73.

[19] The figure for the total population of Aix was worked out by Jacqueline Carrière, *La population d'Aix en Provence à la fin du XVIIe siècle: étude de démographie historique d'après le registre de capitation de 1695* (Aix-en-Provence, 1958), pp. 35, 48; her study then becomes the foundation for the massive investigation of the same tax rolls in Jean Paul Coste, *La ville d'Aix en 1695: structure urbaine et société*, 2 vols. (Aix-en-Provence, 1970), vol. II, pp. 712, 731–995.

Table 1. *Breakdown of the populations of Dijon and Aix*

	Number	Percent of total population
Dijon in 1643		
Clergy	850	4.0
Tax-exempt households	426	2.0
Heads of household	3,654	17.4
Live-in servants	1,800	8.4
Live-in journeymen	350	1.7
The rest (women, children, manual labor, the poor)	13,920	66.3
Total population	21,000	99.8
Aix in 1695		
Religious (male and female)	1,045	3.8
Nobility	452	1.6
Heads of household (trades and professions)	4,677	17.0
Servants	2,442	8.9
Manual laborers (including agricultural)	2,191	8.0
Beggars, disabled, poor	394	1.4
The rest (women, children, apprentices, journeymen, elderly family members)	16,311	59.3
Total population	27,512	100.0

Sources: see note 21.

mostly in transporting people and goods or in agricultural work; another 9 percent servants, mostly living in the houses of their masters; and an undifferentiated mass of other persons subsumed under the households of the professionals and tradesmen, including the vast majority of the women. This breakdown gives us a picture of the total population but it tells us very little about the power structure, since most of the powerful and most of the poor are concealed within the category of heads of household.

If we restrict ourselves to the those households we get a better look at the distribution of professions and trades. In Table 2 I have regrouped Coste's breakdown of the 11,201 households of Aix in 1695 into fifteen descriptive categories. Thus the results represent percentages of listed heads of households rather than percentages of the total population. Aix was an aristocratic capital characterized by large numbers of venal officers (over 300 of them) and a resident nobility numbering in the hun-

Table 2. *Breakdown of the households of Aix in 1695*

Total of 11,201 households from the capitation rolls

		Number of households	Percentage of total households
1	Ecclesiastical	1,045	9.3
	Regular clergy — 828		
	Secular clergy — 217		
2	Nobility	452	4.0
	Nobles with fiefs — 50		
	"Chevaliers," "écuyers," "nobles" — 228		
	Military officers — 124		
	Knights of Malta and other nobles — 50		
3	Royal officers	334	3.0
	Parlement and Chambre des Comptes — 187		
	Trésoriers-Généraux de France — 19		
	Sénéchaussée — 36		
	Secrétaires du roi — 19		
	Other — 73		
4	Bourgeois	199	1.8
5	Commerce, finance	65	0.6
6	Lesser functionaries	174	1.6
	Viguerie and maréchaussée — 11		
	Clerks, secretaries — 31		
	Agents of the city, province — 132		
7	Legal professions	664	5.9
	Avocats — 277		
	Procureurs and huissiers — 352		
	Notaries — 35		
8	Other professions	151	1.3
	Doctors and surgeons — 94		
	Apothecaries — 28		
	Teachers — 29		
9	Hostelry	149	1.3
	Innkeepers, cabaretiers — 90		
	Other — 59		
10	Artisans and shopkeepers	2,388	21.3
11	Unskilled labor	125	1.1
	Drivers, carters, mule drivers — 109		
	Other — 16		
12	Military	192	1.7
	Archers and sergeants — 42		
	Common soldiers — 56		
	Guards, galley soldiers — 94		

Table 2. (*cont*).

Total of 11,201 households from the capitation rolls

		Number of households	Percentage of total households
13	Agricultural		1,998	17.8
	Manual laborers, day laborers	1,756		
	Small farmers	173		
	Millers	39		
	Other	30		
14	Servants		2,871	25.6
15	Indigent		394	3.5
Total			11,201	99.8

Sources: see note 19.

dreds.[20] These were the groups from which emerged the factional leaders discussed in chapter 8. There were also two hundred "bourgeois," living off their lands, rents, or loans, and a smaller number of merchants engaged in wholesale trade. These various elite groups, though belonging to all three estates and enjoying a variety of social situations, added up to about one fifth of the household units. They were not a unified group, since they belonged to distinct hierarchies: the Church, the royal officers, the city magistrates, and the financiers. The last, though private citizens, were investors in public loans, grain supplies, and royal tax farms. Within each hierarchy there was a wide spectrum of wealth and status, but at each summit was a tiny subgroup of power brokers, ranging from the archbishop of Aix to the consuls, the presidents of the Parlement and the Comptes, the intendant, the governor, the chiefs of the leading noble families, and a group of rich citizens. These two hundred or so men belonged to distinct channels of authority, but collectively they controlled virtually all important decisions affecting the community.

Below category five are the intermediate groups: various kinds of legal agents, educated professionals, notaries, innkeepers, prosperous artisans in prestigious trades like goldsmiths, solid local tradesmen like butchers. As intermediaries with both local roots and connections higher up, these people played a crucial leadership role in neighborhoods. Innkeepers presided over centers of sociability where plots were hatched and news was

---

[20] For basic bibliography on Aix, see chapter 8.

exchanged; notaries recorded marriage contracts, business deals or property transfers; avocats and procureurs had a foothold in the law courts;
and those who practiced in the sovereign courts frequented those corridors of power without feeling at home in them; the shops of master artisans were centers of activity as well as neighborhood observation posts
involving journeymen, apprentices, family members, and customers.
Some masters, through their trade associations, had influence in city
councils.

These middling people were probably the heart of the community and
they too had power, but in a more decentralized, unofficial sense. Their
labor or direction of labor affected the lives and work processes of many
people even though they had little input on issues of city-wide importance. If they heeded the call of the authorities to stand guard in their
militia companies and maintain order, the chances were that their neighbors and subordinates would follow suit. But they were just as subject as
those below them to the taxes, threats, and acts of intimidation that came
from above, and they were all the more likely to become outraged at such
measures in that they had some familiarity with the circles in which the
unpopular decisions were made. Being well established, they had a strong
sense of civic pride, but being largely helpless to influence events, they
could easily succumb to indignation.

Still, these intermediaries did not have interests identical to those of the
mass of the population either. Within the category of artisans and
shopkeepers were industrial craftsmen like weavers, tanners, barrelmakers, carpenters, roofers, plasterers, blacksmiths, shoemakers, leather
workers, fullers, dyers, or basketweavers, whose means were meagre and
whose fortunes fluctuated wildly. The Aix rolls cited almost 150 different
trades relating to all sectors of the economy and representing every level
of poverty and prosperity. And below the crafts were the manual laborers
of various sorts – drivers, carters, rural workers, guards, soldiers, and servants – who constituted almost half of the total households without even
counting the invisible journeymen and apprentices or the desperately
poor. This heterogeneous majority was likely to rise up even more vigorously when anger generated in shops and taverns by persons with connections spilled out into the streets, and in many circumstances they were
likely to be joined by angry women and children drawn from the same
households. These popular classes had their own views about those in
charge, including the intermediaries, who in some cases were their
employers, and in a crisis they were perfectly capable of turning on
neighborhood and craft leaders when they sensed a betrayal or when their
perceived interests differed.

If we look at other cities we find a similar picture. Table 3 shows a

Table 3. Social structure of various urban populations

In percentages

	Dijon 1643 (n=4,013)	Lyon 1597 (n=5,317)	Amiens 1624-33 (n=2,429)	Toulouse 1695 (n=10,405)	Montpellier 1640 (n=2,342)	Aix 1695 (n=11,201)
Clergy	—	0.5	5.4	1.7	0.8	9.3
Nobility	—	—	—	3.5	2.7	4.0
Officers	6.2	0.6	3.0	11.3	6.8	3.0
Bourgeois, rentiers	1.3	—	4.0	2.0	2.3	1.8
Commerce, finance	3.9	2.4	2.5	4.7	9.2	0.6
Minor functionaries	3.4	1.7	—	—	0.7	1.6
Legal professions	8.1	3.2	4.7	2.1	4.7	5.9
Other professions	1.1	1.6	0.4	1.6	0.9	1.3
Hostelry	1.2	2.9	3.7	—	1.0	1.3
Crafts, shopkeepers	22.6	56.7	42.1	38.9	26.3	21.3
Unskilled labor	1.6	8.4	—	9.8	—	1.1
Military	1.2	0.5	—	1.0	0.7	1.7
Agriculture	9.8	—	—	15.6	18.0	17.8
Servants	—	—	—	—	—	25.6
Indigent	—	—	—	—	—	3.5
Unknown	39.7	21.6	34.2	7.8	25.7	—

Notes: — indicates a category not used in this source.
Sources: see note 21.

breakdown for five other towns, based on various kinds of enumerations by household.[21] The same general structure is reproduced, depicting some 5 percent nobles and clergy (probably low), a comparable group of royal officers, and a third group of professionals and lawyers, with 3 or 4 percent important merchants. The superiority of the Aix figures is immediately apparent in that most of the other cities fail to capture the highest and lowest sectors of their populations accurately and that all of them post significant levels of "unknowns." We can see that Dijon, Toulouse, and Montpellier, like Aix, have a considerable population of officers because they are regional capitals with sovereign courts, whereas Lyon has very few. The salient feature there and in Amiens is the high number of artisans, reaching 56.7 percent in Lyon and 42.1 percent in Amiens. Add these to the underrepresented manual laborers and agriculturalists, and we have cities with terrifyingly large working populations facing relatively small groups of elites.

The picture is further developed by Olivier Zeller's subtle study of the Lyonnais assessments of 1597 and 1636, which transcends the numerical breakdowns we have examined thus far.[22] Zeller notes that the 1597 survey, the one used in the Lyon figures quoted above, captures quite effectively the trades of the masculine heads of households, but misses the poor and infirm. In the industrial quartier de Griffon, where especially good records list each of the 1,074 inhabitants in 1636, there were 42.2 percent adult men and women (200 men, 253 women), 34.7 percent children under 16, 8.8 percent female servants, 10.9 percent male servants and apprentices, and 3.4 percent elderly and infirm.[23] This breakdown gives us another look at age and status in the sort of neighborhood that

[21] Sources: Dijon (from tax rolls 1643: omits the privileged exempt), James Farr, "Consumers, Commerce and the Craftsmen of Dijon" in Benedict, *Cities and Social Change*, pp. 139, 169–73; Lyon (from a survey of the population in 1597: weak on notables, aged and handicapped), Olivier Zeller, *Les recensements Lyonnais de 1597 et 1636: démographie historique et géographie sociale* (Lyon, 1983), pp. 332–57; Amiens (from the taxe des pauvres 1624–33: omits the poorest 3/5 of the population), Pierre Deyon, *Amiens capitale provinciale: étude sur la société urbaine au 17e siècle* (Paris, 1967), pp. 241–3, 540–1; Toulouse (from the capitation of 1695), using the categories in Micheline Thoumas-Schapira, "La bourgeoisie toulousaine à la fin du XVIIe siècle," *Annales du Midi* 67 (1955), 313–29; Montpellier (from the property tax of 1640: includes only real property owners and omits the poor), Frederick M. Irvine, "From Renaissance City to Ancien Régime Capital: Montpellier, *c.*1500–*c.*1600," in Benedict, *Cities and Social Change*, 114–15, modified and completed with data from Frederick Irvine, "Social Structure, Social Mobility and Social Change in Sixteenth-Century Montpellier," Ph.D. thesis, University of Toronto, 1979, p. 230; Aix (from capitation of 1695), adapted from Coste, *La ville d'Aix en 1695*, vol. II, pp. 712, 731–995.
[22] Zeller, *Les recensements Lyonnais*, pp. 332–57.
[23] Ibid, pp. 166. This is following contemporary classification methods by which "men and women" does not include servants, apprentices, or the elderly and infirm.

often generated popular crowds, where women outnumbered men, and
the servants, apprentices and youths, otherwise invisible, might join in
disturbances. Lyon had several such predominantly industrial neighborhoods: Le Griffon was 61.5 percent textiles, mostly silk; La Croisette was
47.7 percent textiles, mostly hatmaking; on the other hand l'Herberie was
70 percent large-scale merchants with hardly any menu peuple at all.

But Zeller's most important finding is the diversity among neighborhoods. He notes that the printing trades were concentrated in one area,
and hatmaking in another, but that the newer textile trades were widely
dispersed. Trades connected to outside commerce and specialization
tended to be close together, and there was a certain concentration in the
wealthy quarters of trades that served the rich such as doctors, pastrycooks, confectioners, jewelers, and clockmakers. Transportation was
concentrated along the river fronts; most judges and legal auxiliaries lived
in three distinctive quarters, although the élus and trésoriers de France,
who handled taxes and money, lived near the merchants. Most other
trades, especially those needed everywhere such as bakers, tailors, shoemakers, notaries, masons, carpenters, and innkeepers, were distributed
throughout the city. The concentration of wealth is striking. Zeller estimates that at least 22 of the 36 quarters were as poor as Saint-Georges,
where 67.6 percent of the 293 inhabitants were cited as very poor,
meaning that they had no property and were unable to pay anything.[24]
His study of a special tax assessment on the rich in 1640 shows that the
well-to-do were highly concentrated: one single quartier paid 18.5 percent
of the entire city's tax, followed by a second that paid 14.3 percent. Six
others paid between 3 and 9 percent each, while the remaining fifteen
paid under 3 percent each.[25]

Thus the population of a city was as diverse as its neighborhoods, and
no simple characterization can capture "the people." In a limited sense
the entire population was united. After all, they lived within the same
walls, had common institutions, and faced many of the same ultimate
threats of disease, invasion, or famine. Within this totality, however, were
the more significant fault lines that divided the community over issues of
power, security, and subsistence. The term menu peuple captures something of the subordinate nature of the crowd: the "little people" as
opposed to the "great." Protests were "popular" in the sense that they set
the protesters, representing the majority of the community, against the
small groups with all the power. Most of them pitted a segment of the

[24] Ibid, pp. 174–80, 188.
[25] Ibid, pp. 274–5. The districts with low assessments were no less populous than those with
high assessments, in fact the reverse was often the case.

menu peuple against those persons from the ruling group who were associated with a particular grievance. Nevertheless, the menu peuple frequently included important citizens of considerable standing in the community who were *menu* only with respect to the decision-makers above them. And this terminology ignores the split between neighborhood leaders and the poorer, more desperate journeymen, laborers, or farmhands who broke away on occasion from the leadership of their bosses and employers and acted independently. It also fails to capture the women whose active involvement was frequently the impetus behind popular protest.

Thus the concept of "the people" and the distinction between "elite" and "popular" are too broad to serve us well here. But the absence of a single, demonstrable split dividing the city into two warring factions should not be taken to mean that there were no class conflicts in seventeenth-century cities. On the contrary, there were immense disparities in the distribution of power and well-being which resulted in a struggle for influence, if not control, on the part of at least three constituencies: the power-brokers and their circle; the secure, but relatively disenfranchised intermediaries with community standing; and the genuinely poor and vulnerable. Protests began in face-to-face disputes over specific grievances and expanded in widening circles to encompass broader groups and deeper resentments. This is the process we will explore in the following chapters, starting with the simplest, most spontaneous kinds of incidents.

To recapture the spirit behind popular protests we must begin with everyday life. Popular politics was built upon an ongoing interplay of experiences, discussions, and reactions that went on in the streets. The narratives of revolts describe only full-blown events as if the crowd had appeared out of nowhere, but in the real world such movements did not just happen. People had to hear news, exchange views, meet, and organize before the explosion could erupt, and there were usually warnings, false starts, and gradually accelerating incidents and counter-incidents. The place to begin our analysis, then, is before the crisis when people grumbled and plans were hatched. We must ask what induced ordinary citizens to depart from their usual routines and what resources they could call upon in doing so.

Personal indignation

First come expressions of personal exasperation. New studies of "gesture" are beginning to reveal distinctive ways in which seventeenth-century men and women defended their personal autonomy.[1] This is not the place to examine all the subtleties of private interpersonal relations,

---

[1] These studies concentrate on gesture as a cultural language and on forms of personal interaction, often as recorded in criminal complaints. Jan Bremmer and Herman Roodenburg (eds.), *A Cultural History of Gesture* (Ithaca, NY, 1991). The pioneering work was Yves Castan, *Honnêteté et relations sociales en Languedoc à l'époque des Lumières* (Paris, 1980). See also Robert Muchembled, "Pour une histoire des gestes (XVe-XVIIIe siècle)," *Revue d'histoire moderne et contemporaine* 34 (1987), 87–101; Robert Muchembled, *L'invention de l'homme moderne* (Paris, 1988); Gregory Hanlon, "Les rituels de l'aggression en Aquitaine au XVIIe siècle," *Annales ESC* 11 (1985), 244–68; Gregory Hanlon, *L'univers des gens de bien: culture et comportements des élites urbaines en Agenais-Condomois au XVIIe siècle* (Bordeaux, 1989), pp. 65–96; Farr, *Hands of Honor: Artisans and their world in Dijon 1550–1650* (Ithaca, NY, 1988), pp. 177–95; Nicole Gonthier, *Cris de haine et rites d'unité: la violence dans les villes, XIIIe-XVIe siècles* (Paris, 1992); Claude Gauvard, *"De grace especial": crime, état et société en France à la fin du Moyen Age*, 2 vols. (Paris, 1991); Olwen H. Hufton, "Attitudes Towards Authority in Eighteenth-Century Languedoc," *Social History* 3 (1978), 281–302.

but certain emerging themes may prove to have direct relevance to an understanding of popular politics. One is the interplay of face-saving gestures. City people lived and worked close together in shops, spilling out into streets and courtyards. They shared intimate facilities like wells, privies, or market stalls, and they regularly pressed together in cramped public spaces. But at the same time they experienced daily reminders that they lived in a society where gradations of status were central facts of life. Forms of address, preferential treatment or the lack of it, styles of conduct, manners, clothing, all bestowed a stream of small satisfactions or aggravations on persons pursuing their daily affairs. As a result of this exchange of esteem, individuals surrounded themselves with a protective sense of self. This "face" was tied to an envelope of personal space that represented the zone of honor to be respected.[2] A person had an immediate aura of inviolability connected to the head, the hair, other parts of the body, clothes and possessions, and intangibles like name and reputation. He or she operated out of a fixed territory – the house, field, or shop – that represented the individual's private living space, and claimed temporary rights over situational spaces such as rank in a procession or role in a ceremony. The intense sensitivity to reputation attached to these "defense" zones extended as well, though not as clearly, to persons connected to the individual by family, lineage, or patronage, and to larger groups such as neighborhoods, streets, trades, even to a limited degree to entire urban communities.[3]

The result was a constant struggle to maintain one's deserved share of esteem by monitoring the appropriateness of others' responses and according them no more than their due in return. Ideally the resulting give and take would maintain a proper flow of esteem between the parties, but the process often generated conflict since what one party expected was likely to exceed what the other was willing to accord. A challenge would then be issued in the form of an aggressive word or deed, and either the discord would intensify or some sort of peacemaking mechanism would be invoked. Recourse to violence was perfectly acceptable, unless it was considered excessive. On the other hand since insult, not destruction, was the goal of much of this aggressive activity, it was often possible to achieve the desired result by only threatening violence or by assaulting a

---

[2] Further theoretical discussion in J. G. Peristiany (ed.), *Honor and Shame: the Values of Mediterranean Society* (London, 1965); Erving Goffman, *Interaction Ritual: Essays on Face-to-Face Behavior* (Garden City, NY, 1967); David D. Gilmore, *Aggression and Community: Paradoxes of Andalusian Culture* (New Haven, 1987).

[3] Especially useful explorations of these ideas, although in a more rural setting, are Reinhardt, *Justice in the Sarladais*, pp. 161–213; and Malcolm Greenshields, *An Economy of Violence in Early Modern France: Crime and Justice in the Haute Auvergne, 1587–1664* (University Park, PA, 1994).

hat, an animal, a subordinate. Strange gestures and fierce words might have a different meaning from what we would expect. Seventeenth-century people were used to blood. Animals were slaughtered in close proximity; executions were public; hand-to-hand military combat took place within sight of town walls. Seventeenth-century people had little hesitation in brutally attacking an enemy, yet their violence was never gratuitous. When a soldier told the wife of a tavern owner in the Sarladais that "she would die only by his hand and that he wanted to disembowel her from her mouth to her navel" his words probably did not signify intended mutilation as much as an expression of contempt in which the woman was being degraded to the level of a slaughtered animal.[4]

The dynamic tension in a competitive exchange of insults emerges forcefully from a report of an altercation in Amiens in 1689. Charles Corbie, *manouvrier* living in the faubourg d'Hausoye, was angry at Simon Guillier, nicknamed Lamouche, who had been responsible for lodging troops in his house the previous Easter. According to Lamouche, as he was walking out of town he had encountered Corbie on the road and said "bonjour." Corbie had replied "bonjour bougre," and then, "pretending to be drunk, lowered his head to look down his nose at the plaintiff, swearing and blaspheming, and said that he had wanted to kill him for a long time. At that very moment all Corbie's relatives – father, mother, brothers and sisters, picked up rocks and started throwing them at the plaintiff, forcing him to flee." Corbie's account had a different slant. He claimed he had greeted Lamouche civilly with a "bonsoir," and the latter had replied by cursing, "Va te faire foutre (get lost), I will cut up your face." Corbie then responded that Lamouche "was not clever enough to cut up his face," and when Lamouche pursued him with his sword drawn he did admit to having thrown some rocks. In the meantime Lamouche's wife had approached and said that Corbie was "a thief and his sister was a whore." Corbie had replied that her husband was "nothing but a sorcerer." Lamouche had then attacked Corbie with the sword, and Corbie had thrown mud at Lamouche. According to a third account from a bystander, Corbie had said "Bonsoir, bonsoir"; Lamouche had said "I want nothing to do with your bonsoir"; Corbie had called him "bougre de Savoyard." Then the sword had been drawn and rocks had been thrown.[5]

It is easy to see from this veritable catalog of insults how confrontations could escalate. These two men must have had prior altercations that were well known in the neighborhood, and their performance was played before neighbors and bystanders. Both had wives and friends who

---

[4] Reinhardt, *Justice in the Sarladais*, p. 172.
[5] AM Amiens FF 1123.

appeared so readily that the encounter could not have been as fortuitous as the protagonists made it out to be. No one hesitated to have recourse to mud and rocks. The incident was presented as coincidental and largely personal, but it had an official, public dimension in that the pretext for the quarrel was troop billeting.

[When one's autonomy was suddenly challenged, the result might be direct resistance to authorities.] In 1652 when the city of Carcassonne was coming out of a period of quarantine for the plague, Pierre Roux, first consul, received a complaint that Pierre Savy, who had been out of town for two months, had sneaked back into the city without undergoing the requisite check on his medical condition. Roux put on his official robes, took several guards from the patrol and a servant carrying a torch and knocked on the door of Savy's house. Not at all pleased with this nocturnal inquisition, Savy appeared at an upper window and announced that the first person who approached would die on the spot. He then pelted the authorities with rocks, seriously wounding Roux and his valet.[6] Savy's aggression was not at all unusual. We may well wonder why he had rocks stockpiled in the upper story of his residence, but projectiles like these along with the short tempers of their owners, were very common in early modern cities and betray only slightly more premeditation than Corbie's rocks and mud. Savy evidently felt insulted at the suggestion that he might be a bearer of plague, and he was determined to let the neighborhood know about it, especially if the consul was going to violate his very residence, which he treated like a fortress. This incident went beyond a private quarrel. Savy may have felt personally aggrieved and he may well have had prior reasons to dislike First Consul Roux, but here he was attacking a public authority on an official mission, and thereby questioning the municipality and the law – a distinction which makes his rebellion a public, in some sense political, act.

We might note in passing the rocks that appear so frequently in these accounts. Stones seem to have been lying about everywhere, and they were a prime resource in moments of tension. Disputes in the countryside over property were signaled by showers of rocks thrown by one party at another. Crowds might gather and throw rocks at Protestants leaving the city for burial services in rural cemeteries. In 1695 the intendant of Berry described a failed attack by a group of "women and children" who gathered to insult process-servers as they inaugurated a new tax on trades in La Châtre. The women were successfully dispersed, but they left behind a stockpile of rocks situated a bit farther down the street in the direction the process-servers had been moving. In some cities like Bordeaux there were

---

[6] AM Carcassonne BB 6: 2 and 9 November 1652.

periodic complaints about youth groups gathering for battles with rocks and slingshots, but it is noteworthy that slingshots were never mentioned in riots. They were probably not immediately accessible, and required too much aiming in the heat of crowd actions. Rocks, by contrast, could inflict a kind of impulsive, indiscriminate damage that was usually not lethal – in short, they were the perfect weapon for unpremeditated repulsion of an immediate foe. Mud was less dangerous but perhaps more humiliating.[7]

These attacks of rage featuring ostentatious cursing and threatened violence were likely to occur whenever a person representing authority invaded a space considered private. Thus when the inspectors of the say weavers guild of Amiens entered a mill in search of illegally produced merchandise, they encountered the master of the mill holding a club, backed up by his two "boys" wielding wooden and iron hammers, all cursing and saying "Get out of here jeanfoutres, bougres, there's nothing here for you, you won't get the goods." Such antagonism was hardly limited to men. In 1697 when three inspectors of the tailors guild burst into the house of the widow Montfaucon, who had ten girls working for her as dressmakers, the girls all started screaming "Bougres de fripons, bougres de voleurs leave us alone, let's kill these bougres here," and one of them snatched off Louis Canape's wig, tore his clothes, grabbed him by the throat, struck him with sword and fists, and bit his little finger so that blood flowed. These were standard insulting gestures that were intended to humiliate. A baker in Carcassonne who was challenged by the consuls for purchasing grain in the market at too early an hour flew into a rage, calling them "mangeurs" (devourers) and "voleurs" (thieves) – two insulting, incendiary names – and then struck one of the consuls. Arrested, he escaped from the municipal prison and started a law suit against the authorities.[8]

In defending their honor, people flaunted their contempt with a degree of theatricality that is almost incomprehensible to the modern, western observer. When the consuls of Agen saw the royal notary Cabos standing outside his house they called him over to inquire formally (they must have really known) why he had been publicly denouncing them of late. Instead of complying, Cabos made a point of not removing his hat and

---

[7] Davis, *Fiction in the Archives*, p. 84 [countryside]; *Inventaire sommaire des registres de la jurade 1520 à 1783*, 8 vols. (Bordeaux, 1901–1947), vol. I, pp. 507, 508 [slingshot contests]; AM Dijon I 106, fol. 1647 [rock battle in the street by sons of artisans], 12 May 1676 [lackeys attack carriages with rocks]; Farr, *Hands of Honor*, p. 211 [youths throw rocks at a sign]; AN G[7] 1704: letter of 27 October 1695 [women in Berry].

[8] AM Amiens FF 1123: 10 May 1688; FF 1127: 4 April 1697; AM Carcassonne BB 5: 11 September 1648.

announced disdainfully that he wanted to have nothing to do with them. Commanded again to obey, he shouted "Niat, niat," and slammed his door saying "that they made him laugh." Not content with this performance, he leaned out of his highest window a minute later to shout "Niat, niat" at them again. Beside themselves, the consuls stormed upstairs and commanded him in the name of the king to do his duty. Without taking off his hat he retorted that he did not *recognize* their authority and they had no right to order him around. He then struggled against the guards, holding onto furniture, threw the liveries of two consuls on the floor, kicked another in the stomach, tore his robe (more deliberate insults), and punched him in the face. Cabos was adamant in his determination to insult the consuls. After being arrested and thrown in prison, he was still not satisfied and told the jailer to report to his employers that "they are all jean foutres." In 1687 Lefort, an innkeeper from Amiens who also considered himself ruined by the repeated cost of troop lodgings, decided to vent his spleen at Nicolas Tavernier, the lawyer-clerk who was responsible for military billets. Instead of taking advantage of a chance encounter like Corbie, Lefort *planned* a scene. After making a public fuss about wanting to kill Tavernier, he mounted a small, black horse waving a half cocked pistol and rode up to Tavernier's door saying "You gave me soldiers to lodge many times, you're the cause of it, I must kill you." Neighbors disarmed him with great difficulty. In 1672 an échevin of Dijon was on his way to distribute troop lodgings when Daniel Grangier, merchant, stopped him and said "you're a nice fellow to have sent me soldiers" and gave him a punch and several blows, tearing his rabato and throwing his wig on the ground "in front of a large number of people."[9]

This last point is important. Honor was fought out in the public view because it was the verdict of the audience that mattered. Challenging an individual in the street for acts he had performed in an official capacity was bad enough because it invited a questioning of public acts. But invading the city hall was even more disrespectful of local authority. In 1674 a master hatmaker entered the hôtel de ville of Dijon wearing a sword while the échevins were organizing troop billets. He announced that he refused to take in the two soldiers sent to him and that he was going to break someone's head. He then "threatened us by passing his index finger several times up against his nose and pointing it towards us with gestures that expressed his fury." The shocked officials concluded that such gestures "encourage contempt for the magistrates and threaten to stir up an

---

[9] AM Agen FF 90: 22 October 1643; AM Amiens FF 1123: 24 April 1687; AM Dijon I 110: 6 May, 8 January 1672.

uprising to encourage the people not to receive the soldiers sent by order of His Majesty."[10]

Of course these acts of aggression were "political" only in the sense that they publicly challenged duly constituted authorities. But there was a demonstrable connection in people's minds between personal resistance and group rebellion. One year after the bloody rebellion of 1635 in Agen, which we will be examining later on, Michel Besse, gatekeeper at the Porte Neuve, was dismissed from his post for incompetence. Having nowhere to go, he refused to move out, and when the guards came to remove him he said loudly "that he was sorry he hadn't given the keys of the gate to the little people during the uprising so that all of [the authorities] could have been strangled, and that if it ever happened again things would be different." In 1638 a tailor accosted by the tax collector flew into a rage, saying that he knew perfectly well this was a "gabelle" (this provocative word is discussed in chapter 3), and proceeded to assault the guards, along with some friends who joined in, one of whom said that collectors were asking to be beaten up, that he had done it several times before and that he had complete contempt for them. That same year a merchant announced to the tax collector in the middle of a busy street that if he continued to try to sequester his goods, "he would call in sixty men who would beat him up and he would ring the bells to assemble them."[11] These were not idle threats in the aftermath of a major rebellion in which the tocsin had been rung and peasants had been called in from the surrounding villages. They suggest how riots might have started.

This sort of defiance was apparently a long-standing tradition in Agen, not limited to the humble, for in 1695 when the process-server from Bordeaux arrived to seize the furniture of Despallais, lieutenant-assesseur in the présidial, for nonpayment of his *augmentation de gages*, Despallais replied that "one did not treat a man of his condition in this manner and that he would see this comedy brought to an end." He leaned out the window and shouted to his wife who was stationed at the door of their house to tell the neighbors that his furniture was being seized. "Instantly the house of Despallais was filled with people armed with iron bars, clubs and swords, and the sieur Despallais grabbed our person, calling us a rascal of a little huissier, kicking us with his feet and exclaiming 'here is the rogue who demanded an écu for not selling my furniture.'" Standing triumphantly on the huissier's body he then proclaimed, "You won't succeed any more than the others," and when the huissier reminded him

---

[10] AM Dijon I 110: 20 April 1674.
[11] AM Agen FF 89: 28 August 1636; FF 90: 16 June, 28 May 1638.

that he was dealing with orders from the king, he replied that "these k
of orders were from that rascal of a *commis* Cassaing and not from ᴛᴵᴺᴱ
king; that he would certainly never obey; that this came from the cursed
soul of Bezons [intendant of Bordeaux]." Warned that he was speaking ill-
advisedly, he exploded with more kicking of the huissier, saying to those
present, "see how he mistreats me," and then, along with his son and the
other bystanders, beat up the huissier's assistant, calling him "a deserter"
and dragging him off to prison.[12] This incident, which suggests parallels
to the violence in Argenteuil that we saw in chapter 1, gives a fine illustration of the motivations behind such an outbreak. Despallais viewed the
sequestration as a personal insult, not a legal procedure, and he insulated
himself from implications of disloyalty by conceptualizing it as an illicit
move by malevolent intermediaries. He expected his friends to rally to his
cause, and he took pains to dramatize for their benefit the disreputability
and fallibility of his adversaries.

Here in peoples' defensive impulses lay the seeds of actions that could
conceivably add up to full-scale rioting if other circumstances were right.
Faced with a challenge, one reacted swiftly and aggressively, assaulting
the offender with cutting insults, and challenging his autonomy as represented by hat, hair, insignia, clothes. One showered the victim with rocks,
splattered him with mud, expelled him, chased him home, sought out his
possessions for retribution. One threatened humiliating butchery, and in
extreme cases one might knock the victim down, drag his body down the
street like a trophy, deposit it in front of a door with symbolic significance,
even dump it in a well, or in the river – in keeping with the common
expression "He should be dragged and thrown in the river," although this
last extreme was unlikely in private cases.[13] However Farr describes an
incident in Dijon in 1642 in which the wife of a cooper was "ritually
humiliated by the wife of a master cobbler, who dragged her by the hair
and smeared her face in the mud." An attempt to search an inn where
grain was being illegally hoarded in Amiens in 1693 led to an attack on the
huissier by the grandson of the innkeeper who "gave him several punches
on the head with his fist, grabbed his hair, knocked him down, and
dragged him more than ten feet, kicking him in the head and on several

---

[12] AN G⁷ 137: 27 April 1695.

[13] Thus the crowd besieging a tax farmer in Lyon in 1632 wanted to "beat him up and throw
him in the river," AM Lyon BB 182: 25 October 1632. Poachers in eighteenth-century
Languedoc who were challenged by the son of the local seigneur beat him, set his horse
free, and dumped him in the river, Hufton, "Attitudes," 288. According to Bercé agents
were thrown in rivers in Périgueux and Carcassonne in 1664, in Chauvigny in 1633, in
Marennes in 1644, Bercé, *History of Peasant Revolts*, pp. 202, 219. We saw the case of
Argenteuil in chapter 1.

spots of his body."[14] Finally, one stirred up the neighborhood, called for help, rallied others, so that a small incident could become larger.

Did women play a distinct role in these confrontations? We know, of course, that they played major parts in certain kinds of riots involving provisioning and the moral standards of the community. We also know that they were supposed to defend a different sort of domestic and personal honor connected to family and household. Nicole Castan notes that among the urban lower classes wives' honor was limited to "conjugal fidelity," and by virtue of this very fact women could commit acts with impunity that might have been considered threatening to a man's honor. They were also less prosecutable before the law, and for both these reasons may have been pushed by their husbands to challenge authorities. Nevertheless Castan hastens to add that women were perfectly capable of intervening autonomously to protect the interests of the household, and I would extend their sphere even farther.[15]

Wives certainly exploited their advantage of speaking with impunity in many confrontations with authorities, but they also acted as equal partners in anger, and indeed they often appear to be egging on their husbands more than speaking in place of them. In Dijon in 1644 an échevin attempting to requisition post horses from an innkeeper met with considerable reluctance. At first the man said he had no horses. Then he insisted that he did not want to continue his contract because his privileges were not being respected and soldiers were being lodged with him every day. When the échevin commanded that the stables be opened and found six horses, the innkeeper's wife appeared screaming "Devil take me, you won't get them" and insisted that "even if they seized her we would not get any [horses] and that by the grace of God she wished the devil had taken the maire and the syndic and the échevins; that she cared as little about the one as the other and that we [in the town government] were serving the devil." Commanded to respect her magistrates, she ran into the kitchen and returned with a knife, saying "If you come near me I'll plant this knife in your chest to provide myself with nourishment, you meurdefaim (starving beggar)." Angry over troop lodgings which they viewed as a violation of their status, the man and his wife were both uncooperative, but it was the wife who turned the confrontation into an assault on the bodies and reputations of the authorities themselves, using the insulting language of butchery. In the faubourg of Dijon Nicolas

---

[14] Farr, *Hands of Honor*, p. 183; AM Amiens FF 1126: 6 August 1693.
[15] Nicole Castan, "La criminalité familiale dans le ressort du Parlement de Toulouse 1690–1730," in A. Abbiateci et al. (eds.), *Crimes et criminalité en France sous l'ancien régime, 17e-18e siècles* (Paris, 1971), pp. 93–4. See also Hanlon, "Rituels," pp. 251–2 for a good discussion of women's responses.

Collinet, innkeeper, and his wife jointly cursed an échevin who lodging soldiers, and while *he* held his fist in the face of the échevin, *she* threw dishes and pewter platters at him.[16]

Women did fight differently, but they also intervened aggressively just like the men – even, perhaps, with a special, more intense brand of indignation. In Bordeaux in 1643 the governor Saint Luc and the jurats held a meeting in the Château du Hâ to examine the causes of a temporary shortage of grain in the markets. As they were leaving, they were spotted by "a large multitude of menu peuple, especially poor women, who were crying out in the square in front of the château that there was no bread in town; that Minvielle, one of the jurats, was responsible; and that they wanted to cut his throat when he came out of the château" (note again the language). Alarmed, the authorities sent Minvielle back inside for protection and another jurat, Demons, tried to divert the women by saying that if they would follow him he would give them bread. Not fooled, they continued to cry out that they wanted to slit Minvielle's throat. The remaining jurats then did a tour of bakery shops, forcing the bakers to reopen, sell what they had on hand, and start baking more loaves, "especially *du bis* to placate these poor people," but the women still failed to disperse. Soon word arrived that more people were gathering in front of Minvielle's house to "tear it down," so a force was sent which dispersed this group of "poor women." But the original women continued to wait all day outside the château for Minvielle to come out, refusing to budge until Minvielle would be handed over to them. When the jurats finally "talked to some of the loudest shouters of the troop," flattering them and giving them handouts of free bread, they still refused to leave.

The interesting thing about this episode is that it was not just a bread riot. These were not starving women begging for food for their children, but proud, angry women organizing a protest to demand retribution for mismanagement. They were expressing the most compelling desire of seventeenth-century crowds, to *punish* the authorities, and it was the women who were leading. After many hours the crowd drifted away and Minvielle was able to return home.[17]

Common people were also capable of thinking politically. They knew the names of the authorities, they had opinions about daily events, and they had a sharp, though not necessarily accurate, idea of who was responsible for measures that affected them, as we have seen in the case of the women's bread riot in Bordeaux. People participated directly in the lodging of troops, the collecting of taxes, and the organization of guard

[16] AM Dijon B 81: procès-verbal 7 May 1644; I 109: 7 March 1643.
[17] *Inventaire sommaire de la jurade*, vol. II, pp. 343–5.

duty, all of which impinged on them in practical ways involving a knowledge of proper procedures and a set of distinct rights and privileges. They accumulated a body of opinions about rights and duties. In 1608 a vigneron of Dijon, arrested for cutting down recently planted trees for firewood, insisted insolently "that they would never keep him from cutting the willows when he needed to, since he was a resident who had paid his part of the cost of planting them, and now he wanted to take his share [*usage*]." In Châlons an archer sent to investigate complaints about an illegal herd of cattle grazing in the municipal meadow encountered an angry group of "butchers and other inhabitants" muttering "that they had the right to put their cattle in the *jard* because members of the city council did so, and that [butchers] were just as much inhabitants of the town as anyone else."[18]

Political discussions took place in markets, taverns, shops, during guard duty, in neighborhoods. We can occasionally listen in. In 1639 cobblers in Dijon (a border city close to the Thirty Years War) debated the relative merits of the Emperor and Louis XIII and whether the king had any business seizing Lorraine. A table of fullers, tailors, weavers, and cooks sitting in a tavern in Amiens in 1689 agreed, after a good many rounds of drinks, that guard duty only served the rich and was only suitable for beggars. If *they* were on guard duty, they decided, they would let the Prince of Orange into the city and help him pillage the "good houses" so that "the poor would soon be rich." In 1629 artisans in Bordeaux assembled in the Palais de Justice and demanded that the Parlement lower their house rent by a quarter or a half and supply them with food. Asked by the jurats what had made them appeal to the Parlement, they replied "necessity." The same thing happened in Dijon in 1597 when a crowd of master artisans gathered outside the Parlement to protest a new tax and cried out "that it was necessary to take arms." Jean-Jacques Bouchard describes his return to Aix in 1630 in the midst of an urban insurrection. "Passing through the streets large numbers of poor people held onto his bridle and asked him if the king continued to want to establish the élus and swore, tearing their hair and beating their hats on the ground, that they would rather slit their own throats than accept [the élus]."[19] This is interesting evidence of the sharing of crowd objectives by ordinary citizens who were not in the midst of a crowd action.

In many cities demonstrators invaded municipal council chambers to

[18] AM Dijon I 107: 19 July 1608; AM Châlons FF 54: 6 May 1616.
[19] Farr, *Hands of Honor*, pp. 197, 203; AM Amiens FF 1123: 6 May 1689; *Inventaire sommaire de la jurade*, vol. I, p. 505; [Bouchard] quoted in Pillorget, *Mouvements insurrectionels*, p. 403.

complain of particular abuses or to demand action. In 1656 in A[
large a number of unknown people, mutinous and angry, en[
council chamber that it was filled immediately; they began to s[
they wanted no more tax profiteers, no more *pancarte*, and no more *sou
pour pot*, no more guardhouses and salt-tax collectors at the city gates; that
they would have to kill and exterminate all the profiteers, starting with
those on the city council." Citizens intervened in more informal ways as
well. When an échevin in Amiens prohibited a hawker from selling patent
medicines in the marketplace because vesper services were in progress, an
angry baker protested "that it wasn't true that vespers were still being
sung, for he had just come from there," and then started pointing at the
échevin with his finger and shouting "Roux, Roux," as if to stir up the
crowd.[20]

Labor issues naturally stimulated discussion. Questioned about an
illicit meeting of fullers in Amiens in 1695, the participants all denied that
there had been any "assembly to force the merchants to pay a higher price
for fulling the merchandise," but Jean-Baptiste Mallet, master fuller,
noted that "the merchants want to make them work for a lower price than
what they were paid three or four years ago. If they were assembled
together it was only to complain among themselves of the smallness of
their earnings." Louis Guinet added that the payment for pressing a
"double" had gone from 10 to 6 sols and that they wanted to lower it
more; others spoke of the rising cost of tools and taxes and of selling their
possessions to survive.[21] The denials about organizing do not ring true,
but these fullers clearly had strong opinions and were willing to act on
them.

The same was true of the silkweavers of Lyon during a crisis in 1627.
Unemployment was growing and a rumor was going around that the king
was going to prohibit the use of silk, which would put everyone out of
work. On 12 January 400 silkworkers came in person to the city council to
complain that "20,000 people" were unemployed because of this rumor
and invoked the memory of the "late king of glorious memory" who had
introduced the art of silk weaving and caused people to flock to Lyon.
They were told to be patient. But six days later six or seven hundred
silkworkers again jammed into the hôtel de ville, presenting a real threat
to orderly procedures. The échevins' description of what happened gives
a nice feel for the tumultuous politics of the weavers and the contrasting
styles of magistrates and workers. The échevins instructed the silkworkers
that

[20] A. Debidour, *La Fronde angevine: tableau de la vie municipale au XVIIe siècle* (Paris, 1877),
p. 401; Amiens FF 1123: Dec. 12, 1688.   [21] Amiens FF 1126: July 16, 1695.

each of them should indicate what he wanted without the others interrupting him and that they should not all speak confusedly. But it is hard to get the menu peuple to follow orderly procedures, so five or six of them began crying out at once that they were in misery; that they had no work in their trade; that the regulations about clothing were the reasons they weren't working; that they couldn't earn their living and were reduced to hunger; that in the name of God they begged the consulate to establish order in this matter, and other similar statements uttered with such noise and complaining that they aroused sympathy while also giving rise to fears that if the merchants continue to hold back work from the silk manufactures very great disorders may occur in this town.

Ten days later there were still reports of increasingly large meetings of silkworkers which occasioned discussions among the various governing bodies of the city.[22]

Broader movements

How did daily talk and occasional indignation get translated into an angry crowd? The first step was for popular indignation to rise over some particular problem. Common hardships like high prices, shortages, or widely distributed tax exactions had the potential of setting off a groundswell of "murmuring" that required only a spark in a public place to cause a riot. In Lyon on 14 June 1653 when a man named Varillon was heard in the marketplace offering a peasant 3 livres above the going price for his entire stock of wheat, a crowd attacked, beat him until he took refuge in a nearby house and then proclaimed that the house should be burned down because he was a hoarder. This was not an isolated incident, for six days later a sergeant named Bureau was attacked and beaten to death in the Grande Rue de l'Hôpital after the wife of a metal founder screamed out in public "that he was a hoarder of wheat who was causing the price to rise." The atmosphere was so tense that the authorities set up patrols. A porter holding a handful of rocks was soon arrested for "vomiting insults" in front of the house of sieur Des Vignes, an agent of the gabelles. Also picked up was a mason who "ran around the streets carrying a large crowbar on his shoulders, trying to arouse sedition by threatening to strike people he met, calling them hoarders of grain."[23] We have here the conditions for trouble: hardship, public complaining, and self-appointed alarmists repeatedly setting off outcries that died only for lack of the proper crowd chemistry.

Instigators might be faceless individuals spontaneously expressing the fears of the group, but on occasion they might also be persons more consciously acting on behalf of what they viewed as the public interest. We

[22] AM Lyon BB 171, fols. 32r-34r, 44r.   [23] AM Lyon BB 207, pp. 254–66.

hear, for example, of a notary named Marchian in Grenoble who became a virtual tribune of the people during the grain crisis of 1675. Calling himself "syndic of the poor," he kept appearing at the marketplace to make impromptu public speeches blaming the shortage of wheat on hoarding by local notables whom he named, such as Baron, farmer of the *aide* tax. The threat of pillage was serious enough that the consuls conducted a search of the attics of the accused parties, finding nothing. Marchian then went to see the First President of the Parlement and denounced the farmers of the gabelle tax for hoarding grain in their attic, a suggestion disturbing to the court because the money to pay the *gages* of the parlementaires was stored in the same place. If necessary, Marchian claimed, "he would demand justice at the head of four hundred women." The promised riot never occurred, but Marchian was finally arrested after he disobeyed an order to desist and reappeared, still spewing forth accusations, in the place Grenette.[24]

Sometimes the collection of a tax called for such visible public procedures that neighborhood reaction could be almost impulsive. When tax agents descended on the rue Saint Germain in Rennes in 1702 to inspect illicit barrels of cider, neighbors began leaning out of windows, uttering insults, and throwing pebbles, rocks, and bricks from houses and shops. Soon all the facades were crammed with spectators, including a spectrum of the neighborhood community: Pierre Brouillard, archer of the prévôté, a daughter of the widow Denys, printer, La Roze master serge-maker, La Chesnays, journeyman serge-maker and his wife, Artur Bigot and his wife, Master Shoemaker Bourbete and his apprentices, Breisseau and his wife, and so forth. As the mockery and commotion grew, a crowd formed in the street which chased the collectors all the way back to their office, throwing rocks and shouting that if they ever returned to that street again they would never leave it alive.[25]

For a larger and more sustained uprising, advanced preparation was necessary. The participants needed to share a common conception of what the problem was, who was responsible, and what to do about it, and the groundwork for this knowledge was often laid by a series of incidents that served as vehicles for the dissemination of critical opinion. For example, in Troyes in 1627 *coureurs de nuit* rode through the streets hidden by cloaks calling out "We must kill the gabeleurs" and naming citizens of the town. There was talk of meetings in taverns, and fifteen to twenty artisans were seen leaving a private house and passing through the Porte de la Madeleine for an assembly in a garden. Clearly organizers

[24] BN Clairambault 796, pp. 121, 129: 12 June 1675.
[25] AD Ile et Vilaine 1 Bh 14–15.

were at work and plans were being hatched. In Bordeaux after the 1635 uprising, bills posted all over town threatened the tax farmer Montauron for boasting of the large numbers of citizens he was going to hang. Subversive notes were posted on the doors of churches, the hôtel de ville, and the houses of notables, or left on benches or thrown through windows like the "seditious bill" thrown at two of the jurats in a shop by a blond young man who ran away. A man named Laramée was arrested for calling a meeting in the popular quartier Saint Michel.[26]

One of the most common ways agitation could develop was for strategically placed tradesmen to organize a "program" of improvised harassment. In Dijon in 1642 the échevins decided to impose a doubled huitième tax on retail wine sales to raise needed funds. Because this was not a tax imposed by outsiders, they were unusually forthright in denouncing opposition that was directed against their own policies. On 18 September the municipal secretary reported that he had encountered a crowd of people stopped in front of the house of Claude Perard, master apothecary, reading a piece of paper that was posted high on the wall at the corner of the building. Conversation about its meaning was vigorous. One of the more literate onlookers was saying that it was a badly written deliberation of the city council; others who were closer noted that it named the maire and échevin Jacques Clemandot. The secretary climbed up on a large rock that was used as a bench and tore down this "seditious bill against the doubling of the wine tax." He did not reveal its contents, but we know from a subsequent parlementary arrêt that it was one of a number posted by Pierre Oudot, master pastrycook, which began "Monsieur the Mayor" and ended "they must all be massacred."[27]

A few days later the échevins were still greatly alarmed about what seemed to be happening among tavern owners and pastrycooks – the tradesmen whose business would be affected by the tax. "Certain criminals had held assemblies in their houses and drawn up a premeditated plot to assassinate anyone who would undertake the collection of the tax." They were saying

that if anyone tried to go into their cellars and mark the wine . . . they would treat him so rigorously that no one else would dare to go there afterwards . . . They are drawing up libelous statements attacking the magistrates in terms inciting to sedition and posting them in public squares and thoroughfares and on the doors of churches . . . They are trying to make people believe that the doubling of the

---

[26] AM Troyes, série A, no number, "Registre des assemblées générales et consulaires 1623–28": 23 December 1626, 17 August, 2 October 1627; *Inventaire sommaire de la jurade*, vol. v, pp. 125–6, 129–30, 134–5.

[27] The tax was decided on 12 August. By 22 August the échevins were meeting resistance. AM Dijon B 280: 18 September, 30 September, 6 October 1642.

huitième de vin would prohibit inhabitants from selling wine from their own vine-yards . . . Some of these criminals have asserted in various places that the magistrate of this town is the principal *partisan* [incendiary word meaning tax farmer] for the levy of the tax and asserted that neither he nor the *gabeleurs* [another incendiary word meaning illicit extortionists] will be welcomed; that they no longer want to spare anything; that everyone must be massacred [typical defiant language], and that this is going to end up in everyone assassinating each other [obviously an editorial comment by the reporter]. One person, pointing to a shovel for stoking an oven, said that this is how they would accommodate the *maltôtiers* [third incendiary word – extortionist] and that none of them would be spared.[28]

Thus people who sold wine were not only grumbling, but also spreading misinformation designed to capture the popular imagination. It is easy to imagine the indignation as people talked about these growing rumors and anticipated the sort of response they would make.

A major uprising was usually preceded by weeks of this kind of sparring between tax agents, trade groups, anxious consumers, and municipal officials. Popular discontent would be expressed in a series of warnings of varying gravity, some angry, some playful. We can see this process clearly in the attempt to impose new royal offices of *vendeurs et prudhommes de cuir* on Lyon in 1640. On 3 January more than two hundred leatherworkers and their journeymen poured into the council chamber to protest these new offices, claiming that the added cost of the resultant fees would force the closing of shops. Leather merchants from Auvergne were already refusing to bring their wares to the Lyon fair, they said, and if something wasn't done they would all end up in the poorhouse. The prévôt des marchands explained patiently that the council had been working on this problem for a long time and that the only solution was to buy out the new offices. But when the demonstrators repeated that this would force them out of the profession, he got angry and issued a stern warning "that it was necessary to obey and that if any of them broke away from their duty there were means to return them to it." The artisans were ushered out murmuring "that they were not satisfied with this response" and "muttering about some plan of violence."[29]

About six that evening while the council was still in session news arrived that a crowd had gathered in front of the house where the tax farmer Piot had opened his office. Certain "small children" had forced open the door but everyone had fled when Charly, captain of the neighborhood militia, had arrived to restore order. A sign authenticating Piot's authority and bearing the royal arms had been removed from Piot's

---

[28] AM Dijon B 80, fol. 128: 22 September 1642.   [29] AM Lyon BB 194, fols. 10v-12r.

door, but it was later found deposited in Charly's courtyard – a witty challenge, or perhaps a warning?

More warnings followed. On 12 January someone posted a sign on the Saône bridge attacking Piot and Mellier, a councillor from the présidial who had financial ties to Piot's offices. On 26 January an ultimatum from the king demanded immediate satisfaction: the town should either buy out the *partisans* or give proper protection so they could open their collection offices. The échevins protested that they had already taken all possible steps, but they did summon about thirty master courroyeurs and maroquiniers on 28 January and give them a scolding. The town, they warned, had done all it could to protect local interests. Now the leatherworkers should think of the well-being of the whole city and not just their own trade; and – ominous threat – "that they knew how the people in Rouen who had lost control of themselves had been treated, and this set an example that should make anyone behave."[30] This fascinating reference to the brutal repression of the Nu-Pieds uprising the year before demonstrates that the Lyonnais were familiar with similar movements in other cities and saw their conflicts in that light.

Maneuvering continued. On 31 January word came that Jean Dubois, innkeeper at the Golden Lion in the rue de Flandres, had refused to lodge Piot. Was he protecting his property or giving in to neighborhood pressure? Commanded to cooperate, he promised to do so, then backed off. A second command was sent which was refused this time by Dubois' wife. We must imagine each of these steps as a public act, observed in the streets and gossiped about. Getting no satisfaction, Piot complained to the royal council which commissioned Mellier, the man who had already been parodied on the Saône bridge, to enforce the king's wishes. Mellier sparred some more with the échevins, demanding on 4 February that they forbid the townspeople from calling this the "five percent" tax – obviously a pejorative and inflammatory popular name for it.[31] On 9 February Piot was again refused entrance to the Golden Lion, this time by the owner's children, but the next day they agreed to receive him – another case of strategic delay. Trouble continued sporadically for more than a year.

This whole process was really a form of indirect bargaining. Piot was making aggressive moves and flaunting his Parisian support in order to force the reluctant Lyonnais to reimburse his investment. The artisans were mobilizing opposition to remind Piot that milking them would be

---

[30] Ibid., fol. 37r.
[31] Ibid., fol. 44v. The échevins protested that the tax "is in fact a five percent tax on leather as a reading of the edict clearly shows," but that Piot could call it whatever he liked.

neither easy nor pleasant, in hopes that he would come to some accommodation. The échevins were trying to maintain face and keep the lid on the situation while obstructing as much as possible a tax which they also disliked.

Once prepared, larger uprisings were built upon one of three pre-existing associational groupings: guilds, neighborhood solidarities, and militia companies. I will discuss neighborhoods and militias later. Guilds were likely to act in cases where a tax affected their livelihoods directly, and their agitation was most likely to spread when it tied in with some wider source of discontent – wine taxes, food prices, bad times, unemployment. This last point is important because artisans often provided the impetus for a larger community movement, whereas their pursuit of "single-issue" movements had very little potential unless they drew in other groups.

At the most rudimentary level, the members of a trade simply banded together to block execution of an offensive measure. In 1640 Pierre Bourdin, huissier from Le Mans, entered Soissons to serve warrants on the butchers of the city for payment of a tax established by the king in 1638. He headed for the home of Catherin Guillier, doyen of the butchers guild, but as he was approaching the grande boucherie at the end of a bridge across the Aisne, he found a crowd of more than two hundred persons consisting of the butchers, their wives, their children, their servants, and many other allies wielding clubs, knives, and cleavers, and blocking his passage.

They asked where he was going and he replied that he was going to the house of Guillier to serve papers. They responded, "and we are here to tell you that we owe nothing and will pay nothing, and that you would do well to withdraw with the fish you have already caught because if you don't listen to us we will force you to fish some more." [This sort of folkloric resonance is typical of popular intimidation.] One group grabbed Bourdin and his assistants and prepared to cut their throats and throw them in the river, but others intervened and led them to the hôtellerie de la Baumière where they pounded them with rocks, fists and clubs and locked them inside. The butchers surrounded the building until ten o'clock at night, repeating a thousand times "Tête morte et ventre dieu we must set fire to all four sides of La Baumière and burn up the thieves of monopolists who are inside . . ."

Evidently those advocating intimidation had prevailed over those advocating murder, since Bourdin's party, however battered, was allowed to depart peacefully the next morning. As I have noted before, we should always pay attention to the things that did *not* happen in such incidents, which were often more restrained and purposeful than their incendiary language might lead us to believe. Apparently Bourdin was also conscious of this caution, for when he and his assistants were leaving town the next morning they created a new provocation by arresting a butcher and commanding him to accompany them back to Paris. They got as far as Villers-Cotterêts, when a new assembly of two to three hundred consisting of "all the butchers in a body assisted by various valets, boatmen and porters" besieged them in the Unicorn Inn. After being rescued a second time, Bourdin and his party arrested still more persons, but this time what had become an army of butchers blocked all the roads and rescued the prisoners.[32] This is an interesting episode. The butchers must have met numerous times to monitor the situation and mobilize their forces. They flaunted the prospect of serious violence without ever going too far. Perceiving their restraint, Bourdin had the tenacity to keep arresting people. But through brute force the butchers had achieved, at least for the moment, their goal of rejecting the new tax.

Artisans could also be catalysts for action by broader segments of the community. In Amiens labor agitation on the part of the industrial work force was a long-standing tradition. In 1623 wool combers left work as a group and intimidated "new workers." In 1628 say weavers were in the forefront of an attack on a royal intendant who was imposing a tax on looms.[33] In 1636 when a tax farmer tried to impose the *sol pour livre* tax on all manufactured cloth, the response was similar. On the morning of March 29 small groups of weavers and apprentices began roaming the quartier des Minimes in small bands, their faces hidden in cloaks, to engineer a work stoppage by intimidating those still in the shops. The cloaked figures knocked on windows, threatened masters, invaded shops, and cut the warp on looms. By afternoon the movement had expanded. A mixed crowd gathered in the central market "in great numbers" and when échevin Claude de Mons commanded them to return to work, they replied "that they *had* no work and no bread and that was why they would just as soon die." Most of them then started shouting "Let's go to the Red Bull," the inn where an agent of the *sol pour livre* was staying. There they massed in large numbers and began throwing rocks at that establishment and at another inn called the Elephant. A fierce street battle ensued when De Mons' militia company intervened and was repulsed to loud cries of "Bread, bread, or work!"[34] A work stoppage had turned into a wider attack on *partisans* and a call for bread.

The vinegrowers (*vignerons*) of Dijon present another example of an occupational group forming the nucleus of a community movement. Vignerons were among the leaders of the famous lanturelu revolt of 1630

---

[32] BN Ms. fr. 18432, fol. 35.   [33] AM Amiens BB 61, fol. 104r; BB 62, fols. 104v–105r.
[34] AM Amiens FF 1119; narratives in BB 63: 1 April and 2 April. A good analysis of the 1636 revolt is Jean Gallet, "Research on the Popular Movements in Amiens in 1635 and 1636," in Raymond F. Kierstead, ed., *State and Society in Seventeenth-Century France* (New York, 1975), pp. 130–56.

Figure 4 The waterfront in Amiens as sketched by Aimé or Louis Duthoit in 1853. This nineteenth-century view captures the look of the old port. The belfry is on the far right and the cathedral on the left.

discussed in chapter 6. The memory of this formative experience was clearly influential later in the century. Indeed, the organizing skills of the vinegrowers were repeatedly demonstrated. On a November morning in 1639 when the militia company from the parish of Saint Nicolas was late in opening a city gate, they encountered a gathering of over a hundred vignerons muttering about how late it was and blocking the passage. From their ranks emerged a spokesman, François Forrely, described as a perpetual troublemaker, who cursed at the guard's captain, informing him "that he could do whatever he pleased with him." While the gates were being opened someone shouted that they should attack the municipal drummer, and someone else said "No, we mustn't do it, it's the little Bressant." With the gates open, the tension was released and the vignerons streamed out to tend their vines, but Forrely, totally beside himself, couldn't resist coming back to shout "Imbecile of a captain, come out of the guard house, I want to talk to you, come out of there mordieu, imbecile of a captain, come out, ventredieu, I'll kill you, I'm not afraid of you." In this minor incident, rapidly defused, we can glimpse a grumbling crowd in the process of formation, an incipient leader using direct insult to expand a confrontation, and some common sense in the ranks.[35]

Popular memory was long. In 1668 the authorities caused a monitory to be read in all the parishes of Dijon calling for the denunciation of certain evildoing men and women who had

> aroused the people to sedition by saying that it was time to make a lanturelu; carried notices from hearth to hearth to get individuals committed to their party; and enlisted women to start the disorder who went as far as to threaten the taille collector and attack Claude Picard, prudhomme from the parish of Saint Nicolas, an agent in the collection of the tailles . . . They threw mud on him publicly and said that he was an evil man and that they would burn down his house.[36]

We probably have another clue here as to the kind of organizing that might have preceded the appearance of a crowd of angry women in the street. How often did other riots start with notes being passed from door to door and pledges of support being collected? In 1643 in Bordeaux it was reported that people were collecting money door to door for boats that would go down river to Blaye to burn the royal ships that were collecting the unpopular *subvention* tax.[37]

The examples in this chapter are intended to demonstrate the ubiquitous potential for popular revolt. Complaint, protest, and resistance were part of everyday life in seventeenth-century French cities, and in a pinch ordinary citizens had the resources to develop them into a larger, more sustained movement. On a personal level they were deeply imbued with a sense of honor and personal inviolability; on a group level they had ties of trade, neighborhood, or civic guard that gave them frameworks within which to communicate, agitate, and organize. My argument this far has simply been that popular action in major protests is explicable in terms of ordinary people's experiences and impulses. Whatever other forces came into play, no leadership "from above" was necessary to generate the protest.

[35] AM Dijon H 54: 28 November 1639.
[36] AM Dijon I 119: request of 21 November 1668.
[37] *Inventaire sommaire de la jurade*, vol. v, pp. 141–6; Ms. fr. 18752, fols. 35, 37v.

3   The culture of retribution

The consciousness of the crowd is the hardest element to penetrate. How did the demonstrators perceive the social and political arena in which they were acting and what did they think they were doing? Why did they resort to crude violence on occasion, yet most of the time display considerable focus and restraint? To understand the distinctive purposes of urban, seventeenth-century demonstrators, we must set aside prior formulations and explore their intentions with fresh eyes.

There are only a few standard ways of conceptualizing the consciousness of early modern crowds. One model derives from the confrontation of antagonistic sacred communities during the sixteenth-century wars of religion. Then the dominant impulse was eradication of the offending "other" in order to restore religious harmony, producing a form of ritual purification in which symbols were desecrated, sites were pillaged, and individuals or groups were subjected to harassment, intimidation, and symbolic execution, including draggings, disembowelings, and dumpings in the river.[1] Another model derives from the various forms of eighteenth-century food riot in which the crowd intervened to stop the export of grain from a locality, to attack hoarders, or to lower the price of bread or grain to a level considered normal. Thanks to E. P. Thompson's vastly influential analysis of the comparable riots in England, this phenomenon has come to be known as the "moral economy" of the crowd. Thompson's own formulation referred to a rather specific form of confrontation in which crowds defended a set of values derived from the official practice of an earlier age against innovative practices related to the values of the emerging capitalist marketplace. The crowd's actions were defensive, bent on restoring traditional practices and forcing suppliers and sellers to do likewise, and the process was relatively orderly because it relied upon a

---

[1] Davis, "The Rites of Violence"; Barbara B. Diefendorf, *Beneath the Cross: Catholics and Huguenots in Sixteenth-Century Paris* (Oxford, 1991), pp. 28–63; Crouzet, *Les guerriers de Dieu*; Orest Ranum, "The French Ritual of Tyrannicide in the Late Sixteenth Century," *Sixteenth Century Journal* 9 (1980), 63–81; Mark Greengrass, "The Psychology of Religious Violence," *French History* 5 (1991), 467–74.

consensus within the community and set out to regulate not to destroy. Others have extended the concept of moral economy to mean any situation in which crowds acted with moral purpose to correct an indignity viewed as upsetting the proper order of things, and in this more general sense the term can be applied to most early modern crowds.[2]

Seventeenth-century movements contained a curious mixture of elements from these two common conceptualizations. Some of the punishments inflicted recalled the persecutions of the religious wars, but with grievances and targets that were entirely secular. There was also something of a "moral economy" to the indignation of seventeenth-century crowds protesting unpleasant innovations on the grounds that they violated traditional liberties. The only model that has been proposed for these urban revolts is the idea developed by Pillorget and Bercé of the unified community coming together to expel an offending outsider, usually a tax agent coming to impose demands from the increasingly intrusive absolutist state.[3] But this formulation does not seem to me to capture the essence of what seventeenth-century crowds were really doing.

We have already seen that ordinary citizens were never passive when confronted with an attack on personal territory or reputation. The response to such a challenge to honor would be a violent counterreaction entailing refusal, counter-insult, and at least a show of violent resistance as a way of maintaining face and humiliating the opposition. Most important, the challenged party would insult the challenger by invoking infamous punishments: beating, maiming, dragging, carving up, as the form of degradation that the opponent deserved. Thus the face-to-face reaction to an intrusive authority was a reflexive "I refuse," coupled with a rapid "this is illicit," followed by a counter attack of "you are a scoundrel for having abused your authority and violated the rules of proper relations with me, and you should be humiliated like a criminal and purged from the community."

When extended from individual outrage to collective protest, this last impulse, an almost palpable desire to punish the offending authority for

[2] Louise A. Tilly, "The Food Riot as a Form of Political Conflict in France," *Journal of Interdisciplinary History* 2 (1971), 23–57; E. P. Thompson, "The Moral Economy of the English Crowd in the Eighteenth Century," reprinted with new commentary in E. P. Thompson, *Customs in Common*, pp. 185–351; Bouton, *The Flour War*; James C. Scott, *The Moral Economy of the Peasant: Rebellion and Subsistence in Southeast Asia* (New Haven, 1976).

[3] Bercé discusses this concept throughout *Histoire des Croquants*, especially in part 1, chapter 6; Pillorget stresses it in *Mouvements*, pp. 911–61. While both authors see communities united against the outsider as only one of various possible relationships, they both rely heavily on this model as the centerpiece of their analysis.

misdeeds perceived as a violation of trust, is what I call the "culture of retribution." It lay at the heart of the protests of the seventeenth century, regardless of whether they were occasioned by grain shortages, tax excesses, troop lodgings, or other perceived offenses against appropriate traditional procedures. The quest for retribution, defined as "deserved punishment for evil done," is exactly where these crowds differed from the concept of moral economy (restoring a violated norm) or community purification (expelling or exterminating the offender, pure and simple). Moreover, concealed within the desire to punish was the implication that values involving governance and the community had been betrayed. By rioting, these crowds were participating in a dialogue about the management of their city and calling the authorities to task for failing to handle things properly.

Attacking those responsible

But let us return to the evidence and explore crowd motivations step by step. The most obvious indicator of a crowd's intentions was its choice of targets. These were first of all "outsiders," viewed as perpetrators of invasive innovations and treated as scapegoats. They might be legal process-servers sent by a judicial authority to enforce a legal judgment; they might be agents of tax farmers sent to collect a particular kind of fee; or they could be any bearer of public authority, from the governor on down, who was enforcing an intrusive measure. The operative terms here were *traitant* and *partisan*, both of which had negative connotations. The first was derived from the *traité*, a tax farming contract, and the second from the *partie*, the cartel of investors who underwrote the contract, paying a lump sum to the crown for the right to collect a certain type of revenue. These indirect taxes farmed out to private collectors were a feature of the difficult era of Richelieu and Mazarin when the government was straining to raise extraordinary revenues to pay for the Thirty Years War.[4] They took the form of some kind of annoying levy like a tariff on retail sales or a tax on offices and services which required face to face contact between agent and payee, along with inspection of the payee's merchandise, titles, or contracts. The *partisans* encountered by crowds were usually local subcontractors or employees of the central financiers. It is therefore not surprising that these relatively menial, poorly equipped intruders became the

---

[4] On the financial exigency of the state, see Richard Bonney, *Political Change in France under Richelieu and Mazarin, 1624–1661* (Oxford, 1978); Richard Bonney, *The King's Debts: Finance and Politics in France, 1589–1661* (Oxford, 1981); James C. Collins, *Fiscal Limits of Absolutism: Direct Taxation in Seventeenth-Century France* (Berkeley, 1988); Françoise Bayard, *Le monde des financiers au XVIIe siècle* (Paris, 1988).

ommunity animosity or that the terms *partisan* and *traitant*
rogatory epithets, easily linked to more emphatic labels like
extortionist), bloodsucker, and thief.

acks on agents were only the first step of an unfolding process.
example, the demands of a crowd in Vannes, Brittany, in May
1643.[5] Grain was scarce that year, and exports had been banned by an
arrêt of the Parlement. On 18 May, however, a new arrêt reversed the
ruling and permitted export of grain by water. Rapid shifts of policy
which had the appearance of self-interest were suspect in the eyes of the
community. The Parlement was far away in Rennes and there was suspicion that this about-face had been obtained through the intervention of
interested parties. When Leguinio, a judicial crier, proclaimed this
second arrêt in the port where ships were loading grain, he was immediately chased away by an angry crowd. When he returned with La Rivière,
president in the présidial court, the highest judicial authority in the city,
the two men encountered "a very large collection of people armed with
clubs, rocks, hatchets and other tools" surrounding the house of
Alexandre Bigot, nicknamed Villiers. As they approached the house,
people from the crowd complained to them "that grain was being loaded
contrary to the [recent] prohibition, to the prejudice of the needs of the
public which were so great, several of them said, that for the last eight days
they had only been able to feed their children animal fodder and vegeta-
bles without a single piece of bread."

Thus the demonstrators were motivated first by necessity and second
by the challenge of a legal ruling which they rejected as illicit and which
they chose to discredit in favor of an earlier ruling more to their liking. But
their response was not, as one schooled in grain riots might expect, to
seize the grain or attack the ships. Instead, they attacked the man they
"knew" was responsible. When La Rivière suggested that attacking
Villiers was not the proper way to register a protest and that everyone
should go home, "they began to cry out tumultuously that the magistrates
were in league with the merchants and that it was all the same to them
whether they died by the hangman or from starvation, urging us to go
away or else they might have to commit some even more unfortunate
action, since they were determined to pillage the house of sieur Villiers
and several other merchants who were the cause of the shortage of grain."
Thus they respected their local judge and expected that he would agree
with them, but this deference was provisional. When Leguinio and La
Rivière attempted to enter the house, the demonstrators physically
carried them back outside, saying "that they [the magistrates] would have

5 Report in Ms fr. 18598, fol. 113.

to leave because they [the people] were determined to cause disorder, and they held their hatchets and clubs raised, ready to strike the furniture."

La Rivière and Leguinio left and returned with a larger force, although most of the bourgeois refused to assemble. By the time they got back all Villiers' doors and windows and his furniture inside had been smashed; barrels were broken open; and a great abundance of wine was spread all over the building. The majority of the rioters – men, women, and children – were drunkenly proclaiming "that they would burn and pillage everything." They were apparently exacting compensation for being wronged, and no doubt enjoying it. Unable to master the situation, the authorities issued an ordinance forbidding export of grain by the river and setting a maximum price in the market. By all appearances the protesters had now achieved their goal of inducing the authorities to reimpose regulations. But this paternalistic concession to the demands of the crowd did not work because retribution against the merchants loomed larger in the eyes of the crowd than prohibition of exports. Like the Bordelaises we saw in chapter 2, they wanted to punish those who were betraying them, and they were prepared to take the law into their own hands to do it. "This satisfied no one, and after they had beaten up the drummer who was going out to make the announcement, people began to shout that they intended to draw up their own ordinances and execute them themselves and that [the authorities were] only trying to amuse them, saying in a single voice, let's go and do the same thing to the others, let's all go to Duval's"; and they went running off with the magistrates following.

At Duval's house the same scene was repeated, and the authorities, now more alarmed, tried a diversionary tactic by having the wine the crowd demanded transported to a square outside the city as a way of moving them away from their targets. But the conflict intensified. During the night the crowd went to the house of a sieur Laverdin in the marketplace, but Laverdin and his friends had armed themselves and were able to repulse the crowd. The inhabitants of the port had also taken up arms (presumably on the side of order) and the avocat du roi had arrested seven or eight rioters. The next morning a crowd in the faubourg du Marché de Saint Patern gathered and tried to break down the Saint Patern gate where the prisons were located, demanding the prisoners' release and saying that otherwise "they would subject everything to fire and blood." We remember from the personal attacks in chapter 2 that this hyperbole probably meant no more than that they were angry and determined. They smashed the drawbridge, tried to break open the gate, fired muskets at the walls, and threw rocks until the prisoners were released. In their report the magistrates claimed that releasing the prisoners had been the only thing to do, given that "these troubles seemed to be only beginning, and from all directions beggars [*fainéants*] were gathering from surrounding parishes, and even inside the city you could hear the artisans in every carrefour murmuring against the magistrates and accusing them of conniving with the merchants for a grain treaty that would cause shortage in the region and saying that if they were forced to take up arms they would do so to aid those who opposed the export treaty."[6]

This is striking evidence from the magistrates themselves that the menu peuple's objectives went beyond procuring grain. The protesters were anxious about subsistence but they also monitored the legal measures needed to protect it. They did not hesitate to reinterpret the law to suit their purposes, and they would not tolerate even a reading of an edict that seemed to violate their basic rights. They were especially enraged at merchants from their own community who were seen as instigating and profiting from antisocial measures, so their primary motivation became to exact retribution for this betrayal. They were willing to work with the authorities, but quite ready to believe that they were in league with the enemy.

Similar motivations can be explored in two episodes in Troyes.[7] On Friday, 27 June 1586, two *partisans* and their assistants arrived at the Logis du Dauphin and prepared to collect a new tax of 24 écus from each master of each trade.[8] By Sunday people all over the city were beginning to gather and complain. A concerned city council tried to persuade the collectors that it was foolhardy to serve warrants on people on a Sunday "which was a dangerous day" and that it would be more prudent for them to leave town and then negotiate with each trade separately. But the agents were not dissuaded: by late afternoon they had served notice on five hundred persons. They were acting like Regnard in Argenteuil but on a much larger scale: an obnoxious demand was being imposed in a threatening manner on hundreds of well-connected individuals on a day of rest when they were free to confer and organize.

By late afternoon a crowd of reportedly eight hundred men, women, and children had gathered outside the logis where the agents were

---

[6] Ibid.
[7] For background on Troyes, see Théophile Boutiot, *Histoire de la ville de Troyes*, 5 vols. (Paris, 1870–80) [reprinted (Marseilles, 1977)]; Gustave Carré, *Histoire populaire de Troyes et du département de l'Aube* (Troyes, 1881); Jacques Paton, *Le corps de ville de Troyes (1470–1790)* (Troyes, 1939); Kuno Böse, *Amt und soziale Stellung: Die Institution der "Elus" in Frankreich im 16. und 17. Jahrhundert am Beispiel der Elektion Troyes*, 2 vols. (Frankfurt, 1986).
[8] My account is based on Nicolas Dare, "Mémoires et livre de famille de Nicolas Dare," in *Collection de documents inédits relatifs à la ville de Troyes et à la Champagne méridionale publiés par la Société académique de l'Aube*, vol. III (Troyes, 1886), pp. 49–62. These events are also discussed briefly in Boutiot, *Histoire* [1977 reprint], vol. IV, pp. 143–8.

staying. They broke down the door and stormed inside while the two *partisans*, four huissiers and two sergeants hid as best they could. One of the huissiers was found hiding in a horse stall and mercilessly beaten with clubs. Begging not to be killed, he blurted out the names of the local financial backers of the new tax (and presumably his employers): Sanguin, Raguin, and Borne. These names suggested further action. The huissier was dragged to the house of Raguin, who was clerk of the bailliage court, and killed on the doorstep. The premises were then pillaged and all of Raguin's papers were burned, including documents belonging to the court. The violence had been redirected from the agents to the profiteers and their institutional connections.

Recognizing the need to restore order, the urban militia assembled and dispersed the rioters about midnight, while the échevins rescued the frightened agents and got them out of town. But at four the next morning, the crowd reassembled and pillaged the houses of Sanguin and Borne. This time the militia companies refused to rally, complaining coldly that "they did not want to defend gabeleurs." As a result, the demonstrators expanded their targets. A leader emerged, a poor weaver who was reported to have announced, "We need a captain: if you want me to do it, look at the pitchfork I am carrying over my shoulder and call me 'Capitaine La Fourche.'" He was accompanied by his wife and by troops reportedly consisting of children between seven and fifteen years old armed only with rocks – a motley, improvised sort of force.[9]

This group besieged and occupied the house of militia captain Nicolas Largentier where they acquired a veritable arsenal of pikes, halberds, and muskets, intensifying the threat to social order. This was "a very dangerous situation," noted Nicolas Dare, the bourgeois chronicler who wrote a narrative of the event. In addition to being militia captain, Largentier was councillor in the city council and apparently had a reputation as a maltôtier, although the échevins later denied that they had heard any such thing. Largentier must have been unpopular because the neighbors not only failed to defend his house, but they threw logs out of windows which the rioters used to break down his doors. Finally roused to action by this new violence, two hundred armed bourgeois arrived and routed the rioters. Two demonstrators were killed on the spot and thirty died later from wounds. According to Dare, those caught were all poor inhabitants from surrounding villages, except for a certain Martin Callevi, baker. The attack had moved from the *partisans*, to their local bosses, to a prominent citizen who was associated with similar exploitative activities. Dare reported later that Largentier was associated in the popular mind with

[9] Dare, "Mémoires," p. 51. This story sounds embellished.

Sebastien Zamet, one of Henry III's Parisian bankers, to whom he had been dispatched by the city in 1584 to negotiate fiscal business. If Dare was reporting accurately, this would be interesting evidence that the crowd had a long memory. Deputies to court and the connections they revealed were observed and discussed by the community. Largentier was also a militia captain and a city official, and thus an apparent colleague of Raguin, Sanguin, and Borne.[10]

This protest had alarmed the authorities, to judge by the subsequent repression. Searches were conducted of the poorer districts of the city and many pieces of allegedly stolen furniture were recovered. Thirty-two prisoners were taken. On Tuesday Dinteville, the governor, arrived with sixty gentlemen. On Wednesday Dare himself commanded a night watch of 150 footsoldiers and 40 horsemen. At midnight they successfully arrested La Fourche and his wife, who were hanged in secret the following night inside the prison, along with two rioters. This unusual execution was to be remembered by the crowd for a generation.

The June riot had been serious, but its real significance only becomes clear in the context of a second riot, ostensibly over grain shortages, that broke out six weeks later.[11] The crisis developed in measured stages. First some artisans, probably neighborhood leaders, came to the maire and asked him to modify bakery regulations in order to reduce shortages of bread. He granted their request but the situation did not improve. Then a group of fullers, along with needlemakers, weavers and dyers, complained that the "best houses" were buying up the grain in the fields before it got to market; that grain merchants had their attics full, that still others were "gabeleurs." Here is the genesis of a movement from within the community: poorer inhabitants grumble; their more responsible leaders seek corrective measures; a popular explanation develops for the source of the problem. To dissipate negative rumors, the échevins led an inspection tour to the attics where grain was supposed to be hoarded, but found no unusual stocks. Again, they were trying to cooperate but there was no effective way to discredit the strong popular conviction that foul play was occurring.

The next step was direct action. The angry artisans declared that if grain prices did not come down from 22 to 10 sous per boisseau they would break into the storehouses. On 28 August forty or fifty men gathered in the Notre-Dame cemetery with rocks and daggers, but were

---

[10] Ibid., pp. 54, 61–2. Largentier was from a well-known family of financiers. See Léo Mouton, "Deux financiers au temps de Sully: Largentier et Moisset," *Bulletin de la Société de l'histoire de Paris et de l'Ile de France* 64 (1938), 65–105; Böse, *Amt und soziale Stellung*, vol. II, pp. 165–7. I am grateful to the anonymous reader from Cambridge University Press who pointed out these references.   [11] Ibid., p. 59.

stopped by the watch. The next day they tried again. On 29 August at 2 a.m. when the watch was retiring for the night, a crowd headed off to pillage several notables, including the president of the bailliage court and the same Nicolas Largentier who had been attacked in June. The fact that the leaders were five Carré brothers, all fullers, along with some soapmakers, needlemakers, and a blacksmith, confirms the impression that this was a planned masculine movement organized within trades. Again the authorities resorted to force. Dinteville and his forty gentlemen were summoned and the échevins decided to call up forty companies of sixty men each and around seventy horsemen. In another nocturnal sweep, eleven prisoners were taken in their beds. A battle for public opinion followed: while popular rumor threatened reprisals if any prisoners died, the magistrates set up gallows at three key locations, causing sixty people to flee the city, but no death sentences were ultimately issued.

This summer of conflict in Troyes represented more than an isolated expulsion of *partisans* followed by an isolated grain riot. The two movements were linked by underlying exasperation at hard times and a deep distrust of municipal elites. The grape harvest had been mediocre. Grain prices were high. There was no work because of a recent bout of plague, and the poorer inhabitants, Dare reported, had used up their reserves the previous year. Faced with these hardships, the disadvantaged became resentful of their rich compatriots and acted both to punish and to redistribute. Many started murmuring that given the high price of grain, "they should share with the rich."[12] Indeed, in both attacks local notables were seen as the source of the problem: in one case they were the backers of the new tax on artisans; in the other they were hoarders of grain. The enemy, it seemed, was in the heart of the community, and the bourgeois militia companies, though wavering because of their shared hatred of gabeleurs, rallied when they saw that the poorer artisans were going to try to seize weapons and food supplies. In both Vannes and Troyes the crowds looked beyond immediate targets to more fundamental problems concerning rich citizens, and demands for relief were rapidly transformed into demands for retribution.

Moral indignation took many forms. We can see the same impulses in a different guise in an unusual incident that took place in Aix in 1695.[13] A man named Julien was subcontractor to Léopold Roger, *traitant* of the offices of *jurés crieurs publics d'enterrements des morts*, from whom he had

---

[12] Ibid., p. 61.
[13] This account is based on a series of letters and reports in AN G[7] 463 dated from 10 October to 6 November 1695. A slightly different analysis is offered in Pillorget, *Mouvements*, pp. 947–50, using the same sources.

acquired the capacity to issue the legal authorizations required for funerals, a power formerly held by the consuls. Unable to find buyers for the offices, he opened an agency to issue the authorizations himself. This meant involvement in public burials, a sensitive function which had resulted in insults and harassment on several prior occasions. Julien's unpopularity was thus a matter of public knowledge on 9 October when a desperately poor man who lived on the third floor of a house near the place du Marché died, leaving eight children. Attempts to arrange his burial were thwarted by the claims of Julien for payment. Once again we see the moral indignation of the community building through a graduated series of steps punctuated, no doubt, by heated discussion in the streets. First the Confraternity of Pénitents Blancs which usually handled charity cases offered to provide a bier, but was prohibited by Julien. Then a neighbor woman visited Julien on the morning of 10 October and appealed for his sympathy on the grounds that after twenty-four hours the body was beginning to become offensive, but she was turned away. One account claimed that Julien also rejected 6 livres offered by charitable neighbors for the right to allow the Pénitents to provide the bier. Clearly the neighbors were trying to take care of the problem and Julien was getting in the way.[14] Taking matters into their own hands, some local women finally improvised a ladder on which the corpse was carried down to the street, where a crowd of onlookers said angrily that they should take it to the house of Julien. Once again, the impulse of the crowd was to shame and insult the responsible party by bringing the problem home to his doorstep, like the treatment of Raguin's process-server in Troyes. But the confraternity forbade this action, so the body was carried instead to the church for burial. The sight of the poor man's corpse being carried through the streets on a ladder was enough to arouse a crowd of two hundred men, women, and children, who invested Julien's house with cries of "Kill, kill, that thief of a *partisan* of death." They threw rocks until all the windows were smashed, dumped the furniture out the windows, scattered papers, removed clothes and valuables. Julien escaped over the roofs. Prisoners taken by the authorities included the son of a butcher, an apprentice shoemaker, an apprentice braidmaker, a lackey, the pregnant wife of a dyer, the wife of a wood splitter, and a confectioner.

This is a good example of a crowd acting out of moral outrage on an occasion when decency in the community was at issue more than immediate subsistence. The riot had been prepared by a sequence of

---

[14] It is always possible that these preliminary actions never took place, but rather reflect what people were *saying* had happened.

prior conflicts generating news and preparing attitudes.[15] People had tried to cope. Authorities had been consulted and negotiations had taken place but the situation had become intolerable. It was *after* the immediate problem had been resolved that the crowd, aroused by the visible manifestation of their expectations and fears – that death itself was being taxed – stormed through the house and avenged the dead body. They were not reacting to some imaginary myth, but punishing a real person for a specific indignity. If the occupations of those arrested were any indication, these were probably humble people from the immediate neighborhood of the deceased.

When crowds felt betrayed by authorities or violated by exploiters, the punitive reaction was usually relatively benign. However, seventeenth-century crowds did, on occasion, engage in acts of intense brutality. Let us look at one such case in which the familiar attack on the messenger took a particularly dark turn. On the Island of Ré (off La Rochelle) in 1661 the villages around Saint Martin had formed a syndicate to fight a new tax on wine, their chief export.[16] The farmers-general had recently claimed that because very little wine was exported any more without being processed, it was only reasonable to extend a traditional wine tax to eaux de vie and other processed wines. The villagers had launched a countersuit, naming André Boissonière as "syndic of the inhabitants," their official representative. The focal point of their movement was the seigneurial court, where Jacques Baudouin was seneschal and Jean Jamon was procureur fiscal (prosecutor). Clearly there had been meetings and long discussions, allowing popular opinion to coalesce. Although the inhabitants' appeal was pending before the Cour des Aides of La Rochelle, the farmers-general had gone ahead and obtained a ruling from the royal council that all inhabitants were required to register whatever processed wines were in their possession. Like the counter-arrêt in Vannes, this appeared to the population to be an effort to bypass community rights which were still in litigation and pave the way for what looked to the islanders like a grievous new tax.

On 4 July Louis Arlay, sergeant-royal from La Rochelle, arrived on the island to promulgate a new arrêt de conseil. He had been sent on behalf of Claude Revel, fermier-général des aides de France, and while he did not himself perform any inspections, his arrival must have looked like the beginning of a crackdown. Arlay was going to his death. As he made his

---

[15] The intendant accused the consuls of agitating against Julien, and the governor took the side of the consuls. But none of these complications, which helped prepare the popular confrontation, was connected directly with the actions of the crowd.

[16] This episode is found in a set of papers from BN Mélanges Colbert 104.

rounds he began to notice that he was being followed at a distance by Jamon and a group of eight or more local people carrying clubs and striking belligerent poses. Eventually Jamon, the representative of local authority, stopped Arlay and demanded to know why he was wearing a sword. This was a ritual challenge like the insults exchanged in Amiens between Corbie and Lamouche.[17] Arlay replied that it was none of his business. No doubt wondering what to do, Jamon and his followers continued to stalk Arlay, then finally they arrested him and escorted him to the court chamber, where Arlay identified himself to the seneschal and explained his mission. While they were talking an angry mob of eighty or more was gathering outside. Someone was heard to say "that this huissier had come to impose new taxes on eaux de vie and that they should beat him up along with Fanton who had given him support and that they should burn down Fanton's house." The sources give no clue as to who Fanton was, but evidently Arlay, like most similar agents, had found local supporters as well as opposition. Jamon finally disarmed Arlay and told him to leave the island, but when Jamon began to escort him away, the crowd began harassing Arlay and pelting him with rocks, despite Jamon's lame and undoubtedly insincere commands that they desist.

Arlay collapsed, wounded by rocks, outside a church and pleaded with the local priest for sanctuary, but neither the priest nor Jamon would lift a finger to help him, except by administering confession. He was pursued down a side street which turned out to be a cul de sac and died, riddled with blows that "spilled his brains on the pavement." His body was left untended for twenty-four hours and was reportedly gnawed on by dogs. A week later when two women were sent from La Rochelle by Arlay's widow to try to retrieve it, local women advised them that they would be risking their lives if they revealed their identities. Thus not only was Arlay murdered, but his body continued to be an object of contempt and manipulation even after his death.

When Jamon was arrested for this crime by the royal authorities (it was, after all, the reign of Louis XIV), a further meeting held in the house of a local curé gives us another window on the mobilization of a community. The belligerents were outraged: "cursing and taking the name of the Lord in vain, they said that the procureur should be freed and Dolbre and Recq added that they should set fire to the revenue ship [of the Aides] and go to the fort to rescue the procureur [Jamon], whom they called their chief and leader, saying that he had the good of the country [at heart] and that he had been betrayed." This is the same impulse we saw in Vannes: tough talk, an intense sense of betrayal, an impulse to burn the property of the

[17] See p. 30.

offending party, and a desire to rescue the prisoners. There was also retribution against complicit authorities. The crowd stormed out and massed in front of the house of Baudouin the seneschal, saying that he had doublecrossed them and that his house should be pillaged and burned. Curé Louis Rocher, one of the enragés, ran to ring the tocsin, and Pierre Recq raced through all the taverns of Saint Martin, challenging everyone he met to support the party of the prévôt.[18]

This affair frames sharply a vindictive act by an enraged community that can only be called a lynching. The deliberate murder of Arlay and the humiliation of his body were regretted by no one – not by the authorities, the priest, the women – although we do not hear from "Fanton" who, along with other complicit individuals, undoubtedly had to lie low.

Collective sentiments

Several collective sentiments emerge from these examples. The first was the desire to attack and humiliate the immediate perpetrators of an offense. Agents caught at the wrong moment might be beaten or chased, but the universal response – the one seen in virtually every incident – was the pillaging of the responsible party's room, house, or estate, with the emphasis on ceremonial tearing of papers and smashing or burning of possessions, almost as if the act of pulverizing itself was therapeutic. Rocks thrown and possessions smashed symbolized not only the rejection of the offensive measure and the intimidation of its authors, but also the punishment of those immediately responsible.

Something of the intensity of this condemnation is captured by the term "gabeleur," which meant someone trying to impose a "gabelle" on the community. This word was used everywhere, but it had almost mystical connotations in the Southwest where freedom from the salt tax was considered a fundamental right and where its imposition was a source of periodic struggle.[19] In 1645 the duc d'Epernon wrote to the Chancellor Séguier that "the people of this district are so aroused by the very name 'gabelle,' even where it is not aimed at them, that they are beside themselves when they hear it uttered"; and in 1637 the intendant Verthamont was appalled when he realized that the royal council had "inadvertently" used the word "gabelles" in his commission, since "this single term could produce many disorders even if this province is enjoying the most complete

---

[18] Mel. Col. 104.
[19] Bercé discusses the connotation of gabelle and maltôte in *History of Peasant Wars*, p. 226. However, his statement that the former term was used in the south and the latter in the north does not hold up, and my reading of "gabelle" is slightly different.

calm."[20] In Troyes in 1586 militiamen complained that "they did not want to defend gabeleurs," and fullers argued that "gabeleurs" were hoarding grain in the city. In Dijon in 1630 the syndic of the city, making his nocturnal rounds, encountered vinegrowers with their wives and children who "spoke of gabelles, saying that they were so poor they couldn't earn their livelihood."[21] In Agen in 1672 in the dark of an evening when some apprentice printers were posting an announcement of the publication of a new religious book on a church doorway,

> some inhabitants of the quarter started crying out that they were posting the gabelle. They roused the neighbors and in a moment there were almost eighty or a hundred persons, men and women, armed with swords, halberds, clubs, iron skewers, and a few firearms, lighting up the streets with torches of straw . . . and shouting that they wanted to kill the gabeleurs.[22]

Thus the much-feared gabelle was not a specific tax, least of all a mere tax on salt. The term stood for the ultimate assault on the community from the outside – a grievous innovation that intruded on the life of the community, and that was being perpetrated with the assistance of enemies from within. It had the connotation of novelty, of oppression, of betrayal, and most of all it implied action: a gabelle was something one rose up against and a gabeleur was the most hateful of traitors. Bercé speaks of "the psychosis of the gabelle," but before we conclude that some sort of collective myth transformed the crowd's response into a panic release of barbaric impulses, we should consider that popular fears usually had a realistic foundation and that the way the term was used varied with concrete circumstances.[23]

Expulsion and humiliation of agents, pillaging of houses associated with the abuse, fighting back against the gabelle, were all related to the quest for retribution, which was especially applied not to alien intruders but to treasonous neighbors and perfidious leaders. Again and again the sense of betrayal comes through as an intense emotion calling for a specific response. Physical violence should be seen in this context. There was a clear connection between such personal insults as dragging, pulling hair, threatening to cut open, stoning, or showering with mud and the crowd's treatment of bodies. When Jean de Lavergne, an avocat in Agen, accused the consuls of misusing funds, this so enraged consul Ducros that

---

[20] Epernon to Séguier, 21 November 1645; Verthamon to Séguier, 20 May 1637: Hovyn de Tranchère, *Les dessous de l'histoire*, 2 vols. (Paris, 1886), vol. I, pp. 370–2, 316–18.

[21] Dare, "Mémoires," pp. 51, 59; AM Dijon I 117: deliberation of 27 February 1630.

[22] "Relation de la sédition de 1672," reproduced in André Mateu, "Les révoltes populaires de la juridiction d'Agen dans leur contexte socio-économique" (thèse de doctorat de 3e cycle, Université de Toulouse, 1980), pp. 1890–2.

[23] Bercé, *Histoire des Croquants*, p. 324.

he called Lavergne "a perfidious traitor who should be thrown in the river."[24] This, then, was the meaning of dragging and throwing in the river: that the individual in question was a traitor to the community.

Popular punishments also bore clear analogies to official punishments. A servant from Agen who had killed his master with a dagger was sentenced to being dragged through the streets alive, and then he was to have first his fist and then his head cut off (an analogy was being made here between fist [*poing*] and dagger [*poignard*]) in front of the house where the crime had been committed. His body was then to be hung from the gallows, and the head and the fist were to be prominently displayed on a post.[25] These were precisely the procedures mimicked by popular justice, including the display of the body in front of a relevant building, but with the important difference that it was the dead body that was punished by crowds. In spite of many cruel threats, popular demonstrators did not usually torture living victims, except for largely spontaneous beatings administered in the heat of rage. If, as Foucault argues, public executions were a political ritual which "reactivated power" and restored the absolute sovereignty of the crown over the body of the victim, then perhaps it could be argued that popular mutilations and draggings reestablished the claims of the citizens on their leaders and that the punishment of corpses reinforced a sense of the peoples' authority to correct the failings of their superiors.[26]

Agen, 1635

All these themes appear in the most dramatic urban uprising in seventeenth-century France, the massacre of "gabeleurs" in Agen in 1635.[27] Like the inhabitants on the Island of Ré, the people of Agen were braced for the arrival of the agents of a new tax on wine which was viewed as a fundamental intrusion into the lives of every citizen – a classic "gabelle" if there ever was one. Agents were already inspecting local winecellars and

---

[24] AM Agen BB 49: 10 May 1630.

[25] Quoted in *Inventaire sommaire des archives communales antérieures à 1790: Agen* (Paris, 1884), p. 23 (from AM Agen BB 26).

[26] Michel Foucault, *Discipline and Punish: the Birth of the Prison*, tr. by Alan Sheridan (New York, 1979), pp. 32–69.

[27] Bercé does an exhaustive study of this important revolt in *Histoire des Croquants*, pp. 323–37, with which I differ only in interpretive details. It is also discussed in Emmanuel Le Roy Ladurie, *Les paysans de Languedoc*, 2 vols. (Paris, 1966), vol. I, pp. 503–8. By a fluke of historiography the revolt of Agen is not well known to English-speaking readers because, although both these books have been translated, neither abridgment includes the section on Agen. There is an account in Porchnev, *Les soulèvements populaires*, pp. 166–75. Also helpful is the dissertation by André Mateu cited in note 22. The best modern history of Agen is Stephane Baumont (ed.), *Histoire d'Agen* (Toulouse, 1991).

there was ample reason to suspect treachery from persons within the community. Moreover, the city was already filled with royal officers, many of them parvenus connected to two newly established financial courts, the *élection*, established in 1622 and the *Cour des Aides*, established in 1630. These social climbers, many from elsewhere, appeared to the ordinary citizens as rich parvenus trying to link their future to the royal administration rather than defending their newly adopted city.

On 14 May the people of Bordeaux had staged the biggest uprising in recent times against the new wine tax, which they called a gabelle.[28] Echo revolts broke out as the news from Bordeaux moved up the Garonne valley and the populations began bracing themselves for the inevitable counter strike by the crown and the angry response of the citizens. In Agen the consuls began stockpiling weapons. There were several false alarms. On 23 May some boatmen cried out "get the gabeleurs" when they saw some notables crossing the river. On 28 May more rumors of gabeleurs swept through the streets. The scene was set, but the trouble did not begin in earnest until almost a month after the first news. This period of preparation, which allowed time for tensions to mount and rumors to build, helps to explain the suddenness of the outbreak when it occurred. People were fearful and everyone was waiting for someone to make a move.

The occasion was provided at 10 a.m. on Sunday 17 June, in an exchange between Joseph Tissandier and some boatmen in the port.[29] Tissandier was an archer working for Senbel, vice seneschal of the Agennais, who in turn was assembling troops to be used by the duc d'Epernon to repress the rebellion in Bordeaux. Tissandier, who was no doubt nervous, was anxious to embark on the mail boat, but when he tried to get the boatmen to move up their departure time, they replied that they could not leave yet because they did not have the mail packet from the consuls. Tissandier then said to them, "You are delaying so that you won't have to go at all, and you have been bragging that when we are out on the Garonne you are going to drown us, but we will take care of all that; when we're on board we'll tie you to the boat so that you will run the same risk as us."[30] We can see in this challenge the level of tension and suspicion that already existed on both sides. The boatmen, generally a

---

[28] The Bordeaux uprising of 1635 is discussed on pp. 133–43.

[29] My account is based largely on the journal of Malebaysse published by A. Magen as "Une émeute à Agen en 1635," *Recueil des travaux de la Société d'agriculture, science et arts d'Agen* 7 (1854–5), 196–224 (partly republished by G. Tholien, *Revue de l'Agenais* (1893), 441–53) [hereafter Malebaysse, "Journal," referring to the Magen version]. In addition I used the procès-verbal by the consuls reproduced in Bercé, *Histoire des Croquants*, pp. 718–20; and the series of consular deliberations in AM Agen BB 53–5.

[30] Malebaysse, "Journal," 204.

subversive group, had obviously been talking about refusing to transport the potential suppressors of the Bordeaux rebels and Tissandier, who was associated with the repression himself, obviously knew it.

Some women cried out "that the gabeleurs wanted to kill the boatmen," and a crowd set out after Tissandier, who fled into the nearby Jesuit church. This was the moment that had been expected. While a large mob gathered at the church, others assembled at the Saint George gate saying that one had to kill the gabeleurs and crying "Vive le Roy sans gabelle," and another crowd by the river attacked the mail boat. Meanwhile in the church Tissandier begged the enraged crowd to let him at least say confession, then used the opportunity to flee into the sacristy and out into the Jesuits' courtyard where the crowd in hot pursuit killed him with swords and halberds. One of his hands was cut off, and later that evening his body was tied by the feet with a rope, dragged through the streets, and thrown in the Garonne.

An outcry went up all over town. While Guillaume Le Merle, wine porter, climbed up the large belfry and rang the tocsin, another crowd went to the house of David Codoing councillor in the *élection*, who was considered to be a grasping financier. They broke in, destroyed his wooden furniture, tapestries, and bed coverings, threw his linen into the street, took his gold and silver, debts and other papers, and broke all his windows. Pillagers called out the windows that Codoing was hiding in the convent of the Augustine friars, so the crowd rushed there and said to the monks, "Give us Codoing or we will kill you." They searched the church and monastery and all the haylofts in the vicinity until they found Codoing in the attic of Mademoiselle de Savares, mother-in-law of his son, hiding behind a load of wheat. He was beaten to death with iron rods, robbed of 200 pistoles from his pockets and then his body was tied by the feet with his garters, dragged, and dumped in the Garonne. This was an act of retribution for resentments that had a prior history: "This man was so poorly viewed by the people that when he was dragged through the streets there wasn't a good mother's son who didn't give him a blow or a kick," reported Malebaysse, the principal chronicler of the uprising.[31]

When he tried to stop people from ringing the church bells, Guillaume du Périer, canon in the Saint Caprais church, was told "Get out of here, you are a gabeleur." Later he was pursued by rock-throwing women shouting "Kill the gabeleur." He was so frightened that he threw himself off the city wall, broke a leg, and was then killed by peasants massed below. Two peasants from Madailhan cut off a hand and a foot, but they were careful to preserve his right hand because it had consecrated the

---

[31] Ibid., 208.

host. This animosity was no more an accident than the hatred of Codoing. Several months earlier du Périer had reportedly hired day laborers to work on his property for 6 sous per day, and when they were finished had told them "You earned 6 sous a day: I will keep one for the gabelle of each of you." His body, like that of Arlay, was left for three days to rot, and was reportedly eaten by dogs.[32]

Guillaume de Maures, lawyer in the présidial, aged 75, and his son Jean Vincent de Maures, councillor in the *élection*, were killed on the roof of the Carmelite convent where they had taken refuge, and their bodies were thrown down into the nuns' courtyard where the wife of an innkeeper named Petit popped out the eyes of the son and wrapped them in her handkerchief and took them home.[33] These two men, notes Malebaysse, got off easy because the Capuchin monks buried them at night in their church and their house was not pillaged. Malebaysse understood that death was only part of the punishment and that mutilating and exposing the body – like that of Arlay – was a worse indignity. Meanwhile Melot, a local judge, was killed by the peasants while retreating to his house at Clermont de la Magistère. His money was taken and his body stripped naked and thrown in a ditch. Thomas, a barrelmaker who was the local agent of the new tax and who had inventoried the winecellars of the innkeepers of Agen, was killed while being escorted to prison where the consuls were hoping to protect him. Many of the urban attacks were followed by peasant attacks on the same individuals' suburban estates, indicating collusion between townspeople and the surrounding peasantry.

The most spectacular episode was the burning of the house of Etienne Cunolie sieur d'Espalais, jurat and militia captain. Cunolie had been commanded to return to his quarter and mobilize his militia company to fight off the rioters, and he did exactly that. Making his way through the streets with great difficulty because of a barrage of blows from halberds and other similar weapons, he was ultimately felled outside his own door by a blow to the head as he was trying to rally his friends and neighbors.[34] His wife and their servant managed to drag the body into the house – clearly a necessary step to avoid its being dragged and mutilated, but also an invitation to further attack.

---

[32] Ibid., 209.

[33] This is a good place to remind the reader that most of these details are from Malebaysse's journal which, although close to the events and quite specific, undoubtedly recounts stories that circulated after the fact, especially stories unsympathetic to the rioters. The names and events seem reliable, but who can say whether specific details like taking home the eyes in a handkerchief were embellishments or not?

[34] This action by Cunolie should be noted in the context of the shaky loyalty of bourgeois militia officers (see chapter 4). Even in this direst of revolts, some citizens were loyal, and they faced tremendous risks.

The Cunolie residence had by this time become the refuge for a whole circle of officers and persons associated with them. Inside were Cunolie's son Gabriel Antoine de Cunolie, councillor and criminal prosecutor in the présidial court; Maître Gratien de Latour sieur de Saubebère, councillor in the Cour des Aides; the wife of Claude de Barbier sieur de Lasserre, also councillor in the Aides (Lasserre himself was absent); Lasserre's mother; Lasserre's brother, who was a student at the Jesuits; another schoolboy named Guérineau who lived with Lasserre; a clerk, a coachman, and some lackeys. When the crowd broke in the door, Guérineau fired a pistol at them and killed a rioter named Mandou. The enraged crowd then shouted that there were gabeleurs (that is, enemies) inside. While some rioters began setting the building on fire, others stormed in to pillage. The latter were forced out by the smoke, and the residents found themselves trapped in an upper chamber, from which they planned to escape using a portable ladder. First Lasserre's mother climbed out of a window, holding in her arms her infant grandchild. Then her daughter-in-law followed, along with her son the schoolboy, the clerk, the coachman, and the lackeys.

After this exodus two of the rioters climbed back up the ladder and found Saubebère in a bedroom. They prepared to kill him, but he made an eloquent appeal, saying that he was not a gabeleur and had never wanted to accept the royal edicts. This apparently satisfied these particular individuals. However five others climbed back up to finish the job and this time, although they let Saubebère kneel in prayer in front of his mantlepiece, they still killed him with a blow to the head from behind. Guérineau, the schoolboy who had shot a rioter, was also dispatched in that room and his body was thrown out the window. Saubebère's furniture was burned in front of the house and the bodies of Guérineau and Saubebère were thrown into the bonfire along with that of a journeyman spurmaker who had been killed in front of the door. The body of Cunolie, the original casualty, was burned in the lower room, having apparently been singled out as the source of the resistance and symbolically burned in his own house. Also burned there was a "sailor" named Pierre Palendran who had been overcome by smoke while pillaging, perhaps one of the original boatmen.

This attack on the Cunolie residence probably inflicted more damage to persons and property than any other single attack in a seventeenth-century revolt. Containing as it did representatives of the municipality (Cunolie the elder), the présidial court (Cunolie the younger), and the Cour des Aides (Saubebère and the family of Lasserre), this dwelling could almost be said to represent a cross-section of the local power structure. The fierce anger of the crowd and the explosive nature of the uprising had apparently taken its residents by surprise. It was rare for such an extensive group of family members to be trapped in a targeted building, since most "gabeleurs" in a similar dilemma either fled the premises or armed and barricaded them more effectively. The exceptional ferocity of the crowd was no doubt intensified by the original attempt of Cunolie to rally the militia against the riot and by the subsequent shooting of a rioter from inside the house. Pillaging the premises and burning the contents in the street would have been normal practice, but burning the whole house down to the point of overcoming the pillagers with smoke, murdering those inside, and immolating their bodies – even that of a rioter – in the conflagration were exceptional measures. Nevertheless, we should note that seven persons were allowed to depart without harassment, including the women, the children and the servants, and that it was the male officers who were beaten to death, along with one boy murderer.

Barricades went up all over the city. The consuls reported that "these people are bargaining from behind their barricades, stating that they intend to kill everyone if some imagined gabelle is not abolished. They demand a pardon for their murders and a cease-fire, and that the Chamber [de l'Edit] draw up and publish an arrêt to that effect or else they will put everything to fire and blood."[35] As we have seen, this "gabelle" was not an imaginary tax, as the authorities pretended to believe. The crowd was using this term in a comprehensive sense to express their distaste for the *system* of new taxes, the new procedures, and the people associated with them. The gabelle they were fighting was very real, even if it had not technically been imposed yet and the people attacked had not literally been its collectors. As Bercé has shown, the twenty-four victims of the crowd were indeed gabeleurs in this sense: three had a direct role in the new wine tax, twelve were financial officers, and seven had family relationships with gabeleurs, had committed compromising actions, or had been in the wrong place at the wrong time.[36]

The trouble was not over. The next day, 18 June, the crowd reappeared in front of the maison de ville as strong as before and demanded that those who had taken refuge inside be expelled. Then they continued to pillage more houses. They hit Nicolas Duperier, councillor in the *élection*, the brother of the canon killed the day before, who was found hiding in the garden behind the Dean of Saint Caprais' house and killed by a musket shot in the stomach and sword thrusts to the body. One woman allegedly "cut off his private parts and fed them to the dogs, after which a man and two women attached him with a rope and threw him in the Garonne." At 2 p.m. Arnauld Paulmier, sergent-royal in the *élection*, was

[35] Bercé, *Histoire des Croquants*, p. 719.   [36] Ibid., p. 333.

Figure 5 Belfry of the old maison de ville of Agen, drawn in 1833 by
Henri Brécy. Built at the end of the fifteenth century and frequently
modified, it was in use during the revolt of 1635.

killed because it was said that he had executed the commissions of the gabelle and put up the posters at the street corners. He was found hiding in a barrel at the house of Cayron, chaplain of Saint Etienne in the rue du Temple, and there he was killed with blows of halberds and swords and dragged through the streets. The Saint Antoine gate was closed, so they threw him over the walls and the peasants outside dragged him and threw him in the Garonne.

The disorder was getting so bad that only religious symbols seemed potent enough to counteract the rallying force of the gabelle. At 9 or 10 a.m. a general procession was held to pray God to appease the rage of the people, and the reliquaries of Saint Sulpice, Saint Dulcide, Saint Caprais, and Sainte Foy were brought out. The procession left from Saint Etienne and went to Saint Caprais, where archdeacon d'Appil climbed up on the barricade outside the church holding the Holy Sacrament in his hands and exhorted the crowd with tears in his eyes to calm down, which helped a little. Then the procession went back to Saint Etienne and the archdeacon made another appeal in the same manner. Capuchin monks visited each popular barricade carrying crosses and did their best to calm people down. The "hermit of Saint Vincent" went around night and day doing the same thing. Life gradually returned to normal, but the shock had been immense. According to Malebaysse, the "gens de bien" were plunged in sadness at the deaths of their compatriots. He had no comment on how the rioters must have felt. The bells of the city remained silent for thirteen days. No sermon was delivered in any church until the feast of Saint Etienne on 3 August, and for a full month the Holy Sacrament was displayed in rotation in three churches, and processions from the parishes and convents visited them every day.

The paroxysm in Agen was not a typical revolt. Most uprisings were far milder, with much more symbolic protesting and much less crude violence. But although it must have appeared to the notables as if an irrational popular fury had been released, I think we can see that, from their own point of view, the rioters in Agen had acted in a focused, comprehensible manner and that their motivation was just an extreme expression of the same popular sentiments seen in other cases we have been examining. Their attacks were highly selective. The fury of the crowd was concentrated on notables associated in the popular mind with profiteering or persons tied to those individuals. The most striking aspect was the intense desire to punish the people responsible for selling out the community and to do it by attacking their bodies or their property. That this violence was an act of retribution, not mere anger or momentary loss of control, is demonstrated by the practice of degrading bodies. The mutilations and draggings of corpses invariably took place after death, and they often occurred many hours after the murder. What happened to bodies – burial in consecrated ground, ritual punishment, dumping in the river, left to be eaten by dogs – was evidently of central importance, and the narratives always reported how a person had died, what was said, how many blows had fallen where, and in many cases why the person had been attacked. No attack was ever thought of as indiscriminate.

Seventeenth-century demonstrators acted with a mixture of pragmatism and emotion, on the basis of deeply felt values. The most immediate reaction was to eliminate the abuse by expelling the perpetrators. In a day when authority was personal, there was a certain logic to this "out of sight out of mind" strategy. There was also meaning in attacking subordinates. They were stand-ins for their masters in a society where "killing the messenger" made perfect sense in terms of honor. Another motivating value was the concept of a right to demand minimal standards of popular subsistence from those in charge of the community and the crowd's determination to intervene if necessary to see that the process of doing so functioned properly. In both Vannes and Troyes the crowd demonstrated a particular conception of the nature of the problem and an idea of the steps required for a solution. Their appeals to authorities, while respectful, carried an undercurrent of suspicion that there might be collusion in high places, and their prodding was tempered with realism. If stopgap measures were instituted, their immediate response would be that "they are only doing this to amuse us."

The highest level of motivation was the call for retribution, and this was the defining function of seventeenth-century revolts. It was not enough to correct a price, redress a grievance, or expel an offender. Again and again the opinion was expressed that someone had to be held accountable when minimal standards of decency failed. Furthermore the demonstrators had a clear idea of who they thought was responsible. They might not always have been technically correct, but in a deeper sense their conspiracy theories usually contained more than a grain of truth.

The demand for retribution reached fever pitch when demonstrators were killed or dragged away, and more generally when the perception of oppression reached an intolerable level. Then there was talk of gabelles, a sign that the community was reaching a breaking point and that accumulated anger was causing people to watch warily for signs of treason. At such times the vocabulary of violence became more extended, parallel to the defensive insults used on a personal level, and that is when bodies were dragged, mutilated, and humiliated in rituals learned from official justice and, one suspects, from the truly violent legacy of a generation of sixteenth-century religious wars.

It is worth adding that major revolts took on a life of their own in the collective memory. The names "Loricard," "Nu-pieds," "Cascaveoux," "Rebeine" must have struck fear into the hearts of many a municipal councillor.[37] Since most revolts were connected to major repressions that had brought hardship and suffering, it was unlikely that the menu peuple thought of them with great fondness either. On the other hand, there is evidence that they *were* remembered and could serve as a source of inspiration when times got bad again. In 1668 vinegrowers of Dijon started passing the word that "it was time to make a lanturelu," referring to the Lanturelu rebellion of 1630. The Lyonnais were always talking about "rebeines" after the uprising of 1529, and in 1625 during a new grain crisis in Troyes there was talk of the uprising of 1586.[38]

The most unusual piece of evidence I have seen of this collective memory is in a document buried in the archives of the Cour des Comptes of Montpellier.[39] In 1661 Councillor Sartre was sent by the Comptes to the mountain town of Mende in the Gévaudan to enforce a new tax. There he was met by a riotous population which expelled him from the city, and in the heat of this experience he was told by an innkeeper and his wife that "things were not going well for him and they feared the people were so irritated that we would be killed just like the sieur Mas who was left for dead some time ago."[40] And to be sure, an obscure document in the archives of Mende describes how a crowd of women ran a certain Isaac Mas out of town and wounded him with blows to the head by rocks in 1645, sixteen years earlier.[41] Here is evidence that local people remembered even a minor riot that had never left much of a mark in public chronicles and that had not occasioned any serious repression.

[37] These terms refer respectively to riots in Angers 1649 (see chapter 9), Normandy 1639, Aix 1630 (see chapter 8), and Lyon 1529.

[38] AM Dijon I 119: request of 21 November 1668; AM Troyes, série A, sans côte, "Registre des Assemblées générales et consulaires": 15 November 1625, 27 August 1626.

[39] AD Hérault B 9768.   [40] Ibid.   [41] AM Mende II 12: 20 July 1645.

4   The position of the magistrates

City officials were acutely aware of the dangers of popular retribution.[1] They lived close enough to the streets to have a powerful sense of the destructive willfulness of the enraged crowd, and they knew that their own authority was none too solid when everyday respect began to falter. The fragility of their position and their ambivalent feelings about law and order are central to our understanding of the impact of popular disturbances. It was the magistrates who influenced the social climate by their handling of bad news and the degree of vigor with which they repressed disturbances. Their reports give us most of our evidence, and they were the focus of subsequent accusations about complicity. But their position was far more complex than simply opposing or tolerating riots. In the face of trouble, urban leaders wavered between paternalistic sympathy for inferiors, indignation at abuses, self-righteousness about their own administration, and fear for their lives and property. The next two chapters look at popular protest from their perspective.

Facing the population

Cities were governed by a committee of échevins or consuls who held power temporarily, usually for only one or two years.[2] Three to six individuals thus deliberated collectively and had to be assembled before any serious action could be undertaken. Sometimes one of them had the title

---

[1] For general works on French cities see chapter 1, note 15. On the functioning of city governments, see Chevalier, *Les bonnes villes de France*, pp. 197–238; Bonney, *Political Change in France*, pp. 318–43; Robert Descimon, "L'échevinage Parisien sous Henri IV (1594–1609): autonomie urbaine, conflits politiques et exclusives sociales," in Neithard Bulst and Jean-Pierre Genêt (eds.), *La ville, la bourgeoisie et la genèse de l'état moderne (XIIe–XVIIIe siècles)* (Paris, 1988), pp. 113–50; Henry Heller, *The Conquest of Poverty: the Calvinist Revolt in Sixteenth-Century France* (Leiden, 1986) discusses social relations in the previous century.

[2] I will use the generic term *échevin*, although there were a variety of names for municipal officials: *échevin* was common in the north, *consul* in the south, *capitoul* in Toulouse, *jurat* in Bordeaux and its hinterland, etc. In some cities there was a presiding magistrate with a different title such as *prévôt des marchands* in Paris and Lyon, *maire* in Dijon.

of maire or something similar, and in that case he took precedence over the others. Their center of operation, the *hôtel de ville* or *maison de ville*, was a venerable haven of civic symbolism with very few of the attributes of a modern administrative center. Its stark interior contained drafty meeting rooms of various sizes, arsenals, guard rooms, and places for archives connected by dank corridors and protected by heavy portals. This was not a comfortable setting, and the échevins usually worked at home, with the exception of one or two who might be on duty at a given moment. In times of crisis they were informed by a messenger at the door of their residence. If they wanted to be evasive they could wait at home until called, or they could feign ignorance. Once summoned they had to put on robes and gather at the hôtel de ville before any decisive action could be taken.

The persons involved were always eminent citizens with wide contacts. Each city had annual or biennial "elections" at which the new leaders were chosen by a complex process of cooption. Nominating committees drawn from city districts, from métiers, or from preexisting councils were designated to draw up lists of acceptable nominees. The final choices were then determined either by drawing lots or by turning the election over to yet another committee consisting of outgoing échevins, representatives from the other committees, or other notables. Often a judicial official presided; sometimes the governor or intendant intervened. Whatever the process, the final choices were the result of intense politicking and sometimes even illegal manipulation.

Thus the échevins were drawn from a larger circle of notables to which they returned after their year in office. They handled immediate problems, but more important decisions were usually submitted to a larger committee of councillors, and occasionally broad council meetings were held which included representatives from the other corps of the city. During their brief term of office the échevins acquired considerable local prestige and behind-the-scenes power, but their functions were onerous, demanding close attention and requiring difficult decisions for which they could be held liable years after their service was over.

The échevins performed five basic functions: they monitored compliance to "police" matters, that is regulations concerning markets, public morality, upkeep of public facilities, shops and artisanal methods; they defended the city's and their own prerogatives against encroachment by other authorities, usually by managing a dossier of interminable law suits in a variety of local and distant courts; they dealt with fiscal issues – the collection of local taxes, the "protection" of private tax collectors of all sorts, and the incessant raising of money to meet special royal demands; they handled the protocol of relations with local luminaries like the bishop or governor and visiting dignitaries of all sorts; they responded to crises threatening the community, such as warfare, incipient plague, subsistence crisis, and popular uprising. The échevins were assisted in these tasks by a small group of city employees: a procureur-syndic to handle judicial affairs, a secretary to keep records, guards or archers to accompany magistrates on important missions, and criers or trumpeters to announce municipal proclamations. Some cities had a larger corps of paid archers to escort prisoners or back up public acts, but this was never a force that could be used effectively in crowd control.

The city fathers' sense of the dignity of the office was intense, and their responsibility for defending its prerogatives deeply felt. In an appeal to the royal council in 1637 the capitouls of Toulouse noted proudly that they possessed very great privileges including *garde et gouvernement*, ordinary civil and criminal justice, and administration of "police." Disputes concerning their prerogatives, they asserted, were judged only in the grande chambre of the Parlement, and if the Parlement wanted to consult with them protocol required either that the first president summon them to his residence, or that the court send a deputation to the hôtel de ville. If a warrant was to be served, the Parlement's chief clerk was sent, but *never*, they insisted, had a mere process-server ever entered their consistory on behalf of the court![3]

Echevins constantly reiterated their "police" regulations. In Toulouse the capitouls' general ordinances were periodically "proclaimed throughout the streets, trumpets sounding," by a special crier accompanied by liveried soldiers of the watch. This "general cry" prohibiting cursing, gambling, begging, bearing of arms, dirtying of streets, and the use of sick animals, was issued twice a year, and at least ten other similar "cries" were pronounced regulating supplies of salt, transportation of grain, taxes on butter, regulation of fish, repairs on the island of Tounis, various taxes, and the ordering of the march in the procession of the Holy Sacrament. Specific ordinances were also publicized with varying degrees of fanfare, in an attempt to remind the public of the rules and to foster an atmosphere of compliance.[4] The process of getting attention was complicated by the fact that the échevins' sphere of influence intersected with those of a variety of other urban authorities: military commanders, law courts with powers of enforcement, fiscal authorities, emissaries from the king, ecclesiastical dignitaries. Thus municipal ordinances joined a flood of others, producing a cacophony of competing regulations – the seventeenth-century equivalent of an attempt to make an impression on public opinion.

[3] AM Toulouse FF 68, first dossier.
[4] AM Toulouse BB 155: proclamations d'ordonnances.

There were few mechanisms for enforcing these general regulations, short of relying on municipal sentiments of civic cooperation and constant vigilance on the part of the citizenry. The mystique of the hôtel de ville and the élan of the office of échevin were supposed to accompany the individual incumbents as they circulated through the streets. This was why they put on their robes and donned their "liveries" to issue commands to the citizenry. Wherever a consul went he was expected to survey the scene, hear complaints, and challenge visible infractions. Where records survive, as in Dijon, we can see the process at work. Infractions are handled individually. An échevin receives a complaint from an aggrieved party – usually a tradesman reporting illicit methods by his competitor, or family members reporting drunkenness or prostitution. The syndic of the city is then sent to the spot, where he physically confronts the offenders and draws up a report. In Toulouse a peasant passing in front of the hôtel de ville informs the captain of the watch that a quarrel has taken place outside the Saint Cyprien gate over a gabelle guard trying to seize some merchandise. The captain goes and tells the capitoul on duty, who takes some soldiers and visits the scene to investigate; but, of course, arriving long after the excitement is over.[6] Such methods were effective for maintaining a presence and setting occasional examples, but they required the public's acquiescence, which was hardly assured. We have seen in chapter 2 the vituperative backlash which could result when individuals reacted negatively to official actions that were viewed as invasive.

In the course of their term échevins developed opinions about the undisciplined population which they were eager to pass on to their successors. Let us listen to what the consuls of Agen had to say.[7] The consuls of 1623 suggested making sure that "during festivals the butcher shops are closed and women resellers or butchers' wives do not scandalously hawk merchandise; that during those days there is no public cursing in cabarets and taverns, near the small butcher shops by the Saint Antoine gate, or in other places where a large number of lazy bums and even small boys who do nothing but gamble are ordinarily found." The consuls of 1627 observed that "it is completely appropriate to destroy defamatory libels posted as *pancartes* because they denigrate the reputation of fellow citizens and especially those of women and girls . . . and cause conflicts between the inhabitants." The consuls of 1631 warned that,

[5] AM Dijon I 110, I 130, I 143, for example.
[6] AM Toulouse FF 68, second dossier: incident of 12 October 1637.
[7] AM Agen BB 46: "Livre des instructions et mémoires de 1619 à 1639," listed by year of outgoing consuls.

during our year we have found the people to be very rebellious. They have already shaken the respect they owe to their magistrates, perhaps because the times are constantly getting worse or because the people see the sovereign companies as having increased luster and authority, and this causes them to fall into contempt for the consuls; or because of the laxity of those in charge who have not repressed insolent acts and violations to the regulations . . . You know how rigorous the past year was, but beyond the famine, the plague, and the poverty of the maison de ville we have also had to be very cautious. We have been walking on thorns because of the jealousies among the sovereign companies in the city, trying to please the one and then the other, or at least to avoid giving them reason to complain against us.

The consuls of 1633 advised their successors that if they would just maintain their authority, they would

find it easy to make yourselves obeyed by the people, whereas if you allow your offices to fall into contempt, the people will gradually abandon the honor and respect they owe you and will plunge into disobedience . . . Remember the words of the great *politique*, "magnae urbis magistratibus augustos animos non convenire." Therefore stay united not only among yourselves but with the jurade and the corps de ville.

The consuls of 1636, who were ruling in the aftermath of the bloody revolt of 1635, moaned that

we tried to sell bread by weight, which is more just. But we encountered murmuring of the little people even though this would be to their advantage. Because of false rumors that were circulating . . . we couldn't find any neighbor willing to take charge of the scales during the day and set them up and put them away morning and night, because if we left them there all night they would be immediately removed.

And the consuls of 1643 noted that

all important affairs do not take place in the maison de ville. It is extremely important for the consuls to make [public] appearances and show themselves to the inhabitants in the streets, especially those far away like the rue Dupin and the rue Saint Jean where the magistrates are only rarely seen . . . [Then] the inhabitants will respect the boundaries of recognition, duty and obedience that they owe to their magistrates.[8]

Thus échevins were deeply aware of the contingency of their authority. They saw their city as a dense place teeming with potential disorder, where the population would go astray if the consuls did not repeat the rules often, appear frequently, and communicate their importance.

Echevins' reputation also required proper relations with the other local corps – especially the sovereign courts – because they too issued pronouncements, manifested power in the streets, and spoke on behalf of the

[8] Ibid. (for all of the above quotations from Agen).

community. In smaller cities where the highest royal court was the bailliage, matters were relatively simple. But in cities with sovereign courts, issues of jurisdiction and procedure could seriously compromise efforts at law enforcement. We can observe the problem when the Cour des Aides of Guyenne was established in Agen in 1630. This intruding authority whose officers had recently purchased their positions from royal tax farmers nevertheless had to be placated. Quarters were set up for them in the monastery of the frères prêcheurs and a grand welcoming ceremony was staged when they arrived in their carriages at the Saint Antoine gate. But the president of the new court immediately demanded a better location with more "éclat." Soon there were quarrels over the arrest of one of the Aides' huissiers by the consuls, a break-in to the municipal prisons by Aides councillors to rescue one of their lackeys, and a declaration of war when the consuls entered the house of the procureur-général of the Aides to investigate a murder allegedly committed by the man's butler. At this point the consuls protested to the king that the Aides officers had publicly declared themselves enemies of the city and had announced their intention of using their privileges to refuse to pay the taille.[9]

In Bordeaux the give-and-take between city hall and Parlement was an obvious impediment to effective government. Each side liked to think that it made autonomous decisions, but in fact the jurats had to consult the Parlement before they could issue many kinds of public pronouncements, and when the Parlement wanted enforcement of its directives it usually had to summon the jurats. Given the protocol involved, days could pass before action was taken on either side. On 15 February 1642 in the midst of rumblings against the proposed *sol pour livre* tax on basic commodities, the jurats got word that a man named Rivière had received an anonymous letter advising him to "look out for himself since he is one of the *partisans* of the *sol pour livre*." They decided to investigate who had written it and to inform the Parlement. But when their deputies arrived at the Palais they learned that the Parlement had passed a similar resolution four days earlier. On 19 August when new seditious bills were posted, the jurats again tried to act but were told by the Parlement to desist because it had already named commissioners to study the matter. In vain the jurats argued that they had jurisdiction in the first instance because it was their duty to keep the population in check.[10] Echevins or consuls faced such problems in every town. They had to thread their way through the pretensions of the other bodies while maintaining their own prerogatives.

---

[9] AM Agen BB 51 fols. 147r–151r: 23 June to 31 August 1630.
[10] AM Bordeaux Ms. 789, pp. 343–5 ("délibérations secrètes" of the Parlement, 1639–45); *Inventaire sommaire de la jurade*, vol. v, pp. 138–40.

When the delicate equilibrium of deference began to collapse in the face of an emergency, échevins had few means of coercion at their disposal. Their connection to the population was through a network of contacts to neighborhoods via militia captains who were respected residents on each street, or to artisans via the organized métiers. But in moments of crisis the chief actors were the échevins themselves. They might simply assemble in the hôtel de ville where arms and ammunition were supposed to be stockpiled and summon all good bourgeois to take arms at their side – a call that would certainly be heeded by some loyal citizens, especially their allies. Or they might circulate through the streets to restore order. It was relatively simple to occupy strategic locations like the city hall, the belfry, and the gates or ramparts (which, however, might also be occupied by popular forces if they got there first). But it was very difficult to make something positive happen if the protesters were determined to oppose it.

The crowds these men faced were extraordinarily focused on particular actions, persons, or buildings. Their weapons were improvised, and there was very little gunfire. A paradoxical result was that most of the rest of the population was safe if they stayed out of the way – usually by locking themselves up in their strongholds, and there was thus considerable incentive for the notables to disappear from the scene during a crisis. As we have seen in several instances, the authorities could often circulate and even talk to rioters with impunity, provided they did nothing to antagonize large groups at the height of their fury. When things were subsiding it was even possible to arrest individuals, presumably grabbed when they were somewhat separated from the throng. There are few reports of persons resisting arrest or angry crowds coming to their defense on the spot. But it was extraordinarily difficult to *stop* the crowds from their pillaging or to deflect the thrust of an uprising because that would have required active military intervention and considerable personal bravery – just the sort of thing that aging councilmen were not very good at.

Urban militias

The key to such interventionism was the urban militia, a force which requires our close scrutiny because its effectiveness needs to be understood in assessing the zeal of the magistrates in putting down revolts.[11]

---

[11] On militias, see Chevalier, *Les bonnes villes*, pp. 113–28; Albert Babeau, "Le guet et la milice bourgeoise à Troyes," *Mémoires de la Société académique d'agriculture, des sciences, arts et belles-lettres du département de l'Aube* 3e série 15 (1878), 307–61; Robert Descimon, "Solidarité communautaire et sociabilité armée: les compagnies de la milice bourgeoise à Paris (XVIe-XVIIe siècles)," in Françoise Thélamon (ed.), *Sociabilité, pouvoirs et société* (Rouen, 1987), pp. 599–610; and Robert Descimon, "Milice bourgeoise et identité citadine à Paris au temps de la ligue," *Annales ESC* 48 (1993), 885–906.

Every city was supposed to have a citizen guard peopled by heads of households, but such forces were in decline in the seventeenth century for a variety of reasons. Militias performed several functions. The first was routine guard duty. A *guet* (watch) was needed to guard the ramparts, and sometimes the streets as well, during the night. This was an unpleasant task sometimes pushed off on unarmed lesser citizens. *Garde* (guard duty) at the gates during the day was considered more important. The company on duty assembled at a given hour, marched to a place where they ceremonially received the keys from one of the échevins, proceeded to their post, and in the evening reversed the process.[12] Finally in case of emergency every city was supposed to have a general defense force consisting of persons on every street capable of owning and handling arms. This might be all heads of households or it might be a more socially restricted force consisting of prosperous bourgeois and excluding artisans, but it was usually inclusive rather than exclusive.

Lyon can be taken as exemplifying the way the system was supposed to work.[13] The city was divided into thirty-six military districts called *pennonages*, each commanded by a captain pennon and subdivided into companies called *dixaines*. These districts had once elected their own officers, but by the late sixteenth century the pennons were named by the échevins and used explicitly for social control. The officer corps had been expanded to include a lieutenant pennon, a captain ensign, a sergeant and a corporal, and the posts were increasingly restricted to real notables. Each household was expected to provide a militiaman armed with a musket, a pistol, or at least a halberd, but sometimes the officers lent arms to the poorer members of their districts. The pennons were substantial citizens who sometimes served for as long as twenty or thirty years. They led their troops in ceremonial entries and processions and served as the agents of the échevins. For example, in 1632 there were so many beggars in the streets that the pennons were instructed to look into where they were being lodged in the neighborhoods so that they could be arrested and thrown out of town.[14] In 1597 and 1636 the échevins used the pennons to carry out the house-by-house censuses of their districts whose results we examined in chapter 1.

Even in Lyon, however, the system was in decadence. Unpaid, part-time volunteers could not really police a teeming manufacturing city. More and more notables claimed exemption from service, and it was increasingly difficult to rally properly armed companies in time of emer-

[12] Many cities also had trained companies of citizen archers or *arbalétriers* who continued the traditions of the past by holding maneuvers and shooting contests, but their role was becoming purely ceremonial.   [13] Zeller, *Les recensements Lyonnais*, pp. 60–79.
[14] AM Lyon BB 182, fol. 244r-v: 16 November 1632.

gency. In 1627 the pennon from the quartier of la Grenette complained to the échevins that he was having trouble finding men for guard duty because all the richest inhabitants were Protestants who were not supposed to bear arms. In Dijon in 1636 when the prince de Condé required every man capable of bearing arms between the ages of eighteen and sixty to serve, including sons of good family, avocats, clerks, schoolboys, artisans, and valets, he occasioned a protracted dispute with the parlementaires who claimed exemption anyway.[15]

We can see how municipal crowd control was *supposed* to work by looking at the contingency plans set up by urban governments in moments of impending crisis. In Bordeaux in 1637 when there were rumors of a secret revolt being planned to support the rebels of Périgord, the jurats consulted the governor and the Parlement, posted special guards on the Boulevard de Sainte Croix and in the belltower of Saint Michel in the popular quarters, in the château du Hâ, and in the hôtel de ville where a jurat was to remain on duty around the clock guarded by eight bourgeois. The keys to the gates, magazines, arms, and powder were to have special protection. In 1639 when seditious bills appeared all over town, the jurats assembled at 5 a.m., instructed the watch to remove them, and then circulated personally through the quarters checking that all was calm and telling the bourgeois to prepare their arms.[16]

In Agen the procedures were even more explicit. When something happened, the consuls were to take up their positions in the hôtel de ville. Inhabitants were to stay in their houses and shops and await further orders "without parading around armed to no great effect." The canons of Saint Etienne and Saint Caprais and their priests were to secure those churches and lock servants inside the belfries so that the tocsin could not be rung. The same measures were to be taken in each monastery, and if anyone tried to force his or her way in the monks were to inform the consuls immediately. Each consul was assigned an itinerary. The captains of the militia were to go to their rendez-vous points, send their sergeants to the maison de ville for news, and lend aid to any consuls who might pass by.[17]

---

[15] AM Lyon BB 171, fol. 100r: 16 March 1627; AM Dijon H 54 (guet et garde): entries from December 1635 to December 1636.

[16] *Inventaire sommaire de la jurade*, vol. V, pp. 131–4, 135–6.

[17] AM Agen FF 233 (for 1636); BB 55, fol. 243 (for 1639). These procedures were adopted defensively in the aftermath of the 1635 revolt. Among the 108 names of persons who were to be mobilized in the instructions for 1636, I counted 11 judicial officers, 16 present or former jurats, 30 avocats, procureurs and notaires, 3 "bourgeois," 1 regent, 22 merchants, 5 doctors and surgeons, 9 huissiers, sergents and *commis*, 4 apothecaries, 3 innkeepers, and 4 artisans. Thus the majority of the population, including artisans, was excluded.

Such procedures, designed to forestall the strategies commonly adopted by crowds, looked good on paper but they never worked very well in practice. The very terms used illustrate the problem. You could only expect citizens to rally against an enemy if there was general agreement about who the enemy was, and you could only circulate to garner support to the extent that your livery was respected. Protecting targets against seizure required extraordinary coordination to counteract crowds of local inhabitants who coalesced in several places at once and knew the ins and outs of the local topography. It also required better coordination than the scattered échevins with their awkward consultations were likely to provide. Such measures might have suited a theoretical uprising of rogues against whom all sensible citizens were willing to rally. But in reality the rebels were usually familiar local figures who pillaged other neighbors or turned on the authorities themselves. Furthermore, the traditional mobilization procedures assumed that the problem would develop slowly enough for messages to be exchanged while diverse meetings were held to coordinate the defense and that the militia companies would follow their leaders. Most important, it assumed that the militia captains would be willing to venture out into danger instead of defending their houses and neighborhoods.

In fact, citizen militias were always plagued with internal tensions. In Dijon and Châlons-sur-Marne where nocturnal guard duty was still a necessity during the Thirty Years War, we can catch glimpses of these problems from investigations of conflicts. In Dijon a master artisan mocks the shoddiness of a fellow militiaman's weapon, and the latter walks off his post. Guards refuse to let an important personage onto the ramparts even though he knows the password. A dixainier leaves in a huff because a baker in his company refuses to contribute to the collection for purchasing refreshments. One whole company denounces a bourgeois citizen who hasn't stood guard in ten years; the captain of another company complains that he can't assemble his forces because his subordinates refuse to provide a list of enrollees. Four guardsmen are prosecuted for pawning vinegrower Pierre Grillot's sword in a cabaret to buy wine and then lighting a fire so large that it almost burned down the guardhouse. Another soldier who fell asleep on duty is prosecuted for cursing and beating the corporal who tried to wake him up.

In Châlons company captains complain that passersby frequently insult and threaten them or their wives. A man curses and rips his officer's coat for making him do sentinel duty. Nicolas Gaillard, son of a master baker, is found in a drunken stupor in the guard house by Simon Baudouin, merchant, who "scandalously singed his clothes and private parts with a lighted torch" when he and his companions made fun of

Gaillard for being too drunk to be able to tie his own laces. These incidents, though no doubt exceptional, convey an impression of some of the unruliness of militias, seen from below, and perhaps a glimpse of some more playful moments in the lives of the kinds of people who participated in revolts.[18]

As important as patrols might be, it was difficult to get a group of neighbors from diverse trades to appear at the right times and maintain military discipline when they were standing beside neighbors with whom they had other dealings. There were always social conflicts. If service was restricted to men of property, the dangers of arming the menu peuple and teaching them how to organize could be avoided. But respectable men balked at menial duties performed at night or in bad weather, and if artisans were included, then quarrels arose between officers and men, and the ambiance of the tavern was transferred to the ramparts.

On the other hand the journal of René Duchemin, notaire of Rennes, reflects some of the pride taken by respectable bourgeois in their militia service. Duchemin scorns the lower classes. In 1662 he tells how his street and five others were called to arms from 7 a.m. to noon on a certain day because of the authorities' "fear of the rabble from the lower town who wanted to revolt in order to free their comrades who had been taken prisoner for the insults they had uttered against Monseignior of Rennes and the Court." Unfortunately, in his opinion, the offenders "were granted mercy instead of the rope they deserved."[19] In 1664 he notes that his company was one of the seven allowed to take part in the marriage of the young governor, and later that year he proudly records that his street marched third in the ceremonies for the entrance of the duc de Mazarin into Rennes.[20] His notes become especially interesting during the uprising of 1675 when part of the militia mutinied, as described in chapter 7. He records that "our street stood guard for two nights on the ramparts, and the second time . . . I was in command of those from the rue Neuve, when monsieur de Lavardin and monsieur the governor were making their rounds, and when they saw the orderly way we were guarding our post they turned in their tracks, not needing to go any farther."[21] Another memoirist, Morel, procureur in the présidial, recorded carefully by name which cinquantaines stood guard in the city during the troubles of 1675 and which "took arms without orders and guarded the gates of Toussaints

---

[18] All the Dijon examples dating from 1614 to 1644 are drawn from AM Dijon H 54 and H 55. Roles for the guet et garde of 1628 (H 57) reveal a force of about 200 men consisting largely of artisans in over 40 trades. The Châlons examples dating from 1617 to 1636 are drawn from AM Châlons-sur-Marne FF 54, FF 55, FF 56.
[19] "Journal d'un bourgeois de Rennes au XVIIe siècle," a manuscript in AD Ile et Vilaine 1F 306, p. 143.   [20] Ibid., pp. 157–8, 165.   [21] Ibid., p. 199.

and Porte Blanche: the people gathered at the houses of the bourgeois officers and forced them to take up the command."[22] These then are the two extremes adopted by militias: expressions of bourgeois respectability or expressions of unruliness and dissidence.

Toulouse, 1635 and Troyes, 1625–1627

Restricted to largely defensive strategic measures and dependent on the rallying of an extremely fickle urban population, the authorities were limited in what they could really do to head off a revolt. Let us examine some actual cases of crowd control. In Toulouse in 1635, trouble was anticipated after the riots in Bordeaux and Agen. Hearing that one of their employees, a glazier, had been saying that the people should seize the hôtel de ville, the vigilant capitouls had him arrested, and on 25 June he was condemned to death by the equally vigilant Parlement.[23] Evidently the population had been itching for a confrontation like the ones they had heard about down river in Guyenne, but their anger lacked focus. Toulouse was not technically subject to the same "gabelle" as Guyenne, and no such invasive innovation was being imposed at that particular moment. Consequently the authorities had no reason to sympathize with the unruly crowd which, on the contrary, they greatly feared. When the verdict was known, "there was an uprising of the people all over the city, and there was such an alarm that in a moment all the shops closed, the streets were barricaded, and chains hung out."

How did the authorities handle such an uprising? Capitouls Boyer and Dejean, who happened to be in the hôtel de ville, set out on horseback with their valets: at the door they found a crowd of "porters" coming right at them shouting "Vive le Roy sans Gabelle," whom they commanded to go home. Then they rode off in different directions to rally support, but no citizens would follow them: everyone said he wanted to save his own house which the crowd was intending to pillage. Near the Palais de Justice Boyer learned that a crowd was holding hostage a bourgeois militia captain from a quarter behind Saint Barthélemy; he went there and rescued the man from "five hundred or more persons" who demanded that he see to the release of the condemned glazier in return. They grabbed the bridle of Boyer's horse uttering threats, but he managed to escape. Proceeding to the Palais, he found the Parlement's

---

[22] "Relation de la sédition arrivée à Rennes le 18 avril 1675 . . .," a 1782 copy in AD Ile et Vilaine 1F 307, pp. 6–8.

[23] This account is based on the records of the capitouls in AM Toulouse BB 30, fols. 384–411: entries from 31 May to 10 July 1635.

first president assembled with other parlementaires at the nearby city gate which they had closed to shut out people from the faubourg. The latter had already rolled carts of hay up to the drawbridge in order to set fire to the gate.

Meanwhile capitouls Dumas, Araylh, Perrin, and Rougnes were arming the hôtel de ville and closing and guarding the other gates. News arrived that there had been a great disturbance on the north side of town at the Bazacle mill and that people were approaching from there wearing handkerchiefs in their hats as insignia and heading for the palais. Rioters broke into Saint Pierre and rang the tocsin all night long and chains and barricades remained up, but after the glazier had been executed things gradually calmed down. This was a typical seventeenth-century crowd. Turbulent and angry, it occupied public spaces and issued demands without seriously threatening persons or property because its objectives were rather limited. There were no massacres like those in Agen because there were no evident *partisans* to be targeted.

As individuals the various authorities had acted courageously, at least if we believe their own reports, but the fear that had swept the city had demonstrated the complete collapse of the traditional system of citizen defense. The capitouls had only been able to react belatedly to particular situations, whereas trouble was breaking out everywhere at once. In the aftermath they complained that the guard companies were in disarray.[24] The capitouls had not been obeyed. "Certain persons of authority set up their own corps de garde and barricades without permission of their captains." Patrols had been disorganized and insolent. It was decided to draw up new lists of the well-to-do and require them to serve on patrols and guard duty and to prohibit private corps de garde. But several days later there were further complaints that inhabitants were not showing up for guard duty, even though the situation was still perilous: "Boatmen from Agen and Marmande who came here thinking they would bloody their hands the way they did in Agen are still in town, and means need to be found to remove their pretext to come here." After another week there were still complaints that artisans were refusing to attend patrols and that "persons of condition" did not want to serve. "Instead of marching as they should," those on duty were becoming part of the problem: "some beat on doors when they pass by and others cry out incessantly and commit a thousand insolences."[25]

We can further assess the roles of militias by comparing several riots in

[24] In 1635 Toulouse was suffering from the aftermath of a serious bout of plague, floods, and depopulation. To some extent the disarray may have been the result of these factors.
[25] AM Toulouse BB 30, fols. 425v, 427r: 28 August and 3 September 1635.

Troyes in the 1620s.[26] In the first case on 15 September 1625, a crowd attacked four or five carts of rye that were being transported out of town on behalf of the administrators of the hôtel Dieu, saying loudly that the grain belonged to a man named Nicolas Cherot and that they should go to Cherot's house and "do him displeasure." The city council called out several militia companies and restored calm, apparently with no difficulty.[27] Seven months later the second riot occurred on 15 April 1626. This time the maire in his hôtel when persons carrying clubs started making noise outside his house. His clerk reported that twelve or fifteen badly dressed, unknown persons were saying that they'd had no food for three days. They demanded bread or grain, uttered other "insolent and seditious words," and said that "today they wanted to live or die" – that familiar signal of desperation. Soon news arrived of a similar assembly in front of the house of Nicolas Cherot, the man falsely accused of exporting grain the previous September. The authorities rushed there with twenty-five men, but the various captains who were present refused to continue serving and went home after being hit with rocks.[28]

On 16 April the crowd continued to pillage, demonstrating that this was a serious crisis, not an isolated grain riot. Moving at a snail's pace but clearly wanting to act, the échevins and the judicial officers finally decided to inform the king and the duc de Nevers, governor of the province, and at four that afternoon they held a general meeting of notables in the hôtel de ville. The big news was the way the militia companies had refused to assemble. Even the quarter closest to Cherot's house had failed to mobilize and had procrastinated in coming to the aid of the president and lieutenant-général and other officers of the king who were in the thick of it trying to get the crowd to withdraw. Cherot's house had been completely denuded and at that very moment people were carrying all the grain out of the houses of the canon Cornu, rue de l'École, the curé of Saint Germain, the Chartreux monks, and the demoiselle de Sompsois. Even as they spoke news came in that larger crowds were gathering and threatening all the good houses and talking of setting fire to the town.

The notables' alarm was so great that they took a decisive step. Two hundred armed men – not the militia but the magistrates themselves and

---

[26] Unless otherwise indicated, the Troyes narratives are taken from the AM Troyes (located in the Bibliothèque Municipale), fonds Boutiot, série A. The volume I am citing, which has no côte, is the "Registre des assemblées générales et consulaires" for 1623–8 (hereafter "Registre"), whose entries are by date.

[27] "Registre," fols. 85r–87v: 16 September 1625.

[28] Ibid., fols. 113r–119v: 15 April 1626, "Récit de ce qui s'est passé pendant l'émotion populaire de pasques dernier au subjet des bleds."

their friends – set out, led by Feloix the lieutenant-général, along with the lieutenant-criminel, the lieutenant-particulier, the prévôt, the avocats and procureurs du roi, the maire, the échevins, the conseillers de ville and a number of others, in a show of solidarity among authorities that was perhaps unprecedented. They went first to the bishop's house where a crowd had violently entered on the pretext that the bishop's receiver was selling grain, then to Cherot's house which was in an advanced state of demolition and where they made arrests and caused the crowd to flee. Then on to the house of François Tartier, one of the town captains, then to Sieur Guillaume, élu in the *élection* de Troyes, and to the widow of Marc Dieuville. All these crowds were dispersed; then the men reconnoitered on horseback. The following day an exemplary repression was staged. Eleven prisoners were condemned to death and executed in the grain market after a formal procession through town led by Feloix, with the prisoners tied two by two, accompanied by admonishing Cordelier monks, and followed by all the other major officers and the soldiers from the company of Comporté, while the other companies guarded the public squares. Everything was calm because the parade was boycotted by the population.

On 23 August 1627 there was a third riot, this time over the gabelle, the *real* salt tax.[29] About 1 p.m. three desperate officers from the royal salt warehouse came bursting into the hôtel de ville, followed by a large crowd that was storming after them, filling the whole courtyard and screaming that the authorities were going to raise the price of salt. The crowd looked so menacing that the three gabeleurs beat a hasty retreat and the maire and échevins retired to the house of the maire to deliberate. About 4 p.m. the crowd threatened to attack the house of a receiver in the salt warehouse, but was repulsed by several judicial officers along with the neighbors. About 6 p.m. a large crowd assembled in the rue des Bûchettes and a lot of children in front of the house of Louis Berthault next to the hôtel de ville were seen throwing rocks and trying to enter, saying "they should kill, kill, the gabeleurs and all those who would defend them." Reports started coming in that the militia captains couldn't assemble their companies because the men said "their intention was to take arms in the service of the king, but not on this occasion to defend gabeleurs, and that they intended to stay in their houses to guard them."[30] The crowd continued to grow.

By 5 a.m. the next morning the extent of militia absenteeism had become clear: fourteen captains reported that it was impossible to raise

[29] Ibid., fols. 209r–216r: 23 August 1627, "Procès-verbal de l'émotion."
[30] Ibid., fol. 210v.

Figure 6 Outside the tower and gate of the voirie in Amiens as it appeared in 1822 in a drawing by Aimé or Louis Duthoit. This narrow opening in the medieval ramparts was characteristic of the sites patrolled – or seized – by urban militia companies.

their companies, and the other eighteen failed to appear at all. Drummers were sent out to announce in the streets that all militiamen would be held responsible for the consequences of their disobedience, but they were beaten back with rocks and their drums were smashed. The circulation of the four échevins through the streets was no more effective. By 7 a.m. a crowd of some 2,000 people had gathered at Louis Berthauld's house, where the "children" had paved the way the day before, and began destroying everything. Around 2 p.m. after seven hours of summoning and organizing, the authorities left the hôtel de ville reinforced by a few loyal militiamen who had finally turned up, and "went wading straight into the crowd of people despite their efforts to stop us and the blows from rocks they were constantly throwing," and managed to get the rioters to leave the premises.

At 5 or 6 a.m. on 27 August crowds started assembling again saying that prisoners had been killed during the night. We must imagine such rumors (which echoed fears from 1586) circulating in the pre-dawn hours as people rose for work. By 7 a.m. about four hundred demonstrators were at the door of the hôtel de ville shouting angrily "that the prisoners had been killed during the night in the prisons where they were held and that they wanted to see them dead or alive." The President told the crowd that there were only two prisoners and that they were alive and well and would be tried as gently as possible. But the crowd replied that "if they weren't shown the prisoners dead or alive they would throw themselves into extremities to set fire to everything and spread blood everywhere and that someone wanted them all to die of hunger because foreign coins were being refused." They continued to curse and insist "that they would throw themselves onto the magistrates and merchants and would even serve as their hangmen." This crowd was dissipated, along with another of about three hundred which formed near the prisons. At last about two hundred of the summoned militiamen had appeared.

On the morning after the big day of rioting the maire and échevins angrily summoned the captains to account for themselves after the utter failure of the urban militia. Troyes had four quartiers, each with eight companies of around a hundred men, or about four thousand potential soldiers.[31] The officers of ten of these thirty-two companies failed to show up. The rest reported either that all their men had refused to serve or that only a token contingent of eight or ten had appeared. Only one company, the seventh from the quartier de Beffroy, had actually done its duty. The officers' reports were clear enough. "They didn't want to take up arms to protect the gabeleurs." "The soldiers did take up arms but had refused to follow them, saying in loud voices that they did not want to leave their houses." "His lieutenant and enseign couldn't get anyone to obey their repeated commands, and the sergeant received such threats that he refused to go back."[32]

What then could the authorities actually do to stop a crowd? Once they had gathered a sufficient group of notables, their best option was the one adopted in the second riot: to join forces with the local nobility and ride out together to stop the pillagers by a combination of persuasion and group force. But this option was usually not available because of divisions and hesitations within the elite. Even in this optimal situation where they desperately wanted to stop the rioting, the authorities could only do so after many hours by means of the utmost personal energy. The more or less arbitrary grabbing of eleven individuals at the scene of the second riot and their subsequent execution demonstrated the magistrates' determination to have the upper hand, but did little to correct the situation.

In the third riot we again see the unreliability of a militia in putting down a popular cause. Despite their most vigorous efforts the magistrates

---

[31] Babeau, "Le guet et la milice bourgeoise," 315–17; Monmerque and A. H. Tallandier (eds.), *Mémoires du marquis de Beauvais-Nangis* [Mémoires de la Société de l'histoire de France] (Paris, 1862), p. 259.

[32] AM Troyes, series A, "Registre des assemblées générales et consulaires . . .," années 1623–1628, fols. 213v–216r: 25 August 1627.

were unable to rouse their own forces in the face of an angry population
bent on attacking the parties associated with a detested tax increase.
Could the magistrates have ridden out again with their own force as they
had done the previous year? It is true that they faced greater danger from
a more destructive, angry crowd (showers of rocks were directed at
them); but it is also true that they delayed, and they probably did ask
themselves whether it was worth dying for a few gabeleurs. But at
moments like these authorities really had very little chance of stopping
the rioting. They were faced with two unpleasant options: to try to cir-
cumscribe the damage or to do something truly courageous that was risky
and might not work. Not choosing the heroics of the second option did
not necessarily mean that they had sat back and "permitted" the revolt.

A contemporaneous event in Lyon illustrates the same dilemma. On 7
June 1630 two hundred or more angry fustian and velvet weavers, upset
over increases in duties, besieged the house of several implicated
financiers. This time our reporter was none other than Michel de
Marillac, keeper of the seals of France, who was passing through Lyon on
the way back from Italy with the two queens and the royal council and
who sent an eyewitness account to Cardinal Richelieu. How did this stern
advocate of central authority handle the situation? He sent the lieutenant-
criminel of the local bailliage court to see to the matter and sent some of
his own men with an archer from the prévôté de l'hôtel to the scene to disperse the crowd and rescue the financier. The crowd pulled back, then
rallied and repulsed the keeper of the seals' men: "My archer has been
badly beaten up and is in the hands of the barbers [i.e. barber-surgeons],
my upholsterer was severely wounded by rocks and swords." Marillac
finally had to send d'Halincourt, governor of the city, to go in person and
dissipate the crowd. But by 8 p.m. crowds had reformed in multiple locations, demanding the release of a prisoner. Marillac ordered that the
urban militia be called up, but not one captain could muster his company,
so he ordered that the prisoner be released. He wrote to Richelieu that:

it is strange to see how easily these people get worked up and how cool the
respectable people are towards taking care of the situation. I think it is necessary
to draw up procedures for the king to follow to be assured of obedience in these
cities, because these people [i.e. the local magistrates] who are always complaining to the [royal] council have neither the power nor the authority to cause much
harm; but they are chickens without heart and without credibility when it comes
to keeping harm from being committed.[33]

---

[33] Pierre Grillon, ed., *Papiers de Richelieu*, v, 303–4. This letter was cited in a famous article
by Georges Pagès as one of a series of incidents that led Marillac to conclude, in opposition to Richelieu, that internal reform was essential: Georges Pagès, "Autour du 'grand
orage': Richelieu et Marillac, deux politiques," *Revue historique* 179 (1937), 67–72.

In short, France's highest judicial minister did not do much better than the capitouls in Toulouse or the échevins in Troyes when he came face to face with a rebellion.

After a revolt the magistrates faced a new, dual dilemma: how could they restore their own authority and how could they defend their actions before the crown? Regardless of the diffidence or courage with which they had confronted the crisis, they would inevitably be blamed and the royal agents would use the occasion to milk them for funds in the form of new taxes, new offices, or reparation payments. There would also be fierce reprisals against the city and its population that would harm everybody. Their first step had to be to inform the king what had happened and try to justify their conduct. This was not an easy job because local rivals would be sending in their own versions of events, and the partners in Paris of those who had been attacked by the rioters would be lobbying the royal ministers heavily. In the Troyes gabelle revolt the chief victim, Louis Berthault, was an important tax farmer with connections at court. A bourgeois of Troyes, he was also the owner of the gabelle contract since 1612, farmer of the municipal octroi, and important creditor of the city. Even as the échevins were sending their report to Paris, he was obtaining an arrêt de conseil naming commissioners to investigate his claim of 200,000 livres damages and his charge that the magistrates were responsible. According to him, the crowd had pillaged everything in his house and the houses of his relatives, sought out his children to murder them, and wounded his brother.[34] Such recriminations were common. After the Montpellier revolt of 1645 the Falgairolles family was granted 24,000 livres for their pillaged residence and 12,000 livres for its contents, payable by the city. In their petition to the royal council the victims noted that "in all the uprisings that have occurred in the towns of Aix, Rouen, Dijon, Moulins and others the king has granted damages to particular individuals."[35] Evidently by 1645 a body of experience was at the disposal of financiers in Paris on how one handled provincial revolts.

The second step was seeing to the punishment of the rebels, and here the authorities have often been accused of lack of zeal, if not complicity. It is certainly true that échevins had little stomach for the prosecution of individual rioters. Their reports regularly state that they were unable to

[34] These were probably exaggerations, but the version composed by the échevins – the one we have to rely on – was no doubt understated. In December the Parlement condemned the city to pay 20,000 livres of damages to Berthault and his wife, banished five rioters from the city, and sentenced two men to fines and two others to death. AM Troyes H 5, fols. 90v-94r, 113r, 122v-125v.

[35] AM Montpellier FF 533: Falgairolles case, arrêt de conseil of 12 December 1646 and judgment of 8 June 1647.

recognize any of the rioters – indeed that the rebels were all disreputable outsiders. Of course, the rioters were local inhabitants, not mysterious foreigners, and such talk was essentially an excuse. But to the échevins it might well have seemed that the agitated, gesticulating demonstrators were strangers and not compatriots. They would not have recognized the women and youths outside their normal settings, and the poorer quarters that supplied the energy for most protests were clearly less familiar to échevins, even in a small city. With rocks flying and windows smashing it would be understandable if they had failed to notice exactly who had done what. Identification was not easy: cases exist where even the victims reported that they could not recognize any of the persons who had attacked them.

Nevertheless, it strains credulity to believe that public officials were never able to identify rioters, and it makes more sense to conclude that they saw no reason to name names, given the fact that the guilt was collective and the people were viewed as irresponsible, at least in the aggregate. Even when individuals were arrested and jailed they were rarely identified by name in reports. Was it possible to find the perpetrators in the manner of a modern police department? The best evidence we have usually comes from interrogations carried out by outside royal commissioners who used their powers of intimidation to query prisoners and seek out denunciations, but even they never found clear evidence of the organization of revolts or the real ringleaders. The people they uncovered were generally individuals who had been seen at the height of the action egging on the crowd or engaging in particular acts of destruction. Usually they were just persons caught at the scene or heard making seditious remarks.

Thus punishment, for both sides, was largely symbolic. The échevins were always eager to show that they had done their duty, but they had little real interest in punishing the guilty. They deplored disobedience, especially towards themselves, but the best way to stop it was to get the city back into its normal routine and restore the damaged habits of everyday deference, while making sure through exemplary executions that the population realized the seriousness of its transgressions. Besides, they knew that every arrest or execution created the kind of situation that stirred people up again, threatening a new challenge to their authority.

Still, if they had to, the authorities could come up with victims. After the Lanturelu rebellion in Dijon, letters from the king to the mayor and échevins indicated in no uncertain terms that order had better be restored or the town would face the royal wrath. The next morning at seven the general council met in continuous session while 3,000 citizens in arms occupied the gates and streets and a force of 150 performed a house to house search in the vignerons' quarter from which the revolt had emanated. Now the militia companies were working the way they were supposed to work! The troops moved from door to door, seeking a pre-arranged list of about thirty-five rioters – again, scapegoats more than instigators. Some of these were associated with particular actions, like the tapestry maker who had guarded the public square saying "that by the death of God nothing should be saved and everything had to burn", or Thiery the carpenter, seen demolishing roofs with his axe, but most were just people who had been denounced, many of whom had fled or were found, wounded, hiding in dark alleys. This was clearly a command per-formance designed to save the skins of the magistrates.[36]

The third step after a revolt, the one everyone dreaded, was the occupa-tion of the city by royal troops. Regiments would arrive, local power struc-tures would be modified, punishments and new taxes would be imposed. In Rennes after the revolt of 1675 one entire street that was closely associ-ated with the mutiny of the lower city, was ordered razed to the ground.[37] We will see these effects in detail in subsequent chapters.

The dilemma of the magistrates is clear, even when we discount the self-serving nature of their defensive reports. They were not a powerful execu-tive committee with clear options as to how to handle disturbances. Rich and influential though they were, they were only temporary stewards of a complex community that drew its energy from the mutual interaction of groups following unwritten rules about group honor, class distinctions, civic solidarity, and the maintenance of an appropriate moral order. They knew they faced a dangerous community of menu peuple that seemed to them to be irresponsible and prone to go astray. When customary pro-cedures broke down under the stress of unusual circumstances, échevins or consuls could not simply restore order or endorse disorder. During these rare but terrifying moments they felt isolated, and while they took the appropriate steps, they had to keeping looking over their shoulders in a number of directions.

First, they had to think of their own safety and that of their families and properties. Here they had quite a bit of room for maneuver. The top offi-cials were usually held in enough respect that they could circulate through the streets, talk to crowds, even intervene in conflicts without expecting to be directly attacked, and magistrates almost always came through the crisis without personal injury. Still, they had to go out almost alone to face angry demonstrators shouting curses and throwing rocks. Crowds were known to turn on échevins who tried to hold them back and they did denounce the complicity of their magistrates and threaten their houses.

[36] AM Dijon I 117: procès-verbal of 8 March 1630.   [37] See chapter 7.

Disturbances were alarming and seemed unpredictable. If anything was to be done, it was going to require courage and determination that was not always forthcoming, given the uncertain outcome.

Second, they had to act in a way that preserved their authority, that intangible aura that enabled them to issue commands and get things done. This was a difficult factor to assess. Not acting or appearing cowardly would certainly diminish them in the eyes of the population, but intervening and failing to prevail might be just as bad. As we have seen, there was no point in pursuing unnecessary arrests (although some arrests were important in maintaining authority) because jailed prisoners always occasioned new disturbances. It was necessary to prevent serious destruction, especially when the crowd turned on the magistrates, attacked "the rich," or talked of "burning down the city," but it was not wise to be viewed in the eyes of the citizenry as the defenders of gabeleurs, foreigners, or blood-sucking tax farmers. Somehow the line had to be drawn between maintaining respect for law and order and appearing to betray the city and its people.

Third, magistrates had to consider their relations with other authorities. They could not just act; they had to consult with councils and inform the courts, the governor, the intendant. Each of these agencies or individuals could help, but each had its own agenda, its own popularity to consider, and its own axes to grind. Everyone knew that when the crisis was over reports would be written and accusations would be exchanged.

Fourth, magistrates had to contend with the recriminations that they knew would follow a revolt. Their unfortunate job was to maintain public order and protect the king's agents even if the latter were objectionable profiteers flaunting unfair exactions. Whatever the crowd did, the échevins would be held responsible, and law suits, investigations, fines, even constitutional modifications were likely to follow.

The city fathers were conscious of all these perils, which put them in a most unfortunate dilemma. They had inherited traditions and responsibilities that placed them in the role of defenders of a theoretically self-governing community. But the cities they managed were more and more closely tied in with national developments. They had royal officers as colleagues and rivals, intendants intervening in their affairs, military emergencies that sucked away their resources, and shocking new royal fiscal innovations to enforce, but they had no new enforcement mechanisms at their disposal. They were caught in the middle between the traditional interests of their communities and the new demands put upon them by the king, for which they got no credit no matter how successfully they carried them out. They were threatened by social disorder, but they had no help in keeping order.

We have seen that the échevins were not always capable of maintaining order and that their failure to repress rebellions should not therefore be taken as a sign that they sympathized with the rioters. But what about their own efforts to oppose unpleasant innovations? City fathers were just as outraged by oppressive investigations and exploitative levies as their populations, and for many of the same reasons. Might they not have been tempted to curry favor with the crowd by encouraging revolt and shielding rebels from prosecution? The argument of this chapter is that ambivalent as the échevins may have felt, rabble-rousing was not a realistic option for them. They had to set a good example so that they could collect their own taxes and enforce their own unpopular measures. Furthermore, jealous rivals were always looking for ways to discredit the échevins with the crown, and the échevins needed desperately to maintain face with the ministers in Paris on whom they were dependent for protection from disaster. They could tolerate agitation up to a point, but their broader interests made popular retribution an unpalatable and dangerous choice. When they resisted – and they did – it was in their own way, through parallel legal action and by invoking personal contacts, not by fomenting disturbances.

Châlons-sur-Marne

In 1641 the king extended the *subvention* tax to Champagne and the farmer of the tax, Pierre Leduc, began to lay the groundwork for its collection.[1] This process was always a test of authority between local communities and the bearers of royal authorizations. The first round was fired in Paris on 11 May when Leduc reported to the royal council that "bourgeois and inhabitants" of the towns of Champagne were making trouble over the lodging of his agents. The council issued him an arrêt prohibiting any sort of opposition and directing that collections proceed.

---

[1] This 1641 episode has been reconstructed from a dossier in AM Châlons FF 42.

Armed with this ammunition, Pierre Lefebvre, agent of Leduc, arrived in Châlons on 19 June to set up shop.

Châlons, a small city with some 10,000 inhabitants, was typical of many declining manufacturing towns where the craft associations had a tradition of influencing the municipality and the Thirty Years War was disrupting traditional markets.[2] In 1634 drapers and serge-weavers paraded through the dark streets for three nights, causing "noise and scandal," by beating the drum to intimidate the municipal council during discussions of the weavers' status. For three days in 1636 groups of thirty angry butchers protesting a new excise tax roamed the streets carrying clubs, gathered menacingly outside the houses of important officials, committed "disorders," uttered "seditious words," and cursed insolently when commanded to disperse. When the *partisan* of the tax they were protesting left town precipitously, the city council had to rush an envoy to court to counteract the bad impression that his report would undoubtedly make in the royal council.[3]

This was the environment in which Leduc's new tax was to be imposed. On 23 June after his agents had established collection offices inside the Saint Jean and Marne gates, Lefebvre complained to the city council that his employees were receiving threats. The échevins covered themselves by issuing an order forbidding armed assemblies, but they did not take his side. On the contrary they told Lefebvre rather coldly that with regards to the difficulties reported in his statement, "he should address himself to the procureur du roi and the other officers who have jurisdiction over such matters."[4] About 6 a.m. the next morning Lefebvre's agent Collins was besieged by a crowd of "children" in the inn next to the Saint Jean gate. He fled out the back door and went with Lefebvre to fetch the city authorities. The crowd, incited by a man named Pierre Lenoir, had thrown rocks at the doors and windows, broken into the offices, and smashed furniture. But the response of the unsympathetic échevins was again surprisingly complacent. Summoned to inspect the scene, they belittled the whole affair, recording in their procès-verbal that although it was true that a large crowd had assembled in a nearby church for the festival of Saint John, they had found no one in Collins' office and no great damage. All they had seen was thirty to forty rocks "of medium size" along with broken windows, some damaged furniture, and a smashed

[2] There is no complete history of Châlons-sur-Marne. Brief accounts can be found in Georges Clause and Jean-Pierre Ravaux, *Histoire de Châlons-sur-Marne* (Roanne, 1983), pp. 147–51; and Comte Edouard de Barthélemy, *Histoire de la ville de Châlons-sur-Marne et de ses institutions*, 2nd edn. (Châlons, 1888), pp. 330–43.
[3] AM Châlons BB 20: 25 April, 26 June 1634, 1–3 June 1636.
[4] AM Châlons FF 42, acte of 23 June 1641.

container in which Collins' wife claimed the account books had been kept.[5]

Obviously the city was passively supporting the demonstrators. On 28 June the council denounced Collins' further appeals as "slanderous" for claiming that there had been a riot when their investigation had found none. They refused Lefebvre the protection of the municipal archers because "they had very few of them and they were intended for guarding the walls and gates night and day." If he wanted protection, they retorted, he should find his own sergeants and process-servers. They also refused to provide him with sites for his collection offices, noting that plenty of locations were available and that if landlords refused to rent to him it must be because he had not offered them a high enough price. On 3 July when the intendant Herbelay commanded them to reopen the tax offices, they challenged the validity of his order. On 19 July the city council insisted yet again that the royal council was misinformed: there had been no sedition, just "a mild commotion of children."

Here is a case where the échevins were supporting crowd actions by looking the other way and allowing a relatively benign process of community intimidation to take its course. But they would be sorry. In his arrêt of 15 July the king commanded the city to furnish good locations for the tax offices, reinstall the tax collectors in them, and dispatch one of their members to court within eight days with a full report explaining their outrageous conduct. On 1 August the embarrassed city council tried to reopen the *subvention* offices, but now their own authority was threatened as new crowds of "children" (probably adolescents) began to gather, threatening and hooting. Suddenly concerned about order, the échevins at last assured the tax agents that they could expect "all the help and comfort of the authorities" and prohibited public gatherings. But now that they had taken a stand on the side of the law, they were confronted with a real riot. About noon butchers began to assemble all over town. Baugier, lieutenant de la ville, rushed with a colleague and a servant to the Grande Rue, where they confronted about twenty butchers carrying raised clubs and gathering rocks, but other butchers had meanwhile attacked the tax offices, smashed the furniture, and clubbed various agents, including one Antoine Girard whose arm had been broken.[6]

What we have here is a case of "parallel" action. The magistrates had fought a legal battle of delays, appeals, and negotiations while the artisan population muttered and intimidated. Crowds had gathered for festive bonfires on Saint John's eve (23–24 June) and an attack on Collins' house had been organized in the cemetery outside the church. Up to this point

---

[5] Ibid., acte of 24 June.   [6] Ibid., procès-verbal of 1 August 1641.

the city council had looked the other way. As long as protest was restricted to covert threats by small groups against identifiable targets, it could perhaps be tolerated. But life was not that simple and the échevins were walking a tightrope. They may not have liked the *subvention* tax, but they clearly did not want to be challenged by butchers with clubs. When they had to give in to royal pressure and do their duty to defend the *partisans*, they themselves became the target of the population, and it was they who had to capitulate in the face of higher authority. On 2 September at a meeting of the city council presided over by Maître des Requêtes Orgeval, sent by the king, they had to agree to set up the collection bureau in the lower chamber of their own hôtel de ville and to pay damages to Lefebvre.[7]

Their vested interest in law and order was again demonstrated in 1657.[8] On 4 July an arrêt de conseil authorized the levy of 10 sols per livre on each piece of serge produced. But this tax, unlike the *subvention* of 1641, was destined to repay the town's own debts. Thus the échevins, whose credit and possibly personal investments were on the line, had a direct stake in successful collection. On 13 September, the day the tax was to begin, word was received that the "drapers, serge-weavers, combers and other wool workers" were mobilizing. The account of Nicolas Aubertin, lieutenant de la ville, shows once again how difficult it was to organize effective crowd control. Aubertin issued written orders to the captains of the militia to assemble their companies, guard all approaches to the city hall, and keep a close watch on the drapers. But these were the same militia forces whose pranks and quarrels we have noted in chapter 4, and compliance was low.[9] The échevins had to circulate through the streets in ones and twos, commanding each captain to obey his instructions and telling each street-corner gathering to disperse, since, without prodding, unpopular orders would not be obeyed. Aubertin moved around, telling some citizens to go home and arm themselves and others – serge-weavers and combers – to return to work. Interestingly enough, he seems in this small city to have been able to distinguish "friend" from "foe" on sight. One man who was "arousing seditions" by telling onlookers "that this monopoly should be stopped," was seized by Aubertin's archer, but then "many men, boys, women and girls" armed with clubs and stones attacked them and freed the prisoner. Later Aubertin only escaped from roaming crowds "clubs raised, rocks in hand" because a group he encountered, "both men and women making a great noise," turned and headed off in pursuit of another target.

[7] Ibid., arrêt de conseil 8 August; procès-verbaux 2 September.
[8] This account is based on AM Châlons FF 43: procès-verbal of 13 September drawn up by Nicolas Aubertin, lieutenant de la ville.   [9] See above, page 82.

Gradually the authorities fought their way back to the hôtel de ville, which was now beleaguered by the populace. New arrivals were pelted with rocks and pebbles or subjected to a sort of tug-of-war as they tried to squeeze through the crowd of demonstrators and reach the entryway without letting through any rioters. One archer made his way into the building by climbing over the roofs. Several were wounded. After this assault by "serge-weavers, drapers, combers, and male and female spinners," the crowd heard that there was pillaging going on elsewhere and rushed off to participate. Suddenly liberated, the city councillors set up patrols at the hôtel de ville and sought out the military governor, who was himself trying to gather a patrol of nobles and bons bourgeois in another part of town.

Calm returned quickly, but the damage was done. A former councillor, Clozier, had been "assassinated" and the houses of seven councillors, a merchant, and a royal sergeant had been attacked. One of the victims was named Baugier, perhaps the same councillor who had faced the riot of 1641. The vehemence of the rioters can be seen in the report of Paul Marin, sergeant in the militia, who had let the fleeing councillor Nicolas Caillet into his house and slammed the gate behind him.[10] Caillet was being chased down the Grande Rue in front of the hôtel de ville about noon by a crowd of "men, women, boys and girls." Confronted with Marin's locked gate, this crowd of 150 demonstrators turned on Marin, called him a "protector of monopolists," and asserted that "although he was their judge as first officer of the drapers' court, he nevertheless had betrayed them." Once again we see the retributive nature of their sentiments. Marin was a compatriot, known to the crowd, but when he harbored their victim he became a "gabeleur." The crowd battered down the door and pillaged the premises, and Marin claimed later that he had lost furniture, ornaments, linen, gold rings, clothes, deeds, contracts, and various merchandise. His doors and windows were smashed, and his rooms were strewn with broken furniture and torn papers.

In the sentence issued several months later by the intendant Voysin and the royal council, we can read an implicit social analysis.[11] The authorities were not blamed; in fact their power was shored up. Strict limitations were placed on the number of serge-weavers, drapers, carders, and combers who could work in the city, and the size of weaving shops was restricted. Women and girls were forbidden to rent private rooms for spinning except under the authority of their parents. The métiers were placed under the control of the city council: they were forbidden to meet

[10] AM Châlons FF 43: registers of présidial, 18 September 1657.
[11] AM Châlons HH 55: arrêt de conseil of 17 December 1657.

without permission even for festivities or confraternities, and excluded from militia companies. The offending tax was reestablished for the benefit of the city, and – improbable effort at thought control! – everyone was forbidden ever again to use the terms "maltôtier," "maltôte," "monopoleur" or any other words "tending to sedition."

Both Châlons disturbances involved organization by trade groups but the first, in 1641, had started as a playful, heterogeneous effort to intimidate the outsider – an effort which was tolerated, even encouraged, by the échevins until they were forced to assert their authority, at which point they became the enemy. In the second, in 1657, the magistrates proved incapable of enforcing a tax that they wanted to enforce. In both cases the crowd was a disquieting, unruly force not easily manipulated by ambivalent authorities, even when they most wanted to keep order.

Lyon

In Lyon we have a wonderful opportunity to explore the dilemma of authorities caught between state and community loyalties, thanks to the existence of the city's official correspondence.[12] Lyon was an exceptional city by virtue of its size (49,000 in the 1630s), its function as an international crossroads for merchandise, and its teeming industrial population.[13] The city had few nobles and no sovereign court, but many kinds of artisans worked there and a powerful merchant community controlled various manufacturing industries. Of Lyon's 1187 silk looms in 1621, 56.2 percent were controlled by merchants, and two individuals dominated a full quarter of the total silk production.[14] This unusual concentration meant that a great many people – at least 20,000 by contemporary estimates – were dependent on the work provided by a few merchants, who were in turn dependent on the economic conjuncture. Everyone was

---

[12] The best modern history of Lyon is Françoise Bayard and Pierre Cayez (eds.), *Histoire de Lyon des origines à nos jours*, 2 vols. (Roanne, 1990), vol. II, which contains fine discussions of the consulate by Françoise Bayard, pp. 77–103, and of population, neighborhoods, and social tensions by Olivier Zeller, pp. 177–208. The older Privat history is also useful: André Latreille (ed.), *Histoire de Lyon et du Lyonnais* (Toulouse, 1975). Richard Gascon, *Grand commerce et vie urbaine au XVIe siècle: Lyon et ses marchands* (Paris, 1971) is a classic treatment of the sixteenth century. Secondary accounts of the revolt of 1632 are Jean-Pierre Gutton, "La sédition de Lyon en 1632," in *Mélanges offerts à Georges Couton* (Lyon, 1981), pp. 261–70; Pierre Clerjon, *Histoire de Lyon depuis sa fondation jusqu'à nos jours*, 6 vols. (Lyon, 1829–37), vol. VI, pp. 148–58; Sébastien Charléty, *Histoire de Lyon* (Lyon, 1902; new ed. 1972), pp. 497–9; Arthur Jean Kleinclausz (ed.), *Histoire de Lyon*, 3 vols. (Lyon, 1939–52), vol. II, pp. 37–8; Maximin Deloche, *Un frère de Richelieu inconnu, chartreux, primat des gaules, cardinal, ambassadeur* (Paris, 1935), pp. 208–12.
[13] Bayard and Cayez, *Histoire de Lyon*, vol. II, pp. 45, 53.   [14] Ibid., vol. II, pp. 180–1.

aware of the fact that survival was linked to issues of supplies, tariffs, and commercial markets.[15]

For these reasons the municipal government faced the royal fiscal pressures of the 1620s and 1630s with increasing consternation. Lyon's "consulate," consisting of a prévôt des marchands and four échevins, was accustomed to frank discussions with concerned groups about the consequences of changes for their well-being, and its members were perfectly conscious of the social implications of the various possible taxes. Pressure from below was intense. In 1623 an angry crowd chased away agents of the *Douane de Valence*, a customs duty which was viewed as a serious threat to Lyon's commerce. In 1624 a crowd of merchants invaded the council chamber with angry complaints about the damage caused by the same Douane de Valence. In 1627 the council chamber was invaded by silkweavers outraged at the prospect of royal sumptuary laws that might put them out of work. In 1629 and 1630 there were riots of fustian and velvet weavers.[16] Meanwhile the échevins also had to defend themselves at court by taking advantage of every channel of communication. They maintained a team of agents in Paris and sent frequent deputations to the capital to consult with them. When possible they exploited their not always friendly connections with Charles d'Halincourt, governor of the city, who was a member of the powerful Villeroy family, and with Archbishop Alphonse de Richelieu, Cardinal of Lyon, brother of the first minister.

The correspondence of their Parisian agents, Croppet and Chanu, attorneys in the royal council who must have been transplanted Lyonnais, lets us see some of the exasperation felt by those who had to face a constant struggle with royal ministers.[17] After a conference with Sublet de Noyers, intendant des finances, Croppet confessed that "when he proposed this [unfavorable compromise], I fell into a rage against him because I think this proposition is totally unjust, or else they have decided to ruin us totally."[18] Croppet's ire was usually directed at the *partisans* who stood behind all these financial schemes, and notably at Jean de Lagrange, who surfaced as the financial adversary of Lyon every time there was trouble. In 1624 after vigorously opposing the Douane de

---

[15] The magnitude of the problem is indicated by the claim of the rectors of the aumône-général in 1627 that they were faced with more than 17,000 poor persons to feed. AM Lyon BB 171, fols. 186v-189v.

[16] AM Lyon BB 171, fols. 32r-48r. The 1627 protest and another in 1640 were discussed in chapter 2. The 1630 disturbance was the one witnessed by Marillac and the Queen Mother, as we saw in chapter 4.

[17] AM Lyon AA 51: letters to the municipality, 1623–41; AA 85: letters from Chanu 1632–42; AA 118: letters from Lyon 1620–32.

[18] AM Lyon AA 51, fol. 187: 26 June 1631.

Valence, Croppet moaned that he hoped he never encountered another tax farmer who was as aggravating as Lagrange. "Since I have had the honor of being employed in your affairs, there is no detail of our privileges that he has not attacked."[19] In the summer of 1632 Croppet suspiciously watched the proposed merger of five tax farms, wondering what role Lagrange was playing: "I hope that with the help of God all these maltôtiers and devourers of the poor will receive some reverse of fortune that will frighten those who come after." He waited nervously in the ante-chambers of the Cardinal of Lyon, and of Garde des Sceaux Châteauneuf, noting that "Lagrange is clever and nasty and would rather see the best city in France perish than lose 5 sous." On 19 November there were rumors that Lagrange was proposing an increase (*réappréciation*) in the customs duties on all merchandise entering and leaving Lyon, and Croppet exclaimed once again, "May God confound him with his unfortunate and pernicious suggestions."[20] On 7 December Chanu wrote that this increase was proving to be unstoppable: "Those who are pursuing this mandate along with Lagrange have so much influence in the council that although I come and go constantly, I fear the whole thing will be decided before I can find out anything."[21]

We can see, then, that when they talked among themselves these municipal leaders expressed their frustrations in terms not unlike those used by popular crowds. On 10 December Croppet groaned that "this affair is destroying my brain. Lord help us confound all these devourers of the people and *partisans* whose goal is no less than the total undermining of the state for their own enrichment."[22] But when he made this last exclamation he was unaware that he was about to receive the news of the uprising of 6 December which had already occurred in Lyon, and which would make his life even more complicated. To understand this protest, we must return to the city and go back to January 1632.

At that time the prévôt des marchands and échevins of Lyon were in the process of discussing ways to raise new revenues. On 14 January they held a general assembly meeting to thrash out the options. The most promising possibility was a head tax (*capitation*) on everybody, including the privileged, but this was categorically rejected on the grounds that it would "have dangerous consequences." The question therefore was what kind of tax to impose instead, given that any choice favored some interests and harmed others. The clergy and the judicial officers spoke out for a tax on merchandise, not basic commodities, so that the burden would be borne by the merchants and not the poor (or themselves). However the majority

[19] Ibid., fol. 34: 23 April 1624.   [20] Ibid., fols. 195, 286: 23 July, 19 November 1632.
[21] AM Lyon AA 85: 7 December 1632.   [22] AM Lyon AA 51, fol. 298: 10 December 1632.

Figure 7 The so-called "vue de Boisseau" showing Lyon about 1650. We are looking south from the Croix Rousse hill: the Saône river is on the right and the Rhône on the left.

of those present wanted a tax on wine which would spare the merchants, and this was the expedient adopted. Faced with a choice of a "business" or a "consumer" tax, the city's leaders had opted for the latter. The new measure, which was to be levied by the city on all wine entering the gates, was bound to be unpopular with the poor, who would be hit the hardest.[23]

The tax was authorized by the crown in June. On 14 September the city confronted the difficult question of how to collect such a sensitive assessment. Should the city hire a *commis* to collect the tax directly or transfer the rights to a tax farmer? If they hired a *commis*, "they would be exposed to the lies of those who detested the corps consulaire and who would assert, as they already do, that double the legitimate amount was being collected, and they would use this claim as a pretext to denounce the corps consulaire before the royal council." The *commis* would have trouble dealing with important persons claiming exemptions, and the funds raised would be consumed in law suits, making the proceeds uncertain.

[23] AM Lyon BB 182, fol. 25v: 14 January 1632.

By contrast, if the tax was ceded to a tax farmer, then the proceeds would be known in advance, the contract would go to the highest bidder, and lawsuits would be deflected onto a private contractor and perhaps received more favorably at court. Here is a classic statement of the dilemma faced by government agencies trying to raise money. The échevins had opted for the same solution chosen so often by the crown: to receive a lump sum in advance and shift all the dangers of violence and unpopularity off onto a subcontractor.[24]

Their concern was justified because their new wine tax was being levied on top of a much larger increase on wine and salt imposed by Briois, fermier-général des aides, and in addition to another tax, the réappréciation being proposed by Lagrange. Briois had been the target of the riot in 1630; Lagrange, whom we have just met in Paris, had been the focus of the troubles in 1627. Familiar forces were being pitted against one another again, and the échevins were implicated in the process, even as they tried to collect their own revenues.

During September an agent of Briois named Dupleix arrived in town to institute his new tax. "This surcharge was large and thus extremely unpleasant to those who had to endure it," the échevins observed, and although they would do everything in their power to aid Dupleix, "a great multitude of menu peuple were involved and it would be impossible to hold them to their duty unless one proceeded with adroitness and mildness and without publicity."[25] But Dupleix's strategy was exactly the opposite. Like Lefebvre in Châlons and so many other *partisans*, he needed publicity to assert the legitimacy of the tax so that local people would pay it. To the horror of the échevins, Dupleix proceeded to call attention to himself by registering his orders in courts all over the district and announcing that his inspectors would begin on the first of October to visit the cellars of innkeepers and mark their barrels. To make matters worse, he distributed a copy of a letter in which Prévôt des Marchands Pellot had written to the échevins in May that the city was going to have to lend support to Briois' collections. This was exactly the sort of guilt by association that the échevins wanted to avoid because it had the effect of "making us appear suspect and odious to fellow citizens who do not have enough good judgment to recognize the justice in our method, which is predicated on the obedience we owe to the commands of His Majesty."

The predictable outcome of this publicity was that the innkeepers held secret assemblies, discussed various sorts of "evil plans, *even against us*,"

---

[24] AM Lyon BB 182, fols. 189v-190v: 14 September 1632. The decision to farm out the tax was later blocked by the trésoriers de France, so that municipal *commis* were actually collecting the tax during the riot.   [25] AM Lyon BB 182, fols. 214r-219r: 2 October 1632.

and posted subversive bills around town threatening various parties. One of these printed bills was even placed on the porch of the hôtel de ville – a clear threat to the échevins. As if this were not enough, on 30 September merchants came storming into the hôtel de ville to complain of the *other* tax – Lagrange's proposed increase in Lyon's tariffs. It would divert trade and manufacturing to Geneva and other foreign centers, they pleaded, ruin the city, and create massive unemployment. The échevins claimed to be truly concerned.

We assured them that we could not believe that this new increase would be put into effect . . . nevertheless it has so alarmed our fellow citizens, especially the workers who are numerous enough to make up the larger part of our population, that we have been unable to pacify spirits already aroused over Briois' new tax. To avoid embittering or disturbing the public peace we have decided to negotiate this affair amicably as a means of holding everyone to his duty and averting the large uprising which has never been more imminent.[26]

Caught by threats from two constituencies at a time when they were trying to institute their own tax and when the news from Paris was not encouraging either, the échevins had to placate both sides while maintaining authority. In the Dupleix affair they asked the présidial court to investigate the illegal assemblies of the innkeepers, and they asked Halincourt, the governor, to persuade Dupleix to agree to a compromise. Dupleix would get permission for Briois to allow the innkeepers and tavern owners to buy off his rights. In the meantime the innkeepers would promise to keep their establishments open and sell wine at the old prices. The still-pending Lagrange affair was discussed at a general assembly meeting on 4 November, at which the implications of a higher duty on merchandise were explored. Other cities would also be affected, so it was decided to write to other places such as Tours and Marseille to ask them to concert their lobbying efforts at court.[27]

Despite attempts to "handle these affairs amicably and gently," the échevins' compromises appeared exceedingly fragile. On 30 September, even as the merchants were complaining about the réappréciation tax, it was learned that certain wary innkeepers had decided to go back on their agreement and close their establishments anyway, which would "arouse the people, who would rise up when they found no wine in the cabarets; and to agitate them further they were told that they would be made to pay 4 sols per pinte instead of the 1 sol, 6 deniers they pay now."[28] On 25 October the innkeepers and tavern keepers actually did close their doors.

---

[26] Ibid., end of session.
[27] Ibid., fol. 236v: 4 November 1632. This is another instance where the échevins displayed awareness of the situation outside Lyon.   [28] Ibid., fol. 217v.

The échevins hastily summoned twenty of their leaders and reminded them that they were ruining the negotiations, since no barrels had been marked and the farmer was willing to negotiate. But Duval, another agent of Briois had arrived in town for the bargaining and taken lodging in the Lion d'Or on the rue de Flandres. Although he was there to negotiate, the tavern owners were clearly skeptical as to whether the échevins would actually resolve the problem, and they were not willing to take chances. They insisted that they would open their establishments only *after* the deal was signed. By noon a crowd had surrounded the Golden Lion claiming to want to beat up Duval and throw him in the river. The échevins sent their archers and the watch to the scene and, according to their official report, the crowd then dispersed.[29] The tax farmers viewed this crowd as a serious effort at intimidation, but in their report the échevins did not present it as a real riot because there had been no serious consequences. They were again trying to stay in the middle.

In their letters to Paris the échevins complained that Dupleix had proceeded with undue haste:

and seeing that this was not working, he decided to discredit us with the innkeepers by . . . leading them to believe that our dixième du vin [the tax imposed by the city] is a novelty . . . Several of the innkeepers were persuaded to say that our plans should be foiled, and then they posted printed bills in the streets which were not kind to M. Fanfat, our farmer of the dixième tax.[30]

Thus Dupleix the *partisan* had turned the innkeepers against their own magistrates, billing them as *partisans* too. The échevins were trapped defending the city against one tax farmer while defending their own tax farm against the city.

The major riot they had feared broke out on 6 December, but ostensibly it had a different cause.[31] This time the aggravating factor was the arrival in town of Claude de Lagrange, brother of Jean the farmer-general, with lettres de cachet from the king authorizing an increase in customs duties on all sorts of merchandise. For two days there had been rumors of his arrival. On the sixth at 7 a.m. he presented his documents to the prévôt des marchands, who repeated the now-familiar warning about social instability:

that this affair affected all the workers of the town, which was the larger part of the population; that they were already alarmed because people were announcing that

[29] Ibid., fols. 230r-231r: 25 October 1632.
[30] AM Lyon AA 118, fol. 1054: letter to de la Serre, secrétaire du roi, undated but placed between those of 12 and 25 October 1632.
[31] The chief source for this narrative is the procès-verbal drawn up on 7 December: AM Lyon BB 182, fols. 261r-267r.

all manufactures were going to be banned from the town and they would all go hungry; that it was therefore necessary to proceed with prudence and reserve and that Lagrange ought to be a little cautious until they were in a better position to execute the will of His Majesty once Monsieur d'Halincourt had returned.[32]

No sooner had Lagrange left the hôtel de ville than word arrived of 2,000 demonstrators, "silkweavers, weavers of *futaines*, *toiles* and others," massing in front of the customs bureau (*douane*), which was also the building where Lagrange was staying.

In their handling of this uprising, the échevins again demonstrated that they were caught in the middle between royal rules and a dangerous population. Seeing their delicate negotiations again jeopardized and hoping as usual to negotiate a compromise, the échevins marched to the scene. There they moved among the crowd, arguing to anyone who would listen that humble remonstrances to the king were more appropriate than rocks, that they already had a deputy at court to handle this problem, and that Lagrange was willing to suspend collections until the matter was resolved. But instead of dispersing, the crowd or its leaders demanded written confirmation of the promises of suspension and negotiation, and, surprisingly, both the échevins and Lagrange complied. This sort of bargaining suggests that there was relatively good rapport between the city magistrates and at least the leaders of the various trades and that the practice of negotiating had some basis in tradition.

Nevertheless, the agitation did not abate and people began breaking doors and windows. The échevins, who had moved on to the residence of the Cardinal of Lyon to enlist his aid, report that they returned to the scene, repeated their assurances about the efficacy of appeal and added the Cardinal's promise to write on behalf of the city. They even suggested that a few spokesmen from the crowd meet with the Cardinal, and a dozen "workers" returned with them to the Cardinal's palace, where the prelate exhorted them to do their duty and promised he would write to court. These deputies of the crowd then reported back to "their companions" but to no avail: the crowd began attacking the building anyway. A kind of bargaining was taking place but it had weak foundations.

The échevins summoned their archers and commanded each captain pennon to mobilize the guard in his own quarter to quash disorders, and to use their powers of persuasion to reassure neighbor workers about the steps being taken. Again we see the way the neighborhood system was supposed to work. But there was also class fear: because "we were apprehensive about arming the pennonages, being partly composed of workers," the captains were instructed not to arm any silk workers.[33] By 1

[32] Ibid., fol. 261v.   [33] Ibid., fol. 263v.

p.m. the crowd in front of the customs bureau had invaded the building, thrown furniture and merchandise out the windows and lighted bonfires in the public square. The neighborhood militia rallied and expelled the rioters from the area, but in response the demonstrators turned on the échevins themselves as "instigators of the new taxes" and pillaged the houses of Echevin Neyrat and of Prévôt des Marchands Pellot, which they besieged for several hours, crying out that they wanted to burn it to the ground. A real battle apparently took place there between the armed bourgeois, the forces of the hôtel de ville, and the angry demonstrators, in which three or four demonstrators were killed.

We should pause here to look more closely. In subsequent testimony it becomes evident that the house of Neyrat was adjacent to the customs bureau where Claude de Lagrange was living. There was apparent collaboration between the two families, since when Marie Hugalin, Neyrat's wife, saw the crowd getting violent she entered the customs bureau by an inner door for which she had the keys, summoned Madame Lagrange, and with the help of a group of female servants, began carrying valuables into her own house for safekeeping. A long list follows of spoons, forks, cups, silver goblets, mirrors, a large iron trunk, a sack filled with gold and silver, an embroidered blue bedspread, several dozen plates, two chandeliers, even the scales and weights from the customs office. Other neighbors saved items of furniture and clothes; one spoke of snatching items from the bonfire. Charles Gros, silk merchant, recalled asking Madame de Lagrange if she had lost anything and her replying "that praise the Lord she had saved all her rings and jewelry." On the other hand witnesses described articles that *were* burned in the public square: a lute, a violin, a portrait of demoiselle de Lagrange, a gray suit with gold trim, three Turkish carpets, bolsters, papers from Lagrange's study, seven or eight oil paintings, tapestries from Beauvais and Bergamo, and ten or twelve books. There was one report by the wife of a dyer of having seen a customs receiver named Merlat fleeing in a boat across the Saône and seeking refuge in the house of a customs employee while pursued by a crowd of persons "who wanted to kill him."[34]

It appears, then, that this was a moderately violent riot, tempered by the intervention of neighbors and the ultimately successful application of force by the militia. We must imagine the effect of this sort of spectacle on the participants. Claude de Lagrange would have looked like the pro- verbial filthy rich *partisan* to the unemployed weavers who invaded his inner sanctum. As for Echevin Claude Neyret, the attack on him made perfect sense. He was not only implicated through his municipal duties in

[34] AM Lyon CC 4018: 14 February 1633, "Interrogations."

defense of the promulgation of the offensive taxes, but he was a neighbor and literally – via his wife – a protector of Lagrange. Moreover, an account book from 1633 notes that as the farmer of the city's wine tax, Neyrat was subsequently paid 947 livres in damages for wine that was brought into the city tax free during the riot.[35] Thus the crowd was attacking the farmer of the municipal wine tax as well as the farmer of the Lagrange increases. Neyret was also one of the two largest employers of weavers in Lyon, so he represents a dramatic case of a man caught between a tax that hurt his interests and a public position that forced him to defend the perpetrators of the tax to the extent of losing face and suffering damage. As for the attack on the house of the prévôt des marchands, this was the same Claude Pellot whose letter supporting Briois had been circulating earlier.[36] As usual, the protesters displayed an uncanny sense of who was complicit, and they were demanding not just abolition but retribution.

The crowd dwindled away around nightfall. Guard units were stationed all over town "to keep this 'rebeyne' from regaining strength during the night," and we note again the relative effectiveness of the militia in Lyon. At seven the next morning Halincourt arrived in the city with his guards. He met with a group of masters and twelve workers and promised to help them if they would stop their agitation. Once again they asked for a written statement to show to "the assembled people." All the authorities – governor, échevins, cardinal – gathered at the latter's palace to await the return of the artisan-deputies. They soon reported that their "journeymen" had dispersed and asked for forgiveness and for aid in appealing to the king.[37] "But at this same moment a report came in that the population was still assembled and that they had attacked and beaten a man named Hugonin in the quartier du Griffon and were now pillaging his house." The governor and his followers repressed this last wave of violence, but it was clear that the angry crowd was not as repentant as its moderate leaders.

Having lost control over the streets and seen their worst fears realized as the rioters turned on them, the magistrates now had to deal with the

---

[35] AM Lyon CC 1809: "Grandes Octrois de l'année 1633." Given the changes in the way the wine tax was collected, it is not entirely clear what Neyret's position was in December.

[36] Pellot was also a trésorier de France, which meant that he was an officer in the bureau responsible for publicizing and enforcing the customs taxes.

[37] AM Lyon BB 182, fol. 266r. These parleys – the meeting of échevins, governor, and cardinal at the cardinal's palace where they negotiated with representatives of concerned groups of citizens – were repetitions of familiar patterns of governance in Lyon. For example, in 1627 during the silkweavers' agitation, a meeting was called by the prévôt des marchands at the archbishopric with the governor and the présidial: AM Lyon BB 171, fols. 44r-48r: 28 January 1627.

catastrophe at court. Not only would the king be angered at the city's disobedience, but their appeals against the Lagrange tax would now be jeopardized. On 7 December they rushed off a packet of letters and reports to Croppet, observing that "we have risked our lives and the burning of our houses," and apologizing for their haste, inasmuch as "we still have to work on containing this rebeine, since the rabble [*rocaille*] is still assembled in a troop and is threatening to do worse, even to those of us who desire nothing more than their relief." To the king they wrote that they implored His Majesty to believe in their loyalty despite "the excesses of this scum of the people." To de la Serre they added that the letter publicized by Dupleix "gave people a pretext for saying that *we* were the partisans and those who committed the recent violence were thus able to claim that the rate on salt and the rights of douane were being collected *on our behalf*, and this led them to conceive the idea that we should be exterminated." In a subsequent letter they added that "the people are still muttering against us, led by several ill-intentioned people."[38]

Croppet received the news in Paris on Saturday evening, 11 December. On Sunday morning he rushed to Saint Germain where the court was residing to begin what modern politicians would call "damage control." Secretary of State LaVrillière, who was given the packet for the king, proved to be in a relatively good humor and told him that he personally opposed Lagrange's tax, but that the superintendants of finance were indignantly talking of building a citadel in Lyon. "I assure you," moaned Croppet, "all these people are badly disposed towards doing us favors because they think the king should be obeyed." This "absolutist" point of view was threatening to undermine the city's legal cases. "People are pointing out to me what was done in Dijon and what happened in Languedoc and in Provence and none of that augurs well."[39]

The battle of lobbyists was now launched by both sides. Croppet had managed to see LaVrillière first, but half an hour later an agent from Lagrange rushed in with contradictory letters that were "all too well received."

I did everything in my power to demonstrate that neither the consulate nor the persons of standing had anything to do with this mutiny, although people here have been told that it was the principal merchants who caused it, and [Claude de] Lagrange has written many letters to all these messieurs complaining of the great

---

[38] AM Lyon AA 118, fols. 1065v–1071: letters about the riot (italics added).

[39] AM Lyon AA 51, fols. 302–4: letters of 13–14 December 1632. The references are to the execution of Montmorency in Toulouse on 30 October for rebellion, the Lanturelu uprising in Dijon in February 1630, and the Cascaveoux uprising in Aix in November 1630.

losses he has sustained, saying that everything has been stolen from him, and even that he does not know the whereabouts of his poor wife.[40]

Jean de Lagrange himself arrived at Saint Germain on Tuesday, claiming that one of his agents had been killed (which does not appear to have been true). Meanwhile rumors swept Paris that thousands of people had rioted in Lyon, and Chanu made a point of informing everyone that the fault was Lagrange's for not following the advice of the échevins and the governor, "which leads me to believe that he [Claude de Lagrange] deliberately tried to cause [the riot]. These nasty *partisans* are saying that now they can achieve through [the application of] absolute authority what would otherwise have been very difficult to accomplish." Against the tax farmers' claims that the authorities in Lyon had encouraged a revolt against *them* Croppet was countering with the city's position that the *partisans* themselves had instigated the violence in order to get their way. The king was reportedly very angry. Croppet fretted "I think that we will have to lay off two thirds of the workers of Lyon for lack of any livelihood, but they still have to be fed or they will cut our throats." On Friday Croppet and Chanu learned that the tax had been approved and auctioned off to *partisans*. "May God punish the miserable man who advised this," wrote Croppet. "If they didn't rob the king and the people they would be unable to build houses costing a hundred thousand livres at the expense of three or four hundred people who are starving."[41]

By the next week further negotiations were under way over how the king's displeasure with Lyon was to be expressed: whether to say that the échevins had been slow in repressing the disturbance (Lagrange) or that the king was not displeased with the consulate (Croppet); and whether to state that Claude de Lagrange had acted properly with the advice of the consulate (Lagrange) or to deny this (Croppet). When it was decided that Conseiller d'Etat Isaac Juré, sieur de Moric would be sent to Lyon to try the guilty and chastise the city, Croppet tried to soften Moric up by explaining that the cause of the revolt had been misery and that "although the guilt is great, it is in a certain way excusable." Moric promised to be lenient, but the friends of Lyon were not encouraged when he set out from Paris accompanied for seven or eight leagues by Jean de Lagrange.[42] Back in Lyon the authorities were also facing the consequences of their actions. They sympathized with the unemployed population and had

---

[40] Ibid., fol. 304: 13 December letter. In the aftermath of a riot there were always attempts by the victims to claim extravagant damages, while the city tried to disprove such claims. Damage reports, including the items saved and the items burned from the Lagrange residence, must therefore be treated with skepticism.

[41] Ibid., fol. 312: 17 December 1632.

[42] Ibid., fols. 279, 308, 314, 310: Letters of 21, 24, 28, 31 December 1632.

done their best to negotiate a compromise with the various agents who descended upon them. They detested the *partisans* as much as the people in the streets, having said as much privately in terms strikingly similar to those used by rioters. But they also had property and authority to defend and their own tax to collect.

The city fathers had to look in two directions, towards the king and towards their population. Three days after the revolt they began drawing up "good procès-verbaux that will demonstrate their innocence and serve as their justification."[43] But they were also worried about their local reputation. On 16 December they issued an ordinance for public consumption that was nothing less than a budgetary justification of their conduct:

> Certain persons ill-disposed towards the peace of the town are trying to discredit our consular administration on the pretext that we have caused the new aides and gabelles that the agents of Briois want to collect and the increase in salt and the rise in the douane that Lagrange wants to introduce, supposing that we have not taken the necessary steps to oppose these new subsidies, although we could have demonstrated that we have done everything possible by licit and appropriate means. They also target the octroi on the entry of wine, saying that we demanded it unnecessarily to use for our own personal interest.

In order to "disabuse those who allow themselves to be convinced by such lies," they presented a complete list of the debts and expenses of the city, purporting to demonstrate that the total deficit came to a minimum of 155,304 livres. Their wine tax was thus declared necessary, even as they tried to distance themselves from the taxes that fed the coffers of unpopular tax farmers.[44]

Compared to the aftermath of some revolts, the response from Paris was measured. Lyon, after all, was an important border city, very well connected at court, and the citizens had rallied and fought for order more vigorously than in some other cases. Apparently Croppet and his colleagues had done their work well, because the lettre de cachet that was issued on 13 December stated that Louis XIII wanted the authors of the uprising punished, but that he retained affection for the city. On 23 December the prévôt des marchands and échevins sent deputies to court to continue to lobby against the réappréciation tax, the Douane de Valence, and the claims of Jean de Lagrange.[45]

On 27 December at a general assembly meeting to discuss what to do, the recriminations began to fly. Prévôt des marchands Pellot scolded his

[43] AM Lyon BB 182, fol. 270v: 10 December 1632.
[44] Ibid., fols. 275r-282v: 16 December 1632.
[45] Ibid., fols. 288r-312v: 18, 23 December 1632.

compatriots in a speech that could have been delivered in almost any city after a major revolt:

At the beginning of this miserable uprising we had difficulty persuading each person that this misfortune was everyone's concern . . . Some thought they could take advantage of the situation, others thought that although there was misery it would not be manifested publicly. Almost everybody was caught in a profound state of shock and rendered useless, with the result that instead of standing up against this violent popular uprising, many thought of it like a thunderstorm in which you aren't concerned if fire and lightning fall on your neighbor's house, provided your own is protected . . . Instead of devoting all our efforts to reestablishing the king's authority and meeting his demands for justice, we kept our arms folded, and now I see you extraordinarily seized with fear, contemplating the misfortune that hangs over the community, which will envelope the innocent along with the guilty . . .

The prévôt was angry: he and the échevins had informed the assembly of their dire financial straits. Now they were being asked to come up with money to pay for royal troops.[46]

On January 10 Moric arrived in Lyon and began his investigation. Ultimately there were a few executions about which we are badly informed, and the king pardoned everyone except twelve individuals, two of whom were women and one a valet, the rest listed without occupation, but evidently from the menu peuple. After the usual interminable litigation over damages, Lagrange and three other parties were awarded 16,000 livres in compensation, but litigation over this was still continuing in 1637. The city paid 25,930 livres for the upkeep of the royal troops, which stayed from 5 January to 15 March.[47]

These episodes in Châlons and Lyon give us well-documented instances of a classic form of focused protest – the kind of revolt most frequently discussed in studies that stress community solidarity. The movement could be focused because specific groups were targeted by specific agents, and magistrates could communicate with crowds because there was no generalized fear in the air such as the apprehension of the "gabelle." *Partisans* contributed to the scenario by publicizing their arrival, setting up specific locations for collection, and advertising specific starting dates. Once the scene was set, the contest that ensued was almost like a game with rules understood by both sides. Protest would naturally be organized by the trades most directly affected, groups with prior networks of solidarity such as drapers, tanners, butchers, innkeepers, and weavers.

---

[46] Ibid., fols. 313r-324v: 27 December 1632.
[47] Lyon CC 4018: various items.

They held meetings among themselves, posted warnings, and spread rumors about price rises, probable unemployment, illicit practices, or corrupt uses of funds in order to generate anger in their neighborhoods. At each stage of the installation process they tried to intimidate the *partisans*, usually with nasty words, nocturnal threats, or rocks. Once the contest was prepared by rumors and meetings, the incidents could be almost accidental and the perpetrators could be passersby, neighbors, often youths. The clandestine moderation of these initial attacks made them tolerable to city officials who were often waging their own legal wars against the same individuals. After all, they shared the crowd's contempt for "devourers of the people" who built mansions while the unemployed starved.

Such movements have often been studied as prototypical examples of collaboration between magistrates and crowds.[48] But it would be a serious error to picture échevins and protesters united against the agents of external forces because the "community" was more complex than that. Even in these cases of "parallel resistance" there were fundamental divergences between rulers and ruled. Despite a certain civic consciousness tied to common interests and traditions, especially in cities like Châlons and Lyon where the structure of the municipality provided close interaction between échevins and trades, there were undercurrents of antagonism that emerge very clearly in these accounts. The city fathers had broader perspectives than the menu peuple and different interests to look out for. They were integrated into a network of relationships with each other, with people at court, and with their counterparts in other cities. Locally, they had the capacity to make decisions about the structure of tax burdens, and they used it to shield the interests of the privileged while disadvantaging the poor. Some of them also had private interests at stake. They were creditors of the city and they themselves took on its tax farms. They defended their own authority and the interests of property and order. They might grumble and denounce extortionists, but they also made compromises in Paris, collected similar taxes themselves, and remembered that in a pinch, "they will cut our throats."

The menu peuple were not so simple either. They had some respect for their magistrates, and their first recourse was usually to petition for redress by invading council meetings or by sending out signals through slogans, night riders, and bills posted on doors. Their threats were belligerent, but when they moved to action they did so in stages, as if wanting to be persuaded otherwise. At the same time they were deeply

---

[48] For example, Roland Mousnier, *La plume, la faucille et le marteau: institutions et société en France du Moyen Age à la Révolution* (Paris, 1970), 355–9.

suspicious of calls for moderation. When an abuse was anticipated, they
talked, and agitated, and threatened on their own. They demanded guarantees in writing and issued ultimatums that were timed to coincide with
those of the *partisan*. Most important, they anticipated that the magistrates would turn on them, and when this happened they knew whose
houses to attack. If support grew and the official response was unsatisfac-
tory, they were perfectly willing to threaten their own échevins in the
streets, besiege their residences, or storm the hôtel de ville itself.

Thus even in these focused cases where the disaffected and the
échevins spoke different dialects of the same language, the population
was suspicious and the magistrates were two-faced. In more generalized
revolts where the perceived threat was more all-encompassing or the
repression more confrontational, the crowd was likely to demand retribution even more vociferously.

6   Notable uprisings before 1661

The most dramatic uprisings had wider scope than those focused around particular grievances. These were movements with broad-based support and popular inspiration. They lasted at least several days and upset the routine workings of the city, causing the suspension of "business as usual." They transcended immediate circumstances to the point where the participants seemed, for a brief exhilarating or terrifying moment, to be imposing their viewpoint on the city.

There can never be a definitive list of such "notable" uprisings.[1] Documentation has favored some at the expense of others, and existing enumerations are notoriously inaccurate, both for their omissions and for the inappropriate cases that filter through from one list to another. Most important, there is no simple standard of evaluation. Significance should be judged by the degree of popular mobilization and the magnitude of social confrontation: it makes little sense to count houses pillaged or injuries sustained, and there is no way to assess sizes of crowds. Furthermore, there can be no sharp line between "ordinary" and "great" revolts, inasmuch as all uprisings were made up of a sequence of distinct, related incidents and the great ones were simply those in which circumstances combined to lead all the way to a dramatic conclusion. As we have already seen, smaller episodes had many of the same motivations and methods as full-blown crises.

Nevertheless, there is much to be learned from a closer examination of a few full-scale, well documented examples, and in this chapter we will look at three from the first half of the century. Because these revolts occurred in major cities, we should watch for more complex relationships among bourgeois, officers, and menu peuple and be attentive to the policies of the sovereign courts. We can also look again at the motivations of popular crowds and consider the relative weight of popular consciousness and elite complicity in shaping protest.

---

[1] The wildly inaccurate list of revolts that appeared in the French translation of Porchnev, *Soulèvements*, pp. 661–76 has unfortunately been reproduced uncritically in many subsequent syntheses.

Montpellier, 1645

The uprising in Montpellier demonstrates the phases and characteristics of a full-blown popular uprising with unusual clarity.[2] This was an important administrative city of some 20,000 people, the seat of various royal and provincial authorities and the site of a royal citadel. In 1645 the minority of Louis XIV was under way and Cardinal Mazarin was grasping after expedients to pay for the Thirty Years War. Agricultural conditions were poor and prices were high. In Montpellier's province of Languedoc the Estates, meeting in nearby Narbonne, were orchestrating resistance to the imposition of *quartier d'hiver* taxes on the province, and many influential regional nobles were plotting their return to influence after the passing of Richelieu and the appointment of their patron, Gaston d'Orléans, as provincial governor.[3]

Thus there was no lack of resistance in the air when, in June 1645, the hard-pressed inhabitants learned that a new tax, the *joyeux avènement à la couronne*, was being promulgated by the intendant Baltazar and the *partisan* Romanet.[4] This fee for the confirmation of corporate privileges at the advent of Louis XIV's reign threatened guilds and associations and came at a time when a number of other annoying special taxes such as the *amortissements* and *franc-fiefs* were also being levied on designated groups. The agitation began with the widespread serving of summonses to a variety of individuals and associations. We already know that this was a

[2] An earlier version of my analysis on Montpellier was published in William Beik, "The Culture of Protest in Seventeenth-Century French Towns," *Social History* 15 (1990), 4–8. The political context was discussed in William Beik, "Two Intendants face a Popular Revolt: Social Unrest and the Structure of Absolutism in 1645," *Canadian Journal of History* 9 (1974), 243–62.

[3] The history of Montpellier is narrated in the traditional account by Charles d'Aigrefeuille, *Histoire de la ville de Montpellier*, 4 vols. (Montpellier, 1877–82) and the modern study, Gérard Cholvy (ed.), *Histoire de Montpellier* (Toulouse, 1984). Accounts of the 1645 revolt are Alexandre Germain, "Les commencements du règne de Louis XIV et la Fronde à Montpellier," *Mémoires de l'Académie des sciences de Montpellier*, 3 (1859–63), 579–602; Porchnev, *Soulèvements*, pp. 242–60; Emmanuel Le Roy Ladurie, *Les paysans de Languedoc*, 2 vols. (Paris, 1966), vol. I, pp. 496–8.

[4] The major narrative sources are the account by the intendant François Bosquet in Ms. fr. 18432, fol. 344 and reproduced in P. Coquelle, "La sédition de Montpellier en 1645 d'après des documents inédits," *Annales du Midi* 20 (1908), 66–78; two versions of the "Minutte du verbal de messieurs les consuls de Montpellier," in AM Montpellier, liasse FF "attroupements et séditions," nos. 1, 8; André Delort, *Mémoires inédits d'André Delort sur la ville de Montpellier*, 2 vols. (Montpellier, 1978), vol. I, pp. 50–63; Pierre Gariel, *Les Gouverneurs du Languedoc* (Montpellier, 1873); Pierre Sabatier, "Mémorial des choses les plus remarquables arrivées en la ville de Montpellier," AM Montpellier BB 197, fols. 31–41; procès-verbal by Antoine Crouzet, juge mage, Ms. fr. 18432, fols. 336–41; letters from the intendant Baltazar, lieutenant-général Schomberg and others in the correspondence of the Chancellor Séguier, Ms fr. 17383–84; and letters to Cardinal Mazarin in Archives du Ministère des Affaires Etrangères, Mémoires et Documents, France 1632, fol. 1634.

fine way to stir up trouble. The edict, posted all over town, was long and complicated. Many could not read it and its terms were confusing. Though technically restricted to certain associations, this tax must have seemed like a kind of "gabelle," hitting as it did a wide range of groups. Rumors spread that women would be taxed for each of their children and that maids and valets were being individually assessed. Some people complained that the *partisans* were worse than the Turks because they taxed you twice where at least the Turks only taxed you once.

Popular indignation built up over a period of days. All accounts mention repeatedly that the participants were mostly women, not just in the initial protest phase but throughout the violence. Most of them were artisans' wives, possibly joined by female servants. In one report the trouble starts on the evening of 28 June with a band of children throwing rocks at a boy from the Maduron family, financial underwriters of the joyeux avènement, on their way home from a bonfire for the festival of Saints Peter and Paul. This sounds like an echo of the "children" who often stood in for their elders at the beginning of disturbances, and especially after festivities.[5] Most accounts start on 29 June, when we hear of a process-server being chased out of town in the morning by women throwing rocks, of a tailor being arrested for refusing to pay the tax, and of women marching through town beating drums and proclaiming that it was time to get rid of *partisans*. Their leaders were "Monteille," the wife of a tile-maker and another imposing woman nicknamed "la Branlaire".

Antagonism mounted. One report says that the Maduron parents precipitated an exchange with angry mothers by thrashing the ringleader of the children's attack on their son. Typically a counter attack such as this fueled further anger and caused an intensification of conflict. Later that evening (29 June) angry women two or three hundred strong broke into the residence of François Maduron with pikes and hatchets, searching for Romanet, whose office was set up there. The consuls dispersed the initial crowd, but the demonstrators regrouped and pillaged the house of Pierre Maduron, son of François, still complaining of insults and blows proffered by Maduron against women in the crowd. The next morning (30 June) the trouble resumed. More attacks were made on the Maduron houses and roving bands began visiting local inns looking for Romanet, who thus represented an extremely focused target for the protesters. When he was located at the Swan, the entire building was put under siege. Romanet was not found, but his room was broken into, his trunk was searched and the documents it contained, believed by the crowd to be additional tax decrees, were torn into bits. As the day progressed, other

---

[5] For example, the beginnings of the 1641 Châlons riot, pp. 96.

houses were pillaged – always places where tax farmers were lodged – and more papers were destroyed. In mid afternoon the intendant Bosquet found the streets littered with fragments of receipts from the royal *parties casuelles*. Under cover of darkness men joined the sacking operation, two of whom, a locksmith and a miller, were finally seized about 10 p.m. by the guards of Schomberg, the provincial lieutenant general, after a fierce battle inside the pillaged house where Emeré, *partisan* of the amortissement tax was staying.

Phase one had ended on a note of balanced retribution. The *partisans* had been "punished"; the "community" had spoken. However, the arrest of the two pillagers resulted in a predictable phase two. Early the next morning (1 July) the two prisoners were sentenced to death by the présidial court. As the news spread, a different sort of demonstration developed. A little boy marched through the streets beating his drum and crying loudly "that he was announcing that all women and female servants were to go to the palais where two men were going to be hanged unjustly". By late afternoon a large crowd had gathered in front of the hôtel de ville, crying remorsefully "that [the prisoners] were innocent and it was [the women] alone who were guilty." One contingent of women aided by locksmiths and other men slipped outside the town, scaled the prison wall, and released the prisoners with "hatchets, masons hammers and pikes." The convicted pillagers escaped into the countryside and the women returned, "singing of their triumph and declaring that they wanted to keep the peace."[6] The consuls claimed that the avenues leading to the prison had been occupied by large numbers of people and that even the provincial lieutenant governor and his guards had been unable to forestall this action. But it is hard to imagine that the authorities could not have held onto the prisoners if they had really wanted to, and it is possible that they were allowed to escape to placate the crowd. After all, prisoners were more or less pawns seized for symbolic reasons, and the action to this point had been mild enough that placating the city may have appeared more useful than terrorizing the population.

The balance was righted and once again there was calm. Schomberg now held conferences with most of the leaders of the community, all of whom took advantage of the situation to complain of grievances. The heads of the métiers confidently "disavowed the actions of the women and denied that their wives had taken part," but complained about the assessments levied on them and insisted "that they had trouble enough living by the sweat of their brow; that they found the ordinance prescribing *contrainte solidaire* extremely unjust, and that five or six hundred summonses to

---

[6] Sabatier, "Mémorial," fol. 38v; Coquelle, "Sédition," 71–2; consuls, "Minutte."

artisans had been served in one day."[7] This is a more sophisticated version of the same message that was being heard all over town. "People having to pay twice" was contrainte solidaire, the practice of forcing the group to cover the sums not paid by individuals. "Taxing of children and servants" was an extension of the idea that individuals were being unjustly assessed for a tax that was only supposed to be placed on collectivities. The women, no doubt egged on by their husbands, had been expressing in a rudimentary way a genuine grievance about the illegality of the collector's procedures, and this lament had apparently spread through rumors to other women and to the menu peuple in general.

None of the authorities expected further trouble, but they did not allow for the broader class fears that had been set off by the excitement over recent events. This was the crucial extension of the attack from specific individuals to the idea that the town was full of various sorts of exploiters. Those who feared becoming the next victims started calling attention to themselves by fortifying their residences. On the morning of 2 July, passers-by saw the hôtels of Dupuy and Massia, financiers living on opposite sides of the same street, barricaded with barrels and great slabs of wood and teeming with men carrying arquebuses, muskets, and halberds – the first firearms to appear. The men were bustling in and out, making periodic forays into the street. One observer said they were shouting "Kill, kill!" An out-of-town witness was told by bystanders that these were "*partisans*." It is hard to believe that the people passing in the street were as innocent of provocation as some observers later claimed. It does appear, however, that Dupuy and Massia's armed bodyguards were making a show of their defiance, as seventeenth-century soldiers often did. Some observers even reported that they had been firing indiscriminately into the street. Whatever preliminaries actually occurred – perhaps taunts and jeers on both sides – the result was that shots were fired from Dupuy's windows at an unarmed assemblage, predominantly women. Bystanders were wounded and at least two men were killed: Jean Caylar, a "poor plasterer" of thirty years old with three children whose wife was unable to sign her name to her testimony, and Jacques Laurents, nicknamed Resuscitat, a master mason, thirty-five, who also had three children.[8] The body of Caylar, "dead and bleeding," was then paraded through the streets by the indignant crowd, as if to provide tangible evidence of the suspected treason, and "had as great an effect as Caesar's shirt," according to the erudite intendant.[9]

---

[7] Coquelle, "Sédition," 72.
[8] Testimony from eyewitnesses collected for legal proceedings surrounding the later indemnity claims by the Falgairolles family: AM Montpellier FF 533.
[9] Coquelle, "Sédition," 73.

This third round was an expression of class fears on both sides. The crowd was threatening generic *partisans*; the tax farmers were calling attention to themselves by arming; the juxtaposition of bitter demonstrators and nervous bodyguards provided a confrontation. The arbitrary death of "innocents" then produced the age-old response of parading the body to produce solidarity in the neighborhoods through shock. Indignation spread. Storming into the Dupuy house, a large crowd eventually murdered four people: a chamber-maid, two agents of Dupuy, and the widow of a councillor in the Cour des Comptes who, one account stated, had insulted the demonstrators. The body of this widow, the Dame de Falgairolles, was stripped naked and paraded through the streets as if in triumphal retribution for the death of Caylar. Then it was dumped in the cemetery, as was that of Massia's son, a cathedral canon from Narbonne who had been caught fleeing from the house across the street. Montpellier did not have a river suitable for dumping, or perhaps the use of the cemetery indicated that the victims, not themselves *partisans*, deserved an honest burial. Both houses were pillaged and their furniture made a huge bonfire, including "a great quantity of tapestries, silver and pewter dishes, mattresses and linen." Meanwhile the Dupuy family climbed hastily over the roofs and fled from Montpellier.

These seemingly random attacks were vicious but not gratuitous. A contract drawn up two years earlier in the same Dupuy residence shows that Jean Dupuy, brother-in-law of the murdered Dame de Falgairolles, was a secrétaire du roi and collector of the amortissement tax.[10] He had acquired the house in return for repaying a debt which Falgairolles owed to Gabriel Creissels. A witness to the transaction was Guillaume Massia, father of the murdered canon from Narbonne. Massia and Creissels were both financiers and treasurers of the Estates of Languedoc who had lent money to the intendant Baltazar to pay for the passage of royal troops into Catalonia. Thus however improvised their response, the rioters were attacking an interlocking cartel of financiers with ties to the Cour des Comptes of Montpellier, the Estates, the intendant, and the royal credit system, as well as the tax farms. The naked bodies being paraded through the streets were connected through family ties to a cartel of considerable political importance.

Crowds seized the gates and the tocsin was rung continuously for four hours. Chains went up in the streets. Schomberg mustered a number of mounted nobles and forty soldiers from the citadel, but could do nothing against the crowd of "two thousand armed inhabitants divided into several groups . . . stationed at the corners of all the streets," who fired on

---

[10] AM Montpellier FF 533.

them with muskets, pistols, and stones thrown from the rooftops, to cries of "Kill the Marshall," and then retreated down side streets where horses could not follow. "I didn't want to kill for fear of angering them more," Schomberg reported, "but as soon as I had separated them with my club, they regrouped a hundred paces away, and I was obliged to yield to superior force."[11] The rioting went on all night and gradually subsided of its own accord. All the authorities could do was follow these mobs around, making small charges to separate them and then pulling back. The next day Schomberg suspended the unpopular taxes.

The authorities claimed that the rioters were scum (*la lie du peuple*), servants and valets, or, most specifically, starving mountaineers who had come down from the Cevennes for the harvest. But while all of these may have participated in the most general phase of rioting, none of the evidence suggests that unemployed outsiders played a central role. Both the nature of the events and the identity of the few known participants point towards the artisan community, or a segment of it, as the backbone of the revolt. One senses a reasoned improvisation resulting in violent but measured reactions and a crowd that could be rallied semi-spontaneously by street appeals. The intendant's disgust at what the people had done reflects unwittingly the temerity and pride with which they had done it:

The scum of the people . . . have been bold enough to take up arms, seize the gates, force their way into the houses of royal officers . . . mark those thought to belong to *traitants* for pillage . . . attack a duke and peer, marshall of France . . . in a town where he enjoys most of his friendships, dependents, and habits . . . scoffed at the cannons of a citadel, and fought its soldiers . . . Most of all, their great obstinacy and perseverance multiplies the magnitude of the crime.[12]

Perhaps the best expression of the position of the rioters comes when the intendant rails against the failure of "the people" to understand the dictates of raison d'état:

they think they have made an enormous sacrifice to God, the king, and the public by throwing out of town those they suspect of drinking their blood and growing fat on their substance, but they deliver no money to the royal coffers. They have such feeble lights as to make a distinction between the public utility of the state and the particular utility of the tax farmer, but this is just in order to be able to throw themselves down the precipice of rebellion, since they want to provide for the needs of the state by other hands than the *traitants*, an idea which has no relevance to the present state of affairs.[13]

---

[11] Coquelle, "Sédition," 77.
[12] "Advis sommaire sur l'estat present de la ville de Montpellier," Ms. fr. 18432, fols. 330r-333v.   [13] Ibid.

There can be no doubting the intensity of the indignation felt by the demonstrators, the singleness of purpose with which they sought out logical targets and attacked other personages only when they got in the way of this indignation, or the improvised nature of their mobilization, which escalated from small individual acts to large-scale maneuvers. Indeed, the most impressive aspect of the revolt was this solidarity of purpose transmitted predominantly by women and backed up by a large segment of the laboring community. In any event, the Montpelliérains had successfully warded off a scourge which fit the contours of all their worst expectations, and they had discredited all those in authority. The result of the "message" they sent was that the whole province remained on tense alert throughout the "hot" summer of 1645. Peasants guarded the roads and municipal consuls everywhere quaked at the slightest hint of insubordination.[14]

What had become of the forces of order? A fairly complete set of reports, many of them mutually accusatory, give us a good picture of the authorities' reactions, confirming the impression that governmental forces were structurally incapable of handling this sort of emergency.[15] When the attacks on the Maduron house began on the evening of 29 June, the consuls were alerted in their homes by concerned bystanders; they proceeded to the hôtel de ville, put on their liveries and hurried to the scene with the captain of the guet, his archers, and some "honest" citizens collected along the way. After persuading the rioters to retire, they set up patrols in every quarter and apparently went home to bed. The next morning they had to start all over again, with more parties to consult. When new reports of trouble arrived the consuls sent a warning to Jean Baltazar, one of the intendants, who told them to report to the présidial court for advice. They summoned the captains of the militia to arm their sixains and report to the hôtel de ville, but no one showed up except a few of the more loyal captains. The consuls and their immediate entourage were unable to dissuade the crowd from further violence this time (pacification by persuasion was probably something that could only be done once), so they sent to the citadel for reinforcements while the women moved on to invade the Swan. This "military" option was limited. It was wartime, the citadel was understaffed, and consuls generally viewed the calling in of soldiers as an abdication of autonomy. Royal commanders were not too eager to commit their forces to nasty police actions without firm royal orders. The citadel's commander, Villepassier, came out to assess the trouble, but he could not stop the rampaging crowd either. He

[14] Bosquet to Séguier, 18 July 1645: Porchnev, *Soulèvements*, p. 649.
[15] See the sources in note 4.

finally called in a few musketeers whose appearance calmed the crowd, and used them to escort Romanet from hiding, carrying with him 20,000 livres in gold.

It was about then that Juge Mage Crouzet, the most important royal judge short of the sovereign Cour des Comptes, seems to have heard about the rioting for the first time. He arrived at the Swan about noon with his own followers, but too late to do much good. The second intendant, François Bosquet, only heard the news about two or three in the afternoon. He took a walk and saw the damage in the streets, then summoned two of the consuls to tell him what was going on. The city's top military commander, Charles de Schomberg duc d'Halluin, lieutenant general of the province, was off hunting, and none of the royal authorities was willing to do very much without him.[16] By the time he actually got to the scene it was nine or ten at night, but he intervened a little more decisively. Torches were lit and a larger group, now including Crouzet, Baltazar, la Forest de Toiras (seneschal of Montpellier), Villepassier, and a number of soldiers, was able to break up the rioting and seize the two prisoners. Again night patrols were set up and again things appeared calm.

On 1 July Crouzet, Baltazar, and the consuls were tied up from six in the morning at the présidial court where they were trying the two arrested prisoners. Crouzet went from there to the sénéchaussée court, where he spent the afternoon. Schomberg was meanwhile meeting with the métiers. This was the day when the crowd freed the prisoners. All the authorities claimed to have tried to stop this action, but their itineraries make it unclear exactly when it occurred or what they did about it. What seems clear is that they all thought the trouble was over and that most of them were returning to their own, separate affairs.

The morning of 2 July started slowly. The shots and the murders occurred around noon at a time when Schomberg was dining at Baltazar's house along with Crouzet, Toiras, and other notable military officers. When the news arrived, Villepassier hastened to the citadel to get troops, Baltazar took refuge in the citadel, Bosquet stayed home, and the rest, including major officers from the Cour des Comptes, rode out to confront the crowd in general street battle. Schomberg's hôtel gradually became the command center, and all the notables finally rallied, many of them after a night of violence. The sixains were armed, and as citizens arrived to offer their services to Schomberg, he sent them to the hôtel de ville to be armed and positioned, thus confirming a belated collaboration

[16] Schomberg, governor of Languedoc since 1632, was a much-respected local figure, but he had been demoted to lieutenant-général and replaced by Gaston d'Orléans in 1644 – a fact which could have made him less eager to stick his neck out.

between military headquarters and the city. Schomberg issued ordinances suspending the unpopular taxes, guards were stationed at the gates, and notables circulated through the streets explaining the ordinances to anyone who would listen.

Clearly the power structure was defective. Responsibility was diffused. Each agency was locked into its own procedures. When a crowd massed, it was the job of the consuls to disperse it, but they treated this as an isolated incident and went home when it was over. No one had any way of monitoring the ongoing crisis, or even wanted to do so. The courts were preoccupied with their own sessions. The individual consuls, who had recently been imposed on the community by royal fiat, lacked the following to direct a forcible repression. The commanders in the citadel were caught short-handed, and without royal orders crowd control was not their particular concern. The intendants, feuding with each other, had no military expertise. Each authority acted separately, going through the motions of consulting the others, appearing with followers to calm the streets, issuing appropriate orders, but without really taking command. Only genuine, armed soldiers could master the situation through coordinated effort, and only the lieutenant governor – who was out of town, perhaps deliberately, could coordinate the operation. Only fear of anarchy and military leadership ultimately convinced the authorities to come together.

Thus Montpellier shows us a popular movement of impressive force, fueled by a logical sequence of events, and crowned with temporary success. We must imagine each day's events being discussed in shops and homes, and very probably women taking the initiative in organizing the next stage of the protest. Indignation started with the process-serving, then moved on to muttering against the Madurons, attacks on a series of other *partisans*, rising violence capped by the arrest of the prisoners; the move to rescue the prisoners; growing general fear of *partisans* and consequences; the fulfilled prophesy of the counterattack, and a general battle against all the authorities ended by the rescinding of the unpopular measures.

In this atmosphere there was no need for elite instigators.[17] Most of the authorities had reason to be discontented, and many had been expecting a rebellion against the quartier d'hiver that never happened. No one anticipated that the joyeux avènement would cause so much trouble. After the fact, mutual accusations and defensive conspiracy theories abounded. Many of the principals were recent royal appointees who had reason to want to keep order, but there was certainly no unified

---

[17] I discussed this issue more thoroughly in "Two Intendants face a Popular Uprising."

community action. While no leader planned or caused the revolt, few had the desire or the means to put it down effectively. The very procedures used and the rivalries built into the authority structure meant that no one had the motivation to take preventive steps once each immediate disturbance was quelled. And whatever their objectives, the leaders of the community had badly mismanaged the whole affair. Their irreducible reality was that prominent citizens had been murdered, others had fled, houses were ransacked, officers of the governor had been wounded and killed, and every local authority had been humiliated.

Dijon, 1630

With 20,000 people, Dijon was close to the size of Montpellier, and as a former capital of the Burgundian state with a major parlement and a full array of aristocratic authorities, it had considerable civic pride.[18] Among the most interesting citizens of this wine-producing city were the vignerons, vinegrowers, who lived in large numbers in certain quarters. They were poorer than most artisans, but these urban peasants had a strong sense of customary rights. They knew the ramparts well, for they spent many nights doing guard duty there, and their propensity for banding together to defend their rights was repeatedly demonstrated, as we have seen in chapter 2.[19] The 1630 revolt of the Lanturelus has been remembered as a radical protest with picturesque images: a carnival procession turning into a riot; pillagers dancing to the "lanturelu" around bonfires of booty; the portrait of Louis XIII being burned to cries of "Long live the Emperor!"[20] But these graphic moments, possibly apocryphal, do not capture the real significance of the rebellion, which was a fine example of a popular protest linked to a broader constitutional protest.

The issue was the imposition of the élus on the province of Burgundy, a measure which pointed towards abolition of the Estates, centralization of tax collections by the crown, and the creation of new venal officeholders

---

[18] Dijon has been well served by historians. Its artisan community is beautifully analyzed by James Farr, *Hands of Honor: Artisans and their World in Dijon 1550–1650* (Ithaca, NY, 1988). Useful background is provided by Pierre Gras (ed.), *Histoire de Dijon* (Toulouse, 1987); Arthur Kleinclausz, *Histoire de Bourgogne*, 2nd edn. (Paris, 1924) and Jean Richard (ed.), *Histoire de la Bourgogne* (Toulouse, 1978). See also Gaston Roupnel, *La ville et la campagne au XVIIe siècle: étude sur les populations du pays dijonnais* (Paris, 1955), dom Plancher, *Histoire générale de la Bourgogne*, vol. IV (Dijon, 1871), and de la Cuisine, *Le Parlement de Bourgogne depuis son origine jusqu'à sa chute*, 2nd edn., vol. II (Dijon, 1864).

[19] See pp. 46–7.

[20] For example Porchnev, *Soulèvements*, p. 138. Charles Tilly places the same anecdotes in a slightly different context in *The Contentious French* (Cambridge, MA, 1986), pp. 13–15; the carnival demonstration is incorrectly linked to the Mère Folle society in Natalie Davis, *Society and Culture in Early Modern France* (Stanford, 1975), p. 119.

whose existence would challenge local and regional authorities.[21] This institutional reorganization was largely an issue for provincial elites, but the concept of élus had resonance in the larger population because it sounded like a gabelle – an unwarranted intrusion on regional liberties. There were also material reasons for discontent. Troop movements were causing grain shortages, food prices were climbing in early 1630, and wine prices were falling disastrously. Local people, especially vignerons, were hard-pressed to survive. Some may even have been near famine. For them vague rumors about élus agitation could easily turn into stories of terrible consequences, rather like the fatalistic exaggerations heard in Montpellier in 1645. In addition there were reports of a new *aide* tax on wine that would have hit vignerons directly. Rumor had it that the imposition of the élus would clear the way for the imposition of onerous new taxes.

The issue of the *élections*, promulgated by royal edict in June 1629, had been pending for eight months. On 31 January 1630 it was known in Paris that the maire of Dijon's mission to Paris to forestall the promulgation of the edict had failed.[22] Probably this news had reached Dijon by 12 February because on that day the échevins appealed to the Chambre des Comptes in Beaune not to register the élus edict, even as the population was celebrating the last frenzied day of Mardi Gras, led by Anatoire Changenet, vigneron, their festive "Roi Machas." The Chambre des Comptes had recently been transferred to Beaune, but most of its officers lived in Dijon. They were suspect both because their jurisdiction would be enhanced by the reform and because they and the trésoriers de France were prime candidates to invest in the new offices being created. Thus, like the comparable officers in Agen, they appeared to be potential "exploiters." The Parlement, by contrast, had an interest in siding with the people and opposing the moves of their rival officers. On 19 February, a week into a somber Lent, the maire arrived home with official confirmation of the bad news. That same day the city council heard "stirrings

[21] The best recent discussion of the Lanturelu rebellion is Farr, *Hands of Honor*, pp. 201–10. I published an earlier version of my analysis in "The Culture of Protest," 14–20. In addition to the syntheses cited in note 20, the rebellion has been discussed in Charles Fevret, *De la sédition arrivée en la ville de Dijon le 28 février 1630 et jugement rendu par le roi sur icelle* (Paris, 1630); Paul Cunisset-Carnot, *L'émeute des Lanturelus à Dijon en 1630* (Dijon, 1897); and anon., "Le Lanturelu, émeute des vignerons à Dijon en 1630," *Revue retrospective ou bibliothèque historique*," 2 (1834), 454–8. I also profited from reading Xavière Patouillet, "L'émeute des Lanturelus à Dijon en 1630," mémoire de maîtrise, UER, Sciences humaines, Université de Dijon, 1971. I am grateful to James Farr for generously sharing his information with me.
[22] My narrative is based on the city's dossier in AM Dijon I 117, which includes the letter written by Fleutelot de Beneuve on 7 March 1630 and a variety of procès-verbaux, including the report by the échevins and the report by the Parlement. The Bibliothèque Municipale de Dijon, ms. 911 contains the same Beneuve letter plus several other brief commentaries.

among the common people" and decreed an 8 p.m. curfew. The parish captains and lieutenants were called in and instructed to set up patrols. For the next five nights they found no evidence of trouble in the streets, although other sources mention various incidents.[23]

On 27 February rumor had it that the Comptes would register the edict the next morning. That evening about dusk a strange procession led by Changenet marched to the hôtel de ville and massed outside it. He was wearing his mardi-gras costume – bright coat and crown of ivy – with drummers marching in front of him wearing their "carnival rags." Up to one hundred men carrying halberds followed, singing the "lanturelu."[24] Then came disorderly women and children. They demonstrated and shouted peacefully in front of the hôtel de ville.[25] Receiving no response, they became angry, began to utter threats, and moved on, probably to the house of Nicolas Gagne, trésorier de France, where a crowd of thirty or forty gathered about 7 p.m. and threw rocks at the house without gaining admission. They also paused briefly in front of the house of Jean Le Grand, first president of the Comptes. Thus they had already identified the houses that would be attacked the next morning. Fleutelot de Beneuve, a maître in the Comptes who lived nearby, took the news calmly because "the same thing had happened two or three times already a few days previously" – again we get the impression of earlier movements. But a few minutes later he fled out his back door with his family because his servants who had infiltrated the crowd brought back reports that its tone was getting nasty and that pillagers were heading his way. Beneuve gives us some sense of how a budding rebellion looked from the vantage point of the potential victims. Sitting behind closed portals, they were aware that they were potential targets, but they were often able to monitor the progress of the crowd from street to street by sending out their servants. Sometimes they had time to remove valuables from the premises, or at least to depart to a safer location.

As it turned out, the crowd streamed by Beneuve's house and fanned out to gather support in the quartier Saint Philibert where the vignerons lived. This is the interesting part. So far the crowd had consisted of a band

[23] Lackeys were waiting outside the doors of houses where their masters were dining: perhaps there were meetings going on. AM Dijon I 117: deliberations of 19, 21, 24, 25, 26 February.

[24] This is the only instance I know of a song being used in a seventeenth-century revolt.

[25] This famous episode is elusive. Only Cunisset-Carnot reports that the Roi Machas led his troop out of the quartier Saint Philibert "at dusk" on 17 February and that they demonstrated in front of the hôtel de ville. His information is precise, but he has no citations. This version makes sense since Beneuve has a crowd storming down his street that same evening, presumably after the demonstration. Other modern accounts attribute the procession to the morning of the 28th, but this view is hard to reconcile with the blow by blow accounts in the sources, none of which mentions the carnival episode.

of forty or fifty men armed with halberds and clubs but no firearms. Instead of striking blindly, this mixed group of menu peuple dominated by vignerons, spent an entire evening building their forces. About 9 p.m. they beat the tambour to attract attention, gathered behind the Saint Michel church, and sent recruiters to the ramparts where vignerons had the habit of gathering. Popular meetings were held all night on the ramparts, and attempts were made to get the keys to the city from the mayor (who refused) so that vignerons from outside could be brought in through the closed gates. A core of popular organizers was building support and making plans, based on ties with vignerons inside and outside the city. On his rounds later that evening, Philippe Deschamps, syndic of the city, encountered several vignerons with their wives and children who "spoke of gabelles, saying that they were so poor they couldn't earn their livelihood."[26] This must have been the sort of thing that was being said in their meetings.

But at the same time this popular mobilization was a response to the constitutional issue that was not of popular inspiration. On 19 February an affiche had appeared on the door of the Palais de Justice, home of the Parlement: "you, chief of *élections*, beware for yourself and your house."[27] Some sort of premeditated agitation was obviously going on. Beneuve, an unfriendly witness, quotes statements made in the Parlement prior to the disturbances to the effect that certain parties should be attacked: "President Robelin said in the palais that it was shameful to see me in Dijon, that I was part of the faction that supported the *élections*, and that they would have me beaten up."[28] There is no way to determine whether these sorts of insults in judicial chambers reached the streets and what effect they had. The mere fact of their existence does not indicate any sort of conspiracy, but it does suggest that the initial "enemies" attacked by the crowd had been singled out because of the intense personal rivalries deriving from months of conflicts among influential officers. Still, the link between designated targets and popular actions is complex. Beneuve's house was never attacked, despite the accusations. And from the crowd's perspective the issue was fuzzy. Unlike Montpellier in 1645 there was no limited group of outsiders whose removal would end a new tax. And unlike smaller revolts there was no cadre from a particularly affected trade, such as weavers or innkeepers, to organize the resistance. The crowd could have two objectives. The first was "political": to oppose registration of a royal edict by a body of judges in another city. The second was social: to protest hunger or new taxes and to punish the rich

[26] AM Dijon I 117: deliberation of 27 February 1630.
[27] Patouillet, "L'émeute," p. 10, citing AM Dijon B 267.
[28] AM Dijon I 117, Beneuve letter.

or the responsible parties. The colorful demonstration in front of the Hôtel de ville was apparently organized by Changenet either to demonstrate concern about hunger or perhaps to lend support in some way to the authorities' campaign of resistance against the élus. It was a real demonstration, not a riot. But whatever the magistrates may have thought about fomenting resistance, the sight of a ragged band of angry demonstrators in carnival dress, in the dark, in the middle of Lent, was clearly not what they had in mind.

The next morning (28 February) the protesters launched their campaign. Around 5.30 a.m. crowds of "vignerons and unknown persons" gathered in several locations armed with "pikes, halberds, swords, muskets and iron-tipped clubs", rang the tocsins of Saint Michel and Saint Philibert, and set out through the city in semi-military fashion.[29] Their numbers and determination showed the effect of the night of organization. These were now armed men, and they proceeded with a sense of purpose, cheered on by thousands of bystanders. At the house of Gagne one contingent entered, threw the furniture out the windows, and smashed it in the streets, while another guarded the approaches and placed armed sentinels at the street corners. At 9 a.m. another group attacked the house of President Le Grand of the Comptes. When the mayor and échevins tried to intervene, the pillagers threw furniture at them out of windows and bystanders chased them away with rocks and halberds. Meanwhile drummers marched around town rallying new popular forces "with great cries and hoots against the so-called *partisans* of the *élections.*" Five other houses were subsequently sacked by several distinct bands, including the residence of the First President of the Parlement; and in every case valuables, tapestries, and furnishings were thrown into bonfires in the streets while salt, grain, and wine were carted off or consumed. There is only one mention of the burning of a portrait of Louis XIII (by Beneuve), and the story may be hearsay. If this happened, and if salutes to the Emperor were heard, they should probably be taken as no more than an expression of extreme indignation. Actually, Patouillet cites a counterexample which, if not apocryphal, may give a better feel for the royalism of the demonstrators:

It was noted that when these poor devils had entered the houses, they found a portrait of the late king Henri IV attached to a tapestry. They took it down, carried it into the middle of the street, and raised it up, crying loudly, "here is the good grandfather, here is the good king. Let us save him and be careful not to do him any harm . . . and let us each kiss him and carry him towards the crucifix."[30]

---

[29] AM Dijon I 117, procès-verbal of the maire and échevins.
[30] Patouillet, "L'émeute," p. 63.

By noon the pillaging was spreading beyond the original targets to the houses of other visibly rich notables. But if Beneuve is to be believed, the demolition crews were also very scrupulous. At Gagne's house they set fire to the carriage-house in the rear only after they had led two horses to safety. They also escorted Gagne's aged mother out of the house, unlike the vindictive crowd in Montpellier that murdered Falgairolles' widow. They similarly rescued Le Grand's five children, who had been left in the care of two servants. At the house of an officer in the Estates' tax administration named Léonard, they found Léonard himself kneeling on the doorstep with his seven children, pleading that he was not implicated in the crimes they accused him of and insisting that the *élections* would ruin him too. "If they thought he was guilty," he told them, "they should cut his throat on the spot." Léonard was more successful than Saubebère in Agen.[31] His magnificently theatrical gesture obviously swayed the crowd and won over their leaders, one of whom argued in patois "that if he had stayed in his house he must be innocent for otherwise he would-n't have dared." This humane reticence of the crowd may have stemmed in part from the abstraction of the issue at hand, which was responsibil-ity for the élus. Again, this was an administration with fiscal implications, not a new tax or a particular collector, and individuals could be consid-ered scapegoats only by virtue of voting for the edict or investing in élus offices – unless ostentatious wealth itself was to be considered offensive.

As usual, the authorities were unable for many hours to muster a force large enough to take command of the situation. But a more responsible bourgeois force of committed individuals eventually materialized. As the cynical Beneuve put it, "When the bulk of the Parlement saw that this affair might turn against themselves and that in the heat of the night [the rioters] might throw themselves into their houses to seize plunder (some of them had been informed that they were threatened), they came out and armed the bourgeois and went to find these thieves." About noon this group of "good inhabitants" and parlementaires left the hôtel de ville and fired on the crowd in the rue du Potet. Six to eight rioters were killed and the rest fled. Gradually the authorities pushed the rioters back to the quartier Saint Philibert, while the population bombarded the forces of order with rocks from every rooftop. The roving pillagers were retreating into a popular stronghold where their defense became a broader community endeavor. They spent the night on the walls trying to introduce allies from the faubourgs by means of ladders. We can measure the social fear that gripped the city by noting that the First President of the Parlement and his family spent the night in the château, along with Beneuve and probably others.

[31] See the attack on the Cunolie house in Agen in 1635, pp. 66–7.

A tense truce followed in which the vignerons' quarters remained barricaded while the rest of the city was patrolled by the authorities. A measure of the atmosphere is given by the fact that the next day when a carpenter escaped from the grips of two magistrates who were arresting him, vignerons let out a hue and cry, showered the magistrates with rocks, and raised "two thousand armed men in half an hour." Partial calm was restored by two measures: the release of all the prisoners from the day before – a step taken in response to threats by the vignerons that they would "burn down the city"; and publication of the news that the élus edict had never been registered by the Comptes.[32]

Now it was time to wait for recriminations. One week after the disturbance, on 8 March, letters from the king to the mayor and échevins demanded decisive action, and the city responded with a programmed roundup of dissidents in the vignerons' quarter which graphically illustrates the sort of people who had rioted, or at least had been noticed. If municipal leaders had encouraged their constituents to revolt they certainly had no hesitation in turning on their erstwhile allies. On the contrary, what we see in the procès-verbal of the syndic Philippe Deschamps is a class repression against insignificant inferiors on the one hand, and a community of rioters, broken and fearful, on the other.[33] The scene was dismal, reflecting the genuine fighting that had taken place. Many of the participants had fled or retreated into anonymity, leaving behind a variety of evasive excuses with neighbors and family: men killed in the revolt, men who had left town for unknown destinations, men out "working their vines." The ones who could not hide were those wounded by the official armed repression. Pierre Theron, vinegrower, had reportedly died in the rioting and his wife had been wounded as she ran after him down the street. Bernard Grand-Guillaume was near death in the hospital, where his arm had been amputated. A *pareur* who had been wounded in the head with a pike was absent. Philippe Vaudan, whose son had carried a pike at the head of the procession, said the latter had left town. Guillaume Simon, vinegrower, was in his room, wounded and unable to move, still wearing his singed clothes. The wife of Labegne Dumont, vinegrower, a captain of the rioters, said her husband had been killed by a halberd and pleaded that her three small children be placed in the hospital since she could no longer feed them. Sabatier Dioton, a wounded vinegrower who had already been arrested and released, was recaptured. It was noteworthy that the neighbors and residents of the quarter offered no resis-

---

[32] Beneuve charged that this release was intended to keep the prisoners from revealing their connections to elite instigators, but it is hardly plausible that the particular individuals arrested would have had such information or that it would not have come out in later investigations.   [33] AM Dijon I 117: procès-verbal 8 March 1630.

tance to the searchers. Faced with a strong symbolic repression, their resignation was complete. It is also interesting that the two instances of denunciation to the authorities involved "outsiders" – a *garde de sel* who was denounced by the whole neighborhood, and five "strangers" who were found hiding in the attic of a "poor beggar's" lodging. Changenet, the "Roi Machas," was reported to have fled. Only two men were ultimately executed, a vinegrower and a furrier.

In the aftermath of the crisis, all the parties suffered and recriminations multiplied. On the one hand the king restricted the city's privileges. On the other the vinegrowers were collectively banished from the city and only gradually allowed to return – probably a greater hardship for them. For years the city fought a nasty legal battle with the claimants over indemnities.[34]

But these repercussions just underline the salient characteristics of the Lanturelu episode. The participants were poor. They came from a variety of trades, but the majority were vinegrowers, and although master artisans played a major role in the city's cultural identity, they were largely absent from the rioting. The revolt was clearly prepared by elites who may have encouraged its outbreak and who faltered in its repression until persecution became a political necessity. But if they were foolish enough to foment actual resistance, they certainly unleashed a dangerous force which none could manipulate, least of all the Parlement which stood to gain the most by the abolition of the élus. Unlike the women of Montpellier, who expressed more or less spontaneous indignation at an obvious intrusion and then at the enemies who overreacted in response, the vinegrowers of Dijon demonstrated, planned, and then attacked with some sophistication. The *élections* were never installed, but if the poor got any satisfaction from their revolt, it was more likely from the memory of having punished some "élus" and struck fear in the hearts of the elite, a fact that was remembered for the rest of the century. For most the result was increased suffering.

Bordeaux, 1635

Bordeaux was a larger, "tougher" city which was the home not only of the major uprisings of 1635 and 1675, but of the Ormée movement during the Fronde.[35] One of France's most impressive urban centers with a

---

[34] AM Dijon I 117, third folder: procès-verbal of François Auguste de Thou, maître des requêtes, on his investigations in Dijon.

[35] Bordeaux has two magnificent general histories: Robert Boutruche (ed.), *Bordeaux de 1453 à 1715*, [vol. IV (1966) of Charles Higounet (ed.), *Histoire de Bordeaux*, 8 vols. (Bordeaux, 1962–74)]; and Charles Higounet (ed.), *Histoire de Bordeaux* (Toulouse, 1980). The revolt of 1635 is thoroughly analyzed in Bercé, *Histoire des Croquants*, pp. 294–316.

population of about 40,000 consisting of a minority of vinegrowers and a majority of craftsmen, shopkeepers, merchants and officers, it was a geographically ambivalent city, serving on the one hand as a regional market center and on the other as an international port exposed to merchants and sailors from Spain, England, Holland, and Brittany. It also contained a full range of governing agents and corporations: Parlement, Cour des Aides, sénéchaussée, archbishopric, military command, intendant. The *jurade* or "elected" municipal government of six jurats, had been established under English rule to ward off the French, and municipal distinctiveness had been further reinforced by the deal struck with Charles VII in 1453 which incorporated the city into France with favored status.

Perhaps because of this long-standing particularism, the people of Bordeaux were uncommonly wary of measures perceived as threatening their sense of autonomy. As the intendant Lauson put it in 1644, "here men throw themselves blindly into rebellions if you push them beyond what is just; and uprisings, reproaches to gabeleurs, and murders follow if you don't handle things with a measuring scale in your hand."[36] This urban chauvinism tinged with defensiveness was a popular tradition. Neighborhoods repeatedly demonstrated the capacity to mobilize relatively spontaneously, using the cadres of the militia. For example, on 11 July 1625 false rumors that the duc de Soubise's rebel navy was in the Gironde set the whole city moving. Although the Parlement forbade assemblies and bearing of arms, there were stirrings of schoolboys anyway, and then armed gatherings at the Porte Médoc and throughout the quartier Saint Michel.[37] In the Saint Projet neighborhood the patrolling jurats found people standing in doorways bearing arms and told them to stay inside, while at the market near the Château du Hâ butchers barricaded three street corners – and all this for a false alarm that the authorities had deliberately tried to squelch.

All of these elements came directly into play in the events of 1635.[38] In August 1634 the king had instituted a new annual tax on wine retailers which required that agents visit and mark the wine barrels. These agents had immediately been run out of town by angry innkeepers, and now on

---

[36] Lauson to Séguier from Bordeaux, 26 May 1644: Porchnev, *Soulèvements*, pp. 629–30.

[37] Paul Courteault and Alfred Leroux (eds.), *Inventaire sommaire des registres de la jurade 1520 à 1783*, vol. V [vol. X of *Archives municipales de Bordeaux*] (Bordeaux, 1913), pp. 110–12. This invaluable series, a printed collection of entries from registers that were subsequently burned, will hereafter be cited as *Inventaire sommaire*.

[38] The chief sources for this narrative are the account by the jurats in *Inventaire sommaire*, vol. V, pp. 115–25 and the secret deliberations of the Parlement in AM Bordeaux ms. 788, pp. 230–539. See also the letter from Guillaume Millanges, bourgeois, in Bercé, *Histoire des Croquants*, vol. II, pp. 716–18; and the account by Guillaume Girard, secretary to Epernon, *Histoire de la vie du duc d'Espernon, divisee en trois parties* (Paris, 1655), pp. 515–30.

10 May 1635 a man named Laforêt, archer of the grand prévôt had arrived with letters to all the appropriate authorities from the royal council renewing the command that the king should be obeyed. To the population this was a frustrating reappearance of an outrage they had already disposed of, but to the jurats it was a serious second warning direct from the crown. Popular grumbling resumed, and an informant told the authorities that the hôteliers and cabaretiers were deliberately stirring up an uprising by taking down their signs and telling people that the gabeleurs wanted to make them pay an écu per barrel of wine – a strategy similar to what we have seen in Lyon and Dijon.[39]

The response of the jurats was naive or incompetent. They summoned the militia captains and the *bayles* of the hôtelier and cabaretier trades to command them to keep order and control their constituencies, but only nine captains and two hôteliers showed up. When the Parlement offered to suspend the tax pending remonstrances to the king, the city, incredibly, opposed this move for fear that it would stir up more trouble. Perhaps the jurats were jealous of the Parlement, but they had rejected an obvious way to obstruct the tax and transfer responsibility to the sovereign court. They do not seem to have understood the gravity of the danger, or else they thought they could handle it or that it would not threaten them personally.

By now the popular quarters were seething with indignation, and armed gatherings were forming like those in 1625. Large meetings were being held in the open, no doubt led by the innkeepers, and serious action was being planned. The rioting began on 14 May, the day Laforêt began his collections. However later reports typically focused not on this obvious cause but rather on a particular incident: a nobleman named Jean Desaigues, who was apparently connected to the tax farms, became exasperated with all this agitation and challenged one such armed assemblage that was meeting in the cemetery of Sainte Eulalie.[40] Desaigues was asserting the sort of personal influence that might have been accepted in normal times but that turned out under the circumstances to be provocative. He told these militants that they were asking to be hanged, and they

---

[39] See pp. 42–3, 105.
[40] The role of Desaigues is something of a mystery. First President d'Aguesseau later described him as a man "wearing a sword by profession who intervened by his own volition in this affair without having any post in the hôtel de ville (Porchnev, *Soulèvements*, 586). The jurats described his intervention as if it had been a simple act of civic duty. But the fact that he spoke out so energetically against the demonstrators and was later murdered for his trouble only makes sense if we pay attention to a single hint in one of the accounts which suggests that he was himself connected to the tax collections ("Desaigues et Eymery qui avoient certaines commissions" [*Inventaire sommaire*, vol. v, p. 120]). He was also apparently a client of the governor.

replied "that they were respectable men and not gabeleurs but that they would certainly manage to locate the latter."[41] Here is the confrontation of world-views in a nutshell: those viewed as "rogues worthy of being hanged" would oppose those viewed as "authorities harboring gabeleurs."

The response of the jurats illustrates again the inadequacy of municipal procedures in the face of a crisis. Caught between a growing storm from below, the need to mobilize bourgeois peers, and the necessity of maintaining liaison with a rather standoffish Parlement, the jurats were trapped in a veritable ballet of consultations and reactive reconnoiterings. First Jurat Constant was sent at 8 a.m. to inform the Parlement that trouble was brewing. The Parlement instructed the jurats to call out the militia. But by the time he got back Desaigues had forced the issue by confronting the meeting in the cemetery and reporting the demonstrators' disobedience to the hôtel de ville. So Jurats Constant and Fouques were sent out with twenty archers to reconnoiter, but predictably the illicit assembly had left the cemetery by the time they got there. Then the jurats heard of trouble in Saint Michel, so Fouques was sent there, while Constant was sent back to the Parlement to report on developments. He had just returned to the hôtel de ville when the news arrived that there had been more trouble in Saint Michel and that one of Fouques' subordinates had been wounded with rocks and chased into the Capuchin monastery. At 10 a.m. Constant therefore returned to the Parlement a third time, and the court finally suspended its regular proceedings and assembled in the Grande Chambre in emergency session to deliberate. Constant waited outside the chamber, but when he heard that the hôtel de ville had been attacked by demonstrators, he barged right in "with a shocked expression, saying that the matter was getting urgent."[42] By this time the hôtel de ville had been besieged, so he spent the rest of the day at the palais separated from his fellow jurats.

Earlier Desaigues had grabbed one of the innkeeper-ringleaders and brought him along to the hôtel de ville to be placed under arrest in the guard room. The embarrassed jurats immediately had the man released – another sign of their compelling desire to avoid trouble. But popular indignation at the arrest, an impulse we have seen in both Montpellier and Dijon, had already spread. News came in that a growing mass of several thousand armed demonstrators, plus a constantly growing contingent of sympathetic bystanders was approaching the hôtel de ville. Soon the crowd was assaulting the building, crying out that the gabeleurs were

[41] *Inventaire sommaire*, vol. v, p. 118.
[42] "Délibérations secrètes," 14 May: AM Bordeaux ms. 788, pp. 250–76.

inside and that they should be turned over or the whole place would be burned down. Their message was that they meant no harm to their magistrates but that they would not tolerate the harboring of evil tax agents.[43] And, indeed, the jurats *were* collaborating in the collection of the new tax and Laforêt *was* one of the men inside. Only then did the desperate magistrates (seventeen bourgeois and nine archers or sergeants) begin to set up a real defense. Windows and doors were barricaded and the call was issued to muster arms. But the muskets in the arsenal proved to be inoperable and there was no supply of powder or fuses – an absurd situation for town leaders who had had four days to prepare!

Church bells were rung to attract the residents of the faubourgs, and bonfires were lighted in the streets. Parleys proved futile. The crowd demanded to see a captain from the quartier Saint Michel, Hugla the Younger, a popular merchant who was apparently viewed as a prisoner inside the hôtel de ville. Hugla was lowered down a rope and tried to mediate, but the crowd's demands were that Desaigues and Laforêt be turned over to them to kill – familiar demand for retribution – so no progress was made. Towards the end of the afternoon the crowd burned down a side door to the building and set fire to a small courtyard, using tar and turpentine, substances that would be readily available to barrelmakers and shipbuilders, as the city clerk and his servants desperately dragged the city's archives into the audience chamber and tried to keep them from burning up by collecting pans of water.

Having only pikes and possessing no provisions whatever, the defenders of the hôtel de ville were finally forced to capitulate. One group, including Desaigues, Laforêt, the captains, and the archers, made their way out a window of the guard room and fled through the house of a neighboring shoemaker. Laforêt, caught fleeing in disguise, was killed by the crowd in the adjacent cemetery of Saint Eloi, and Desaigues, dressed as a gardener, was also killed along with two other persons associated with the tax. The bodies of Laforêt and the clerk who had posted his commissions were dragged through the streets and thrown in the river. Meanwhile another group of beleaguered defenders had taken refuge in the prisons of the hôtel de ville. Around 6 p.m. the rioters stormed through the burned door carrying "poles, wheels, taillefons, hatchets and other tools used by artisans," rang the great bell, and demanded that the prison gates be opened so that the gabeleurs could be finished off.

While the crisis was fanning out through the southern popular quarters, the Parlement was also reacting.[44] Upon hearing of the siege of the hôtel de ville, the judges responded with a routine that was just as stylized

[43] *Inventaire sommaire*, vol. v, p. 120.   [44] AM Bordeaux ms. 788, p. 238.

and inadequate as that of the jurats. They sent their own repeated delega-
tions of parlementaires out to survey the trouble and to command the
bourgeois to obey, notably in the Chapeau Rouge quarter which was far
away from the rioting but close to their homes. They found shops closed
and bourgeois recalcitrant. Those whose doors were pounded on produced servants who claimed that their masters weren't home; only three
agreed to help. This delegation of judges was almost attacked by the
crowd at the hôtel de ville, and when Avocat-Général Duffaut commanded a man with a hatchet to retire, the man replied "that they should
retire themselves," and pointed his weapon directly at Duffaut.

The Parlement did suspend the tax, but their expediency was received
by the crowd with suspicion and hostility. Rioters surrounded the horse of
the huissier who was trying to pronounce the suspension, forced him to
dismount, tore his robe, and snatched the document from his hand,
asking who in the crowd could read it. An unidentified person then read it
and told them "that it was an attempt to fool them; that the edict was not
signed by the First President or the clerk, that it was only on paper, and
that the suspension it spoke of was only for a certain length of time and
only applied to the innkeepers." So the crowd tore up the arrêt, declaring
that they wanted a new one "on parchment signed by the First President
and properly sealed, with no limitation of time, covering all sellers of
wine, and that it be publicized using the silver trumpets." There are hints
of informal legal advice here – perhaps from a procureur or avocat. Soon
the Parlement's palais was invaded by a group of forty armed demonstrators demanding that the revised arrêt be issued or they would besiege the
premises. The court capitulated, promising to make the required changes
in good faith and to get the king to relieve the inhabitants.[45]

The judges had lost what control they had of the situation. The citizens
refused to obey them; the popular demonstrators were scornful of the
judges' power of command, and conciliatory legal acts were rejected as
ruses. Parlementaires put a great deal of stock in their personal power of
command, and they were in for a shock. Presidents Daffis and Pommiès
were sent out once again to rally municipal forces and lead them to the
hôtel de ville, while Presidents Pichon, Lalanne, and Pontac were
instructed to return home to see that trouble did not spread to their part
of the city – clearly a diplomatic way of saying that they were afraid for
their own property. But these efforts were in vain. Crowds of several
hundred started moving through the Chapeau Rouge quarter. Once
home, Daffis refused to come back, saying that he was indisposed. Most
of the parlementaires must also have drifted home, since there were only

[45] "Délibérations secrètes," 14 May: AM Bordeaux ms. 788, pp. 250–76.

five judges left in the Grande Chambre at the end of the afternoon when the sound of the grosse cloche ringing told them that the hôtel de ville had fallen. After this success, the crowd announced that it was heading for the Palais to get rid of First President d'Aguesseau and Jurat Constant because they favored the new tax. As usual they were after their own responsible leaders. While a few bourgeois prepared to defend the building, d'Aguesseau fled in a carriage to the Château du Hâ, where he stayed until the following evening.

Meanwhile the rest of the city was in turmoil. The crowd roamed through the streets "with an audacity and threats that terrified all *gens de bien*."[46] Seven murders took place in all, including Aical, another clerk of the tax commission, whose body was dragged through mud and dung and thrown over the wall into the Capuchins' garden. For the rest of the night the crowd rang the great bell without anyone venturing to expel them from the hôtel de ville, which was guarded by their sentinels placed in key streets. Girard talks of nocturnal drinking and a feeling that enough was enough, provided the past was forgiven. The next day crowds still thronged the streets again, periodically calling out "Vive le roi," as they had during the murders of the previous evening, but their emphasis did turn to consolidation of their position, and cries were heard for a general pardon as well as for the gates to be opened or they would burn everything down.[47]

Once again it took intervention by a military commander and real soldiers to end the standoff. Informed of events at his château of Cadillac, the octogenarian governor, the duc d'Epernon, took his time mustering forces. Eventually on 17 May he entered the city with a large train of nobles, as was his custom, and was apparently received by the population with considerable enthusiasm, the mood having completely changed with the attainment of the most immediate goals. Epernon immediately deposed the jurats who had handled the situation so badly, telling them to go home and not appear in their livery until further notice. This could be one reason for his popularity: he seemed to be ratifying the rebels' actions. He summoned the militia, set up patrols and guards along the main thoroughfares and in the tour Saint Michel and the Château du Hâ. Powder, ammunition, wine, and provisions were laid in, cannons mounted, and the keys to the city delivered to the château. But this was at best an uneasy truce and, as Maître des Requêtes Verthamon reported on 28 May, the city was "in the power of inhabitants whose affections cannot

---

[46] Girard, *Histoire*, pp. 518–19.
[47] D'Aguesseau to Séguier, 20 May 1635: J.-A. Hovyn de Tranchère, *Les dessous de l'histoire*, 2 vols. (Paris, 1996), vol. 1, p. 287.

Figure 8 The rue des Fauves in Bordeaux, sketched by Charles Marionneau in the late nineteenth century. This sixteenth-century street was a main artery connecting the quartier Saint Michel to the center of the city, and may have been the site of barricades.

be relied on, and the common population is threatening both there and in the countryside to rise up as soon as we arrest somebody.[48]

The ferocity of the popular movement was still intact, as we can see from two final explosions on 15 and 30 June. On 15 June without recorded warning, artisans in the quartier Saint Michel took up arms and built barricades blocking off the quarter. Perhaps they were responding to rumors of coming repressive measures. The Parlement seems once again to have evaded any decisive action, but this time the militia was more than willing to mobilize itself. About noon Epernon arrived with twenty-two cavaliers and twenty-six foot soldiers and went to the first barricade, where he found chains raised. Showing courage and restraint, he leaped over the chains and persuaded the defenders to surrender peacefully, a move that was widely noted and admired. They told him "they were his and the king's good servants but they didn't want to hear of the gabelle because the king knew nothing about it and had never intended to oppress his people with such tax increases."[49] Then it was on to the barricade in the rue Saint Michel, where things did not go as well.

---

[48] Porchnev, *Soulèvements*, pp. 587–8.   [49] *Inventaire sommaire*, vol. v, p. 123.

The excited defenders fired off several wild rounds and the governor's guards fired back, killing nine and wounding twelve in the first salvo. Epernon's foot soldiers then charged the barricade, and he followed on horseback, forcing the defenders to retreat behind five additional, stubbornly defended barricades. In the account written by the governor's historian Girard, the communal intensity of this neighborhood resistance from Saint Michel stands out:

It looked as if he [Epernon] were the target of the musket and pistol fire and the showers of rocks. The threat did not come only from those who fired at him from the barricades: the greater danger came from the windows, since the narrowness of the streets robbed him of all means of protecting himself from blows that came from the side. Even the women put him in no small peril. One of them almost crushed him with a pot of carnations that hit the rump of his horse; a man in a window ten paces away was aiming at him and would have fired a musket if he hadn't been picked off by a guard named Caudère who saw and killed him. We had never seen the like of the determination manifested that day among these people. Even when a barricade had been seized it was hard to make them retreat, and even if you took away their arms or they threw them away in despair, they asked to be killed rather than live and see the gabelle imposed.[50]

Epernon had now become the gabeleur, like the jurats and the Parlement before him, because he was taking the side of repression. Many were killed on both sides including two of Epernon's pages.

On 30 June the quarter of Sainte Eulalie rioted. The house of Maurin, élu, was set afire and razed completely to the ground, and the same treatment was given to Lateste, a royal sergeant, to Jurat Constant, still singled out as the principal traitor by the crowd, to his colleague Dupin, and to others. The governor sent his guards to protect Constant. The first time they dispersed the crowd, but when pillaging resumed on 1 July they killed two pillaging "crocheteurs." Even larger patrols were now successfully organized with guards on every street corner "because of the burnings and murders that threatened principal houses."[51] It was about this time that the story originated of the existence of a list of four hundred of the richest houses to be pillaged – a suggestive myth "from above," although, as Bercé correctly argues, the list probably never existed.[52] That evening houses began to burn in the faubourg Saint Seurin. Epernon, who could see the fires from the building where he was staying, got out of bed and hastened there with one hundred musketeers, forced his way into the church of Saint Seurin, and fired on the rioters who had taken refuge inside, killing some thirty while the others were mowed down as they fled into the fields.

[50] Girard, *Histoire*, pp. 523–4.   [51] *Inventaire sommaire*, vol. v, p. 124.
[52] Bercé, *Histoire des Croquants*, vol. I, pp. 307–8.

Thus the uprising in Bordeaux left behind a legacy of class hatred. The notables would never forget the ferocity of the attack from below, and the rebels remained bitter. On 29 October a bill posted all over town threatened Montauron, the *partisan* of the tax, for boasting of the large numbers of citizens he was going to hang.[53] On 1 November boatman Jean Lureau was accused of trying to start a riot against a man he thought was a tax collector at the Chapeau Rouge gate. Lureau denied the charges, but when Constant urged him to be loyal because the king had pardoned the town, he mobilized a different kind of loyalty, repeating proudly "that it was true that he had served the public and he was ready to continue to do so, and he could always find five hundred men to oppose taxes." On 24 November someone posted a satire on Constant's door: "Constant, ton esprit et ta volagerie, te menera à la bougerie."[54]

Sentiments such as these should dissipate any impression that the authorities and population of Bordeaux were unified against the "gabelle." It is true that at the outset few people had wanted to lift a finger to defend an unpopular tax. But many persons did side with the authorities and even risked their lives doing so: councillors and jurats on patrol, militia captains who served, bourgeois who tried to defend the palais from the crowd, the considerable number of persons affiliated with the tax farms who lay low during the trouble or fled. Still, it was painfully clear that the jurats had prepared badly for the crisis and that the Parlement's response was not very constructive either. Most militia captains had refused to assemble; most bourgeois had avoided taking arms, except at the end. Perhaps they had thought they could look the other way and allow the crowd to expel the gabeleur, thereby currying popularity while pleading impotence to the king. But if this was prevarication, it was a naive response leading to death and destruction – a response that Bordeaux would never repeat.

The demonstrators were more sophisticated. They thought of themselves as respectable citizens who honored the king, but they were ready to do whatever it took to purge the gabelle in law and in fact, and they were willing to die in the process. Their definition of the gabelle was tangible and personal. It started with the collectors and their servants, then extended outward to those holding indirect responsibility, either through a rumored financial interest in the tax farm or through actions that aided and abetted the gabeleurs. Certain responsible parties – Constant among the jurats and d'Aguesseau among the parlementaires – were subjected to direct denunciations and fierce attacks on property that generated class fears. Popular leaders saw through the authorities' gestures and under-

[53] *Inventaire sommaire*, vol. v, pp. 125–6.   [54] Ibid., pp. 128–9.

stood that the jurade and the Parlement were really on the side of the crown; that much as they would like to defend local interests, their position required them to take the side of king's agents in the long run, and that any concession would be temporary.

The movement thus grew from a specific community protest to an expression of distaste for legitimate leaders. The difference from Montpellier in 1645 was that the anger was so immediately intense and the organization so focused. The mobilization in Bordeaux was similar to the climax of the mobilization in Dijon, except that the innkeepers were more centrally placed and more powerful than the dijonnais vignerons and they displayed their might from the beginning of the protest. The demonstrators, all apparently male, were deadly serious. There were no playful antics here, no festive protests, no preliminary incidents involving women or children or accidental confrontations. Their analysis was also more developed than that of the Montpéllierains or Dijonnais. They correctly interpreted the command structure, understanding that the Parlement had authority to decree in the king's name, whereas the jurade had immediate responsibility for protecting the king's agents. Therefore they imposed terms on the Parlement, but took over the hôtel de ville. They also held the leaders of each body up as accountable scapegoats. The flaw in their politics was of course that the demonstrators set up no alternatives. There was no way for them to maintain the new status quo except by vigilance, and no channel for influencing what the king's external agents might do in retaliation.

But they had severely humiliated the authorities. On 11 August the secret minutes of the Parlement observed that "during this public calamity the court of Parlement found itself not only deprived of all authority but, even worse, almost all its officers were reduced to taking up arms and going to assigned stations to defend their lives" – supreme humiliation! "The most pressed had to take refuge in the hôtel of my Lord duc d'Epernon."[55]

Each of these cases illustrates a different facet of popular mobilization. In Montpellier it was the step-by-step logic of the conflict and the predominant role of women who marched, organized, and prodded their communities to action. In Dijon it was the organized determination of the vinegrowers of St. Philibert and the all-out battle fought on their own terms against the authorities, while redefining an issue (the élus) that had been raised by threatened elites for different reasons. In Bordeaux it was the even greater capacity of a broader-based group from the popular

[55] AM Bordeaux ms. 788, p. 347.

quarters to occupy the hôtel de ville, terrorize city leaders, and manipulate the Parlement.

In all three cases the two most striking features were the inadequacy of municipal policing measures and the ferocity of the crowd. Once again, the system of policing that entailed carefully rehearsed patrols carried out by loyal échevins, forays and directives from multiple power centers, and mobilizations of citizen militia service had proved insufficient to protect property and stop popular retribution. Although hesitation on the part of the authorities certainly existed, and with good reason, these inadequacies of policing were manifested even in later stages of the rioting when the authorities would have done anything to stop the disorder.

When the demonstrators were truly enraged they organized a planned, but fierce attack. They went after selected targets connected to the hôtel de ville, the sovereign courts, the merchant community or the financial backers of edicts. But a primary characteristic of the power structure of these cities was the degree to which the power of these agents was divided, even during an emergency. Their only military successes came when a real or self-appointed military commander led out a contingent of real soldiers along with the most dedicated (or frightened) urban leaders and attacked the crowd head on. When this happened they always won, but at the cost of casualties and with the effect of arousing greater resistance in the popular neighborhoods. The second wave of retribution that was turned against principal local dignitaries was nothing to laugh at: houses pillaged and burned, rural farms ravaged, relatives murdered or chased away, pitched battles in narrow streets, rumors of longer lists of targets. Yet in the face of all this the response of the authorities remained woefully inadequate.

Louis XIV is not usually associated with popular uprisings because his entire state apparatus was devoted to projecting an image of order and majesty, and historians either treat his revolts as episodic annoyances or leave them out altogether.[1] This approach is misleading for two reasons. In the first place, the Sun King was faced with at least seven major insurrectionary movements that spanned his long personal rule.[2] These were predominantly rural rebellions in backward regions, but they were nonetheless highly significant. In the second, we should remember that from an urban community perspective the phenomenon of popular protest continued, albeit at a reduced rate. There were petty grumblings, cases of insubordination, and crowd actions just as before, with an equivalent impact on governmental processes.[3] There also continued to be important urban riots. To name a few, there were uprisings in Saint Tropez in 1678, in Arles and Marseille in 1679, 1692, 1696, and 1709, in Mende in 1660, in Lyon in 1667–8 and 1692, and in Dijon in 1668, 1684, 1696, and 1709. Amiens experienced labor insurgency in 1685, 1695, 1704, and 1711. Thus every decade except perhaps the 1680s saw

[1] The pioneering corrective to this view was Leon Bernard, "French Society and Popular Uprisings under Louis XIV," *French Historical Studies* 3 (1963–4), 454–74. A summary with a different emphasis is Tilly, *The Contentious French*, pp. 147–61. Another list is provided by Ernest Lavisse, *Histoire de France depuis les origines jusqu'à la Révolution*, 9 vols. in 15 (Paris, 1903–11), vol. VII–1, pp. 345–58, "not a year of the reign passed without revolts, some of which were very serious" (p. 345).

[2] In late 1661 the county of Benauge near Bordeaux saw an uprising of some 3,000 peasants. In the summer of 1662 some 6,000 "Lustucru" besieged châteaux in the Boulonnais and opposed the abolition of tax privileges. In 1664–7 the region of Chalosse-Labourd in the Southwest near Béarn saw the Audijos rebellion, a guerrilla-type struggle against the gabelle that culminated in an army of 6,000 and a related uprising in the city of Bayonne. In the summer of 1670 the Roure revolt in the Vivarais region north of Languedoc culminated in the domination of the area by a rebel army of several thousand. In 1675 the whole of lower Brittany rose up. Louis faced the wars of the Camisards in the Cévennes between 1702 and 1710 and the Tard-Avisés of Quercy in 1707.

[3] See, for example, Guy Lemarchand, "Crises économiques et atmosphère social en milieu urbain sous Louis XIV," *Revue d'histoire moderne et contemporaine* 14 (1967), 244–65, translated in Kierstead, *State and Society in Seventeenth-Century France*, pp. 233–64.

important conflicts. To be sure, most towns seem to have been quieter
after 1670. The one comprehensive long-term survey, Pillorget's study of
Provence, found 264 "incidents" between 1596 and 1660 as compared to
110 incidents between 1661 and 1715, or half as many per year during the
personal reign of Louis XIV. Bercé reports similar findings in Guyenne,
where 60 percent of the cases from 1590 to 1715 fell between 1635 and
1660.[4] Nevertheless, popular protest continued to be important, and
Louis XIV still faced major waves of trouble, especially in difficult years
such as 1675, 1693, and 1709.

I will concentrate here on the wave of uprisings that took place in 1675,
specifically those in Bordeaux and Rennes. Given the reputation of Louis
XIV, it is worth asking whether things had changed by 1675: were authorities more effective or crowds less vociferous? This question is especially
opportune since we are returning to the same streets of Bordeaux, forty
years after the events of 1635 that we have just finished examining.[5]

Bordeaux, 1675

In 1673 the king began to impose a comprehensive series of novel
consumption taxes: fees for legal transactions (*contrôle des exploits*), obliga-
tion to use stamped paper for many of these transactions (*papier timbré*),
monopoly on the sale of tobacco, and a sou per livre on pewterware manufactured by pewterers (*marque d'étain*).[6] In the face of this new set of
provocations, popular agitation was not slow in appearing, but the striking new element in the relationship between authorities and taxpayers
was the new climate of cooperation that prevailed among the authorities
themselves. On one occasion the intendant De Sève, now resident in
Bordeaux, spotted insulting signs posted in the place Saint Projet and
conferred immediately with the jurats, who hastened to prosecute the
offenders. On another occasion the Parlement consulted the jurats about
rumors of placards; on a third a passing paver dutifully removed a poster
from the door of a merchant's shop and delivered it to the jurats, who took
it to the Parlement and reported on the incident to Châteauneuf, the
king's secretaire d'état.[7] Now not only were the various authorities more

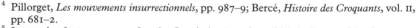

---

[4] Pillorget, *Les mouvements insurrectionnels*, pp. 987–9; Bercé, *Histoire des Croquants*, vol. II,
    pp. 681–2.
[5] It was also fourteen years after the Ormée insurrection which is discussed in chapter 10
    because it was a more sophisticated movement of a different nature.
[6] For histories of Bordeaux, see chapter 6, note 35. An excellent analysis of the 1675 revolt
    is François Loirette, "La sédition bordelaise de 1675, dernière grande révolte urbaine de
    l'ancien régime," *Actes du 102e Congrès national des sociétés savantes, Limoges, 1977; Section
    d'histoire moderne et contemporaine*, vol. II (Paris, 1978), pp. 237–60.
[7] *Inventaire sommaire*, vol. V, p. 155: 13 Mar 1673, 13, 20 June 1674.

sensitive to the danger of popular dissidence, but the separate elements of the system seemed to be working better together.

The first serious incident took place on 26 March 1675 when a fierce group of female peddlers wielding knives (another report called them fishwives) attacked the agents of the *traitant* of the marque d'étain in a house in the rue Saint Loup and chased them to the nearby rue d'Arnaud Miqueu, throwing rocks and calling them gabeleurs.[8] Fonteneil, Roche, and Minvielle, three of the jurats, rushed there with the commander of the municipal watch and some archers and dispersed the crowd; then they rescued the agents from a house where they had taken refuge and "walked" them through their duties by escorting them back to the original house to finish the marking, and home to the inn where they were staying. This was a more impressive performance than in 1635. The jurats were actually willing to take responsibility for the collections and they were able to defuse a tense moment and enforce royal orders.

However, their success was ephemeral. The next day (27 March) the authorities were confronted with a major insurrection, the organization and style of which suggested that the rioters had learned as much as the magistrates about the nature of the local power structure. That morning reports came in from several informants that artisans were planning to meet in a shop on the rue Saint Loup, stronghold of the pewterers, to decide what to do about the tax agents. So at 4 p.m. Jurat Jean de Fonteneil set out with the commander of the watch and four soldiers to accompany three tax agents into the shops and proceed with the marking of the pewter. This was a deliberate challenge to the dissidents. The jurats had worked for about half an hour marking pots in the shop of a man named Cigouille when Fonteneil began to notice that a crowd of "menu peuple" was gathering and murmuring outside the shop. He warned those within not to pay any attention, but "rabble" holding rocks and clubs came out of an alley, along with some female "orange sellers" carrying knives, all shouting "Vive le Roy sans gabelle!" These people asked Fonteneil to leave so that they could give the tax agents a thrashing (note the familiar tone of provisional respect). He grabbed his livery and exhorted them to disperse, saying that everything he was doing was by order of the king and the city, and that their temerity would cause their

---

[8] The main narratives for the 1675 revolt are the jurats' account in *Inventaire sommaire*, vol. v, pp. 156–64 which is essentially the same as the procès-verbal of 27 March in AM Bordeaux FF 68. There are also the long account by Lombard in BN Mélanges Colbert 171, fol. 112; the jurats' report of 30 March to Colbert: Mel. Col. 171, fol. 122; and the account of 30 March by Ferrant, agent of the Receveur-Général LeMaigre, Mel. Col. 171, fol. 126. Additional documents can be found in *Archives historiques du département de la Gironde*, vols. XLI, XLVI (Paris, 1906–11) [hereafter *Archives historiques de la Gironde*].

ruin. It would have been inconceivable in the 1630s for a magistrate to be found in the street in this way, helping *partisans* to mark merchandise.

The crowd started to throw rocks, hitting both Fonteneil and the agents. He hastily sent for reinforcements, then tried to make his way back through the confusion to the hôtel de ville. Municipal justice was still so improvisatory that a jurat and his guards would try to escort hated *partisans*, plus two rioters arrested in passing, through glowering crowds, aided only by several public-spirited citizens. Approaching the market, Fonteneil saw people converging on him from both ends of the street. He pushed the agents into a nearby house, placed himself on the threshold, spread wide his cloak and declared, livery in hand, that he would die before he would let anyone touch one of the *commis*. However exaggerated the account (after all, it is Fonteneil reporting), this was a better performance than any jurat under Louis XIII had displayed. But belligerence had its price: in this tense moment one of the demonstrators, barrelmaker Jean Laveau, punched one of the tax agents, whereupon one of the accompanying soldiers, Captain Calle, shot him dead. This was a pivotal moment. A traditional pummeling had been cut short by a swift repressive response. Laveau's death provided the spark that set off the general mobilization. Chains went up everywhere with shouts "that they should beat up all the gabeleurs."[9]

The other jurats arrived with two captains of the watch and more archers, and the whole troop made for the hôtel de ville while the people "losing all respect" threw rocks and fired muskets at them. Once inside the hôtel de ville, the jurats sent messages to the Parlement and the governor and barricaded the building as they had in 1635. They claimed later that more vigorous resistance was impossible because some of their archers were wounded and the militia captains had not arrived. After dark, under cover of a heavy rainstorm, they sent the procureur-syndic and the city clerk out through a false door in the back to escort the agents to the Château Trompette. This time, unlike 1635, the *partisans* made their way to safety.

The jurats had only seen a small part of the action, which was much more massive than Fonteneil's pointillistic account would suggest.[10] Actually, the Saint Michel quarter was already mobilized and had attacked two rich pewter merchants seen as traitors for having obeyed the king and paid the tax. Their houses were pillaged and demolished in three hours. As one of the observers, Ferrant, put it, the crowd acted in a rage

---

[9] The authorities apparently felt some guilt about this use of excessive force because Laveau's wife Simone Boucherie was later granted compensation by the city for his killing: *Archives historiques de la Gironde*, vol. XLI, pp. 188–9 (April 17).

[10] The Lombard letter, Mel. Col. 171, fol. 112, gives this added information.

without desire for profit, since they loaded the merchandise onto carts
and dumped it in the river. Then the crowd rang the great bell of Saint
Michel and started marching in arms, tambour beating, towards the hôtel
de ville, insulting anyone who opposed their "desperate plans." This foray
begins to sound like a military campaign, as opposed to the crowds of
women and others who had accosted the *partisans* in the rue Saint Loup –
evidently the fruits of prior organizing. Having successfully halted the
marking of pewter, the movement was now punishing traitors and exacting approval from bystanders, as if to legitimize their alternative justice.
When they encountered a wine merchant from La Rochelle they beat him
up for refusing to cry out "Vive le Roy sans gabelle." They also demolished the house of a tobacco agent – note the shift from pewter.

The jarring ferocity of the next action wakes us up to the intensity of
the crowd's anger, which we would not have guessed from the narrative so
far. Another nameless victim, encountered in the street, was murdered by
the crowd, which mutilated his corpse and started dragging it around.
Clearly the crowd's indignation encompassed more than a single tax on
pewter. One report says that this victim was a bourgeois who had told the
crowd (like Desaigues in 1635) that what they were doing was wrong.[11]
But another says that this man was believed to be an agent of François de
Vivey, subdelegate of the intendant.

As drums beat, the body was dragged by the feet on a symbolic itinerary that seemed designed to rebuke the authorities: from the Porte de la
Grave where the murder took place to the rue Fossé des Tanneurs, past
the windows of First President d'Aulède, down the rue Sainte Catherine,
the rue Saint Maixent, and the rue Margaux, where they pounded repeatedly on the door of Ferrant, an agent of the receiver general of finances,
one of our narrators, who was cowering inside; then on to the rue
Castillone and the place Puypaulin, where they administered blows to the
body in front of the intendant's door, and then on to the house of Vivey
the man's alleged employer in the aristocratic end of town. By this time
Montaigu, second in command to the governor, César-Phébus d'Albret,
was circulating in his carriage, surveying the situation. He effected a dramatic rescue of Vivey, who was standing in his doorway as the angry
crowd approached, by rushing by, pulling Vivey inside the carriage, and
racing off, even as Madame Vivey, unable to jump on in time, went
running down the street in the opposite direction.

The crowd broke into Vivey's house, placed the by-now much-muti-
lated body of the earlier victim into Vivey's carriage, and burned it in the
courtyard while the lavishly furnished house was pillaged. It is hard to

---

[11] Jurats' letter: Mel. Col. 171, fol. 122.

Figure 9 A crowd pillages the Hôtel de Castries in Paris on 13 November 1790, engraving by Berthaut. There are no seventeenth-century depictions of crowds exacting retribution, but this scene captures the spirit of such an event.

imagine a more symbolic way of saying that the intendant and his local allies were now important enough locally to be considered directly responsible for unpopular taxes. Vivey was hated because he had long served as subdelegate to three intendants, including the current one, De Sève. He was also a trésorier de France suspected of involvement in the tax farms, and as first jurat in 1669 he had been "continued in office" by order of the king because he was a supporter of royal fiscal policies. He had then advocated consumption taxes that harmed the poor.[12] Thus he was correctly associated in the popular mind with new taxes and anti-popular behavior. The crowd subsequently pillaged the maison du domaine du roy across the street from Vivey and burned papers relating to the royal judicial administration and especially the stamp tax, with "cries and howling, an inexpressible rage." Drouet, the intendant's secretary, whose sister-in-law was married to the director of the domaine, was living in the pillaged building, where his apartment was sacked.[13]

Nightfall left "everyone surprised, each wary of his neighbor, not daring to speak, everyone locked up in his house." Around 8 p.m. Montaigu brought in two companies from the Château Trompette and battled the armed crowd the length of the rue du Chapeau Rouge, in the heart of the aristocratic quarter. Two rioters were killed and eight others arrested in and around Vivey's house. Then heavy rain began to fall. About a hundred captains and bons bourgeois did arrive at the hôtel de ville and organize patrols, so at least some citizens were apparently willing to cooperate.

The rest of the night "all you heard in the streets was cries of 'Vive le roy sans gabelle,' and even the children were singing the same tune," reported Ferrant, who spent the time hiding out in the house of his brother-in-law because he was unable to get to the château.[14] The next morning Albret wrote to Colbert that "the bad-intentioned have filled the little people with rumors of new taxes on copper, beds, shoes, and bread" and reports that they "were going to mark pewter dishes belonging to every private individual."[15] Here is another expression of what the protest meant to the participants. A fee on certain shops was being expanded in the popular mind to an attack on all ordinary people like the tax on children in Montpellier. At the same time the opposition was broadening its sights to a whole range of impositions, no doubt under the impetus of other affected groups.

---

[12] Loirette, "La sédition bordelaise," pp. 253–4.
[13] De Sève to Colbert, 17 April 1675: Mel. Col. 171, fol. 195.
[14] Ferrant had been the object of placarded death threats in 1673 and 1674: Loirette, "La sédition bordelaise," p. 254.
[15] Albret to Colbert, 28 March 1675: Mel. Col. 171, fol. 118.

March 28 was to be unique for the organized force of the opposition. The city was now intensely angry. Pillagers in the Vivey house continued doggedly to tear it down, returning every time they were chased away. Armed rebels seized major avenues and the Sainte Croix gate, where peasants were allowed into the city, and soon rebel squadrons were parading through the streets. Probably there was a connection between these forces and the regular militia, although none has been recorded. One report says that "this rabble named captains chosen from among the company of tanners."[16] The rebels demanded that the prisoners from the previous evening be released and that Calle, the killer of the barrelmaker Laveau, be released to them. Crowds became more and more insolent and began to seize the initiative. Jurat Laurent Boisson was taken hostage and told that he would not be released until Albret and the Parlement freed the prisoners, otherwise there would be blood and fire. When one of the Parlement's commissioners, Tarneau, who was also the nephew of Jurat Beauroche, tried to reason with rioters at the door of his house, he was shot with musket fire, stabbed repeatedly with daggers and "his body was beaten with a thousand blows." According to Lombard, a portefaix who tried to rescue the body was also killed by the crowd in the presence of Tarneau's wife and the wife of First President Daulède. Some merchants and their wives took refuge in the château, bringing their furniture with them. First President Daulède de Lestonnac and councillors Lalanne, Andraut, and Marboutin from the Parlement were also taken hostage.

Overwhelmed, the authorities drew together. The jurats reported to the Parlement, which instructed that they summon Albret and Montaigu to the Palais and assemble the bourgeois militiamen to guard the hôtel de ville and the avenues. But as the insurrection took over the city, the bourgeois refused to come or else sent their valets, who just shouted "Vive le Roi sans gabelle" and sided with the rebels. When the jurats circulated through each jurade accompanied by archers and commissioners from the Parlement – an unusual joint effort – the militia still refused to appear and there were hints of mutiny in the ranks. Outmaneuvered and terrified, the jurats sent Fonteneil to ask Montaigu to release the prisoners. Fonteneil had a dramatic trip. On his way to the Château Trompette he was stopped by a crowd which threatened to murder his whole family if he failed to get the prisoners released within the next half hour. He went on and was stopped by another troop with the same demands. No sooner had he reached the château than Lalanne arrived, along with Lachèse and Minvielle, to demand the same thing on behalf of the parlementaire

---

[16] Lombard to Colbert, 27 March 1675: Mel. Col. 171, fol. 112.

hostages being held by a different rebel band. Both the municipality and the Parlement were being manipulated by the rebels.

After a parley in the Château Trompette, Montaigu released the prisoners into the hands of the unnamed chief of the rebels, who was waiting outside the château. He had the prisoners promenaded through town "in all the battalions" so that they could be recognized. This gesture of "informing the public" by parading was the counterpart to the displaying of friendly victims' bodies and the dragging of enemies' bodies. The rebels then retired, as promised, to Saint Michel and Sainte Croix, but they did not let up their pressure. Sentinels still guarded the streets all night while people met by lantern light in the cemeteries of Saint Michel and Sainte Croix, and letters were written to nearby parishes to induce more peasants to come to their aid the next day. On 29 March, as peasants from all around the city were beating drums and heading for Bordeaux, Albret, who was recovering from a paralysis in his side, sent word that he was coming in person. When he reached the hôtel de ville four to five thousand rebels were already gathered at their rendez-vous points (the numbers are obviously exaggerated) and more persons were waiting outside the gates. An ultimatum from the rebels was brought by the curés from Sainte Croix. The rebels wanted Albret to meet with them in person. If their demands were met they would lay down their arms, otherwise they would burn everything down.[17]

The governor decided to humor them. With the approval of the assembled chambers of the Parlement, he proceeded to the place Saint Michel, accompanied by some gentlemen and guards, and reportedly found three to four thousand troops in battle formation. Lombard says the rebels there got down on their knees to ask pardon for the murder of Tarneau, an interesting, archaic gesture apparently signifying that they distinguished between justified and unjustified killings. Then they demanded a general amnesty and the abolition of "taxes." Albret proceeded to the cemetery of Sainte Croix where more troops were ranged and the same demands were presented. Ferrant's description of the dialogue between Albret and the rebels there is worth repeating, although it may err in the direction of literary license:

At twenty paces, a Pelloustre dressed all in rags stepped out of their ranks saber raised high, and approached up to three paces from the head of Monsieur le Maréchal's horse. The Marshal [tutoying]: "Very well my friend, who are you angry at? Are you intending to speak to me?" At which this miserable person, without flinching replied "Yes, I am the deputy of these people of Saint Miquau to inform you that they are loyal servants of the king but that they want no more

---

[17] *Inventaire sommaire*, vol. V, pp. 159–63; procès-verbal of the échevins 28–9 March: *Archives historiques de la Gironde*, vol. XLVI, pp. 145–66.

gabelles nor tax on pewter, nor tobacco nor stamp tax, nor contrôle d'exploits, nor five sous per boisseau of wheat, nor greffe d'arbitrages." The Marshal (very softly): "Very well my friend, since you assure me that the people of Saint Michel are loyal servants of the king, I am here to assure them that I would like to take them under my protection provided that they disarm themselves and go back to their duty; and I promise them that I will intercede for them before the king." "Very well," replied the Pelloustre, "in that case give us an arrêt of Parlement to that effect and we will be satisfied, provided you also obtain an amnesty for every-thing we have just done, without which we declare to you that we are going to spare nothing and that we are resolved to perish rather than to suffer any more."[18]

An impressive segment of the people of Bordeaux, armed and mobilized in the popular quarters, no doubt with reinforcement from the rest of the city, was demanding abolition of a comprehensive list of new taxes, a list so well informed that some observers suggested it must have been drawn up by more educated persons – certainly a real possibility. They were speaking from a position of strength, and while they respected the gover-nor, his word was not sufficient. They wanted official confirmation from the Parlement *and* from the king.

D'Albret returned to the Palais, encountering along the way "2,000" men in bands of 150 – more or less the configuration of militia companies – with swords raised swearing that they would kill everyone if their demands were not met. The Parlement was likewise besieged by a crowd shouting that no one would leave the building until their demands were met. Meanwhile word was coming in that those guarding the gates on the Graves side of the city – evidently there were some loyal militia companies – were giving way and that the peasants, who were already cutting vines and burning houses outside the walls, were starting to push their way into the city. As the governor arrived to inform the Parlement of the popular demands, the curé of Saint Michel rushed in "all flustered" to announce that his constituents were impatient at the long delay and would burn down the houses of the parlementaires if he failed to return with the arrêt they were waiting for. Much of the city was in insurrection, and there seemed to be quite a bit of coordination.

The assembled chambers capitulated, issuing an arrêt that petitioned the king for a general amnesty and for the end of the contrôle, the papier timbré, the marque d'étain, and the tax on tobacco; and in the meantime suspended collections. Merchants were to be permitted to sell as before, women resellers could offer lard and foodstuffs in the place des Salinières (we recall the "orange sellers"), butchers could sell lambs, there would be no 5 sous per boisseau of wheat and flour, nothing would be demanded of artisans; and notaries could continue to draw up acts as they had before

---

[18] Ferrant to Colbert, 30 March 1675: Mel. Col. 171, fol. 126.

the creation of special officers for certain kinds of acts. These were references not only to the taxes on legal acts but also to a group of unpopular consumption taxes on items used by the poor that had been instituted by the city to pay debts and that had been renewed in 1674.[19] Thus the whole panoply of recent fiscal measures was being abrogated, and the municipality was threatened as well as the crown. The crowds disbanded and the next day, 30 March, the city was calm.

This initial popular movement, grounded in certain trades and quarters, had surely been influenced along the way by other constituencies to the point where the final mobilization might be considered a coalition of disaffected groups. As Lombard put it, "the bourgeois do not want to obey their magistrates, and they are making it known that they are not displeased at this disorder, because now that the people have retrieved their prisoners they are insisting that we abolish the tax on wheat and other impositions, which is equivalent to saying that someone is causing them to act this way."[20] Putting the matter less conspiratorially, we may conclude that a wide range of citizens was capitalizing on the initial belligerence and energy of the crowd to expand their goals to a whole range of measures.

Such a massive protest seemed almost unthinkable under Louis XIV. In 1674 Colbert had written as much to De Sève:

We are living under the greatest king who has ever borne a scepter . . . In times like these if a city like Bordeaux showed signs of the slightest movement of rebellion, it would assuredly feel the mark of his ill will longer than it did under the reign of Henry II . . . Judge for yourself whether, after those master strokes, we should fear the ill will of the rabble of Bordeaux.[21]

But this "rabble" had successfully embarrassed the Sun King.

For a while the rebels could bask in their impunity while the authorities fumed. Louis XIV sent a declaration of amnesty for all participants that was registered by the Parlement on 6 April, and Châteauneuf sent congratulations to the jurats for their conduct.[22] But no one had any illusions. Albret made it clear that he was going to humor the rebels only until he had the means to crack down on them. De Sève noted on 17 April that despite the amnesty each rumor of approaching troops caused the artisans of Saint Michel and Sainte Croix to set up night patrols. He almost

---

[19] Loirette, "La sédition bordelaise," pp. 242–3.
[20] Lombard to Colbert, 27 March 1675: Mel. Col. 171, fol. 112.
[21] Colbert to De Sève, 25 May 1674: Pierre Clément (ed.), *Lettres, instructions et mémoires de Colbert*, vol. II (Paris, 1906), pp. 338–9. The reference is to a serious revolt in 1548: Colbert was apparently well informed! Jonathan Powis, "Guyenne 1548: the Crown, the Province, and the Social Order," *European Studies Review* 12 (1982), 1–15.
[22] *Archives historiques de la Gironde*, vol. XLI, pp. 180–5.

wished they would cause some real trouble so that he would have a pretext for arresting the guilty parties without violating the terms of the peace.[23]

Indeed, the insurgents were doing their best to achieve the hopeless task of permanently warding off the repression. Provocations in the form of placards continued the dialogue, on the door of the Saint Michel church:

Messieurs you are warned that a man named Despasse, procureur in the Parlement, Pierre Maquran, clerk of Monsieur Bussaguet, councillor, belong to the party of the gabelle and a man named Taranque, surgeon. This is the advice given you by a friend of the patrie and of the public tranquillity,

on the door of Etienne de Mullet, sieur de Voluzan, councillor in the Parlement, whose house was the site of the stamp tax office:

Messieurs, I advise you that the order has come from Paris that the stamp tax should be burned this evening and the *partisans* who sell it as well. DE VOLUZAN, [Here the seditious were putting into the mouth of the traitor the words he *ought* to have been saying.]

and on the door of the hôtel de ville:

We know that the intendant has issued an ordinance to reestablish the stamp tax. We are just waiting for this to happen so we can act like before and kill and burn the jurats who enforce his tyrannies, and even Marshall Albret and all his supporters. [signed] The Lost Children.[24]

In mid August bales of stamped paper were discovered in a boat coming from Bergerac, and a crowd burned the boat and tore up the paper before sounding the alarm in Saint Michel and Sainte Croix, initiating a riot in which the jurats arrested twelve men and one woman and hanged two masons and a tailor.[25]

Of course the crowd was right about the future, but there was nothing they could do to stop it. On 17 November 208 companies of infantry and

---

[23] Albret to Colbert, 28 March: Mel. Col. 171, fol. 118; De Sève to Colbert, 17 April: Mel. Col. 171, fol. 195.

[24] The precise statements are: (1) "Messieurs, vous serez advertis qu'un nommé Despase procureur au parlement, Pierre Maquran cler de monsieur Bussaguet conseiller sont du party de Gabelle et un nommé Taranque, chirurgien. C'est ladvis que vous donne un amy de la patrie et du repos public," *Archives historiques de la Gironde*, vol. XLI, pp. 172–5: 31 March 1675. (2) "Messieurs je vous adverty que l'ordre de Paris est venu que le papier timbre sera brulé ce soir et les partisans qui le debittent aussy. Monsieur de Voluzan vous donne cet advis. DE VOLUZAN," ibid., pp. 176–8: 2 April 1675. (3) "Nous savons que l'intendant a donné eunne ordonnance pour restablir le papier timbré. Nous natandons que cela pour faierre comme avenc et tué et brulé les juras qui preste la main a ses tirannie et mesme le marechal dalbret et tous les adherans. Les anfans perdu," ibid., pp. 196–7: 19 June 1675.   [25] *Inventaire sommaire*, vol. V, p. 165–7: 17 August 1675.

cavalry from Catalonia entered the city to be billeted on the citizens for the winter. The inhabitants of Saint Michel, Sainte Croix and Sainte Eulalie, and later all inhabitants, were ordered to turn in their arms. On 18 November the Parlement rescinded its suspension of the new taxes and two days later was exiled from the city, not to return until 1690. An extension to the Château Trompette was announced, requiring demolition of property and forced labor, and the bells of Saint Michel and Sainte Eulalie were removed along with the cannons from the hôtel de ville. The city was subjected to a new taillon of 15,000 livres plus all the taxes it had rejected. In July, 1676 Vivey was granted 112,030 livres to pay for damages to his property during the riot, with interest at denier twenty (5 percent). It was estimated that two thousand houses were deserted by the exile of the royal courts and that the troop lodgings had cost the city 961,000 livres.[26]

A ferocious uprising had been answered with an intense punishment that was clearly different from the days of Louis XIII. But the protesters had also gone farther. They had started like their predecessors, but with an increased propensity for armed confrontation that was perhaps related to the experiences of the intervening Fronde. Then, in response to the show of counterforce from the château, they had demonstrated their strength by terrorizing certain notables and seizing eminent hostages to be exchanged for prisoners. Instead of subsiding they held further meetings, drew in reinforcements from the countryside, formed companies, and orchestrated a greater mobilization in order to achieve broader, more comprehensive demands. They negotiated with the governor from a position of strength and forced the Parlement to ratify a package of demands that by this time encompassed not only the crown's new taxes, but municipal taxes as well. They had displayed superior ability to effect a broad range of changes, but they still had no technique for fending off the repression from a better organized and more powerful king.

The anger spreads

News of the Bordeaux uprising spread apprehension up and down the west coast of France. Revolts had been contagious before, but this was an unprecedented response, perhaps encouraged by new conditions. Novel taxes were being applied more effectively over a wider range of communities in a shorter period of time; authorities were more vigilant;

---

[26] *Inventaire sommaire*, vol. v, pp. 169–78: 16 November 1675 to 4 May 1676; AM Bordeaux FF 68; Loirette, "La sédition bordelaise," p. 258.

populations were more conscious of what they were up against. To appreciate this phenomenon, it is worth just for a moment changing our perspective and imagining how these multiplying problems must have looked to Colbert as we leaf through the letters he was receiving from the provinces:[27]

24 April: seditious bills have been thrown into the Palais of the Parlement in Toulouse and the residence of First President Fieubet. *3 May*: seditious women in Bergerac have thrown all the stamped paper into a stream. When attacked, they pillage other offices and invade churches in search of the responsible parties. *5 and 7 May*: there may be trouble in Périgueux, where tax agents have fled to Bordeaux and the peasants are massing. *9 June*: peasants in the region of Montségur have pillaged and burned stamped paper. *11 June*: an uprising has occurred in La Réole, resulting in the burning of all the stamped paper and the destruction of the country house of the farmer of the contrôle des exploits. *12 June*: grain riots in Grenoble are linked to agitation over stamped paper. *16 June*: trials of the rebels are under way in La Reole and Montségur, but new trouble is breaking out in Marmande. *24 June*: the receiver of taxes of the diocese of Cornouaille sends a chilling report from Quimper: "Monsieur, we have been obliged to withdraw all our agents from the bishopric . . . Today, after multiple insults and attacks, we have decided to abandon our office to protect ourselves from the rage of the people and take cover in the houses of particular friends . . . If we manage to save our lives today, the director of the grands devoirs and I are determined to leave tonight for a place of greater safety . . ." *25 June*: a similar report is sent by a *partisan* in Nantes: "In Châteaulin they beat up the huissier who brought the arrêt of reinstatement right in the court session, chased away the judges, mistreated the criminal judge, pillaged our stamp tax office and razed the house of la Garanne Jouhan who ran the tax farms." *29 June*: new placards in Bordeaux. *30 June*: the intendant is trying those guilty of an uprising in Tours. *July*: serious trouble throughout rural Brittany. *6 August*: the pewterers of Toulouse have closed their shops. Intendant Aguesseau [the same man who had employed the pillaged Vivey in Bordeaux] is reluctant to hurry back to Toulouse for fear of setting off rumors.

Evidently the news from Bordeaux had intensified popular fears of new exactions and turned stamped paper, which had not been a central issue in the early stages of the uprising, into a new manifestation of the evil "gabelle" that had to be sought out everywhere and eradicated. One intendant's explanation is helpful: "The people believe these [stamped paper and contrôle taxes] have been established for the sole purpose of preparing them to accept the gabelle, along with annual taxes on all kinds of artisans and manual laborers."[28] By this report the protesters saw the imposition of the new taxes on legal procedures as a way of softening

---

[27] These references are all from BN Clairambault 796, a collection of Colbert's correspondence from 1675. I have not included every incident.
[28] De Sève to Colbert from La Réole, 16 June 1675: Clairambault 796, p. 147.

them up for a gabelle on the poor which would hit ordinary people's daily transactions the way these taxes hit legal documents. Again the spectre loomed of an intrusion on daily necessities.

Rennes, 1675

The impact of these sentiments was soon felt in Rennes, a large city of some 49,000 people with an independent-minded Parlement, sitting in a particularistic province where there was as yet no intendant.[29] Because Rennes had a city council but no formal échevinage, much power lay in the hands of two royal appointees who were at the same time patrons of local interests: the duc de Chaulnes, governor of the province, and René marquis de Coëtlogon, governor of the city. On 3 April when the news of the Bordeaux revolt reached Rennes, the reaction indicates that both the population and the authorities were watching. On the popular side stones were thrown and windows broken. Meanwhile the duc de Chaulnes, who was in Paris, warned Colbert that "after what has happened in Bordeaux, nothing must be overlooked with regard to the edicts," and First President Argouges from the Parlement warned the principal authorities in the towns of Brittany to watch for trouble. He also told the pewter and tobacco agents in Rennes to suspend their operations for two weeks, but to keep their offices open to maintain the principle of obeying royal authority.[30]

The real uprising took place on 18 April after everyone had had time to

---

[29] For histories of Brittany and Rennes, see Jean Meyer (ed.), *Histoire de Rennes* (Toulouse, 1972) which, however, barely mentions the events of 1675, presumably because they were covered in Jean Delumeau (ed.), *Histoire de la Bretagne* (Toulouse, 1969), pp. 291–2. In many ways a more satisfying general history is Barthélemy Pocquet, *Histoire de la Bretagne*, 6 vols. (Rennes, 1905–14), vol. v. A new examination in depth is James B. Collins, *Classes, Estates, and Order in Early Modern Brittany* (Cambridge, 1994). On the events of 1675, the best modern account for all of Brittany is Yvon Garlan and Claude Nières, *Les révoltes bretonnes de 1675: papier timbré et Bonnets Rouges* (Paris, 1975). Poquet's older, more traditional account is also excellent, *Histoire de la Bretagne*, pp. 480–534, as is Jean Lemoine's in *La révolte dite du papier timbré ou des Bonnets Rouges en Bretagne en 1675* (Paris, 1889), pp. 1–83, which built upon Arthur de la Borderie's royalist study, *La révolte du papier timbré advenue en Bretagne en 1675* (Saint-Brieuc, 1884). The latter is reprinted along with a translation of Porchnev's 1940 essay, "Les buts et les revendications des paysans lors de la révolte bretonne de 1675," in Groupe ESB (ed.), *Les Bonnets Rouges* (Paris, 1975). See also Jean Tanguy, "Les révoltes paysannes de 1675 et la conjoncture en Basse Bretagne au XVIIe siècle," *Annales de Bretagne* 82 (1975), 427–42; Claude Nières, "Boris Porchnev et les révoltes bretonnes de 1675," *Annales de Bretagne* 82 (1975), 459–75; and Roland Mousnier, *Peasant Uprisings in Seventeenth-Century France, Russia, and China* (New York, 1970), pp. 123–60.

[30] Huchet to Chaulnes 3 April, Argouges to syndics, 5 April, Chaulnes to Colbert, 6 April: Lemoine #1–3, pp. 85–7 (see next note).

prepare.[31] This was a period of popular anxiety over provisioning, and rumors were circulating of taxes on bread and wheat. Crowds began threatening to break into shops if they could not buy tobacco, the supply of which had been cut off by the Parlement's suspension of the taxes.[32] Around two in the afternoon a crowd stormed up to the bureau in the Champjacquet square where, by unfortunate coincidence, the cobblestones were in piles because of a repaving project. They smashed all the windows with rocks, took the tobacco and dragged out the furniture, searched the cellars, and carried off the wine and cider. Their next stop was the nearby bureau du contrôle et affirmations, where they threw documents and cahiers into a bonfire. They then went on to the bureau of the domaine in the nearby rue de la Filanderie. Coëtlogon's son, who was acting governor of the city, went to the hôtel de ville and summoned the militia; then he set out with twenty or thirty gentlemen followers who routed the demonstrators by firing on the crowd, killing twelve and wounding nearly fifty, according to his estimate, including Jean Bernier, turner, and a servant from the Petite Harpe tavern. As we have seen, this vigorous response was characteristic of the 1670s.

The crowd moved on to the grand bureau des devoirs in the rue aux Foulons and to the stamped paper office which was in the actual palais of the Parlement. There more shots were fired and the crowd was repulsed after the death of another demonstrator. La Courneuve, an eyewitness observer, said "there were more than two thousand pillagers all crying 'Vive le Roy sans gabelle et sans édits.'" That evening the enraged population spoke of burning down the houses of a group of rich merchants, specified by name, including First President Argouges.

[31] My account is based on the following narratives: "Relation de la sédition arrivée à Rennes le 18 avril 1675," by Morel, procureur in the présidial, which survives in a copy made in 1782: AD Ile-et-Vilaine 1F 307 [hereafter Morel]; "Délibérations de la maison de ville 1675": AM Rennes 511C [hereafter Delibs]; "Registre secret du Parlement de Rennes" for 1675: AD Ile-et-Vilaine Bb 244–5 [hereafter Registre secret]; "Journal d'un bourgeois de Rennes au xviie siècle," which is the livre de raison of René Duchemin, notaire royal: AD Ile-et-Vilaine 1F 306 (in the papers of la Borderie) [hereafter Duchemin] [this source has recently been published as Bruno Isblad (ed.), *Moi, Claude Bordeaux: journal d'un bourgeois de Rennes au 17e siècle* (Rennes, 1992)]; Journal of René Cormier sieur de la Courneuve, notes by La Borderie: AD Ile-et-Vilaine 1F 1637 [hereafter La Courneuve]; letter from Procureur-Général Huchet, 28 April 1675: BN Clairambault 796, p. 59; "Relation de la sédition de Rennes en 1675 extrait du journal de René Monneraye de Bourgneuf": AD Ile-et-Vilaine 1F 1032. There is an invaluable collection of original documents in Jean Lemoine, *La révolte dite du papier timbré* [hereafter cited as Lemoine, with document number and page].

[32] The grocers reportedly asked Argouges for permission to sell tobacco in small quantities, but he told them to wait to see if there would be violence. They then diverted the demonstrators' attention from themselves by directing it towards the general tobacco office. Registre secret, 20 April: AD Ile et Vilaine 1Bb 244; Coëtlogon fils to Louvois, 19 April: Lemoine, #4, p. 87.

Things were moving fast. The willingness of Coëtlogon's contingent to fire on the crowd so early in the game had nipped the movement in the bud, at the expense of turning the demonstrators immediately against natural leaders like the First President, who was no longer viewed as an ally. The crowd does not seem to have been armed or highly organized. It had originated in a relatively naive demand for access to tobacco and sub-sistence goods and moved on, perhaps with prompting, to target the offices of all the various "edicts." There were deaths among the demon-strators, but no prisoners, so there was no impetus for a subsequent attack on the prisons. Since the edicts had already been suspended by the Parlement and both governors were out of town, the city was left in a state of suspended animation. The action moved to the faubourgs where Procureur-Général Huchet discovered attacks in progress on smaller excise stations when he returned that evening from Saint Malo.[33]

Then, a week later, a curious incident renewed the protest. On 25 April around 1 p.m. a group of schoolboys, butchers, and some women, set fire to the Protestant temple at Cleuné, which was a suburb within sight of the walls of Rennes, on pretext that several of the tobacco agents were Protestants. Coëtlogon arrived again with a troop of nobles but the per-petrators dispersed "down narrow paths inaccessible to cavalry." A baker from the faubourg named Simon Ollivier and a young schoolboy from the class of cinquième were arrested and thrown into prison. Later that day rumor had it in the streets that schoolboys were going to burn down the prison where the prisoners were held, so the militia was called up, the gates closed, and night patrols organized.

This attack suggests that frustration against bad times, blamed on new taxes and gabeleurs, was still being ventilated. But scapegoating of Calvinists was hardly fortuitous, for it had a long history in Rennes. The temple at Cleuné had been burned in 1613, 1654, and 1661, and an arrêt de conseil d'état of 19 June 1661 had condemned the city to pay for the rebuilding. The Protestants later complained that the 25 April burning had been completely preventable:

The rumor circulated for several days in advance. The date and the time . . . were announced by these mutineers. We informed the principal persons of the city, who assured us of their protection. In fact, fearing that this disorder would be committed by schoolboys they instructed the regents [of the collège] to keep them under control.

This report is confirmed by Huchet who states that on the 24th

The rabble had broadsheets carried into the classes of the collège where there are easily two thousand students . . . inviting the schoolboys to report at two the next

[33] Huchet to Colbert, 28 April: BN Clairambault 796, p. 59.

afternoon to the [Protestant] temple . . . to help set it on fire. When we learned of this we [the Parlement] assembled, but no one took this news seriously, treating it as if it were something floating in the air, in the belief that such a public announcement was a sign that nobody would really do anything about it.[34]

This episode establishes a curious link between the attack on gabeleurs and deep-seated religious antagonism rarely if ever expressed in tax revolts. According to the Protestants, "they have violated the tombs of our dead, thrown their bones and remains into the fire, and dug up some of the most recent bodies to expose them to their anger."[35] This form of desecration is reminiscent of the religious wars of the sixteenth century, as if the linking of new enemies to old prejudices had revived an earlier mode of behavior linked to religious fervor. And, in fact, the Jesuit collège from which the student pillagers came was in 1675 the focal point of a Catholic revival in Rennes. The defense of community against gabeleurs seems to have been transformed for a moment into the archaic (or revived?) defense of the sacred against pollution.

Up to this point the Rennes revolt had been serious but not unusual. Its next phase, however, was going to be quite original. A confrontation was brewing between the royal authorities, who were not going to tolerate open rebellion to Louis XIV himself, and the Rennais who were determined not only to reject a takeover of their city but to continue their campaign against taxes as well. The protesters were going to challenge the governor, and indirectly the king himself, by seizing the militia and expelling the troops sent to intimidate them. This move was possible because disturbances had broken out in Saint Malo and Nantes, and in early June insurrection began to spread through the countryside of Lower Brittany. Given the state of the province, the protesters had reason to believe that they might have some breathing room.

On 2 May the duc de Chaulnes, who had rushed back from Paris without any troops, arrived in a hopeful and fearful city. He was met outside the walls by two hundred noblemen and treated to the ringing of the great bell and the firing of cannons, while militiamen from every street mounted ceremonial guard. The next day it was on to a banquet in the hôtel de ville with more toasts and salutes.[36] This was a far cry from the way governors were usually received after revolts. The city was buttering up the governor in hopes that he would take their side, but instead, on 4 May, Chaulnes presided over the promulgation of a parlementary arrêt ordering that the tax offices be reopened – the first hint that a crackdown was in the offing. La Courneuve reports that when they heard the news

[34] Huchet, ibid.   [35] AM Rennes titre 344, titre 354 (Protestants 1601–54 and 1661–1720).
[36] Duchemin, 200; Delibs, 25r.

people began to murmur, and manifestos and threats began to circulate again. Support for Chaulnes evaporated. He had entered the Palais with three hundred nobles in attendance, but only a dozen left with him.

Next the governor began to work on a force to patrol the streets. We know that this was a central problem in all seventeenth-century cities. His first plan was to recruit two companies of soldiers in the city, but when the potential recruits learned that they were to protect the bureaux of the *partisans* "they gave back the money and no longer wanted to serve."[37] Chaulnes decided instead to call up all the militia companies in rotation and name two hundred "well-known men capable of service" to guard the hôtel de ville.[38] Then he went off to Nantes, leaving the city in the hands of its own citizen patrols for a month – ample time for the citizens to gain confidence and contemplate future dangers.

They had reason for alarm because the news had arrived that the king was sending the regiment of La Couronne to repress the disorders in Nantes and Rennes. Louvois and the authorities at court were determined to repress all dissidence, but they viewed the problems elsewhere as more serious than Rennes and so they allowed the duc de Chaulnes, who was trying to defend his city and his own popularity, to persuade them to go lightly. Chaulnes had promised the notables of Rennes that if they would keep the city loyal he would hold off the cavalry and bring only three companies into the city for show, out of the sixteen that were available. He even asked Louvois to route the troops away from Rennes out of fear that their approach would stimulate new disorders.[39]

On 8 June Chaulnes marched the three infantry companies into the city where "so many troops had never been seen before." The situation was highly volatile. Allegedly benign troops were entering a city that had revolted against the king, where a citizen militia was still on duty. The royal troops entered in battle formation and took up positions in front of the hôtel de ville where command was to be transferred from the citizen forces guarding the square to the soldiers. A large crowd of onlookers began taunting the troops, saying "are these the fine soldiers that we were so threatened by?" and in the confusion it looked for a moment as if the citizen forces were going to resist the royal troops.[40] There was a scuffle, people started throwing rocks, and the troops almost fired on the citizens.

---

[37] Chaulnes to Colbert, 15 June: Lemoine #41, p. 125.
[38] Delibs, 26r. See also 32v–34v: 30 May.
[39] Royal orders of 8 May, Louvois to Chaulnes 8 May, Chaulnes to Louvois 15 and 19 May: Lemoine #12–13, #17, #19, pp. 100–1, 104, 106.
[40] This and many other negative details come from the complete account Jonville wrote to Louvois on 29 June. However Jonville, who was commissaire des guerres, was in Nantes and negatively disposed towards Chaulnes. Lemoine #64, pp. 153–62.

Now it was a question of who was threatening whom. Afraid to demobilize his men because of the volatile atmosphere, yet pledged to protect the city, the governor took up residence in the bishopric surrounded by his soldiers. That night there was excitement in the faubourgs, the most visible manifestation of which was a march by "sixty or eighty rascals with weapons" into the city, purportedly to aid the urban militiamen. They were sent away by the municipal captains with a warning that they would be fired upon if they did not retire. The next day (9 June) it seemed to Chaulnes that insubordination was "everywhere"; that he faced not one municipal force, but a separate unit in each of the five faubourgs, so that "when you punished one [company] it had no effect on the others; since even in the same faubourg they were separated into groups, and everyone was drunk."[41] He spent the day trying to get the loyal militia companies to discipline the rebels and found that many of the companies were willing to cooperate but they would not fire on their more independent compatriots. A split was developing between the respectable militia units in the center of town which were obeying the governor's orders and the more plebeian units from the faubourgs.[42]

That evening things got worse. The bishopric was besieged by a rock-throwing crowd from the faubourgs, and when Chaulnes came out he was confronted, cheek to jowl, with three hundred inhabitants all crying "Kill, kill," according to la Courneuve. They were mostly "women and children" and the militia corps that was guarding the bishopric asked him not to fire "because they would be held responsible." Another account says the rioters called him "fat pig, fat beggar"; and complained "that he had come to enrich himself at the expense of the province, that this was a fine dog of a governor." Here is another expression of popular indignation at authorities. Two of the captains of the regiment of La Couronne later said they had never seen the like, "talking to Monsieur le duc de Chaulnes as if he were the lowest of men."[43] Chaulnes himself reported that when he surveyed the situation he found mostly "women and children ten to twelve years old," and attributed the agitation in the faubourgs to rumors of the approach of additional troops spread especially by women. He noted that they were threatening to smash the tax offices, ring the tocsin, and march to the Parlement to demand arrêts similar to those obtained in Bordeaux.[44] Popular crowds (the women and children) and mutinous militia companies were mutually encouraging each other in the popular

---

[41] Morel, p. 8.
[42] Chaulnes' longer account is in his letter of 15 June: Lemoine #41, pp. 125–30.
[43] The quotations are from Jonville, 29 June, cited in note 40.
[44] Chaulnes to Colbert, 12 June: G. B. Depping, *Correspondance administrative sous le règne de Louis XIV*, vol. III (Paris, 1852), pp. 255–6.

sections of town, with the aim of expelling not just a *partisan* but a treasonous governor and the forces of repression.

On 10 June, having received his authorization to depart, Chaulnes paraded the three companies out of the city. The mutinous militiamen, especially those from the seditious rue Haute, were reported to have thrown rocks at the troops as they left and boasted that they had chased away three companies of soldiers. But this apparent success did not blind the agitators to their original purpose. That night disorder started again "from the effect of the wine." There was talk of more pillaging of offices and of marching the next morning "tambour beating" to the Parlement to demand a revocation of the edicts. Chaulnes claimed to have headed this off by an assemblage of nobles around the palais, but other outcries continued. When a woman shouted "to arms" because she thought more troops had been sighted in the faubourgs, "butchers and bakers" rallied and rescued the baker who had been imprisoned after pillaging the temple at Cleuné (the schoolboy had already been released). People "uttered another multitude of insolences, especially persons from the rue Haute, who wanted to burn down the procureur du roy, Duclos, Bessart, Ferret, La Feve Cotton, Gardin, Des Plantes and others they thought had betrayed them."[45] The calls for retribution thus continued after the troops were gone. Indeed, Morel states that on 12 June the inhabitants in the cinquantaine of Champjacquet and the rue aux Foulons rejected their captain, the sieur Desplantes-Avril, saying they didn't want to be commanded by him any more "because in the preceding days he had killed several persons during the tumultuous disturbance and smashing of the offices in the Champjacquet." The same thing happened to the captain of the company of La Cordonnerie. Desplantes-Avril was also one of the rich merchants threatened by the original rioters: probably all of those names had been associated with the original repression of the crowd.

Thus from 9 to 20 June the city was split into two camps, represented roughly by the respectable militia companies in the center and the dissident companies in the faubourgs. There were twenty-six militia companies in all, eighteen inside the walls. Thirteen relatively safe companies were guarding the hôtel de ville in rotation, but within these were soldiers who were not so "well intentioned," reported Chaulnes. The other five internal companies were of questionable loyalty, and most of them had joined forces with the dissidents. Thus power was evenly divided between thirteen relatively loyal companies and thirteen unsafe companies, whose base was in the faubourgs. "There are even gates where there

---

[45] La Courneuve, 11 June.

are municipal guards stationed by our orders on one side and guards from the faubourgs on the other side," marvelled the governor.[46]

We can get a sense of the people and activities in this dissident force by jumping ahead to the list of those persons who were later prosecuted for this resistance: Pierre Trehol nicknamed La Chesnaye, merchant fripier from the rue Tristan who forced his way into the courtyard of the episcopal residence with a rifle and tried to fire at the governor; Gaudin of the rue Haute exiled for sedition; Jean Rive, innkeeper of the rue Haute who was broken on the wheel as "chief" of the rebels and Pierre Boissart, both of whom had taken command of the militia company of the rue Haute; Jean Blé of the rue Haute who had forced his officers to take up arms and punched his captain in the cheek when he ordered them to take arms against the mutineers; Le Mounier, carpenter from the rue Haute, condemned to the galleys; a man named Hellandais who had taken up arms and beaten the drum; Julien Lepretre, slate roofer from the rue Haute who had forced other inhabitants to take up arms and who had wanted to set fires.[47]

Chaulnes worked gingerly to restore order. On 21 June he reported that he had finally persuaded all the dissident captains to demobilize themselves and issued an ordinance forbidding inhabitants to take arms except by orders from him or from those commanding in his absence.[48] However, as one observer put it on 21 June, the people would rise again at the slightest provocation, having "sensed their power and discovered that there is nothing here that can hold them back."[49] Indeed, another report on 29 June indicated that dissidents were still standing guard despite Chaulnes' orders and that the zealous were intimidating the cautious. If a neighbor was shirking guard duty they would arrive at his door and exact a fine of twelve to eighteen livres which was then put towards mutual wining and dining. Thus it appears that dissident guard duty was being treated like a convivial association and sanctioned accordingly.

This unprecedented situation of a town resisting the crown with impunity after a revolt was the result of the crisis in the rest of Brittany. Chaulnes was in the embarrassing position of appearing weak. Rumors circulated that he was being paid off by the cities of Nantes and Rennes.[50] On 30 June he denounced a new royal plan to send him archers from Normandy: "There are too many of them to risk punishment with these

---

[46] Chaulnes to Colbert 16 June: Lemoine #44, p. 132.
[47] Compiled from Morel, pp. 41–70.
[48] Ordinance 20 June, Chaulnes to Colbert 21 June: Lemoine #48–9, pp. 137–8.
[49] Guédameuc to Colbert, 21 June: Lemoine #52, pp. 141–4. This account, sympathetic to Chaulnes can be compared with Jonville's letter of 29 June, cited above, which is quite negative.   [50] Again, it was Jonville who reported this.

archers, and when an entire town is complicit one must take more precautions."[51] Instead he was putting his hopes in the calming effect of a projected meeting of the Estates of Brittany. Clearly he cared more about maintaining face than about imposing the full weight of the directives from Versailles: "In the present circumstances it is convenient to close one's eyes to many things and to reassure people's minds until it is time for a just and strong punishment." But there is no doubt as to his real sympathies. As early as 12 June he had written to Colbert that "the remedy is to ruin the faubourgs completely; it is a bit violent but in my opinion it is the only [solution]."[52]

Chaulnes blamed instigators for his dilemma. He pointed the finger at the Parlement and more specifically at the procureurs from the palais. It was they, he argued, who were encouraging people to hold onto their weapons and march on the Parlement to demand a revocation of the edicts. The proof, he thought, was that the movement was focusing attention on the stamp tax which affected the legal profession rather than on the tobacco tax which concerned the masses. Moreover the Parlement had never taken serious measures against the rebellion because it was happy to see his authority diminished.[53]

These claims should be taken seriously. Procureurs, notaries, and clerks may well have played a role in encouraging and orienting the revolt. They would have been important intermediaries between artisans little versed in legal niceties and the authorities being attacked. Nevertheless, the popular movement *had*, in fact, started with tobacco, and we have seen that the stamp tax and other edicts rapidly became a rich symbol evoking subsistence issues which had little to do with legal procedures. Resistance was in fact broad-based and centered in the popular quarters; the elites were split, not unified around resistance. But the parlementaires did indeed have something to gain from letting events unfold, especially since their lives and property were never seriously threatened, in contrast to their counterparts in Bordeaux where the Parlement had been treated as part of the enemy.

On 17 July around noon there was one last, mysterious episode. A crowd suddenly materialized outside the palais of the Parlement and invaded the ground floor office where the stamp tax office was located, doing what damage they could, allegedly because the *partisans* had beaten a clerk outside. A few inhabitants rallied and fired on the crowd, and one

---

[51] Chaulnes to Louvois and to Colbert, 30 June: Lemoine #65–6, pp. 162–4.
[52] Chaulnes to Colbert 12 June: Depping, *Correspondance administrative*, vol. III, p. 256; Chaulnes to Colbert 19 June: Lemoine #47, p. 135.
[53] These claims are made most forcefully in Chaulnes to Colbert, 16 June and 30 June; Depping, *Correspondance administrative*, vol. III, pp. 258–61.

person was killed while the rest fled. But all the reports agree that the office was empty, that the office of the bureau des exploits upstairs was found locked and deserted, and that the *partisans* were nowhere to be found. Therefore speculation grew that the riot had been provoked by the agents themselves. There is no way to unravel the mystery, but this incident must surely have been an attempt either by provocateurs to force the government to act or by dissidents to reinvigorate the process of expulsion. It demonstrated that the city was still tense and that people on all sides were fearful. When the militia captains offered to mobilize their companies, the governor told them on the contrary not to leave their own streets – we can imagine why. Morel, a procureur in the Parlement, saw the threat as coming from the crowd: "This pernicious enterprise is deplored by all the members of the Parlement, and the respectable inhabitants are in such fear of the rioters that they do not dare leave their houses, threatened as they are by a seditious cohort of vagabond and libertine persons." The Parlement declared that "the ability of these criminals to undertake such serious violence in the light of day" indicated that "this venture had been planned, organized and prepared for a long time, since it is evident that a few particulars could not have thought up such a dangerous enterprise without advance planning."[54] Three days later the duchesse de Chaulnes, writing to Colbert in the manner of her husband, said more or less the same thing:

I can't tell you, Monsieur, what a miserable state we're in in this town, being at the mercy of a people who want only fire and pillage and who need only one badly intentioned person to say that troops are coming to the town and everyone takes up arms without anyone being able to stop them.[55]

This standoff could not go on forever, even in Brittany, and the cruel rigor of the ultimate repression expresses better than anything else the indignation felt by the authorities and especially by the governor. On 3 October, five months after the revolt, Chaulnes sent word that he was coming with occupying forces and the city had better reestablish the tax bureaux without delay. The next day the bureaux reopened. By 8 October many prosperous inhabitants were moving their furniture out of the city, especially beds that might be used for lodging soldiers, to the extent that the Parlement had to decree that all inhabitants were to keep their apartments furnished with beds and accessories, otherwise the poor would be overburdened by the lodgings.[56] On the 10th Chaulnes arrived in town and on the 12th some 4,000 to 5,000 troops entered the city and were

[54] Morel, pp. 14–15; Registre secret, AD Ile et Vilaine 1Bb 244, fols. 77v-78r.
[55] Duchesse de Chaulnes to Colbert, 20 July: Lemoine #91, p. 193.
[56] Registre secret, Ile et Vilaine 1Bb 245, fol. 23v-24r.

lodged at the citizens' expense. The marquise de Sévigné, who was staying at her Breton estate of Les Rochers, commented:

They say there will be a lot of hanging. Monsieur de Chaulnes has been received there like the king, but fear is what has changed their language, and Monsieur de Chaulnes has not forgotten any of the insults that were said to him, of which the sweetest and most familiar was "fat pig," not to mention the rocks in his house and garden and the threats that only God himself seemed capable of preventing: *that* is what they are going to punish.[57]

All the militia companies were disarmed except for a small core; the individual citizens were also disarmed; then a graduated tax was laid on every household. The Parlement was exiled to Vannes (like Bordeaux, not to return until 1690), and large-scale arrests began. On the 14th, as troops were being reviewed all over town, the duchesse de Chaulnes entered the city and passed through the rue Haute, where dissidents threw a rotten cat carcass into her carriage, no doubt a commentary on the love which this street felt for her husband.[58]

Executions of rebels, which extended over several weeks, must have made quite an impression since the chroniclers identify each victim. The entire rue Haute, home of many of the most belligerent protesters and symbol of the dissident militia, was ordered razed to the ground. Madame de Sévigné again wryly commented:

An entire street has been chased out and banished, and everyone is prohibited from taking them in on pain of death, with the result that you could see these unfortunates, old men, pregnant women, children wandering about in tears at the exits of the city not knowing where to go, without food or a place to sleep. Day before yesterday they broke a violin player on the wheel who had started the dancing and pillaging of the stamped paper. He was drawn and his four quarters exposed at the four corners of the city like those of Josseran in Aix. As he was dying he said that it was the farmers of the stamped paper who gave him 25 écus for starting the uprising; they couldn't get anything more out of him. Sixty bourgeois have been arrested and tomorrow they begin the punishments. This province sets a good example for the others, [teaching] especially that you should respect your governors and governesses, not insult them, and not throw rocks in their gardens.[59]

---

[57] Letter of 16 October: Madame de Sévigné, *Correspondance*, ed. Roger Duchêne (Paris, 1974), vol. II, p. 132.

[58] This incident is reported by both la Borderie, *Les Bonnets Rouges*, p. 104, and Poquet, *Histoire de Bretagne*, pp. 492–3. Neither author cites a source; Poquet seems to be paraphrasing la Borderie, who attributes the story to oral tradition. Both place the incident in July after the riot of 17 July, but the only mention I have seen is by Morel, who alludes to it in October when the duchess was indeed back in Rennes.

[59] Letter of 30 October: *Correspondance*, pp. 146–7. The editor's note explains that Josseran was a servant who had killed his master, a noble from the house of Pontevès, in Provence.

Other arrests and executions were massive for a seventeenth-century revolt, hitting close to a hundred persons who were seriously prose-cuted.[60] In addition, the absence of the Parlement for fifteen years was said to have brought the city's ruin, a claim which has recently been supported by François Lebrun's demographic study.[61]

These movements of 1675 demonstrate that serious uprisings were still possible under Louis XIV and that popular crowds could be more vociferous than ever in demanding proper treatment. However, both the official actions and the popular responses had become more sophisticated. The obvious difference was the determined and coordinated posture of the authorities. Faced with the prospect of disturbances, they were now capable of consulting with one another and taking precautions in a businesslike manner. No longer did the jurats of Bordeaux falter in their own defense or waste their time sparring with the Parlement; instead they felt obliged to appear alongside the hated inspectors in the very streets where women were wielding knives, not only to participate in the marking of merchandise but also to confront the crowd and escort the agents to safety. In Rennes the responsible authorities were also united and willing to act, in fact the original rebellion was swiftly and effectively repressed. Now the guiding principle in the minds of all authorities was the necessity of complying immediately with Louis XIV's wishes. Correspondence with royal ministers was swifter and more direct and came from a wider range of responsible parties. Agents, in their turn, were able to coordinate policy better, with minimal delays, compared to the era of Richelieu. And instead of the equivocal compromises that followed many earlier revolts, both Bordeaux and Rennes were subjected to pun-

---

[60] A loose examination of the 72 persons from Rennes cited as executed or exempted from the king's general amnesty, minus 21 names without occupations, yields 51 remaining names. Of these, 21 were procureurs or other minor legal personages and 24 were from various trades: innkeepers (6), butchers (9), construction and road (4), carpentry (2), blacksmith (1), barber (1), violin player (1). One was a merchant, one was a junk-dealer (fripier), four were women. This is more or less what we would expect, given the fact that the resistance was centered in militia companies: half relatively humble artisans, half legal functionaries. Innkeepers play their habitual central role; butchers have a distinct prominence. This was a community movement, but its soul was in the lower half of the community. The size of the repression is indicated by two lists of prisoners held in the conciergerie of the Parlement in 1675 and 1676. They cite respectively about 100 and 125 names without occupations, few of which are repeated in both lists. "Abolition générale" of 5 February 1676: AD Ile-et-Vilaine 1Bh 14; Lemoine #139–40, pp. 248–58.

[61] Lebrun calculated the population as 49,420 in 1671–5, 39,144 in 1676–80, 38,584 in 1681–5, 37,072 in 1686–90, and 47,040 in 1691–5 – that is after the Parlement had returned in 1690. François Lebrun, "L'évolution de la population de Rennes au XVIIe siècle," in Daniel Aris (ed.), *La Bretagne au XVIIe siècle* (Vannes, 1991), pp. 543–53.

ishment that was comprehensive and long-lasting. The exile of the two parlements made a real impact.

Nevertheless, the royal authorities were temporarily hampered by the concurrent Dutch war and by the existence of several simultaneous insurrections, leaving room for the protesters to expand their influence. The governors of both Guyenne and Brittany were forced to negotiate with rebels under humiliating circumstances because the limited forces at their disposal precluded for the moment more decisive action. In Rennes only a few troops were sent to make a show of force before being rushed off to other trouble spots. In Bordeaux the garrison in the Château Trompette made concessions to the crowd.

Taking advantage of these openings, popular demonstrators also acted with greater sophistication. Crowds still demanded retribution by pillaging and tormenting the responsible parties in more or less the traditional manner, but there was more scope to the unfolding uprisings, in part because Louis XIV had threatened a number of constituencies at once, engendering wider support for the protests. The insurgents took hostages and occupied the streets more systematically in Bordeaux; they took over units of the militia and occupied the gates in Rennes. In both cases they showed greater subtlety in the range of abuses they attacked and the guarantees they demanded. One might almost say they had a program of reform, albeit a purely negative one. These changes suggest broader participation. Someone was organizing military-style shows of force in Bordeaux, distributing subversive bills to schoolboys in Rennes. A multi-faceted protest led by traditional interest groups (pewterers and hungry families) was gradually being extended to other constituencies, notably the more educated procureurs and legal agents affected by the new judicial fees. The presence of a more diverse segment of the population was signaled by a more legalistic formulation of demands, by more subtle posted threats, and by greater involvement of formal militia units.

In addition, the greater unity of authorities now required the protesters to challenge the king's agents themselves. The pillaging of Vivey in Bordeaux, which signalled the new importance of the intendant, and the direct assault on the governor and his troops in Rennes, are cases in point. The taking of hostages in Bordeaux was a way of dealing with the garrison in the Château Trompette. Crowds mobilized in more military fashion to counter official military forces and they challenged governors and officials directly.

Thus the popular impetus behind these rebellions was still evident in the crowd's traditional forms of action, but these later movements had perhaps moved a half step closer to becoming revolutionary parties in which educated citizens who had some personal experience of the way power was exercised began to join forces with groups of angry artisans and indignant gatherings of neighbors. As the government's forces became more organized, so too did the popular groups responding to them.

These explosions of genuine popular fury did not exhaust the possibilities of urban protest. In the next two chapters we will explore other kinds of movements which had superficial similarity to the previous episodes, but were significantly different in scope, language, and motivation. It is essential to recognize this difference in order to avoid confusing aspects of one form of protest with another and blurring the distinction between popular motivation and elite instigation. Sometimes the movements we will examine involved battles between factions of prominent citizens, drawing popular crowds along with them; sometimes the factions were organized around princely leaders who brought personal allegiances and national perspectives into the equation. We might still find angry crowds doing some of the same things they did in revolts, but the circumstances were demonstrably different.[1]

In 1615 Échevin Antoine Pingré of Amiens was called to his door after midnight by five or six unknown armed men stating that the duchesse de Longueville wanted to see him at once. When he appeared in the doorway someone fired shots at him and then retreated across the public square shouting "To arms, to arms" in an attempt to arouse the population. Although the échevins then organized patrols to prevent what they called "a large popular uprising," the context makes clear that Pingré's experience was really a skirmish in a battle for position between the forces of the duc de Longueville, provincial governor, and the maréchal d'Ancre (Concini), governor of Amiens. Longueville was allied with the rebellious princes; Ancre was the favorite of Marie de Medicis against whom they were rebelling; Amiens was an important border city whose citadel was controlled by Ancre. The anonymous soldiers were hardly raising an

---

[1] On parties and factions, the most useful survey is Jacques Heers, *Parties and Political Life in the Medieval West* (Amsterdam, 1977) although it concentrates on medieval Italian cities. An essential recent study is Wolfgang Kaiser, *Marseille au temps des troubles 1559–1596: morphologie sociale et luttes de factions* (Paris, 1992). For the larger picture of client ties, see Sharon Kettering, *Patrons, Brokers, and Clients in Seventeenth-Century France* (New York, 1986).

improbable popular uprising in the middle of the night. Their purpose
was rather to undermine the authority of the échevins, who were loyal to
the crown, and in so doing to demonstrate that the princes had a following in Amiens strong enough to be able to pull off an escapade. Such displays of bravado signaled that a group powerful enough to throw its
weight around was feeling excluded from the normal channels of authority. This "uprising" was "popular" in a completely different sense from
the ones we have been examining.[2]

In Montpellier in 1656 fifty or sixty armed gentlemen led by a certain
Colonel Baltazar and a recognizable group of local citizens rode through
the streets "insulting the officers of justice, saying things which tended to
foment popular sedition and crying out loudly 'Vive la liberté,'" as they
pulled Protestant ministers from their beds and warned them to "abjure
their evil plans." Several days earlier this same group had humiliated and
beaten a city guard. On the following Sunday they again rode through the
public squares allegedly carrying sacks of money "to seduce the people,
saying haughtily that they should seize the bells in the large belltower, that
no municipal judge should be recognized, that it was time to free themselves, and there there was an écu in it for everyone who would join
them."[3]

Here the context was a dispute over the religious composition of the
consulate. The agitators, opposed to a restoration of Protestant consuls,
were engaging in a campaign of harassment. They were not a formal
party, but they were organized enough to hold meetings and improvise
incidents. The slogan of "liberty" was designed to arouse local support,
and the failure of this tactic was underlined by its replacement with
bribes. But the real message was not "free the town," it was "follow me,"
and it failed. Despite these efforts, the "people" did not rise.

On 21 July 1632 an armed force of approximately thirty men forced
their way into the hôtel de ville of Lyon, led by the sieurs Laure and
Béraud who were trying to occupy the courtroom of the police court.
They skirmished with city guards and broke into the locked room
through a window, aided by the "cadet" Laure, a merchant, Margot, a
canon of Saint Nizier, who "claimed to be ready to kill five or six people,"
and a group of others waving swords. This incident occurred in the same

[2] AM Amiens BB 59, fols. 234v-235r.
[3] Two months later a larger meeting of a group now identified as "la médaille grasse" –
note the factional label – was meeting in an inn outside of which was a crowd of valets
wearing Baltazar's livery. Ms. fr. 17435, fols 357–9, 371–3. For background Charles
d'Aigrefeuille, *Histoire de la ville de Montpellier*, 4 vols. (Montpellier, 1875–82), vol. II, pp.
153–4; and A. Arnaud, "Fonctions et juridiction consulaires à Montpellier," *Annales du
Midi* 31 (1919), 35–67, 129–56.

year as the serious revolt we examined in chapter 5 but it had no connection to those events. Rather, it was the result of a dispute between the présidial court and the consulate over who had the right to nominate the juges de police. Thus a struggle in the hôtel de ville which, reported out of context, looked like a popular takeover, was just a tactical maneuver in this battle of authorities for legal jurisdiction.[4]

Béziers and Albi in the 1640s

All these brief incidents illustrate the sort of factional conflict that historians have sometimes mistaken for a popular revolt. The most interesting cases were long-standing rivalries in which two locally based factions developed an identity over time that transcended any particular issue. Take Béziers, for example.[5] The town was traditionally dominated by the family of Henri du Caylar, baron de Puisserguier, whose family had served the Montmorencys since the 1580s as governors of the city, and who led a coterie of rich, allegedly lazy local nobles in dominating local affairs.[6] The rival group, which appears to have consisted of notables only slightly less eminent, claimed to be interested in cutting out corruption in the management of municipal contracts and opening up the election process.

The crisis began to build at the time of the election of November 1644 when disputes in council meetings became heated and people bearing weapons began to appear – a sure sign that the group out of power was flexing its muscles.[7] Municipal elections were ideal moments for factional agitation because they required the ruling oligarchies to hold public meetings and move through a series of prescribed procedures which

[4] Procès-verbal 21 July: AM Lyon BB 182, fol. 145v-150v; letter from Croppet 30 July 1632: AA 51, fol. 206; Pierre Clerjon, *Histoire de Lyon depuis sa fondation jusqu'à nos jours*, 6 vols. (Lyon, 1829–37), vol. VI, pp. 152–3.
[5] I examined this episode in more detail in "Urban Factions and the Social Order during the Minority of Louis XIV," *French Historical Studies* 15 (1987), 42–6. The latest history of Béziers, Jean Sagnes (ed.), *Histoire de Béziers* (Toulouse, 1986), does not even mention these events. Older works are sketchy: Madame Bellaud Dessales, *Histoire de Béziers des origines à la Révolution française* (Béziers, 1929); E. Sabatier, *Histoire de la ville de Béziers et des évèques de Béziers* (Béziers, 1854); Antonin Soucaille, "Le consulat de Béziers," *Bulletin de la Société archéologique de Béziers*, 3e série 1 (1895–6), 217–504. A partial account of these events based on municipal deliberations is Anonymous, "Episode de la vie municipale à Béziers en 1646," *Mémoires de la Société archéologique de Béziers*, 2e série 5, 188–200.
[6] Soucaille, "Consulat," 333–45; BN Languedoc (Bénédictins) 12, fol. 172.
[7] The factional agitation resumed in 1643 because Puisserguier, who had been deposed for participating in the Montmorency rebellion of 1632, was restored to power in 1643 after the death of Louis XIII. The events in Béziers are reported in several documents from Ms. fr. 18830.

provided opportunities for challenges. In order to avoid trouble the intendant Baltazar suspended the election and continued the incumbent
consuls for a second year, but this move just exacerbated the antagonism.
The outsider group appealed, and the royal council and the intendant
Bosquet, who was an enemy of Baltazar, responded by scheduling new
elections on 24 October 1645. The split in the local oligarchy had now
been legitimized by contradictory rulings from higher authorities. This
time the reformers were elected, led by Gabriel d'Arnoye, seigneur de
Perdiguier, a rich citizen with a large popular following. But the regular
election day, 2 November 1645, was only a week off, so the ousted anti-
reformers began agitating themselves. They concealed "unknown men
with swords and firearms" in local taverns and outlying farms while the
reform consuls barricaded themselves in the hôtel de ville and surrounded the building with a crowd of popular supporters. As election day
wore on the supporters of d'Arnoye began to mass in the streets, "four or
five hundred persons from the populace – artisans and others," crying
that they wanted no other consul but d'Arnoye and chanting "Vive le roi
et monsieur d'Arnoye."[8] Bosquet rushed to Béziers and arranged a compromise election in which d'Arnoye and a reform colleague remained but
the rest of the slate was changed. This was a recipe for disaster. Now the
consulate itself was split between the two factions.

A few days later the newly empowered reformers appointed a board of
"policiens" to investigate the abuses of the previous anti-reformer
regime.[9] They heard testimony about monopolistic contracts with butchers, failure to regulate weights and measures, graft in sales of wheat, illegally high market prices, bakers selling "short" loaves, and kickbacks to
the authorities. These were the sorts of suspicions that had fueled factional dissidence in the first place. Honestly or cynically, the reformers
were using popular outrage at high prices and wartime taxes to undermine their entrenched rivals.

But the anti-reformers were also represented in the consulate. No
sooner had the reformers begun to act than they obtained delaying orders
from the Parlement and the other intendant, Baltazar. Then they began
their own campaign of intimidation, which was carried out in a series of
boisterous insults by swaggering friends of the governor. On 9 January,
while the reformers were in the council chamber hearing testimony from
women who had just bought fresh pork at illegally high prices in the

[8] Bosquet's report: Ms. fr. 18830, fols. 230r–237r.
[9] This narrative is based on a copy of an unattributed letter to Séguier in Ms. fr. 18830, fols.
     240r–243v. The author, sympathetic to the reformers, who may be the intendant Bosquet
     or another official from Béziers, states that he was not present during these events. See
     also Ms. fr. 16800, fols. 11–25.

market, the anti-reformer Second Consul Pouderoux noisily disowned the proceedings and provoked a scuffle with the aid of armed friends who were waiting outside the building. One of the "policiens" was beaten and wounded. That evening the same allies of Pouderoux tried to ambush d'Arnoye in the hôtel de ville and, when accosted, fled through the streets while someone rang the tocsin. They were trying to provoke a riot but the populace did not stir. The next morning Pouderoux was arrested by order of the sénéchaussée court and thrown into prison with the aid of d'Arnoye. Predictably, the allies of the governor rescued him by force from the prison and "promenaded him as if in triumph through the streets" in front of the houses of d'Arnoye and other adversaries.

The split consulate formalized an impossible cohabitation in which each side had some claims to legitimacy. The reformers were supported by an intendant and the royal council; the anti-reformers were backed by the other intendant, the Parlement, and the local governor. The former were relying on the popularity of their muck-raking, while the anti-reformers tried to delegitimize their rivals through humiliation. We must imagine armed young gentlemen on both sides, acting like swaggering youth gangs, trying to score points against their rivals as the rest of this rather small city watched and gossiped.

Their solidarity was reinforced by banqueting. Later that day (10 January), seeing a group of "reformer" opponents led by the cadet Cassan walking down the rue de la Patisserie on their way to dine together at an inn, the baron du Pujol leaned out the window of Moiseau's tavern and invited the Cassan party, no doubt sarcastically, to eat with him and his friends. They replied "that they would willingly do so," but when they entered the establishment they asked the innkeeper whether he had enough meat for them, and when he replied no, they left. They had almost finished their meal in an upstairs room at another tavern when Pujol and his friends arrived to return the compliment. "You didn't want to drink our wine so I have come to drink yours," Pujol announced. The banqueters responded "that they were their servants," and drank a toast to Pujol's health. Pujol replied by returning the toast, then announced: "this wine is no good," and, showing them his sword, said "if you will step outside I'll make you drink this, which is better."

This final provocation, the last in a long series, had the desired effect. Accepting the challenge, the "reform" banqueters followed Pujol to the door of the inn where they were ambushed by "a large troop of 'anti-reformers' armed with swords and pistols" rushing forward to attack them. A large crowd gathered in the street and the news swept through the city that "Sartre and Cassan and their friends were being assassinated in the cabaret," so d'Arnoye put on his consular livery, summoned some friends, and headed for the scene. When they appeared at the end of the street, largely unarmed except for swords, Pujol's followers swung around and attacked d'Arnoye's forces, firing a round of pistol shots which killed three persons and wounded at least ten. Pujol's friends, accompanied by "foreign cavaliers and a quantity of valets" carrying "three or four pistols each and even hunting arquebuses," took the lightly armed magistrates by surprise, knocking them down with rocks and then stabbing them on the ground with swords. All the victims were from d'Arnoye's contingent, and he was himself wounded in the head. The crowd was on d'Arnoye's side.[10]

This was a typical factional conflict, a local rivalry over power that was encouraged and amplified by contradictions among the royal authorities, which then culminated in an armed brawl among prominent leaders and their followers. It was not a popular revolt. The street action, which would be inexplicable without the backdrop of the split consulate, was military. The stakes were the reputation of the two sides. Each challenge – at the hearing on prices, in the streets the night of 9 January, at the prison, in the tavern – was improvised. Exactly what would be said or where each provocation would lead was not known in advance, but nothing was accidental: armed friends were always waiting close at hand to take advantage of any opportunity. The governor's people were trying to dampen the popularity of the reformers through humiliation, but try as they might they could not mobilize any popular following because of d'Arnoye's successful use of the reform issue to win over the people in the street.[11] The crowd took sides and played a supportive role without instigating or channeling the disorder.

A similar situation in Albi in the 1640s provides a more intensive look at the tactics of factional mobilization. Here the issue was independence from the authority of a powerful bishop.[12] As temporal lord of the city Gaspard de Daillon du Lude directed every aspect of local government by means of his clients within the hôtel de ville. He had inherited the position of his predecessor Alphonse d'Elbène, who had been deposed by the king for supporting Montmorency's provincial rebellion in 1632. The resulting six years of episcopal interregnum had provided the opponents

---

[10] The details and quotations are from Ms. fr. 18830, fol. 242v. The banquet episode has the ring of a story told and retold.

[11] Similar factional conflicts with recognizable connections to the parties of 1646 continued in Béziers until 1660. See for example Ms. fr. 17343, fol. 73 and Ms. fr. 18601, fol. 307.

[12] This case was also discussed in Beik, "Urban Factions," 46–54, where the larger political context is more fully delineated. This episode is summarized on pp. 185–6 of Jean-Louis Biget (ed.), *Histoire d'Albi* (Toulouse, 1983); Emile Jolibois, "Troubles dans la ville d'Albi pendant l'épiscopat de Gaspard de Daillon du Lude," *Revue du Tarn* 9 (1892), 49–61, 135–45. Both these accounts take the side of the dissidents, in part because the authors did not use the pro-episcopal documents in Paris.

of episcopal authority the opportunity to launch a counteroffensive. Calling themselves "directeurs," this group appealed to the king to establish a présidial court which would provide royal justice to rival the bishop's and the opportunity for local notables to purchase offices that would give them independent standing in the community. When Daillon was finally installed in 1637 he had other ideas. He induced the diocesan assembly to abolish the newly announced présidial court and to borrow 90,000 livres to pay off the *partisans* who were peddling the offices. The result was the emergence of a vigorous party opposed to these new debts, strengthened by popular antagonism towards the growing tax burden, which could now be blamed on the bishop's malice.[13]

In 1646, during the minority of Louis XIV, the reform movement was able to flex its muscles.[14] The elections of September 1645 had produced a conflict not unlike the one in Béziers. Three anti-episcopal consuls had been chosen along with three pro-episcopal consuls, in an election usually controlled by the bishop. The first consul, Jean de Bages, was an episcopal nominee, but he betrayed the bishop and became the leader of the opposition. On 7 May he persuaded the city council to suspend taxes supported by Daillon. A new committee of "directeurs" was named to appeal to the royal council against the taxes. Clandestine meetings began to be held by persons whom the bishop called "men of evil affairs charged with debts and crimes." They extended the meaning of "directorate" from a technical term to the name of a party by putting laurel leaves in their hats as a symbol, swearing on a missal to remain united, and staging parades through the streets to the sound of violins, accompanied by shouts of "Long live Bages and the laurel leaf!" These were the attributes of a faction flaunting and developing its popular support: emblems, a name, and an issue – all aimed at garnering support for the group and its leader.

Attention turned to the election of the consuls for 1647 on 15 September 1646. On that day the directeurs, armed with favorable rulings from the Parlement of Toulouse, managed to take over the proceedings and impose their own slate of candidates. When the bishop charged that this had been a popular rebellion, the intendant was sent in to investigate. His interrogations of forty-seven persons produced fascinating evidence of the way the town had become split between two groups utterly loyal among themselves. Sixteen persons reported detailed evidence which implicated the directeurs in premeditated conspiracy. Thirty-one friends of the directeurs denied categorically that anything unusual had taken

---

[13] On these earlier developments, AM Albi BB 29, fols. 654–707, 713v–734v.

[14] The basic narrative of this conflict can be found in two factums of 1652: Daillon's position is in Ms. fr. 18601, fols. 297–300 and that of the "consuls and inhabitants" starts on fol. 305.

place. Two contradictory stories were being told under oath and one party, most likely the directeurs, had to be lying.[15]

According to the friends of the bishop, word was spread in the streets on the day before the election that the bishop's nominees should not be accepted because they would impose new taxes, and that the first person to speak of voting the bishop's way "would be killed and his house pillaged." This is the familiar mixture of incentive and intimidation used by factions: we note that despite the evocation of pillage, the objective is loyalty to a leader, not elimination of an abuse. All day soldiers were seen gathering in inns or patrolling in twos and threes, and secret meetings were held at the home of the *viguier*, a local judge. Another characteristic was thus a military presence because the objective was the seizure of legitimate power. A priest from a neighboring village had stayed at an inn where he had heard twenty-five armed soldiers saying that "they had come to serve some of their particular friends in the election of the consuls." Others saw soldiers leaning out of windows or tossing rocks back and forth in the street. A lawyer claimed he had overheard one of the directeurs saying "that if they followed his advice they should stir up disorder and especially work on those in the faubourg of the *bout du pont*, who were manual laborers." Another directeur reportedly stopped peasants returning from the market in Albi and told them "that they should stand by in case there were disorders and that when they saw . . . torches in the belfry of Sainte Cécile they should not fail to come and help" – shades of a rudimentary plot that was never carried out. Another man had been at Valence "hiring some people to come to Albi for the choosing of the consuls." Thus peasant followers and potential mercenaries were being mobilized to stir up trouble and reinforce the presence of the directeurs.

On election day, still according to the bishop's allies, the directeurs in the hôtel de ville stalled until nightfall and then locked the main gate, separating the intimidated electors inside from a noisy, armed crowd of several hundred demonstrators outside in the square. The desired slate was imposed by intimidation. If recalcitrant electors tried to object, their statements were torn up, or they were threatened. Meanwhile Jean Pelletier stayed at the window, shouting down news of what was happening, as the loyal directeur supporters in the square roared approval or pounded on the door with cries of "Vive Bages." Again, leadership was being invoked.

The friends of the directeurs denied all this categorically. A merchant from Lescure had been in Albi on the 15th and had gone to the hôtel de ville at eight or nine p.m. "out of curiosity." He had indeed seen a

---

[15] *Informations* by La Margerie and accompanying documents: Ms. fr. 18601, fols. 241–96.

Figure 10 Typical street near the cathedral in the heart of Albi.

hundred or so inhabitants "promenading" outside, but he saw no weapons and no shouting. After the election he claimed that he had gone home for supper with Barthelemy Blanc, one of the aggrieved former consuls, the same man who had testified that Antoine Roussière had raised his sword against him, muttering "Rascal, you really made us dance here, now you must die for it." But according to the merchant, the trip had been uneventful and Blanc had told him that the election had unfolded "without noise or disorder." Salvy Cransac, valet of the consuls of Albi for fifteen years, had gone home with Jean Larroque who had also claimed to have been attacked and insulted, but Cransac said that the trip had been accomplished "with great peace and silence" and that afterwards members of the rival factions had "laughed and supped together." Many others testified that the crowd had been small and there had been no noise. Again and again merchants, priests, students, artisans repeated that there had been no mobs, no violence, no irregularities. The accused instigators denied all the charges concerning illicit meetings and recruiting. They charged that on the contrary the bishop's vicar-general had tried to force the electors to vote for his own slate of candidates.

A classic faction with widespread support had used its followers and the uncertainties of the royal minority to take power from an unpopular clique. Whatever the truth of the claims about soldiers and intimidation, various witnesses made the point that no one had been wounded or killed, and there certainly had been no lasting damage to property or persons. Unlike the bloody skirmish in Béziers that was provoked by a minority of strongmen without adequate popular support, the directeurs had succeeded because they seemed to be popular. The directeur leaders were all prosperous citizens from the more prestigious ranks. Among the identifiable forty-two names mentioned by witnesses we find the viguier and his two sons, thirteen merchants or bourgeois, four financial agents, four avocats, four notaries, three surgeons, three otherwise unidentified city councilors, one medical doctor, two "écuyers," one "sieur de," one priest, and three unknowns. This is a remarkably cohesive group of insiders, with few nobles and no artisans.[16]

Their followers are harder to identify, but the "soldiers" brought into town were evidently inhabitants from nearby villages. Of the forty-one identifiable names, thirty-one came from villages less than twenty kilometers from Albi, and all in the same northeastern direction; the other ten listed no place of origin. The fifteen whose occupations were given consisted of three "sieurs de," three surgeons, four tailors, two carders, two finishers (pareurs), and one merchant. Thus they were about half artisans and half persons of higher status. It is interesting that as many as forty-one persons were known and recognized by the witnesses, a result strikingly different from that found in most popular uprisings where few persons ever seemed to be known.[17] These were clearly people who had

---

[16] Compilation of names from all the sources and interrogations.
[17] Recruitment in the region was probably made easier by the fact that townsmen and peasants were all subject to the same diocesan taxes which were at the center of the conflict.

come to support a party, to "serve some of their particular friends," not to fight for a cause. No anger was displayed and no issue was discussed by them. The crowd was playful rather than threatening; its only slogan was "Vive Bages."

This was only the first round in a conflict that expanded to the point where, by 1649, the bishop was using royal guards to arrest the leading dissidents, and the directeurs were responding by parading through the streets with clubs and expelling "eighty" important families who supported the bishop from the city, using armed "bâtonniers de la direction" stationed in front of their doors at night – sign of a faction in power using fear to promote its aims.[18] Here, as in Béziers, conflict resulted from a struggle for power between two groups, each led by prominent citizens with a claim to power, each drawing in wider circles of followers and seeking popular acclaim by calling for reform, trumpeting municipal liberty, and currying favor with popular groups through parades and demonstrations of force.

Marseille

Marseille and Aix offer the ultimate examples of factional conflict, with the difference that here there was a greater emphasis on permanent rivalries between powerful patrons.[19] Whereas other cities developed loosely fluctuating interest-groups which combined personal rivalries with practical issues like fiscal mismanagement, these cities were animated by rivalries between clans led by "godfather"-like figures who seemed to view everything – even popular uprisings – as an expression of the struggle between clientèles. The fact that the nobility, sword and robe, resided in the cities and participated actively in civic affairs was one reason for this phenomenon, along with the distance from Paris and the vitality of long-standing traditions reminiscent of Renaissance Italy. Provençal aristocrats grouped themselves into intensely loyal networks and surrounded themselves with "cadets," those aristocratic youths who seemed always ready to mix mockery with assault in defense of their party's honor. At moments of confrontation parties asserted themselves in military fashion, while cultivating their public reputation with displays of verve and wit. In Marseille the focal point was the Valbelle family, led by Cosme de

---

[18] AM Albi BB 30, fol. 24v; Ms. fr. fols. 297–300; Daillon to Mazarin 7 July 1647: AAE France 1634, fol. 312.

[19] For the movements in Provence see René Pillorget, *Mouvements*, an exhaustive study whose conscientious research into each incident is unsurpassed, even if some of the author's conclusions can be challenged. For background, see Edouard Baratier (ed.), *Histoire de la Provence* (Toulouse, 1969).

Valbelle, consul in 1618 and 1631, and after his death in 1638 by Antoine de Valbelle, lieutenant of the admiralty.[20] Through the memoirs of Antoine de Félix, a habitué of these aristocratic circles, we can glimpse Marseillais politics and examine the connections between clan leaders and the crowd.[21]

Rival aristocrats jockeying for position by mocking one another or carrying out public vendettas were a fact of life in Marseille. When the Parlement held special hearings (*grands jours*) there in 1623, friends of Félix who were angry about being fined hung a dummy with horns from the gallows wearing a sign that said "The First President" and covered the area with satirical verses and pictures mocking other parlementaires who had insulted them. In 1627 when two cadets were arrested for dueling and murder, one of Félix's cousins "incited the people" to rescue them. In 1634 when his own brother killed another man in a duel, he noted that his colleagues in the présidial had "had enough regard for me to disguise the affair and pass it off as a casual quarrel."[22]

That same year Félix, who belonged to the opposing faction, was delighted to see the Valbelle consulate embarrassed by a rise in salt taxes which greatly antagonized the populace, especially fishermen whose livelihoods were dependent on salt. Félix describes how he and his friends decided to make trouble for the consuls:

> We went in a troop as far as Saint Jean where my brothers had some power, and after the party had been expanded by the addition of Gressy and some fishermen who carried oars and poles and those long rods that they call *grapes*, we were shouting "Vive le Roy" and the group that was at Saint Victor was shouting that these people were thieves and that we should go and attack them; then we retired into the fortress of Notre-Dame de la Garde.

Here is a faction stirring up popular opposition, although not apparently instigating it. Félix clearly relished the enterprise and noted with satisfaction that the consuls were forced to spend the night barricaded in the hôtel de ville, "not without some difficulty at restraining the boldness of certain unknown persons who appeared with axes and hammers to go and break down the doors and pillage the houses of the consuls allied with Cosme de Valbelle and the enemies of [Félix's] party." A month later when royal soldiers arrived to implement the rise in salt prices, Félix describes how they were besieged in the house of the second consul and

---

[20] For Marseille, in addition to Pillorget's *Mouvements*, Edouard Baratier (ed.), *Histoire de Marseille* (Toulouse, 1973) provides useful background and a synthesis on the period of revolts by Pillorget himself. Adolphe Crémieux, *Marseille et la royauté pendant la minorité de Louis XIV (1643–1660)*, 2 vols. (Paris, 1917) has additional documents and quotes many sources.

[21] Aix-en-Provence, Bibliothèque Méjanes 939 (RA 25), "Mémoires d'Antoine de Félix," a copy made from the original in 1839.   [22] Félix, "Mémoires," pp. 20, 23.

MASSILIA. MARSEILLE.

Figure 11 Panoramic view of Marseille around 1650. The port is visible,
dominated by the commanderie Saint Jean, the fortress at its mouth.

how his brothers had to come and decoy the crowd away from the building so that the besieged gabeleurs could escape over the roofs.[23]

Thus Félix and his friends saw themselves as charismatic figures who used the crowd to orchestrate their humiliation of the faction in power. They flaunted their popularity and revelled in the other side's embarrassment, but they also drew back from excessive crowd violence. In fact, Félix was frequently scornful of the real menu peuple, and when he said "the people," he usually meant his aristocratic friends. Speaking of a crowd of lower-class supporters, he observed cynically that "it was difficult to get this multitude to give way, but if there is nothing to steal, all popular uprisings evaporate at nightfall or when it is mealtime."[24]

The important thing was popularity. On 2 January 1635 Félix waxes ecstatic over the support he received when he returned from a trip to Aix to negotiate with the royal agents on behalf of the city. Outside Marseille he found "such a crowd of friends and enemies that the horses could

[23] Ibid., pp. 23–5. Pillorget indicates that the Glandèves-Félix party was responsible for organizing this attack, on the basis of AAE France 1702, fols. 420–3, which I have not consulted. Pillorget, *Mouvements*, p. 368.   [24] Félix, "Mémoires," p. 24.

hardly move, and there was a tumultuous sound of people crying 'Vive le Roy et fouero lairons.'" That evening he and his friends spent the time carousing and drinking toasts, and when they were all drunk they took a turn through Valbelle's street, serenading him with insulting songs – shades of the Puisserguier faction in Béziers.[25]

As the Fronde approached, party rivalries led to increasingly bitter confrontations which illustrate the consequences of a political culture in which clans of nobles in formations that were not congruent with formal institutions were prepared to take up arms. On 5 November 1644 the new consuls, nominees of Provincial Governor Alais and enemies of Valbelle, were planning to use city funds to pursue a law suit that the previous consuls had instituted against Antoine de Valbelle for fraudulent practices. Deciding enough was enough, Jean-Philippe de Valbelle, cousin of Antoine, assembled a large company in Valbelle's hôtel and drew up a legal act protesting this use of public funds. They then proceeded to the hôtel de ville, in an orderly fashion by their own account but as sixty to eighty armed men waving swords according to their enemies. The consuls met them on the steps and the first consul accepted the document – all in good order. Then someone shouted "Vive lou rey et fouero larrons"; armed friends of the consuls came running out of the building; Alais appeared with his guards; and there was a confused melee in which a young Valbelliste, the cadet Bonnet, was killed. This sort of confrontation was part of life in Marseille. Eyewitness merchants from Lyon reported hearing "tumult" and seeing people fleeing the length of the rue de la Bonneterie crying out "Close the shops, because they're killing each other at the Loge." Thus confrontations which, in some cities, might have led to pushing and shoving, in Marseille led to assemblages of armed men likely to lose their tempers because honor as well as power was at stake.[26]

In January 1651, during yet another struggle for control of the hôtel de ville, Félix describes how the allies of Alais turned the house of the baron de Bormes into a fortress from which they rushed, swords in hand, shouting "Vive le roy, fuore larrons," towards the hôtel de ville which was occupied by the Valbellistes. Félix had now gone over to Valbelle's camp. His account gives the improvisatory flavor of a campaign by factional agitators who knew the city well:

Without considering our safety, I drew the pistol I was carrying in my pocket and started shouting 'Aux armes,' as soon as we reached the four corners of the

[25] Ibid., p. 26.
[26] Account by Félix, now a supporter of Valbelle, "Mémoires," pp. 62–4; another report, Ms. fr. 18976, fol. 609; *Informations* by the intendant Champigny, 5 November 1644: AM Marseille FF 33.

chapelle Saint Victor. The chevalier de Temple, the cadet Saint Jacques and two others joined us, and monsieur de la Salle left us at the corner of his street to go home. I continued down the rue Droite shouting to everyone to arm and that we had to preserve the city for the king. I went to monsieur le lieutenant [Valbelle]'s house where other people were gathering. The objective was to occupy and fortify the [city] gate . . . We made a lot of noise as we passed through the streets to give the impression that there were more of us.[27]

These cohorts of aristocratic men thus fought battles for position which entailed both military control of strategic territory and charismatic control of the people in the streets.

But were there no genuinely popular riots in Marseille? A case in 1644 gives us an opportunity to explore the connection between popular protest and factional agitation.[28] Complaints were mounting over the shortage of grain and the refusal of bakers to accept doubles tournois (new coins) in exchange for bread. Let us first listen to Félix, who is siding with Valbelle and against the anti-Valbelle consuls:

Certain women assembled in the place de Lenche and, since hunger has no counsel, one of them took up a drum and another a long pole called a fichouire used by the fishermen which is as long as a half pike with a point at the end, and they went through the city gathering other women and a few men who became involved, crying 'Vouleu de pan! Vouleu de pan!' And this troop of amazons came right up to the corner of the house of Superte where Sieur Isnard-Marion lives at present. The sieur de La Salle and the sieur de Septêmes, cousin of the second consul, prepared to resist, but not being able to succeed, they promised that they would arrange for [the women] to be issued as much bread as they wanted. But while this cooled some down from their original ardor, others continued the effort by pushing through another street and investing the house of the second consul, Jean François Berenguier, suspected of speculating in the grain trade – which is a filthy thing for a consul to do. He was lucky to have escaped with difficulty via the roof into the adjacent house, since they would have killed and dragged him. They broke down the door of his shop and set fire to the door of his house.

This sounds like a typical bread riot. We note the way the women refused to be pacified by bread alone, like their counterparts in Bordeaux. The movement grew and men joined in. First Consul des Pennes' house was attacked. His wife grabbed their valuables and took refuge in the house of a relative of Félix. This man, "placing himself at the head of our friends, forced the people to leave, although they had not been able to break in the door which was barricaded from within."[29]

[27] Félix, "Mémoires," pp. 112–14: 17 January 1651.
[28] This episode was discussed in detail in Crémieux, *Marseille*, vol. 1, pp. 190–8, which stresses the political ramifications. It is also mentioned in Pillorget, *Mouvements*," pp. 503–5 and Porchnev, *Soulèvements*, pp. 225–35.   [29] Félix, "Mémoires," pp. 58–9.

Thus Félix views this episode as a spontaneous uprising carried out by a group of "amazons" whom he finds mildly entertaining. And while he takes pleasure once again in the discomfiture of his enemies, he also enjoys the role played by his relatives, who could save the day by gallantly stepping in to rescue their competitors from their own folly and protecting them from an admittedly dangerous crowd. He especially enjoys noting how "people said loudly that this wouldn't have happened in the time of Valbelle" and describes how during the riot the great patron "never went out of his house and kept his door constantly open, [where he could be seen] promenading back and forth in the courtyard." This wonderful gesture by Valbelle, made it clear to the public that while Valbelle washed his hands of this affair, no one was attacking *him*, and he was free to do as he pleased.[30]

Later testimony before the intendant Champigny also confirms the impression of a genuine popular disturbance.[31] Pierre Mortier, écuyer, had encountered many unarmed men, women and children in the rue Negredaux shouting "Long live the king, and close the gates because we have to drag the consuls." He recognized a fishwife leading the others. A large group of men was throwing rocks at the hôtel de ville, incited by a tall porter named Nicolas. François Blache, sergent for consul Berenguier, heard them saying that the consuls should be killed and that they wanted to strangle them; that there was no wheat or bread, and "that they had better watch out and that they were all thieves." Pierre Ricard, procureur, had heard a large number of women incited by four female leaders insulting the first consul, throwing rocks, and saying in provençal, "We want to kill Monsieur Des Pennes." One participant named Françoise Bertrande begged his pardon when he asked her why she was throwing rocks at his windows; another came up screaming "See, we have to kill them and do the same thing they did at the house of Monsieur de la Barben."

These elements – the familiar anger, the improvisatory tacts, the primitive weaponry, the punitive impulses – that we have seen in so many other

---

[30] Ibid. In his own memoirs, cited by Crémieux, Valbelle described his relationship to the riot in a similar way: "I can say without vanity that many of these women cried out during the disorder that this would not have happened in the days of Valbelle, and certain poor individuals who passed in front of my house blessed my conduct and cursed those who were governing at that time. I was nevertheless annoyed and angered at this violence and, if it had not been for the advice of one of my friends, I believe that my presence would not have been without utility in getting these women to withdraw. But I was correctly told that I had better not do it for fear of being suspected of having lighted a fire that I could extinguish so easily. I nevertheless sent my compliments to Madame des Pennes who had withdrawn and was hiding in the house of my father-in-law." Crémieux, *Marseille*, pp. 194–5.   [31] *Informations* by Champigny, 28–9 June 1644: Ms. fr. 18976, fols. 475–509.

places, indicate a spontaneous popular protest, and there is no reason to doubt this interpretation, which even the intendant endorsed by concluding his hearings with the arrest of seven lowly rioters. But a month later when Champigny was pressured by friends of the consuls to collect further testimony from their allies, he got a different story. Nicolas du Villages had heard Durant, a creature of Valbelle, telling the crowd in front of the Palais, "Well well, what is this? Go and drag the consuls who caused all this misfortune." Later, Durant taunted that "they had thrown people in prison, which was something even a Turk would not do to a Moor and that they were taking up arms against the people." Gaspard de Villages had been slipped an anonymous letter dated 28 June threatening that "these past days you have deceived the poor, promising them more than you have delivered. Believe me, do not get involved with the crowd of poor people: it will cost you your life." And a note passed to Pillandre de Vincheguerre on 3 July warned that he should "tell Monsieur le comte d'Alais to carry his last confession in his pocket if he returns to this town to meddle in the maison commune."[32]

After these new reports Champigny wrote to the Chancellor Séguier that his investigations "show clearly that those of [Valbelle's] party were the authors of the uprising that occurred in Marseille."[33] Of course the new charges were from patently unfriendly witnesses like the ones in Albi and could have been totally fabricated. But there is every likelihood that Valbelle's followers had indeed taken advantage of the situation to egg on the crowd, insult the authorities, and trumpet their own popularity, as they had done on other occasions. This then was a case where a spontaneous riot was amplified and channeled by a factional party; or perhaps there were equal measures of popular mobilization and elite fomentation. The issue and style were genuinely popular but the crowd was susceptible to suggestion. A riot which elsewhere might have been a straightforward subsistence conflict, in Marseille became enmeshed in factional politics.

Aix-en-Provence

The same factionalism was even more pronounced in Aix, which was a hotbed of aristocratic honor and manipulative ostentation, due to the importance of the robe families attached to the sovereign courts and the

---

[32] *Informations* by Champigny, continuation on 25 July 1644; memoir by Champigny; later threats and *informations* 28 June–5 July 1644: Ms. fr. 18976, fols. 475–509, 596–601.

[33] Champigny to Séguier 26 July 1644: A. D. Lublinskaya, *Lettres et mémoires adressés au Chancelier P. Séguier* (Moscow, 1966), p. 285.

rivalries between their presidents and chambers.[34] Aix's three serious revolts in 1630, 1649, and 1659 illustrate brilliantly the characteristics of aristocratic factional quarrels, while illuminating their complex connection to popular disturbances. A perfect example is the famous "Cascaveoux" revolt of 1630.[35] The situation was similar to the contemporaneous Lanturelu uprising in Dijon, in that there was general dissatisfaction against the intrusive new regime of the élus that was being imposed by the royal government at a time of widespread suffering resulting from a recent bout of plague and high prices. But in Aix the battle was structured around rivalries between two factions in the Parlement: those championing President Coriolis and those supporting First President Maynier d'Oppède.

When the intendant Dreux d'Aubray arrived on 19 September 1630 to get the edict of the élus registered, the familiar process of resisting the intruder began, but the forms of action had a distinctly aristocratic flavor. On 8 September First Consul Le Barben, who was viewed as a traitor for supporting the élus and abandoning the town during the plague and who was the cousin of Oppède, had already left town because of rumors that cadets were threatening to throw him into a victory bonfire. During the night they did in fact lay a trail of straw leading from his door to the gallows.[36] On 19 September Aubray was immediately chased out of town, his hôtel was pillaged, and his clothes and carriage were "piled up and a bonfire lighted, like a sacrifice which they claimed to be making to the public liberty." This movement was started by "angry young men, swords in hand" who gathered at the hôtel de ville and marched towards the hôtel chanting "Vive lê roy! Fouero Elus et larrons!"[37] It was clearly different in form from that of the vinegrowers of Dijon or the women of Montpellier, nevertheless it set off a riot with a popular dimension. When Oppède set out for the Parlement "with what he had of people" to put an end to the

---

[34] The best book on seventeenth-century Aix is Sharon Kettering, *Judicial Politics and Urban Revolt in Seventeenth-Century France: the Parlement of Aix, 1629–1659* (Princeton, 1978); on the aristocratic milieu, see Donna Bohanan, *Old and New Nobility in Aix-en-Provence, 1600–1695: Portrait of an Urban Elite* (Baton Rouge, LA, 1992); for a detailed analysis of the social structure, see Coste, *La ville d'Aix en 1695*. The two seventeenth-century histories are Jean Scholastique Pitton, *Histoire de la ville d'Aix, capitale de la Provence* (Aix, 1660); and Pierre-Joseph de Haitze, *Histoire de la ville d'Aix, capitale de la Provence*, 6 vols. (Aix, 1880–92).

[35] I make no effort here to cover all the ramifications of this revolt. Excellent accounts of the context and events can be found in Kettering, *Judicial Politics*, pp. 150–81 and Pillorget, *Mouvements*, pp. 325–54. An earlier version of Pillorget's account has been translated as "The 'Cascaveoux': the Insurrection at Aix of the Autumn of 1630," in Raymond F. Kierstead (ed.), *State and Society in Seventeenth-Century France* (New York, 1975), pp. 96–129.   [36] Haitze, *Histoire*, vol. IV, p. 164.

[37] Ibid., p. 177; Kettering, *Judicial Politics*, p. 157.

violence, "he heard so many unpleasant words on his way that, despite his effort at self-restraint, his face could not conceal his fear."[38]

On 13 October a straw effigy of Surintendant des Finances d'Effiat was burned in the place des Prêcheurs while satirical songs were sung. Shortly thereafter Haitze, the leading chronicler of Aix, speaks of night meetings on the boulevard de la Platte-forme, where "everybody," (meaning his aristocratic counterparts) wanted to die for the "patrie" but no one wanted to lead the movement. Finally Paul de Joannis, seigneur de Châteauneuf, took command and invented their insignia: a bell (*cascaveou*) attached to a strap with his coat of arms on it. An avocat was made "chancellor" of the movement and a list of adherents was drawn up.[39] All these activities – satiric verses, insignia, debates over leadership, officers and lists – were clear signs of elite direction, like the ones in Marseille.

Nevertheless, the connection between party leaders and crowds was complex. As Pillorget correctly points out, once the movement had been launched it took on a life of its own in the popular consciousness: the name "cascaveoux," the bells, the hatred of élus – with overtones of "the selfish rich" – all acquired symbolic force. The attack on the intendant was perhaps symptomatic in the way it moved from a formal humiliation of the individual to the more popularly inspired burning of his furniture. As Haitze put it, "The cadets of good family are always inclined to whip the cat and even put on charivaris because of the amount of leisure time they have. And following their example many artisans went by night to the houses of those they suspected of favoring the *élections* to make noise and utter threats." Another chronicler, Pitton, described the relationship between cadets and populace more cynically: "As soon as the little people have tasted the pleasure of being insolent, it is impossible to contain them. They become a torrent against which the dikes have no force; private vengeance is cloaked in the public good, and one begins to sack houses with impunity."[40]

In fact, as the movement developed there was increasing disparity between the motivations of leaders and crowds. On the one hand we hear of parlementaire banquets featuring pies with live birds in them that were "liberated" – evidently aristocratic party celebrations. On the other, when the newly elected consuls were insulted by priests in the cathedral, there was mumbling in the crowd about revenge against priests and threats "to stop paying the tithe and to go and break into their common cellar to carry off the wine" – a seemingly popular sentiment as much expressive of rudimentary anti-clericalism as of immediate party loyalty.[41]

[38] Haitze, *Histoire*, vol. IV, p. 178.   [39] Ibid., pp. 182–4.
[40] Ibid., p. 182; Pitton, *Histoire*, p. 386.   [41] Haitze, *Histoire*, vol. IV, pp. 185–7, 188.

On 17 October the house of councillor de Paule, viewed as an ally of Oppède, was sacked by two hundred lower-class persons. Also present were Châteauneuf and some mysterious masked figures, obviously instigators. On Sunday 3 November, peasants from the surrounding region flocked en masse into Aix to participate in the attacks. Pillorget claims that they were summoned by Châteauneuf, but this is not entirely clear.[42] In any event, a mass influx of villagers from miles around indicates consciousness and a certain agreement, whatever the impetus. Crowds massed on the place des Prêcheurs, solicited on all sides. In the evening they began to sack the houses of several officers viewed as *partisans*. The notables were alarmed, but neither the Parlement nor the consuls were able to stop the violence, which threatened to spread.[43] It may be for this reason that a large group of several thousand was deflected back to the countryside the next morning, led by Châteauneuf and accompanied by "all the youths, wearing bells," to pillage Le Barben's estate – perhaps a "safe" target removed from the city.[44] This troop returned at nightfall proudly carrying "a few sacks of grain and salt, some large furniture, some sculpted doorways and some bundles of pine which they burned to celebrate the memory of the day."[45]

From this point on, aristocratic alarm at the threat from below led to a closing of the ranks, but not to an abandonment of the two factional groupings. The authorities took elaborate steps to mobilize the bourgeois guard, but skirmishes were fought between the followers of the consuls (the "blues") and the followers of Coriolis (the "whites"). All sides fortified houses, collected arms, and solicited popular support. The city ended up as an armed camp with barricades, refuges, and sword battles between the blues, who opposed the élus but saw themselves as the party of order, and the whites who continued to maintain a more popular orientation – another way in which the Cascaveoux revolt differed sharply from the revolts in Bordeaux, Lyon, or Agen.

In 1649 the factions had regrouped themselves but the style of conflict was the same.[46] Instead of the élus, the issue was now the creation by the crown of a new "semester" parlement which sat alternately with the original body. The champions of the "old" parlement, led by Oppède and now called "sabreurs," were bracing themselves against the new semester officers, the consuls, and the governor Alais, who was preparing for a showdown by bringing in troops from Marseille to enforce

---

[42] Pillorget does not give his source for this information, and Kettering does not mention it.
[43] Haitze, *Histoire*, vol. IV, pp. 184–5.   [44] Cited by Pillorget, *Mouvements*, p. 334.
[45] Haitze, *Histoire*, vol. IV, p. 190.
[46] Accounts of this uprising in Kettering, *Judicial Politics*, pp. 251–97; and Pillorget, *Mouvements*, pp. 569–602.

the royal will, even as reports arrived of the flight of the royal family from Paris in January 1649. On 18 January after an incident concerning an insolent lackey set off rumors of a coup, armed forces assembled to resist the governor led by judges from the old parlement, including councillor Signier who shouted "at the top of his voice that everyone should follow him and not the governor." The fact that the parlementaires were wearing their red robes suggests that this was as much a play for public support as a military operation. The tocsin was rung – Haitze claims by Oppède's mother – and peasants returning from the fields were invited to come and eat at Oppède's table, in the courtyard of his hôtel.[47] Such "open tables" were a sure sign of aristocratic recruitment. A truce was declared, but two days later on Saint Sebastian's Day (20 January) during a solemn mass and procession, someone spotted Alais' guards in the tower of the hôtel de ville, and shouts of "A l'alarmo! A l'alarmo!" were heard in the place Saint Sauveur. Haitze may overdramatize the ensuing scene, but his account conveys a vivid impression of the style of factional instigators trying to drum up support for their cause by every means possible:

You could hear nothing but confused, tumultuous voices; everyone was alarmed and wanted to arm himself against the imaginary treason. At this word "treason," the great and the unimportant all armed themselves, some with halberds, some with firearms, some with iron-tipped clubs, running here and there around the city, wherever the clusters of people were the largest. You could even see disheveled women, who always have extreme manners, running around the streets, wild as the followers of Bacchus, some with pistols or bare swords in their hands, to stir up the people; others with sacks of silver to win them over; many crying at the top of their voices "Vive la liberté, point d'impositions." The least courageous women armed themselves at home with rocks to throw from their windows onto the poor semester people and those who supported them. Moving around the town, the proclaimers of the uprising pointed some of these armed and furious people towards the carrefour Saint Sauveur, as if that were the chief parade ground. A large number of these people, excited by their weapons, collected of their own accord along the Rue du Grand Horloge to block those who had seized the hôtel de ville. The baron d'Ansouis, a very popular personage, after regaling three hundred artisans with refreshments, armed himself and led them chez the President d'Oppède.[48]

Haitze does not really mean "everyone," but rather the group of instigators who interested him and who were using every possible means to win adherents, including payoffs, scare tactics, and banqueting. Contrast this account with what we know about popular insurrectionary movements and the difference is dramatic. Despite the evident concern of the

---

[47] Haitze, *Histoire*, vol. V, pp. 14–21.   [48] Ibid., p. 27.

population, this is a picture of extreme rabble-rousing, displaying little of the focus or collective rage found in popular disturbances.

The battle for position raged. Alais and his ally the duc de Richelieu were captured in the Palais de Justice without bloodshed and placed under arrest. Semester members took refuge in convents outside the walls; friends of the governor holed themselves up in his hôtel, and the friends of Oppède did the same in his. The "old" officers, principally Avocat-Général de Cormis and councillor Bonfils, rode through the city in red robes haranguing the people, arguing that the semester had been Mazarin's idea and that he would use it to pass any edict he wanted to oppress the people. Other parlementaires tore down the shed which was used to collect the piquet tax on flour – an important gesture to curry popular favor. There were shouts of "Vive la liberté and no more paying taxes."[49]

In 1659 the "Saint Valentine's Day Revolt" provided a climax to Aix's ongoing battle of factions.[50] In his latest factional about-face Oppède had constructed a new power base by becoming the creature of Mazarin, who made him acting intendant of Provence. Perceiving that the future lay with effective royal service, he became the architect of new taxes and increased royal control, to the disgust of his former allies, led by President Charles de Grimaldi-Regusse and President Louis Decormis. Once again a faction was going to defend itself against loss of political influence by fomenting opposition. Once again the city was watching, expecting a coup, planning to take sides or watch passively.

When news arrived on 14 February that a young Oppèdiste had wounded a member of the opposite faction in a private quarrel, rumors swept the city that an Oppède coup was under way, and a crowd of armed opponents circulated through the streets trying to rally support by saying that it was time to end his oppression.

Eyewitness accounts give us another opportunity to watch the interaction of faction leaders and crowds. Oppède made his way to the Palais in his carriage, stony-faced, amidst crowds calling him "the thief Oppède, traitor, tyrant," and assembled the court for a special session.[51] About an hour later a troop of around twenty young cadets entered the building armed with pistols, drawn swords, and muskets. They were followed by a larger crowd of unarmed observers. Witnesses identified a man named Taxil who seemed to be playing a prominent role, and in the course of the

[49] Pillorget, *Mouvements*, 593.
[50] This uprising is discussed in Kettering, *Judicial Politics*, pp. 298–328; and Pillorget, *Mouvements*, pp. 783–801.
[51] Haitze, *Histoire*, vol. v, pp. 436–46; *Informations* taken 4 March 1659 by commissioners of the Parlement: Aix, Bibliothèque Méjanes 1273 (RA 1155), fol. 216.

day the names of eleven or twelve *cadet* leaders were consistently mentioned. They were shouting in Provençal, "Lou fau ave," "We must have
him." They stormed around, going from room to room, trying to force
their way into the various chambers, not heeding the councillors from the
Parlement who came out to ask them to leave. Oppède was eventually
ushered out through the crowd, "held in an embrace" by his enemies
Cardinal Grimaldi, archbishop of Aix, and President de Bras, who had
come to rescue him. Outside, people surrounding the coach shouted "we
must kill him, We must kill him," but instead he was taken to the archbishopric and held hostage for ten days until a compromise was worked
out.

Cadets with swords and their artisan recruits were seen roaming
through the city. Jean Suchet, weigher of flour, saw twenty-five men with
swords drag the two cannons that were stored in his building down the
rue Saint Jean. Joseph Borreli, master carpenter, saw many men in the
Grande Rue firing at Oppède's house. Berard, called "Cantonnel," made
a round through town with a crowd, waving his sword, "trying to arouse
the people but they did not want to budge." Brother John, Augustine friar
and doctor of theology, saw men with swords and a large hammer enter
his monastery and break into the refectory where the city arsenal was
stored. Vincent Ragot saw a crowd of seven or eight young men armed
with swords and pistols and followed by twenty or so other persons,
apparently of lesser status, some carrying clubs and others with pastrycooks' rolling pins. On the morning of 15 February Taxil tried to get
merchants in front of the Palais to close their shops. Then he fired shots at
the Jesuit collège to get the students to come out. Storming inside, he held
a gun to the head of Louis Guicheron, 20, who was teaching the qua-
trième class, and said "Ventre dieu, are you a servant of the king or not?"

Thus there were no large uncontrollable crowds and no women.
Instead, small troops of heavily armed cadets were seen performing military maneuvers and dominating key command points, followed by less
well armed artisans and youths. Jean-Baptiste Merle, 40, a recent arrival
in Aix who could not sign his name, had heard the cadets in the place des
Prêcheurs shouting "To arms! To arms! We must go to the palace and kill
that thief of a First President." Later he saw the son of President Regusse
and others dragging a cannon through the square and constructing a
guard post out of the benches belonging to a miller. The view from inside
the shops gives an impression of passivity, contingent loyalty, or curiosity.[52] The wife of Bertrand, glazier, had seen a butcher she knew carrying

---

[52] *Informations* 4 March 1659. There is some danger of exaggerating the passivity, since
these are statements from interrogations in which the witnesses had every reason to minimize their involvement.

a rifle and going towards Oppède's house; many men had gone by her shop. Rimbaud, master tailor, had seen crowds led by cadets shouting "Close the shops." A laundryman who lived nearby had passed armed with a musket accompanied by other persons "exciting sedition."

A similar sense of contingency seems to have motivated respectable householders. Michel Rabelin, bourgeois, returned to town that evening and saw that the guard posts and two cannons were stationed in the place des Prêcheurs. He went home, got his sword, and reported to the archbishopric where Oppède was being held, presumably because his own company was already on duty there. He found Michon, captain of his quarter guarding the First President, along with cadets de Melu, de Perrin, de Regnac, Taxil and others. They told Rabelin to sleep there and help guard "this thief of a First President," but he went home instead. The next morning on his way to the place des Prêcheurs, cadet Rigret had said to him, "Monsieur Rabelin, I'm amazed that a man like you who has fought in the war has not taken up arms on this occasion"; and he had replied, "I only take up arms on good occasions."[53]

The rebellions in Aix were dominated by cadres of closely allied notables who used political issues and personal rivalries as pretexts for personal advancement, and who drew the crowds along with them. Popular groups were recruitable because the issues had resonance with them, but their anger was never the motivating force behind the movement. Nevertheless, followers from the menu peuple did bring their own opinions to bear on the question of loyalty to the factional bands that were roaming their city. Most, of course, were passive: they went about their business, watched from a distance, opened or closed shops according to the prevailing opinion. But many did take sides. There was genuine indignation that could be stirred up around the defense of municipal liberties or opposition to behavior viewed as tyrannical. Some came willingly or were available for hire; others came begrudgingly, or turned up in the context of their militia company; some refused to be persuaded.

As for the leaders who seized the opportunity to struggle against the impending domination of Oppède, these were men who were very sure of themselves. They brandished swords, felt free to command subordinates, and had no compunction about being seen. They talked "tough," partly out of genuine anger and partly as a way of rallying a following. They probably believed that they meant what they said when they proposed to kill and drag Oppède, but the chances of this happening were relatively remote, and they were really out to seize power for their group, not to destroy lives or pillage property.

---

[53] Of course Rabelin may have been covering his tracks.

The conflicts in this chapter were markedly different from the community-style protests studied earlier. They formed around issues of leadership in which prominent patrons or spokesmen for factional interest groups rallied bands of followers as a way of asserting their importance in relation to equivalent rivals.[54] These agitators employed distinctive forms of public display, with much blustering and occasional real violence, but they also exhibited restraint – a knowledge of how far to go and when to hold off – because the goal was to manipulate the rules, not to arouse social antagonism. All the parties were operating within the context of a monarchy with acknowledged authority. Factional movements were attempts to capture and redirect some of that power or to modify the link between a higher authority and a broader "public"; they did not aim to transform power itself.

On the other hand, factional agitation did signal a breakdown in the hierarchical system. Something was going wrong that allowed ambiguity to enter the picture: jurisdictional quarrels between agencies might be brewing, oligarchies might be splitting into warring camps because their holds on power were not firm enough, or higher authorities might themselves be quarreling and encouraging rival groups to compete on the local level. In fact, most of the best examples stem from the minority of Louis XIV when precisely these conditions prevailed. The sudden emergence of brazen street displays or conspiracies to seize power almost invariably took place when the way was paved by external political conditions.

Since my analysis of the nature of popular politics rests upon this difference between community revolts and factional conflicts, the question naturally arises whether the distinction might be simply a function of the nature of the evidence. In most factional conflicts we have accounts from the principal factional leaders bragging about their exploits and mocking their opponents. By contrast, in popular uprisings we hear only of anonymous, collective actions as described by third parties, usually persons responsible for the repression. Is it possible that popular revolts were simply factional coups in which the leaders have successfully covered their tracks? Could the revolts in Bordeaux or Montpellier have had chroniclers in the style of a Félix of Marseille or a Haitze of Aix whose reports have simply been lost?

This possibility – that there was no difference between popular,

---

[54] It is probably no accident that all the major examples in this chapter come from southern France, since it does appear that the extreme public sociability of the Midi, its urban culture, and its Mediterranean sense of honor and shame must have contributed to the flowering of this phenomenon, although it did also exist in other places.

community revolts and factional conflicts – can be ruled out. The two kinds of public disturbances displayed very different modes of behavior. As we have seen, the major popular revolts expressed their own distinctive goals, made different uses of violence, unfolded with a characteristic rhythm. Factional conflicts also had their own style. They were invariably carried out by men, often with swords, sometimes on horseback, and they relied heavily on military styles of mobilization. They did not throw rocks, enlist women and children, storm from place to place, cry out in desperation and indignation, or engage in vindictive mutilations, draggings, or pillaging – although they might tolerate these tactics as byproducts of their principal activity. Instead they paraded around, held banquets, rallied around leaders' residences, ambushed or insulted rival authorities. Their activities were aimed at looking grand, brave, powerful, or clever – popular crowds never aimed at these objectives – or alternatively at humiliating their rivals in a similarly sophisticated way. They were rarely hesitant to be identified, since that was the point of their enterprise. Even masks and disguises conferred only relative anonymity and suggested the status, if not the identity of the wearer.

When such movements evoked a popular response, it was by appealing to sentiments of civic patriotism and factional loyalty. They were likely to promote abstract slogans concerning civic liberty, to display symbols that mirrored their style, and to have names that reflected group leaders like "directeurs," or "sabreurs." They rallied popular followers and pointed them towards enemies, but they were always out front leading the way, and their goal was always personal advancement for their chief or chiefs. They focused on issues of leadership, whereas popular uprisings focused on issues of subsistence or community safety.

9   Princely leaders and popular parties

In their simplest manifestations factional conflicts took the form of contests for power between two rival segments of the local elite, each trying to enlist the support of the larger community. Such conflicts could be exacerbated by links between the local factions and competing higher authorities, as when the struggle between the princes and the favorites of Marie de Medicis led to disturbances in Amiens. If this outside linkage was ongoing, one faction might build its identity around its association with an external leader; then there was at least the possibility that princely protection might provide a shield behind which a local interest group could develop in the direction of a real popular party, provided there was also genuine grass-roots support.[1] The next two chapters explore the possibilities and limits of such alliances.

Factional quarrels and popular protests were "popular" in different ways. Popularly inspired revolts expressed deep-seated values about self-preservation, and they asserted commonly held beliefs by punishing persons perceived as having double-crossed the community, sometimes even eliciting more fundamental criticisms of the way things were normally run. Such revolts were also "popular" in the sense that they emanated from the body of the community and set out to nullify official acts performed by legitimate authorities. They drew their strength from parishes, trade organizations, or neighborhoods, and they targeted tax collectors, rich hoarders, échevins, governors, intendants, judges from the courts, or even unsympathetic militia captains. Their weakness was the absence of any procedure for organizing sustained action and their inability to develop a broader critique of the way things worked. They especially lacked influence over the external power centers where many decisions affecting their lives were made.

Factional movements enlisted the support of some of the same people and tapped some of the same fears and indignations, but they emphasized

[1] I am using the term "princely" here to designate groups led by nobles with national stature and positions of command. The title "prince" recalls the Princes of Condé and Conti, but I do not intend the concept to be limited to them.

a different set of values. Factions stressed the loyalty to persons that was so ingrained in early modern society. They enabled their followers to revel in the group's triumphs by vindicating a leader, supporting a clan, or associating with a particular faction's slogans, symbols, and festivities. This was a more masculine, more celebratory version of success. It implied that community identity would be enhanced not by defending traditional norms but through the triumph of leaders. The strength of factional movements was that they connected the crowd to elite leaders who had resources, contacts, and leadership skills. Their weakness was the likelihood that these same leaders viewed the followers as little more than pawns to further their ambitions.

Thus popular crowds and factional groupings were each an expression of a distinctive early modern social practice. Popular uprisings drew upon the sociability of urban sub-communities; factional conflict was built upon client loyalties. Combine these forms of action and add the leadership of a great noble with a reputation and a following, and the organizational possibilities will be enlarged. Princely leaders were immersed in their own affairs, but they were natural figureheads, links between local factional parties and outside forces, personalities around whom to rally. Princely leadership complicated the culture of retribution by heightening the celebratory opportunities available to popular followers while increasing their risk. Instead of squabbles over local elections, they were now likely be to drawn into real civil war. Real armies would enter the picture, real sieges, and the possibility of real treachery from fellow citizens. Such experiences could help to focus popular movements, but the real question was whether the objectives of the crowd would be lost in the shuffle.

Governors and crowds: Troyes and Agen

Let us shift perspective for a moment and look at urban squabbles from the point of view of an outside figure arriving in a client city. In June 1641 the marquis de Beauvais-Nangis was appointed governor of Troyes and sent there to guard the city during the princely rebellion raised by the duc de Bouillon. He described the experience in his memoirs.[2] Beauvais-Nangis considered this assignment to be an unavoidable recipe for dis-

[2] Marquis de Beauvais-Nangis, *Mémoires du marquis de Beauvais-Nangis*, ed. Monmerqué and A. H. Taillandier [Mémoires de la Société de l'histoire de France] (Paris, 1862). For bibliography on Troyes see chapter 3 and Jean-Marc Roger, "Ollier, intendant à Troyes (1641)," in *Actes du 102e Congrès national de sociétés savantes, Limoges, 1977; Section d'histoire moderne et contemporaine*, vol. II (Paris, 1978), pp. 189–203; and Jean-Marc Roger, "Luillier d'Orgeval intendant à Châlons (1641)," *Actes du 103e Congrès national des sociétés savantes, Nancy-Metz, 1978; Section d'histoire moderne et contemporaine*, vol. II (Paris, 1979), pp. 199–222.

aster. He was being sent without troops to a city he barely knew just at the moment when an unpopular *subvention* tax was about to be imposed:

These people were embittered by the tax, and mylords the Count [of Soissons] and the princes were about to enter Champagne with an army composed of foreigners and discontented Frenchmen. Most of the large towns were plunged into despair by the new tax, and the discontented nobility was already starting to rise up in territories far from the court.[3]

So Beauvais-Nangis entered Troyes on 6 July, inspected the walls and gates, and instructed the échevins to set up patrols. He was aware of his political danger. If the princes had approached, the crowd in Troyes might have supported them out of animosity for the new tax. As it turned out, the princes were defeated. But instead of being awarded the post of lieutenant-général of Champagne that he coveted, Beauvais-Nangis learned that the son of the maréchal de Praslin had been granted the position and that the latter's family, which had originally intervened to keep Beauvais-Nangis out of their bailiwick, was now lobbying to keep him there until after the *subvention* tax had been instituted. As the maréchale de Praslin put it, her son "was not the sort of man to establish the *subvention*." This is interesting evidence that families who frequented the court were conscious of the implications of urban politics and ready to use popular animosity towards *partisans* for their own purposes.[4]

Isolated and unprotected, Beauvais-Nangis was stuck in the middle of a growing tax crisis. He avoided speaking to the *partisans* who were already gathering their forces "because my commission did not instruct me to meddle in this affair which would have made me odious to everyone in town." On 10 July, however, when the collectors complained directly to him about threats to their safety, he put on a gallant front, saying "that if someone tried to displease them all I could do was to go there in person and try to calm the people, preserving their lives at the risk of my own."[5] He continued to perform his duties as local commander; he sparred with the échevins over precedence issues; studied the animosities that existed between the présidial and maison de ville; inspected the ramparts and the militia companies. He found the latter to be in mediocre shape, but he decided not to complain since there was no immediate military threat.

Soon his friend Ollier who had been sent to serve as intendant of Champagne arrived in town, and on 30 July the city received notification of the arrêt officially establishing the *subvention*. On 13 August Beauvais-Nangis finally obtained the papers authorizing his departure that he had been desperately soliciting, but before he could get out of town the *partisans* rushed to begin their collections so that he would have to protect

[3] Beauvais-Nangis, *Mémoires*, p. 250.   [4] Ibid., p. 264.   [5] Ibid., pp. 252, 265.

Figure 12 Panoramic view of Troyes as it appeared in 1621. Anonymous nineteenth-century lithograph of a seventeenth-century painting. This is more or less the way the city would have looked to the apprehensive Beauvais-Nangis as he approached his assignment.

them. The crowd responded immediately. Word arrived that there was a disturbance at the Beffroy gate, where "children" had pursued the agents up to Ollier's door. Here in a commander's own words is his reluctant handling of the sort of popular disturbance that we have seen many times from the other side:

Although my commission was terminated and I had already said goodby to the maire and the échevins, I felt honor bound to go there: royal service required it and Monsieur Ollier was my friend. Anticipating that this [disturbance] would bring on the town's ruin and wanting to demonstrate that I was not afraid, I hurried there with three or four gentlemen. I saw that people were beginning to come out of the shops; I gently persuaded everyone to go back in, and by the grace of God my presence appeased the turbulence a bit . . . Several of those accompanying me heard people saying loudly that Ollier should be grateful because if it hadn't been for me they would never have retreated, but that my arrival had made it impossible for them to cause trouble without discrediting me, and most of them did not hate me.[6]

For Beauvais-Nangis, a riot was a matter of honor, and he saw his relationship with the crowd as one in which he expressed paternalistic concern for their well-being and they defended his personal reputation. At a hastily assembled council meeting Beauvais-Nangis also heard the authorities openly express their fears:

not only that the gabeleurs would be killed but that the many impoverished outsiders present [in the crowd] would attack in the night and pillage the houses of the richest and might set the town, for the most part built out of wood, on fire. News came in that at the Comporté gate schoolboys coming out of the collège had confronted a *subvention* collector and called him a gabeleur; feeling insulted, he threatened them with the whip; they threw rocks at him and other habitants joined in.[7]

The magistrates' alarm in the face of revolt contrasts sharply with the indifference of Beauvais-Nangis. This outside testimony confirms the reality of the sorts of class fears we have encountered many times before. The authorities in Troyes were really afraid that the demonstrators, stereotyped as destitute strangers, would demand retribution by pillaging the rich and burning down the town, just as they had said in their more self-serving reports in the 1620s.[8] As an outsider unaffected by such oral traditions, Beauvais-Nangis was not particularly alarmed, except for his own reputation. He hated the idea

[6] Ibid., pp. 265–6.
[7] Ibid., p. 266. This is the third case we have seen of adolescents from a collège being solicited in popular protests, a little-noted and intriguing phenomenon. The others were in Rennes (chapter 7) and Aix (chapter 8).
[8] See chapter 4.

of being associated with gabeleurs, and he wanted the town to know that he was acting for their own welfare, not on behalf of tax farmers. He had no regrets several nights later when, after three or four volleys of musket-fire had been shot through their windows, the *partisans* left town uttering threats about appeals to the royal council. He departed from Troyes, eager to record in his memoirs for his son the advice that one should never get drawn into these municipal feuds.

After this case of casual contact, we turn to an example where an outside leader interacted directly with citizen groups in order to generate a following. On 12 March 1652 the prince de Condé arrived in Agen in advance of the princely forces which were fleeing the royal army com-manded by the comte d'Harcourt. We know what happened from the rather self-serving memoirs of the Agenais bookseller Bru, who was on the royalist side.[9] On 21 March, no doubt after days of extensive network-ing, Condé formally requested that the consuls permit him to leave his brother the prince de Conti with a garrison of four hundred men inside the city while he went off to rally new support. The consuls were split. Condé was a popular leader who had led Bordeaux against the duc d'Epernon, and he clearly had support. But the Fronde was drawing to a close and military lodgings were unpleasant, particularly lodgings of rebel forces about to be overtaken by a royal army.

We can watch Condé trying to build support – the opposite of the standoffish posture of Beauvais-Nangis in Troyes. At the meeting of the consuls, First Consul Boissonnade spoke on behalf of Condé, but when Fourth and Sixth Consuls d'Espalais and Labouroux expressed opposi-tion, an angry Condé swore to avenge himself on Labouroux "up to the fourth generation." Princely rage could be intimidating. Condé then demanded a meeting with the captains and sergeants of the militia, to whom he delivered a long harangue about his need for support. Again opinion was divided. Lescazes, captain of the Saint Etienne quarter, said that if it were up to him everyone would blindly obey Condé's orders; but our narrator Bru, sergeant from the same quarter, said that people were grumbling and would never tolerate a garrison; others agreed. Condé angrily called Bru a "Mazarin." The Prince later wooed some repre-sentatives of the soapmakers and the butchers, with whom he apparently had connections. Then he went sauntering through the streets accompa-nied by a large number of nobles, asking bystanders "whether they loved

---

[9] "Mémoires de Bru libraire: récit de ce qui se passa dans la ville d'Agen le jour que mon-seigneur le Prince de Condé y voulut establir garnison," AM Agen 2J 67 [nineteenth-century copy]. My entire narration is drawn from Bru's account, which has no pagination. For background on Agen see chapter 3 and Louis Couyba, *Etude sur la Fronde en Agenais et ses origines*, 2 vols. in 3 parts (Villeneuve-sur-Lot, 1899–1901).

him and whether they wouldn't like to do whatever he wished, without explaining further, and they responded with cries of 'Vive le Roy et Monsieur le Prince.'" But – sign of independence – many added "and no garrison."

Condé was still not getting unanimous support, but he commanded the regiment of Conti to advance towards the city with every expectation that they would be welcomed. Once inside, the soldiers started marching towards the maison de ville until a militia company numbering fifteen or sixteen from the rue de Garonne commanded them to stop. Shots were fired, causing the officers, who were not looking for trouble, to retreat. Barricades went up all over the city while women collected piles of rocks inside their windows and prepared boiling water: here is a community uprising in the making, complete with rocks. Condé again tried to take advantage of his personal influence in the manner of a charismatic leader:

His highness . . . started going from barricade to barricade, requesting them to take each one down and saying that if the garrison was not permitted he and his followers would be at risk. Some dismantled them to let him pass on condition that he command the garrison to leave the city. Others refused, saying that they would never lower their barricades as long as the garrison had not left and that those who had done so would rebuild them stronger than ever as soon as he and his party had passed. He traveled virtually all the streets without getting anything and became extremely angry.

He was faced with a city split by neighborhood and by militia company, and the only remedy was persuasion. The citizens, in turn, were torn between loyalty to a persuasive leader and a deeply ingrained reaction against troop lodgings reminiscent of the reaction in Rennes in 1675. A compromise was reached in which the troops were removed to the faubourgs.

A week later Conti also left, but with the approach of Harcourt's army, the internal split between Condéistes and royalists intensified in the city. An "assembly of the three orders" was held at which those shouting "Vive le Roy, les consuls, et la liberté" prevailed over those who tried to start chants of "Vive Monsieur le Prince." The urban allies of the princes then began organizing resistance. As Harcourt's army arrived outside the city on 29 March, another stormy meeting was held at which the dissidents flaunted muskets and pistols and shouted that they should "stand by Monsieur le Prince or die"; but they did not prevail. Then they circulated through the streets "with their servants and some bad inhabitants" shouting "Vive le Roy et Monsieur le Prince." They assembled armed men at the houses of wealthy supporters and had tables set out to wine and dine anyone who would join them in toasts to the princes – again those banquet tables. Meanwhile, certain ladies of high condition who supported the same party and the same interests as Monsieur le Prince decided to give presents to those who would support their party. They distributed ribbons colored light brown and blue, and thus committed the recipients . . . to go and shout out "Vive Monsieur le Prince" all over town.

Here are all the elements of a factional struggle, now connected to princely revolt: banquets, slogans, ribbons, client loyalties on the one side; municipal defensive procedures on the other. Bru's description of this night of agitation gives a wonderful picture of the way local solidarities worked:

Through the whole night from Good Friday to Saturday they never stopped trying to debauch the carters and butchers, most of whom let themselves be blindly won over. But along with some of the consuls, Messieurs de Saint-Gilis, and several good and faithful inhabitants of the rue de Garonne, there were other faithful [i.e. royalist] inhabitants: from the parish of Saint Hilaire, Monsieur de Sevin the younger did wonders to hold the loyalty of those of his quartier, as did Monsieur Ducros the elder, avocat, in the quartier de la Porte Neuve. Dufort, priest, held those from Carné loyal, and in Pont de Garonne messieurs de Maurès and de Loret seized and preserved the church of the Jacobins, aided by some faithful inhabitants from their neighborhood who had taken refuge there. Almost everyone at the Porte du Pin was perverted, and in the rue de Saint Jean as well, and in the parish of Saint Caprais almost everyone was in the other party except for several captains and sergeants from the quartier.

Tension mounted in the succeeding days. The rebels dragged a cannon to one of the gates and fired across the river at royal forces. The royalists packed themselves into the maison de ville and aimed their weapons out the windows. There were personal confrontations between captains from the two sides, and barricades were built in every street – 233 of them according to Bru.

The ladies and their band continued to circulate through the streets distributing their ribbons to attract the simpleminded to their party, which caused such a great problem that the common people revolted against the consuls and magistrates. These mutineers threatened the consuls that they would come and cut the throats of all those who were in the maison de ville, crying "Vive Monsieur le Prince," and claiming that they would perish before they would allow Harcourt to enter the city.

Here is the tough talk and over-dramatized agitation commonly employed by the losing side in a factional struggle (although Bru's account slants the tale against the Condéistes).

The city became an armed camp in which the posture of each side was largely defensive and the balance of power was critical. Militia companies patrolled and exchanged passwords. Houses near the maison de ville were posted with musketeers. Condé's support gradually diminished. On 2 April his local ally Galapian decided to try to seize the maison de ville by force, but failed, and here we can again see the improvisatory nature of the situation:

He left his house with twenty men, leaving another eighty behind. All he could do was circulate through town to gather as many men as he could to force the maison de ville, telling them "that nothing could be easier; that there were only a few rascals and they would not resist." In many areas he was denied passage: Sevin at the barricades of Saint Hilaire, Dufort at Carné and Corporal Margouillait, weaver, who commanded a barricade in front of [the house of] Monsieur Le Président Boissonnade all made him turn back, saying that if he approached they would fire on him. He headed towards Saint Caprais past the belltower and straight to the du Pin gate and the rue de Saint Jean, inviting everyone to follow him. But people were beginning to come to their senses and they replied that they wanted to maintain their barricades, so all he could do was bring along sixty or so small children, and he and the baron de Moncaut made them shout "Vive Monsieur le Prince."

On 3 April Condé's allies were asked to leave the city, and the next day Harcourt entered and was greeted by the consuls and the parishes in arms, except for Saint Caprais and Sainte Foy which abstained from sending anyone.

This account reveals the popularity of princely leaders, and it shows how neighborhoods and individual leaders made semi-autonomous decisions about what to do when a split town provided a viable choice of options. The process was similar to the factional recruiting in Aix, except that an external leader had to build loyalties on the spot or rely on local intermediaries rather than calling out a permanent faction led by young nobles. Let us now examine another movement during the Fronde which inserts popular pressure from below into the picture.

The Loricards of Angers

Angers is a fine example of a city vulnerable to princely seduction and popular agitation because of a long history of factionalism.[10] Two segments of the elite had been battling for power at least since the turn of the

---

[10] The history of this period is lightly covered in François Lebrun (ed.), *Histoire d'Angers* (Toulouse, 1975) and examined comprehensively in A. Debidour, *La Fronde angevine: tableau de la vie municipale au XVIIe siècle* (Paris, 1877). Also invaluable is Celestin Port, *Inventaire analytique des archives anciennes de la mairie d'Angers* (Paris, 1861) which includes among its documents the "Journal de M. Jousselin, curé de Sainte-Croix d'Angers (1621–1652)," pp. 424–84, an essential eyewitness account. An excellent study of Angevin government which begins after the Fronde, is Jacques Maillard, *Le pouvoir municipal à Angers de 1657 à 1789*, 2 vols. (Angers, 1984).

century in a manner not unlike the factions in Béziers and Albi. On the one side a small circle of officers from the royal courts, notably the présidial, virtually monopolized the government through cooption. On the other, a group of excluded professionals and merchants tried to break their way into the charmed circle by defining themselves as reformers. The Fronde then provided an opportunity for the growth of an interesting popular movement with ties to both the reformers and the princes.

The traditional dispute was defined in terms of a constitutional conflict which had resonance for ordinary citizens.[11] Angers was supposed to be exempt from taille, gabelle, and troop lodgings, but under Louis XIII the gabelle had been introduced and troop lodgings were increasingly common, especially as a tactic to enforce obedience. These annoyances gave the opposition faction ammunition with which to launch legal appeals charging that the maire and échevins were acting selfishly against the town's best interests. In 1601 one such appeal had resulted in a reform mandated by the Parlement of Paris which weakened the authority of the hôtel de ville without really satisfying the opposition. When special taxes were promulgated, the maire and échevins were now required to present them to a general assembly for ratification. This procedure set up a dangerous process of grassroots consultation. The sixteen parishes would be instructed to meet on a Sunday after Mass in their parish churches to discuss the issue and then send deputies to the general assembly where the final outcome would be voted. This procedure provided the opportunity for the parish communities to discuss local politics and offered a point of contact between opposition leaders and parishioners.

To make matters worse, Angers' exemption from the taille meant that there were no established tax rolls, so that when the king demanded wartime subsidies the maire and échevins always had to resort to the kind of special taxes that required ratification. The échevins were caught in a fiscal trap rather like their counterparts in Lyon. Unwilling to levy a *capitation* on themselves and unable to raise the sums the king was demanding through loans, the maire and échevins would try to impose a pancarte on consumption. They would summon the parishes which would respond with absenteeism and abstention, making collection impossible; the town would fall into arrears; the king would send a regiment to enforce obedience; then the whole resistance process would start again. This cycle intensified hatred of three intrusive procedures: gabelle,

[11] The Loricard revolt is discussed in detail in Debidour, *La Fronde angevine*; and in Tilly, *The Contentious French*, pp. 79–103. It is placed in the context of earlier revolts in François Lebrun's excellent article, "Les soulèvements populaires à Angers aux XVIIe et XVIIIe siècles," *Actes du 90e Congrès national des sociétés savantes, Nice, 1965; Section d'histoire moderne et contemporaine*, vol. I (Paris, 1966), pp. 119–40.

pancarte, and lodging of troops, each of which aroused intense popular indignation as a violation of traditional privileges. The opposition was then able to attribute these perennial evils to the regime in power. The maire and échevins, they charged, were exempting their friends from taxation and troop billeting and calling in the army to punish the town for resisting them. Thus lower-class grievances relating to subsistence rights paralleled the constitutional complaints of opposition merchants and lawyers – a potent recipe for resistance.

An institution parallel to the parish assemblies was the militia, organized within each parish by the same sort of merchants and lawyers who led the parish assemblies, lending potential force to the grievances of popular assemblies. Resistance was not an abstraction, as the city had turbulent experiences to draw on. In 1620 during the revolt of the Queen Mother, crowds of artisans assisted by a few nobles had attacked the house of an échevin accused of hoarding arms. In 1629 tanners had besieged the agents of a new tax on skins. In 1630 avocats and procureurs had gone on strike to protest taxes levied on them by the hôtel de ville and angry crowds had murdered several agents of the gabelle. In 1641 and 1643 there were new troubles.[12]

We first get hints of the popular movement later called the "Loricards" in the undercurrent of resistance to the expedients proposed by the maire to resolve the financial crisis of 1647 and 1648. Parish assemblies repeatedly resisted any suggestion of a new pancarte; inflammatory news was announced from pulpits; there were meetings and occasional attacks on tax collectors. Then in the summer of 1648, no doubt in response to the news of the revolt in Paris, there was a unilateral refusal on the part of rising numbers of citizens to pay the pancarte at the gates. Agitation appeared sporadically in different locations and circumstances. It was surely no accident that when the prévôt Martineau pursued a man into the church of La Trinité during Mass in May, the worshippers protected the man by raising an outcry against Martineau, a member of the unpopular oligarchy; or that four months later the city gate was menacingly slammed and locked while the maire was outside the walls reviewing unpopular royal troops, and that this humiliation was perpetrated by the militia company from the same parish of La Trinité.[13]

Since Urbain de Maillé-Brézé, governor of Anjou, had always supported the oligarchy against the reformers, it was not surprising that when the first war of the Fronde broke out in early 1649, Brézé and the oligarchy supported the crown, while the parishes and reformers rallied

---

[12] These movements are discussed in Lebrun, "Les soulèvements populaires."
[13] Jousselin, "Journal," pp. 432–3; Debidour, *La Fronde angevine*, pp. 67–8; Deliberations, 17, 20, 30 September, 24 November 1647: AM Angers BB 81.

behind the Parlement of Paris and supported the duc de La Trémouille's campaign on behalf of the frondeurs. While the maire and échevins avoided calling up the militia for fear of insubordination and tried in vain to assemble the deputies of the parishes to declare loyalty to the crown, the parish militia companies began organizing themselves, calling for a tightening of security, unilaterally setting up their own units to guard the ramparts, and firing on suspicious parties.[14] Gradually overtaken by events, the maire had to ratify this fait accompli as enthusiastic citizens blockaded the river, manned the ramparts, and isolated the chateau where Brézé's garrison was stationed. Once again the militia was proving to be an instrument of neighborhoods *against* magistrates.

This opposition was closely linked to the reform party. On 16 March 1649 as the maire and échevins were leaving a regular council meeting, they were surrounded in the marketplace by a tumultuous crowd led by a prominent reformer, Claude Voisin, regent of the university, who insisted that they return to the hôtel de ville and name a "major" (special commander) for the militia. Back inside the building a "large number of inhabitants of various conditions" cried out "with great noise and a dreadful clamor" that they insisted on having Philippe Lemarié, councillor in the présidial, and Claude Dupas, merchant, as commanders of the militia. The doors were blocked for an hour while these men were summoned and sworn in – our first concrete indication of the leadership behind the agitation. Voisin was already popular because he had defended the taxpayers against earlier *subsistance* taxes. Ten days later a general council meeting dominated by Lemarié swore allegiance to the Parlement and to La Trémouille, and for three weeks until a hasty peace left Angers vulnerable again, a joyful insurrectionary mood reigned, as barricades went up, the clergy raised money for the cause, and the militia exchanged daring volleys with the garrison in the château – evidence once again of the defensive impulses of an unchained population. On 7 April, after the peace had been promulgated in the sénéchaussée, the maire was attacked by a crowd and forced to flee the city.[15]

Thus an insurrection tied to the Fronde and to reform leaders was also enlisting enthusiastic support from the population. There is no way of knowing when Lemarié and his friends took over the leadership, but there is every indication that the movement had started with popular sentiment in the militia companies, expanded because of the atmosphere of the Parisian revolt, and then adopted leaders who were positioned to carry on the constitutional struggle against the oligarchy. These leaders tried to

[14] Jousselin, "Journal," p. 434.
[15] Deliberations, 16–31 March, 8 April 1649: AM Angers BB 81.

enact the popular program as a way of asserting authority and gaining popularity. They stopped grain export on the river and sponsored forays against the gabelle which were led by the sieur de Grandmaison, merchant and militia captain from the parish of La Trinité. Grandmaison's company gathered arms, pillaged the lands of enemies from the château, and attacked gabelle agents in order to organize free distribution of salt – the exact opposite of a "gabeleur."

Although the movement was led by Voisin, Lemarié, Dupas, and Grandmaison, all prominent citizens, it also left hints of lower-class feelings and actions. The term "loricard," which emerged about this time, had a distinctly popular ring. It was borrowed from a lower-class district near the port and the Cathedral Saint Maurice, as well as from the "Loricard company" of the militia of that same parish. Later it was applied to the entire pro-Fronde party of Angers, but it retained the connotation of "lowly" in the minds of its enemies. Much of the agitation in the militia and in parish assemblies came from this and neighboring parishes which were the poorest in the city.

These supporters were difficult to control. On 26 March during the general council meeting in which Lemarié would have wanted to monopolize all attention because he was carefully maneuvering the city into a declaration of allegiance to the Parisian Fronde, a rock was thrown through the window with a note attached which accused Grandet, lieutenant of the maréchaussée and captain of the gabelles, of harboring armed men in his residence.[16] This was an unexpected diversion "from below." Soon an angry crowd had pillaged Grandet's residence from top to bottom despite the forces under Dupas which Lemarié sent to control the situation. Evidently the popular movement was not under the firm control of its leaders, and the impulse to attack the gabelle was not being successfully subordinated to the move to establish an elite-led frondeur party.

Stories about these rioters' motives suggest a different mental universe from that prevailing at the hôtel de ville. The pillaging crowd cried out that "Grandet's wife had been nicknamed 'Mary without Pity' because of her treatment of the porters of salt who were also harshly handled by her husband, and that on this day of Our Lady of Pity, it was necessary to be without pity towards them."[17] This popular recollection of a victim's prior treatment of employees is reminiscent of the attack on canon du Périer in Agen in 1635. The gossip about Grandet and his family was so tinged with revulsion that word of mouth accounts readily slipped into folkloric formulas. A second story was that a poor saltmaker

---

[16] Jousselin, "Journal," p. 436.			[17] Ibid.

had been found in the house covered from head to foot with toads – another metaphor for Grandet's exploitation of humble workers? Some observers thought that a catcher of frogs had emptied his sack in order to fill it with loot, but others claimed that this was evidence of Grandet's sorcery.

The authorities, fearing further trouble, had to put up chains in the streets and organize patrols. The subsequent expeditions to seize salt, mentioned above, were probably an attempt to channel these same energies in a less threatening direction. Two hundred men from Angers pillaged the gabelle station at La Pointe, freed a number of prisoners, and seized the royal salt, which was brought triumphally back to Angers and distributed free of charge. As La Trémouille's army approached and the city was subjected to a barrage of fire from the château, the angry citizens went into a fury of supportive military activities, patrolling, barricading, threatening suspects. Money was raised – this time with the support of the parishes – and angry crowds effected spontaneous sorties to pillage houses belonging to soldiers in the château. When a truce was arranged, conciliation was apparently not part of the popular agenda, since signs of agitation continued in the streets, along with mutterings against the maire, who was forced to flee. Even La Trémouille was greeted coolly by the crowd, and people were noticeably undemonstrative at the Te Deum service and the bonfires he organized to celebrate the peace because the population felt that he had sold out their cause.

This mobilization had shown the elite reformers what they could do with a little popular support.[18] In 1650, as the arrest of the princes made it clear that the opportunities of the Fronde were far from exhausted, further discussions were held between the merchant community, the corporation of avocats, and the deputies of the parishes to find ways of nullifying the royal officers' hold on the hôtel de ville. Out of meetings in the cloister of the Cordelier monks emerged a committee of eight – four avocats and four merchants – who styled themselves *procureurs-généraux des habitants* and instituted a law suit on behalf of five parishes being sued for funds by the town's creditors.[19] One of these parishes was Saint Maurice, home of the Loricards. This quasi-legal committee of eight, formed in semi-clandestinity and reminiscent of the directeurs in Béziers, posed an immediate threat to the maire, who complained that people were saying that these "so-called procureurs-généraux would look after

---

[18] The deliberations of 8–9 November 1647 describe the position of each parish and the appeals: AM Angers BB 81.
[19] The eight procureurs-généraux were Laurent Gault, Germain Nivard and Antoine Deschamps, all avocats; and Claude Dupas, Nicolas Marguaritteau, René le Crespy, Jacques Theard, and François Tartaret. Deliberations, 3 June 1650: AM Angers BB 82.

the affairs of the inhabitants and take care of them."[20] The familiar tactic of a legal appeal initiated by a syndicate of inhabitants was taking on the flavor of a popular party.

The maire's fears were justified, for the committee was deliberately trying to win popular support. In late May 1650 the reformers obtained an arrêt from the Parlement which insulted the city administration by directing that the municipal account books be presented for public audit in the open air *in front of the cathedral*. The maire replied indignantly that such an unprecedented procedure would endanger the safety of municipal records and humiliate the city, since this spot in front of the cathedral, not far from the Loricards' stronghold, was the place where criminals did their penance![21]

The battle for popularity intensified. While Lemarié held military drills of friendly militia companies in the fields outside the city, supposedly to prepare a welcome for the new governor Henri de Rohan-Chabot, all the royal courts rallied to support the status quo by agreeing to collaborate with the présidial in opposing "factions" holding "illicit assemblies." The présidial even took steps to expel the turncoat Lemarié from its ranks, protesting to the First President of the Paris Parlement that Lemarié's claims "dishonor and discredit all the officers [in the eyes of] the people."[22] Meanwhile the hôtel de ville asserted "that the title *procureur-général of the inhabitants* is injurious to the honor and authority of the officers; it tends to divide the people and separate them from the obedience they owe to their *popular magistrates*."[23] The reformers meanwhile launched a new law suit aimed at excluding all members of the judicial companies from the hôtel de ville and listing nine offenders by name – a veritable honor roll of the traditional leadership.[24] The authorities filed a counter-suit charging them with being "perturbers" of the peace.

The "princely" element of factional relations – the authority of figurehead nobles – was also in play. It should be remembered that Anjou had been the stronghold of Marie de Medicis during her rebellion against Louis XIII and a center of other princely rebellions. Because Maillé-Brézé was an ally of the oligarchy, Lemarié's movement had supported

---

[20] Deliberations, 27, 29 May 1650: AM Angers BB 82.
[21] Deliberations, 31 May, 5 August 1650: AM Angers BB 82.
[22] AD Maine et Loire I B 10 bis: Présidial d'Angers, papier des conclusions de la chambre du conseil, 8, 21, 28 June 1650 (fols. 30–2).
[23] Registre du présidial d'Angers, 1 June 1650: published in *Revue de l'Anjou et de Maine et Loire* 3e série 3 (1861), vol. I, 53; Debidour, *La Fronde angevine*, p. 143 [my italics]. The Parlement did subsequently rule that the title was inadmissible, but then the eight simply changed their name to "deputies of the inhabitants." Arrêt du parlement cited in deliberation 21 June 1650: AM Angers BB 82.
[24] Debidour, *La Fronde angevine*, p. 155.

the duc de La Trémouille in 1649, but this alliance involved no special bonds of loyalty.[25] At this point, however, a remarkable reversal in sentiment took place, raising the formerly despised Brézé to the role of popular hero almost overnight. Fevered negotiations between Brézé and the newly appointed bishop Arnauld had deflected the impending occupation by royal troops and bestowed instant popularity on the governor. On 20 April 1649 the magistrates and the bishop rode through the streets to spread the word to the public that the troops would be sent away. That afternoon Brézé's entry was made even more triumphal when he insisted on saluting Voisin, Lemarié, and other leaders of the popular rebels, telling them that "he admired their firmness."[26]

As if to solidify this unwritten union of governor-turned-clement and rebels-turned-respectable, the Loricard company soon proposed to honor Brézé with a pyramid, for which he consented to lay the first stone. This act of flattery was also an intriguing use of symbolism, for the pyramid was to replace a broken-down post marking the edge of the port, which had held an image of the Virgin called the Notre-Dame du Loricat. The new stone pyramid was to contain the image of the Virgin, the arms of Brézé, and the arms of the city, linking the identity of the popular quarter, a militia company, and the whole rebellion, to the newly sympathetic governor who was adopted as a popular figurehead after the departure of La Trémouille.[27]

This process of identification repeated itself in the spring of 1650. By then Brézé had died and been replaced by the duc de Rohan-Chabot, a future ally of Condé. By a process that is not fully known, Chabot and Lemarié joined forces. On 29 March 1650 when Chabot made his formal entrance into Angers, he was escorted by none other than Lemarié and his wife. The dissident leader had assumed a rank equal to that of the municipal authorities, even though he had no official status. And Chabot had guaranteed his own popularity by linking himself to the popular movement, a luxury which the cautious Beauvais-Nangis in Troyes had not been able to afford. The welcoming cavalcade "composed of some sixty persons of honor, avocats, good bourgeois, merchants, and notaries," was followed by an interesting throng: "a large number of clerics, shop clerks, innkeepers, and second-hand dealers, most of them mounted on unshod farm horses which were about as well equipped as the people riding them."[28] The next day Chabot pardoned citizens who were in prison for being unable to collect their share of taxes and held a

[25] Jousselin, "Journal," pp. 440–1.   [26] Ibid., pp. 443–4.
[27] Ibid., p. 444; deliberation 4 May 1649: AM Angers BB 82.
[28] Jousselin, "Journal," pp. 447–8; procès-verbal of 29 March 1650: AM Angers BB 82.

large ball (the tell-tale patron's banquet), saying that no one was to be excluded because everyone had a right to be in the hôtel de ville. As if to clinch the matter, it was soon proposed, one year after the pyramid for Brézé, to set up a maypole in honor of Chabot in the courtyard of the Logis Barrault where he was staying. This bit of folklore illustrates the use of tradition to cement a relationship between a popular group and a noble figurehead. The ceremony was proposed by none other than Grandmaison who had led the popular forays of 1649, and who personally supplied the tree. The event was martial: companies of guards and all the captains of the militia, along with drums, trumpets, and musicians, escorted the tree from the city gate to Chabot's door, where the governor thanked them and offered wine to the soldiers and served dinner to the maire and the officers. It was noted that no may pole had been erected in this spot since 1620, and on that occasion that the pole had been erected in the presence of Marie de Medicis, who was herself in rebellion.[29]

In early 1651 the city's woes intensified, first because of a disastrous flood that hit the port and the Loricard stronghold especially hard and then because of a massive lodging of royal troops on the parishes, even while the "deputies of the inhabitants" continued their law suits. Agitation between the factions grew during the municipal elections of Spring 1651. The reformers wanted Voisin, the agitator of 1649, chosen as maire, but Chabot and the bishop persuaded the crowd to accept as compromise candidate Michel Bruneau, a venerable avocat who was popular without being seditious.[30] Shortly after, with Bruneau in power, we hear again of murmurings against the gabelle, refusals to pay taxes, and a crowd of women attacking a péage collector.[31]

From December 1651 to 29 February 1652 Chabot led Angers into open rebellion on behalf of the princes. This time a resident governor had initiated the revolt, but it was clearly desired by much of the population, and the local militia companies pitched in with evident relish. We learn that the boatmen of the Port Ligny, heart of the Loricard quarter, were enthusiastic supporters and we can presume that the reformers enjoyed the affair as they had in 1649.[32] Voisin was constantly at Chabot's side. The governor, though firmly in command, still needed the support of the population. He flattered the urban militia officers by allowing them to accompany him "acting like almost as great masters as himself," but he

---

[29] Deliberation of 6, 10 June 1620: AM Angers BB 65; procès- verbal of planting of the mai, 3 May 1650: BB 82, fol. 122.   [30] Debidour, *La Fronde angevine*, p. 390.
[31] A pastrycook was arrested for uttering "insolences" that were "called sedition." Jousselin, "Journal," p. 456.   [32] Ibid., p. 457.

was privately rather contemptuous towards them, and they did not completely trust him either.[33]

When the royal army actually approached to support the traditional authorities, the popular movement understandably lost its initiative. There were heroic acts of defense, but in the end the rebel cause began to appear hopeless, and crowds of women and desperate citizens began to plead for an amnesty. A capitulation was signed on 28 February, followed by the inevitable troop ravages, new taxes, and the installation of mazarinists from the présidial in all important posts.

The Loricard rebellion had been unusual in the way it combined the forces of an impulsive popular movement and the direction of an organized faction. One senses that the elite reformers would not have achieved as much as they did without the autonomous protests of the popular parishes, which already existed and did not have to be called into being by the sort of streetcorner recruiting we saw in Aix or the reliance on personal loyalties so evident in Marseille. On the other hand the popular movement would have remained improvisational without the leadership of the militia captains and the merchant reformers and their constitutional pretexts for government restructuring. Finally, both parties profited from the legitimation and military expertise provided by princely figureheads like Maillé-Brézé and Rohan-Chabot.

Once the frondeur figureheads were gone, the close alliance dissolved and the elite reformers and popular protesters were left to pursue their separate paths. The leaders of the reformers, now in exile in Paris, resumed their former strategy by initiating a new appeal to the Parlement and expressed in pamphlets their frustration at being excluded from power. One polemic accused Bishop Arnauld, who had turned against the frondeurs, of "having no master but the Mazarin," of "advantaging those who have established their fortunes on our ruins," and of "abandoning your flock to follow wayward lambs, by which we mean the maltôtiers, cheats, extortionists, simoniacs, and counterfeiters." Royal troops had been called in, the author asserted, because "it was state policy to force the Loricards, who were known by name at court, to submit to the yoke of the magistrates" when all they wanted was to "reestablish the officers in their posts according to the terms of the peace . . . stop the levy of taxes on us, restore to us the freedom to pursue our appeals in the Parlement, see that the inhabitants are safe in the city."[34] Thus the elite reformers consid-

[33] Abbé Arnauld, *Mémoires de l'abbé Arnauld* [*Collection des mémoires relatifs à l'histoire de France*, ed. Petitot, 2e série, vol. 34] (Paris, 1824), p. 297; Debidour, *La Fronde angevine*, pp. 207–8.

[34] "La plainte de la response à la lettre pastorale de l'Evesque d'Angers, bruslée par les Mazarins de la ville d'Angers," reproduced in Debidour, *La Fronde angevine*, pp. 396–9.

ered *themselves* to be the Loricards and defined their movement as a constitutional battle for their own participation and freedom from fiscal oppression. Except for the polemical reference to maltôtiers they made no allusion to the needs of the broader community.

But community groups also continued, in their own way, to express adversion to the authorities' complicity in favoritism, mismanagement, and unfair distribution of fiscal burdens. In October 1656 crowds started once again attacking tax collectors and causing disturbances.[35] Totally exasperated and, since the events of the Fronde, fully conscious of their inability to rally popular support, the maire and échevins wrote to the absent lieutenant governor asking for a firm repression on the grounds that "you will be better obeyed than the popular magistrates [themselves] whom the common people often accuse of everything that doesn't go their way, to the point of blaming them for war, epidemics, and drought."[36] These words were confirmed soon after by the riot which occurred on 22 October.[37] Perhaps the crowd which invaded the hôtel de ville, a "great quantity of persons of both sexes most of them unknown persons of low condition," recalled Lemarié's coup of seven years earlier. In any event they had no such respectable leader, and their demands were far less constitutional: "that they wanted no more maltôte or maltôtiers, no more pancartes nor sou pour pot, no more guardhouses nor gabeleurs at the gates of town; and that all maltôtiers had to be killed and exterminated, *starting with those in the corps de ville.*"

This compelling popular view of the problem (invoking retribution against authorities) was reinforced by direct action: "Monsieur de la Daulmerye, it was your father who imposed the first maltôte in Angers, and you must be the one to remove it," said an aging "beggar." Another man, brandishing a shoe with a spike in it, tried to strike the échevins, crying "What are we waiting for, why aren't we thrashing these maltôtiers from the corps de ville?" One man grabbed the contrôleur Rousseau, while another, cursing and trying to drag the échevin Syette from his seat, asked him "Was it you, Monsieur, who said that half a dozen inhabitants should be hanged?" Meanwhile others tried to restrain them, saying "No, it wasn't him, it was that one next to him," and one man, illustrating the other side of this very intimate form of rebellion, told échevin Gaultier: "Monsieur, you will not be harmed; I will answer body for body for your life because you are not a maltôtier like the others." The échevins only

[35] "Registre du Présidial," 1 December 1656.
[36] Debidour, *La Fronde angevine*, pp. 314–15.
[37] "Sédition du 22 octobre 1656," reprinted in Debidour, *La Fronde angevine*, pp. 400–4, from AM Angers BB 86.

escaped by issuing an order on the spot meeting all the demands, which the crowd carried off after asking for many copies.

These cases provide us with a better understanding of how popular and elite urban movements and princely rebellions fitted together. In Troyes Beauvais-Nangis faced popular unrest that he wanted no part of, but he nevertheless had a reputation with the crowd which played a role in the situation, and he was well aware of his influence, as were his rival noble commanders. In Agen Condé and Conti tried to stir up support for their own purposes, but although they had clients and supporters in the city, they never succeeded in rallying the critical mass needed to swing the city to their side. Meanwhile consuls, métiers, and militia companies imposed their own agenda by taking over meetings, raising barricades, and preparing for street-by-street resistance.

In Angers the comparable popular movement was prepared by years of aggravation to link up with both local leaders and outside figureheads. Elite insiders helped legitimize the movement by encasing it in legal appeals and formal complaints, while princely outsiders added the crucial dimension of military leadership, gallantry, and support from outside the walls. To extend themselves, popular movements seemed to gravitate towards this sort of identification which raised them up in esteem but at the same time made them subject to forces beyond their control. In Angers, as elsewhere, the most interesting popular movements had a life of their own and expressed their concerns in their own distinctive ways. They were not merely mobs responding to the call from leaders, but independent forces that momentarily blossomed, then were smothered, through their princely connections. The greatest example was the Ormée of Bordeaux, to which we now turn.

10   Popular politics in Bordeaux's Fronde

Bordeaux was a city with a strong tradition of self-generated popular revolt marked by periodic clashes between the popular quarters and the Chapeau Rouge.[1] It already suffered from chronic rivalries between the jurats, the sovereign courts, and the governor over jurisdictional authority. Suddenly during the Fronde the population was drawn by the Parlement into two wars against the king which tested everyone's notion of community. Condé and the princes meanwhile tried to enlist this collective energy on behalf of their own battle against the crown. But none of these movements was possible without building popular support, and the people of Bordeaux were anything but passive in their ability to seize the initiative and impose their own views about their community. Their experiences from 1648 to 1653 included all the elements we have seen in other places: spontaneous movements, battles for factional followings, and princely leadership. But out of the crossfire emerged a popular party, the Ormée, which turned out to be the most sophisticated popular movement since the Paris League.[2]

[1] We examined the revolt of 1635 in chapter 6 and the revolt of 1675, which came *after* these events, in chapter 7.

[2] Beyond the histories of Bordeaux cited in chapters 6 and 7, the Ormée has been discussed many times in a variety of ways. I have leaned heavily on the pioneering synthesis in English by Sal Alexander Westrich, *The Ormée of Bordeaux: a Revolution during the Fronde* (Baltimore, 1972) and on the expertise of Christian Jouhaud, both in his "Idées et mentalités d'opposants Ormistes (Bordeaux 1651–1653)," TER, Université de Bordeaux III, 1973; and in his synthesis, *Mazarinades: la Fronde des mots* (Paris, 1985), pp. 127–53, 185–208. Another recent study is Helmut Kötting, *Die Ormée (1651–1653): Gestaltende Kräfte und Personenverbindungen der Bordelaiser Fronde* (Munich, 1983). Important documents are reproduced in Eckart Birnsticl, *Die Fronde in Bordeaux 1648–1653* (Frankfurt, 1985). Two classic discussions are Ernst H. Kossmann, *La Fronde* (Leiden, 1954), pp. 245–58; and Philip A. Knachel, *England and the Fronde: the Impact of the English Civil War and Revolution on France* (Ithaca, NY, 1967), pp. 179–214. For a broad, readable account, see Orest Ranum, *The Fronde: a French Revolution 1648–1652* (New York, 1993), pp. 215–41, 244–70; for further details and insights, see Yves-Marie Bercé, *Histoire des Croquants*, vol. I, pp. 496–503, 511–16; another synthetic view is Perez Zagorin, *Rebels and Rulers 1500–1660*, 2 vols. (Cambridge, 1982), vol. II, pp. 216–19. An old but detailed history of the Parlement is C. B. F. Boscheron des Portes, *Histoire du Parlement de Bordeaux depuis sa création jusqu'à sa suppression (1451–1790)*, 2 vols. (Bordeaux, 1877).

The first war, 1649

When the Fronde in Paris created a power vacuum in Bordeaux, the obvious issue was who could seize command: the Parlement or the governor.[3] Bernard de Nogaret de la Valette, duc d'Epernon, governor of Guyenne, had a long history of unpopularity. He had first been known to the Bordelais as the man called in by his father to enforce the repression after the 1635 revolt, and he was later associated with attempts by the jurats to impose unpopular taxes. In 1638 he had been disgraced in Spain and condemned to death in absentia by Louis XIII. During the interim from 1638 until 1643, when Epernon was rehabilitated, his replacement had been the prince de Condé, a popular figure who rarely appeared in the province. Thus the reputations of Epernon and Condé were established in the popular mind before 1648. Epernon was a proven scoundrel; Condé was a benevolent hero.

In early 1649 when Epernon started raising troops in the region and building a strategically placed fortress at Libourne which threatened Bordeaux, there was general indignation. Seeing themselves as the primary administrators of the city, the parlementaires seized the opportunity to intervene. Their joint chambers began meeting daily and issuing directives. They dispatched commissioners to Libourne to investigate, called for the abolition of their rival the Cour des Aides, created a war council which met in the hôtel de ville to plan an offensive against the "soldiers" threatening the region, invited nobles to come and help defend the city, and set up a council of finances.[4] They saw themselves as leaders of a civic coalition of corporate authorities. Thus their war council consisted of eleven judges from the Parlement, one trésorier de France, one representative from the sénéchaussée court, someone from each ecclesiastical chapter, two jurats, one bourgeois-avocat, and one "bourgeois de

---

[3] The Fronde in Bordeaux can be explored in several important series of printed documents, including Paul Caraman, "La Fronde à Bordeaux d'après le registre secret du Parlement de Guyenne," in *Archives historiques de la Gironde*, vol. LIII (Paris, 1919–20), pp. 34–86, and vol. LIV (Paris, 1921–2), pp. 1–84 [hereafter *Registre secret*]; *Inventaire sommaire des registres de la jurade 1520 à 1783*, vol. V [vol. X of *Archives municipales de Bordeaux*] (Bordeaux, 1913) [hereafter *Inventaire sommaire*]; *Mémoires de Pierre Lenet* [*Collection des mémoires relatifs à l'histoire de France*, ed. by A. Petitot and Monmerqué, vols. LIII–LIV] (Paris, 1826), covering the year 1650; and Pierre Lenet, *Mémoires concernant l'histoire du prince de Condé* [*Nouvelle collection des mémoires relatifs à l'histoire de France*, vol. XXVI] (Paris, 1854), pp. 527–615, covering the years 1651–9 [these two different collections will be cited as Lenet, *Mémoires*, with volume number]; Cayrac, "Récit de la Fronde à Bordeaux," ed. by F. Gebelin, *Revue historique de Bordeaux* 7 (1914), 5–17, 195–209, 261–71; 11 (1918), 171–81, 230–45 [hereafter Cayrac, "Récit"]. Many documents are also reproduced in Gabriel-Jules comte de Cosnac, *Souvenirs du règne de Louis XIV*, 8 vols. (Paris, 1866–82).

[4] Cour des Aides to Séguier, 3 February 1649: Mousnier, *Lettres et mémoires*, vol. II, p. 909; *Registre secret*, vol. LIII, pp. 76–84, vol. LIV, pp. 1–10.

robe courte." These actions were predicated on the assumption that the parlementaires would control the movement themselves; that they were simply undertaking a preemptive strike against Epernon in order to strengthen their hand in preparation for an eventual negotiation. Notably absent from their deliberations were representatives of the trades and the militia captains, groups which were expected to follow, not participate.

Nevertheless, the people were watching closely and their support was necessary. On 31 March after a delegation of parlementaires had been fired upon by Epernon's soldiers during a touchy negotiation at the Château Trompette, the deputies returned to find the streets filling with citizens angrily arming themselves and building barricades. This popular initiative was not part of their plans, so they replaced some of the militia captains with men loyal to the Parlement. Meanwhile rumors of treachery raised apprehensions in the streets, and there was talk of closing shops and storming houses where armed men were supposed to be hiding in cellars – echoes of 1625 and 1635. On 1 April demonstrators in the quartier Saint Michel demanded the removal of the jurats.[5]

On 1 May the Parlement took a momentous step by organizing a "solemn oath of fidelity and union for the defense of the city." The oath was administered by councillors from the Parlement after Mass in every parish church, with special arrangements for Protestants (who took the oath in the hôtel de ville) and parlementaires (who took the oath from each other).[6] This quasi-civic ceremony, which was to be the prototype for subsequent, more radical oaths, must have aroused strong emotions even as it built new ties between the Parlement and the community. Such a procedure was not unprecedented in times of imminent invasion, but the Parlement was in effect preparing the citizens for rebellion as a way of strengthening its own influence.

This was a dangerous course of action because parlementaire leaders were actually seeking negotiations, not war. By early May the Parlement was talking with René de Voyer d'Argenson, Mazarin's envoy, about a settlement. But the court was splitting between moderates and radicals over how far to carry the rebellion, and on the 12th when the vote was taken to accept an accommodation between the city and Epernon, it was by a majority of only one vote. To the people in the streets this decision smelled of a sellout. The citadel was still being built at Libourne and Epernon was even rumored to be planning to take over the Château du Hâ. Why would the Parlement make a deal? That afternoon a meeting of the conseil de bourgeoisie was boycotted by many of the bourgeois

---

[5] *Registre secret*, vol. LIII, pp. 71–4.
[6] Fonteneil, *Histoire des movemens de Bourdeaux*, vol. I [the only volume written], (Bordeaux, 1651), pp. 121–2.

notables, and instead the room was filled with "unknown persons," while at the door "a large number were shouting that they should not surrender the Château du Hâ or disband the city guard; on the contrary that it should be doubled and that they themselves were ready to serve."[7]

Fearing a loss of popularity, the Parlement undertook an unprecedented series of consultations with civic groups, not unlike Condé when he was trying to rally support in Agen, and with similarly troubling results. Commissioners were sent to meet with the bailiffs of all the trades. These men insisted that they were loyal to the Parlement but didn't want to give up the Château du Hâ or lay down their arms. A second meeting was held with artisans in Saint Michel who went one step further, adding that they themselves wanted to go to demolish the citadel at Libourne and "if the Parlement didn't permit this they would go anyway."[8] On 14 May the conseil de bourgeoisie again discussed an armed march to Libourne, and the raising of a municipal army was proposed by avocats Constant and Laroche.

The Parlement, or at least its conservative leadership, was losing control of the situation. That same day armed protesters jeered and threatened First President Dubernet's carriage as he left the Palais, and followed him all the way to his refuge in the Château du Hâ. The next day, while the conseil de police was meeting in the Parlement's Salle de l'Audience, a noisy group of demonstrators forced its way into the room and demanded authorization to go to Libourne. Every day popular pressure mounted.[9] Virtually all the leaders of the Parlement began absenting themselves from the sessions. On 26 May with only the most half-hearted authorization, an enthusiastic municipal army materialized and marched out of the city with 7,700 infantry and 300 cavalry, including some parlementaires and their sons. This was a loosely organized civic force that obviously reflected planning by neighborhood leaders and parlementaire radicals, but it was beyond the control of the original planners. The consequences were disastrous. On 28 May word reached the city that Commander Chamberet was dead and more than 3,000 others had been killed in action or drowned in the Dordogne.[10]

Negotiations with the crown continued. When Epernon returned to the city on 23 July to enforce a royal pardon and settlement arranged by the archbishop of Bordeaux which called for the exile of the Parlement, he had a very unpleasant visit. First there was a struggle among authorities to avoid holding the keys to the Saint Julien gate where the governor was

[7] *Registre secret*, vol. LIV, pp. 42–65, 74–6; Fonteneil, *Histoire*, p. 144.
[8] *Registre secret*, vol. LIV, p. 76.   [9] Ibid., p. 80.
[10] *Registre secret*, vol. LIV, pp. 74–82; D'Argenson to Séguier, 27 May 1649 summarized in Mousnier, *Lettres*, vol. II, p. 1015.

expected to enter. Popular groups built barricades which forced Epernon to divert his party to another gate. Meanwhile, continuing its outreach into the neighborhoods, the Parlement forbade anyone to ratify the "pardon" and sent commissioners into every quarter to organize resistance. When Epernon arrived at the hôtel de ville only eight out of four hundred bourgeois turned up to answer his summons – a measure of the popularity of the opposition.[11] He left angrily, passing through crowds shouting "to arms, justice is being attacked," and barged into the Palais de Justice, where the Parlement refused to deliberate under duress. When the royal huissiers de la chaîne read the proclamation establishing their exile, the parlementaires voted only to continue sitting pending new remonstrances.[12]

Two days later Epernon made a second attempt to enforce the royal orders, but when armed crowds again assumed insurrectionary postures, the badly shaken governor decided to get out fast. Ignoring the pleadings of the jurats that if he left they "would be exposed to the fury of the people, who neither feared nor loved them," he led his forces down alleys to a side gate and left the city unceremoniously by the back door because the usual portals were blockaded by angry citizens. Fonteneil, who relishes this episode, claims that children who were fighting a war with slingshots outside the walls rallied and showered the governor's retreating forces with rocks as they rode away, while the ramparts filled with angry citizens shouting curses at the receding governor.[13]

Meanwhile Quinqueboeuf and Herbin, the two resplendent huissiers de la chaîne who were accompanying Epernon, faced a horror show of their own. Returning to find an angry crowd gathered outside their lodging, they hastily packed their bags, slipped out a side door, and made their way to the port, where boats filled with arriving Epernon supporters were being attacked by angry citizens. Battered by these "barbarians," the two Parisian process-servers somehow managed to flag down a boatman who was headed up river and pay him 15 pistoles to save their lives. Quinqueboeuf claimed to have been almost torn apart by five or six angry women while Herbin jumped into the water up to his waist and clambered into the boat with people firing rifles at him, shouting "Those are the huissiers of the great chain who suspended the Parlement, kill them!"[14]

---

[11] Fonteneil, *Histoire*, pp. 188–233; Dubernet to Séguier, 28 July 1649: Mousnier, *Lettres*, vol. II, pp. 960–2; jurade, 23–4 July 1649: Bordeaux FF 68; D'Argenson to Séguier, 29 July 1649: Hovyn de Tranchère, *Les dessous de l'histoire* (Paris, 1886), vol. II, pp. 32–3.

[12] Procès-verbal of Pierre Quinqueboeuf and Nicolas Herbin, 24 July 1649: Ms. fr. 18752, 137; jurade 23–4 July 1649: AM Bordeaux FF 68; *Inventaire sommaire*, vol. V, p. 151; Boscheron des Portes, *Histoire*, vol. II, pp. 46–8; Fonteneil, *Histoire*, pp. 233–53.

[13] Fonteneil, *Histoire*, pp. 253–4.

[14] Quinqueboeuf and Herbin to Séguier from Cadillac, 28 July 1649: Mousnier, *Lettres*, vol. II, pp. 964–7.

Figure 13 The waterfront of Bordeaux around 1650 as portrayed by resident Dutch artist Hermann van der Hem. The medieval wall separating the city from the port is visible. Just to the right of center is the old Château Trompette before its reconstruction after the 1675 rebellion. The tiny twin pointed towers to the left of the center of the skyline are the great bell tower (grosse cloche) attached to the hôtel de ville.

Bordeaux continued in rebellion for the rest of 1649. The Parlement replaced the jurats, raised a navy on the river, and on 19 December during the height of a royal siege, administered another mass oath in all the parish churches.[15] The war was characterized by skirmishes in the countryside, pillaging of the rural estates of Bordelais notables by Epernon's men, and mutual exchanges between the city and the Château Trompette, which bombarded the city for weeks causing fires and deaths until it was taken by triumphant citizens in October. An amnesty was ultimately signed on 5 January 1650, reflecting the Peace of Paris of 23 December in the north.

Already Bordeaux had produced an unusual movement. Unlike Angers, the city had a Parlement to focus its resistance. But the sovereign court's carefully orchestrated coalition was too fragile to contain the upsurge of popular indignation that greeted any attempt at compromise once the resistance was under way. New civic leaders were planning journées, taking over meetings, and rejecting compromise solutions. We

[15] Boscheron des Portes, *Histoire*, vol. II, p. 62.

might take as typical the avocats Constant and Laroche, solid citizens who demanded the march on Libourne on 14 May, both of whom were later members of the Ormée.

The second war, 1650

In May 1650 the news arrived that the princesse de Condé and her entourage were coming to seek refuge in Bordeaux.[16] Mazarin's imprisonment of her husband in February, along with Conti and their brother-in-law the duc de Longueville, must have confirmed many of the Bordelais' negative suspicions. But the princess's arrival presented a dilemma for the authorities. The jurade and the Parlement would face rival command centers, and splits would widen between those advocating obedience to the crown ("mazarins"), those advocating behind-the-scenes resistance to Mazarin and Epernon led by the Parlement (the "petite fronde"), and those who wanted to join the princes overtly in all-out rebellion (the "grande fronde"). For weeks the population enjoyed the pageant as the regional nobility in all its finery flocked into the city to pay respects to this courageous lady and her young son, Condé's heir, as she made daily trips through the streets in her carriage, flanked by well-wishers, on rounds of visits to leading parlementaires and nobles. She was assisted by Pierre Lenet, a shrewd robe noble from Burgundy who was Condé's chief strategist and who left detailed memoirs of these events.[17]

As weeks passed and Epernon's army moved closer to the city, an internal power struggle was waged in the streets, in city council meetings, and in the Parlement over how deeply the city would be committed to rebellion on behalf of the princes. It was a factional struggle not unlike the comparable battles in Aix, but there were also signs that a segment of the population was asserting its will over and beyond the demonstrations arranged by one party or another.[18] On 21 June the fall of the nearby Saint George Island to Epernon precipitated an invasion of the Palais by

---

[16] The princess was soon joined by the duc de Bouillon and the duc de la Rochefoucauld, and the duchesse de Longueville and other members of the Condé party came and went at various times. For simplicity, I refer to this changing group as "the princes" or sometimes "the princess."   [17] Lenet, *Mémoirs*, vol. LIII, pp. 282–3.

[18] There were, indeed, crowds organized as pressure groups by the various factions. Lenet describes proudly in his memoirs how he used a crowd to drive Alvimar, Mazarin's chief negotiator, out of the city. Another attack by a crowd on Thibaud de La Vie, procureur-général of the Parlement, on 5 June gives the impression of a fomented crowd (led by the marquis de Sauveboeuf, one of the city's commanders in 1649) that got out of hand, pillaging the house of La Vie and threatening his wife and family. Lenet's comment was that "truthfully all wise men opposed the violence in this action"; and he observed "it is not always easy to excite seditions, but when they are aroused, it is difficult to stop their course." Lenet, *Mémoires*, vol. LIII, pp. 324–5; Cayrac, "Recit," p. 202.

crowds denouncing traitors. On 22 June the "general assembly" of the city demanded a new "union" which, in this context, meant a general oath on behalf of the princes. On 24 June another crowd invaded the Palais calling for Union and the killing of anyone opposed to it, focusing particularly on conservative Presidents Daffis and Pommiers, who complained to Lenet that "they were being exposed at every moment to the fury of the people."[19] On 27 July after the Saint George Island had been retaken and the prisoners brought triumphantly to Bordeaux, one soldier who cried out "Vive le roi et M. d'Epernon" was murdered and dragged through the streets by crowds that cut off his nose, ears, and "shameful parts," according to Lenet. "Thus it is dangerous to speak or act against the current of the inclinations of a mutinied populace," he concluded.[20]

A showdown on 11 July suggests the existence of a semi-autonomous civic force.[21] The princess was still demanding to know whether she was to be "received" by the Parlement, which would be tantamount to the court's declaring a rebellion. That morning a large, disciplined crowd stormed into the Palais for the third time in two months and pushed its way into the salle de l'audience, saying noisily that "we want a union with messieurs les princes otherwise you'll be sorry." The scandalized judges pushed the crowd out of the room and tried to adjourn their session, but five hundred men with drawn swords blocked their exit from the building, declaring that the parlementaires could not leave until they had proclaimed the union. So they retreated back into their chamber where they remained semi-captive until five in the afternoon.

The Parlement had been beleaguered by an organized force that might or might not have been linked to the princes, who certainly stood to gain by the action. Lenet saw this as a day of great "disorder," and claimed that the princes were not responsible for it. He describes going to the Parlement by himself and passing crowds lining the streets with men shouting "Vive le Roi et les princes," swords in hand. Inside the Palais he found the parlementaires fighting mad. A disoriented President Daffis was pacing up and down cursing "that they were about to be slaughtered."[22] Lenet went out and urged the assembled multitude to go home, but they refused to budge, displaying that characteristic wariness of promises that we have encountered before, and still insisting on a *union*. Finally Jurat Pontac-Beautiran arrived with a contingent of the militia which fired on the crowd, killing about five people, after which the occupiers beat an orderly retreat and the Parlement went home.

[19] Lenet, *Mémoires*, vol. LIII, p. 351.   [20] Ibid., p. 358.
[21] Major account in ibid., pp. 385–92. See also Boscheron des Portes, *Histoire*, vol. II, pp. 95–107. Additional details in Ms. fr. 18752, fols. 234, 238.
[22] Lenet, *Mémoires*, vol. LIII, p. 389.

This journée suggests the existence of a nascent third force. The crowds supporting the princess may have been stirred up by the princes' agitation, despite the denials of Lenet, but they had an independent existence. They were massive and organized, thus evidently constituting semi-official contingents of the citizen militia, and they were capable of parleys and orderly retreats. But they were only a segment of the militia because the jurats still had forces that could be called up against them. Their purpose was political in that they came to demand allegiance to the princes, but it was distinctive in that the "union" they insisted upon meant something more to them, something civic and emotive that transcended a mere deal between the Parlement and the princess. We can only conclude that this military demonstration represented a segment of the bourgeoisie in arms, resuming the form they had taken on the march to Libourne the previous year and in the skirmishes with Epernon a few weeks earlier. The city could now muster at least an informal force without the aid of the jurade (which opposed it), the Parlement (which was entrapped by it), or the princes (who were compromised by it).

On 15 July reports that Mazarin would come to Bordeaux led to new rounds of feverish negotiations in which all sides tried to take advantage of the militant citizenry. On 19 July the princess summoned the "leading bourgeois and captains of quarters" to her residence and asked directly for their "friendship," which was warmly granted. On 20 July an assembly at the hôtel de ville agreed to tax the inhabitants for war, and the jurats agreed to ask the Parlement to grant the princess's request. On 21 July the Parlement caved in and ratified a "union" against Mazarin.[23] Thus the city had reinvented its "union," this time with the impetus coming from the "bourgeoisie" instead of the Parlement. As the military emergency deepened, it appears that popular groups, acting as an independent civic force but closely allied with the princes, were monitoring the city on their own. On 26 July a courier who had delivered royal letters had to take refuge in the archbishopric, where an angry crowd threatened to throw him into the Garonne; and when the jurats dispatched Pontac-Beautiran (who had fired on the crowd besieging the Parlement) as envoy to the king, a crowd kept watch at his house all night and told him in the morning that if he went on this deputation they would burn down his residence while he was gone and kill him when he returned.[24]

To this popular vindictiveness was joined a good measure of civic patriotism, as we can see in the enthusiasm with which bourgeois soldiers

[23] Ibid., pp. 403, 407.   [24] Ibid., pp. 431–3.

prepared to defend their city.[25] Cayrac, a city receiver and militia captain, looked back on those days with relish. During the night there were special rounds, procedures, and passwords, with pride of place going to those who occupied the hôtel de ville and those guarding the Château Trompette. Meanwhile peasants who took refuge in the city were put to work building fortifications and paid daily out of a fund collected from the bourgeois, who thereby bought exemption from work services. As the siege emergency grew, companies on duty volunteered themselves to work on the fortifications, and women also pitched in, supposedly including the princess.[26] A truce was arranged on the 16th and a peace signed on the 28th. The terms granted amnesty to the city, a respectable retreat for the princess and her followers, and the removal of Epernon as governor.

For two years the people of Bordeaux had undergone a remarkable apprenticeship in civic politics. Summoned first by the Parlement to oppose Epernon and then by the princes to oppose Mazarin, they had learned how to mobilize a powerful civic force that came out of, but did not equal, the traditional militia companies, and they had used it to impose upon the jurade, the Parlement, and the princes something of their own interpretation of the problem. Twice they had mobilized their forces against the "enemy"; twice their leaders had negotiated settlements, but the same problems always seemed to return.

Genesis of the Ormée

From 1651 to 1653 an even greater collapse of national unity provided new opportunities for independent power struggles in Bordeaux. Here are the circumstances that confronted the city. In February 1651 the princes were released. Mazarin left the country, and that May Condé was officially named governor of Guyenne, replacing Epernon. Thus the spring of 1651 was a time of cautious rejoicing in Bordeaux. Then in August the queen turned against Condé and in September he and his party returned to Bordeaux, followed soon after by the princess and her entourage, to lead a new rebellion. The whole cycle of resistance was starting again. In November Condé departed to raise an army, leaving his brother Conti in charge. Mazarin returned to France, and fighting resumed. Thus the winter of 1651 and the spring of 1652 were devoted to

---

[25] The number of bourgeois companies had been increased by the committee of direction from twelve to thirty-six, with twelve serving on any given day. This expansion would have permitted the naming of supporters to key posts and produced a higher intensity of neighborhood involvement.

[26] Lenet, *Mémoires*, vol. LIII, p. 510. Cayrac, "Récit," gives a colorful account, however his inaccurate dates make it difficult to pinpoint the events he is narrating.

civil war, much of it close to home. In July 1652 Condé took control of Paris; but the various parties at court started quarreling again. The king's party gradually grew stronger; Mazarin left again for Germany to clear the air; and Louis XIV reentered the capital triumphantly in October, effectively ending the Fronde in the north. But Condé continued to fight on with Bordeaux as a base and Spain as an ally. So from the autumn of 1652 until their ultimate capitulation in August 1653 the Bordelais were drawn into an active rebellion against the crown, and it was during this most intense phase of the conflict that the Ormée dominated the city.

The beginnings of the Ormée are obscure. In the course of the spring of 1651 a group of citizens started meeting hundreds strong on a platform planted with elm trees (hence the name Ormée) that was situated on the popular end of the city near Sainte Eulalie and not far from the Château du Hâ. Jouhaud pictures this autonomous space, separate from the city with its partisan quarters, as capable of inspiring feelings of municipal unity and papering over conflicts of class and neighborhood.[27] According to Filhot, the first gatherings had taken place in the open ditches near the hôtel de ville when citizens reacted negatively to rumors that Epernon was being reinstated as governor. When the jurats threatened to fire on them they moved farther away to the Ormée platform "where they would be in liberty."[28] Thus from the very first the ormistes presented themselves as a shadow government paralleling the jurade.

The meetings of the Ormée were unique. Most seventeenth-century riots had been organized by menu peuple on ramparts and in cemeteries on the spur of the moment. Some had been plotted by instigators in taverns. Factional coups had been organized in the mansions of aristocrats. But most of these meetings had been impromptu gatherings immediately preceding some anticipated event. The ormistes, by contrast, met for almost a year before turning to direct action; they gathered on neutral ground, and they gradually developed a critique of the entire local political structure without limiting their targets to a specific tax or a particular scapegoat. From the outset they must have been led by respected members of the community. As the apologist Lartigue put it, they were "the most distinguished [les plus apparens] people from the bourgeoisie, those not tied down by necessity to their work or confined to the shops."[29] Lartigue may have exaggerated, but it stands to reason that crowds of menu peuple would have had neither the confidence nor the

---

[27] Jouhaud, *Mouvements populaires*, p. 36.
[28] A. Communay (ed.), *L'Ormée à Bordeaux d'après le journal inédit de J. de Filhot* (Bordeaux, 1887), pp. 172–3.
[29] "Apologie pour l'Ormée," reprinted in Birnstiel, *Die Fronde*, p. 275.

leisure time to gather so conspicuously in a place away from their usual haunts.

Such people, many of whom had begun to assume responsibility during the mobilizations of 1649 and 1650, must have consolidated their ties with civic groups during the festive revelries of early 1651. When the news arrived at carnival time of Condé's release from captivity, shops closed for three days and "there were nothing but bonfires, dances, and other public celebrations."[30] A "person dressed in red with a two-horned bonnet of the same color, wearing a mask representing His Eminence, and mounted on a mule with a torch in his hand" was paraded boisterously through the streets by "two or three hundred persons armed with naked swords, pistols, and guns," after which a mock decapitation was performed in the ditches of the hôtel de ville, future site of the first Ormée meeting. This festive humiliation of the Devil Mazarin was thus organized by an armed crowd not unlike later Ormée troops and probably linked to the militia companies.[31] When news arrived of the princes' entrance into Paris, bourgeois in the rue de la Rousselle served wine to passersby who would drink to the health of the princes – again we see banquets – and on the first Sunday of Lent (26 February) there was a bonfire in the place du Palais, scene of public executions, at which a mannequin of the Cardinal was immolated wearing an actual cap that Mazarin had left behind during his recent visit.[32] The following Sunday the militia companies planned and financed their own symbolic bonfire in front of the hôtel de ville in which the captains and their companies paraded in full regalia, resplendent in ribbons, wearing slingshots, symbol of the Fronde. Cayrac reports that every company created a float and that "certain avocats" helped devise themes based on the *Metamorphoses* of Ovid.

Banquets, parades, learned satire, popular ribaldry: all of these provided ideal occasions for potential leaders, such as the avocats mentioned above, to build emotional ties with artisanal followings. It must have been shortly afterwards that the meetings on the platform began. Later in the spring there is further evidence that the Ormée was flexing its muscles. When news arrived in May that Condé had been appointed governor of Guyenne, Cayrac describes more celebratory street banquets with long tables seating a hundred and food catered by innkeepers.[33] The Ormée is

[30] Cayrac, "Récit," p. 174.
[31] Anonymous letter published by Francis Loirette, "Une Mazarinade en action: le carnaval de Bordeaux (1651)," *Bulletin et mémoires de la Société archéologique de Bordeaux* 66 (1972), 82–8.
[32] The cap had been kept by a local *callotier* from whom Mazarin had ordered new *calots*, and it is tempting to imagine this subversive local artisan deliberately setting aside this relic of the hated enemy and passing it along to his friends.
[33] Cayrac, "Récit," pp. 176–7.

associated with these festivities by a document found by Westrich in which the "illustrious frondeurs of the Ormée" invite the bearer to a mass in Sainte Eulalie in honor of peace, followed by a dinner at the Château du Hâ on 14 June.[34] By July the Ormée was corresponding officially with Condé.

The princes took up residence again in Bordeaux at the end of September 1651 and laid plans for a real rebellion. They signed a treaty with Spain, arranged with the Parlement and the jurats to collect tax revenues for a war chest, denounced and expelled enemies from the Cour des Aides, and set up a Council of Direction with representatives from the Parlement, the princes, and the jurade. In a sense these measures simply revived the steps taken during the previous war, but the context was fundamentally changed by the active direction of the princes and the pressuring of the Ormée.

But as the authorities proceeded with their planning, voices began to be heard from "below." Certain "bourgeois" were rejecting the assumption that business could be conducted without consulting them, especially when finances were involved. On 20 December 1651, when the Parlement's assembly of chambers decided to take their own *gages* out of public funds, these "bourgeois" protested to the point where a different system had to be set up. Fiscal matters were now to be audited by two parlementaires, two representatives of the jurade, and two other "bourgeois" – probably budding ormistes. On 3 January 1652, the day the Parlement was to vote on a formal declaration against Mazarin, Procureur-Général Pontac was waylaid by a crowd of one hundred to two hundred persons who said they were acting on behalf of "some bourgeois." They commandeered packets from the king and threatened to burn down his house.[35]

That same day, in the presence of the princes and the jurats, the Parlement declared a new "treaty and contract of the union." In this document the princes took the city under their protection and princes, jurats, and Parlement swore to kill Cardinal Mazarin and "post his head on a principal gate of the city" on behalf of all "bons français."[36] This was

[34] As Westrich points out in *The Ormée*, p. 23, note 7, Labadie in *Nouveau supplément à la bibliographie des Mazarinades* (Paris, 1904), no. 199, places this invitation in 1653, but the stated date, Wednesday 14 June (Westrich incorrectly says Thursday) occurred only in 1651.

[35] BM Bordeaux ms. 1501: Registre secret of the Parlement, 20 December 1651 and 3 January 1652. This manuscript source should be distinguished from the printed excerpts published by Caraman.

[36] The text of the union is reproduced in Birnstiel, *Die Fronde*, pp. 231–41. The agreement also stipulated that finances should be reformed; intendants and tax farmers abolished; rentes and gages paid regularly; capable persons named to governorships; and governors denied the right of succession within families.

a "unity" program to the extent that it embraced the widespread opposition to Mazarin and Epernon, but it was still a program designed for princes and royal officers which contained little for the commoners of Bordeaux and which absolutely ignored the Ormée.

Such arrogance was no longer going to be tolerated. On 22 January the Parlement set up a committee to rule on "suspects" but preserved its own jurisdiction over "privilégiés" – that is, persons like themselves. Three days later the unnamed "assembly" of bourgeois sent emissaries to insist on more rigorous prosecution of six notorious individuals, some of whom *were*, in fact, parlementaires. The Parlement responded by reminding the jurats to disperse illicit meetings of "bourgeois."[37] When news of Condé's defeat before Agen and of that city's uprising in favor of the royalist army of Harcourt further outraged the Bordelais in March, the Ormée offered to raise their own independent regiment to help Condé.[38] On 10 April the Parlement once again instructed the jurats to monitor the "daily assemblies being held at the ormée" as threats to public tranquillity. The next day the Ormée held an armed meeting "to force suspect persons, even some of messieurs of the Parlement, to leave town." The Parlement sent the jurats to break up the meeting. The ormistes dispersed, but before doing so they handed the jurats an ominous sealed message containing the names of nine prominent parlementaire suspects.[39]

These heady days in the spring of 1652 must have marked the high point of Ormée enthusiasm. In *La Colombe Miraculeuse*, Geoffroy Gay, an aging priest, litterateur and loyal ormiste, describes a miraculous event that occurred on 15 April, just at the time of the budding conflict with the Parlement.[40] He pictures a large meeting at the platform convening at 7 a.m., consisting of several hundred "generous and faithful bourgeois from the city who aimed at nothing more than the glory of God, the service of the king and of Monsieur le Prince, and the welfare of the people." They sat in a circle and spoke by rank, in a style reminiscent of official meetings. During their deliberations a dove appeared, perched for a long time in the elm tree under which the meeting was being held, flew

---

[37]   Registre secret, 25 January 1652: AM Bordeaux ms. 1501.

[38]   *Le Courrier de la Guyenne*, quoted in Birnstiel, *Die Fronde*, p. 259. On 22 March Condé wrote to "messieurs les bourgeois de l'Ormée de Bordeaux" thanking them for their offers sent via Villars, who was thus already one of the Ormée leaders: AM Bordeaux FF 68.

[39]   Registre secret, 10, 11, 12, 13 April 1652: AM Bordeaux, ms. 1501. The proscribed were councillors from the "petite fronde" according to Westrich, plus Pontac, procureur-général.

[40]   Text in Birnstiel, *Die Fronde*, pp. 242–7; on Gay see Christian Jouhaud, "Geoffroy Gay: une lecture de la Fronde Bordelaise," *Annales du Midi* 91 (1979), 273–95 and Jouhaud, *Mazarinades*, pp. 194–201.

Figure 14 Bordeaux at the time of the Fronde as portrayed by resident Dutch artist Hermann van der Hem. We are outside the wall on the west side, looking south. To the left are the cathedral and the bishop's palace, headquarters of the princes. In the rear is the Château du Hâ and the spire of Sainte Eulalie, behind which was the platform where the Ormée assembled.

off to the cathedral, circled other churches, then returned to its original perch at the Ormée, just as news arrived that Condé, who had disappeared from view after the defeat at Agen, was safe. Gay claims that the very same dove, harbinger of good news or perhaps divine favor, had appeared to the Ormée a year earlier when it was believed that Condé would be denied the governorship and Epernon might return. In this way he connected the early meetings at the platform with the party of 1652 and lent a prophetic tone to the movement. Gay also captured the more apocalyptic mood that was emerging, at least among the most belligerent participants. It was necessary, he editorialized, for those seeking the "good of the people and the glory of God" to expel from the city "the crows, the Cains and Judas, the parricides, I say, those denatured traitors who still remain in the agencies [ordres] of the city."

The Ormée was becoming a militant party led by agitators like Christophe Dureteste, a minor legal functionary, and Pierre Villars, an avocat in the Parlement. In early May armed men started massing in front of the houses of targeted parlementaires and demanding that Conti issue "passports" which would exile questionable individuals. A rumor campaign inspired by ormistes gives us a glimpse of the network of lawyers who must have been instrumental in the movement. Investigating the source of rumors accusing parlementaires of treason, the Parlement discovered that the accusation had originated in a note slipped to Councillor Raymond by Procureur Galibert; he had heard it from Bastide, procureur in the sénéchaussée, who had heard it from Quentin, avocat, in the presence of Rocques Bacqué, also procureur in the sénéchaussée. Bastide and Rocques were ormistes, connected to a network of legal functionaries. About the same time, President Pichon attended a meeting at the Prince de Conti's residence, where he found the room filled with persons "from among those who assemble at the ormée, who called him a Mazarin and an Epernoniste several times, saying that he should be killed."[41]

On 13 May the Parlement threw down the gauntlet and issued yet another order banning illicit assemblies. That same day a crowd led by Geoffroy Gay threatened President Daffis with attack if he enforced the order, and certain ormistes issued their own proclamation in the style of an arrêt, threatening the Parlement directly:

Notice having been received by the company of the Ormière assembled in service to the king and Monsieur le Prince, of a certain injurious and unreasonable arrêt of the Parlement of this city which impedes and obstructs the good intentions of the aforesaid faithful assembly, we say that if the aforesaid arrêt is published by the aforementioned municipality, the authors, adherants and accomplices of the arrêt will be directly attacked. The Parlement is prohibited on pain of death from using such procedures in the future, to oppose which the Ormière will take arms, enjoining and exhorting all loyal bourgeois of the city to lend aid on pain of being declared traitors to their patrie and as such being banished in perpetuity from the aforesaid city and their goods confiscated. [signed] Lormiere [followed by various signatures and sealed with a great seal of red wax].[42]

This document may have been pure bravado on the part of a few militants, but it demonstrates the thinking of the extremists. On 17 May a straw dummy wearing parlementary robes was found hanged from an elm tree (*ormeau*) outside the Palais; soon there were joyous processions of

[41] Registre secret: 17, 20, 22 April: AM Bordeaux ms. 1501. To establish membership in the Ormée I am using Westrich's published list, which he took from a letter sent to Condé on 13 May 1652: Westrich, *The Ormée*, pp. 142–7.

[42] This widely quoted document may have been drawn up by only a few radicals, as Jouhaud believes, but it marks an important transition to action against the Parlement. It was reproduced in "La manifeste des Bourdelois," published in Paris around June 1652 and reprinted in Birnstiel, *Die Fronde*, pp. 248–52; but the version translated here, a copy deposited in BN Dupuy 775, fol. 183, was obviously from a different source, since the wording varies.

ormistes to erect a maypole in honor of the princes – note the parallel to Angers.[43]

Making good their threat to banish their enemies by 3 June, the Ormée waited until the deadline had arrived and then acted directly, ignoring Conti's request that they desist.[44] Two thousand ormistes wearing elm branches in their hats marched through the Chapeau Rouge past the houses of the proscribed:

> Dureteste, taking with him fifteen or sixteen fusiliers who had been picked from his troops, descended first on M. de Mons, councillor in the Enquêtes, ordering him in the name of the Ormée to leave before six the next morning or risk losing his life. They then went to see M. Le President Pichon and all the others in the same manner, adding to their announcement a deluge of threats so outrageous and scandalous that even those who were with them were horrified.[45]

In all, fourteen parlementaires were expelled. Then the ormistes drew up new accusations against two jurats, another dozen parlementaires, and various bourgeois, and set a new deadline of 10 June for *their* departure.[46]

It was becoming necessary for the traditional leaders to counterattack. Conti commanded the radicals not to meet, and conservatives in the Chapeau Rouge and Chartreux quarters made plans to take up arms and seize the ormistes as a way of preempting another journée of expulsions. Conti himself promised that on the night of 9–10 June he would fetch the "bons bourgeois" from the Chapeau Rouge district and help them occupy the hôtel de ville. But that night a suspicious Ormée sent a patrol into the quarter at 1 a.m. and saw people assembling armed in front of the house of a man named DuCornet. Shots were fired, and the counter-conspirators took refuge in the DuCornet house and fired back, killing seven or eight persons from the Ormée. An intense street battle ensued. At five the next morning Conti tried to arrange a pacification while the princess, the duke, Conti, Longueville, the juge de la bourse, and other gentlemen began at 6 a.m. to circulate in carriages through the streets, telling shops to open up and dissuading people from arming to join the Ormée. Conti and Longueville made a point of announcing loudly that, contrary to rumor, they did not favor the Ormée assemblies.[47]

Although the princes and the Parlement recalled the exiles and

[43] Anonymous letter 23 May 1652: *Archives historiques de la Gironde*, vol. LVIII (1929–32), pp. 29–31.

[44] Letter of 3 May 1652: Ms fr. 6707, fol. 158; Registre secret, 15 May 1652: AM Bordeaux ms. 1501; letter from Bordeaux, 16 May 1652: BN Dupuy 775, fol. 182.

[45] Anonymous letter quoted in Westrich, *The Fronde*, p. 30.

[46] Lenet letter 10 June 1652: Lenet, *Mémoires*, vol. XXVI, pp. 548–51.

[47] Letter 10 June: Ms. fr. 6707, fol. 163, reproduced in Cosnac, *Souvenirs*, vol. III, pp. 488–91; Lenet to Condé, 10 June 1652: Lenet, *Mémoires*, vol. XXVI, pp. 548–51.

renewed the official oath of "union" on 13 June, they continued to leave the Ormée out of their plans. In fact, a group of conservatives, led by jurats Fontenel and Guirault, were emboldened enough by their apparent success at quashing the radicals to organize what one author calls a counter-party "of the Chapeau Rouge." On Sunday the 23rd news arrived that Condé's forces had lost the nearby town of Cadillac to the royalists and were besieged in the château.[48] It was the eve of Saint John's Day and there were scuffles "between individuals from the Ormée and from the Chapeau Rouge" at the traditional bonfire. Early the next morning eighty to a hundred ormistes gathered near Sainte Croix, apparently to march to Cadillac and save the château – another repetition of the march to Libourne in 1649. The Counter-Ormée saw this as a potentially disastrous resurgence of influence. Jurat Guirault went to Saint Michel to command the group to disperse, as jurats normally did. But according to Lenet "he threatened to hang them" and said "that he bet 100 pistoles that if they would wait for him he would go and find the means to tear them to pieces." While Guirault rallied an armed force of "conseillers and bons bourgeois" in the Chapeau Rouge and Saint Rémi quarters, the princess and Madame de Longueville had themselves carried through the streets, hoping to head off the confrontation by persuasion, but they were too late. Guirault had confronted the rebels in the rue du Pas Saint George, and another fierce battle ensued. "Stirred by the presence of the jurats, the bourgeois unleashed such a withering fire that the rebels were obliged to barricade themselves inside the houses and fire from behind the windows."[49] After three hours of fighting, Guirault's forces withdrew, leaving estimates of five to forty ormistes dead and the rest fuming. This was the bloody confrontation that was to bring the Ormée to power.

The next morning 2,000 armed men from Saint Michel and Sainte Croix accompanied by women and children – a traditionally popular force demanding justice – marched on the hôtel de ville, where jurat du Bourdieu who was on duty collapsed and let them in.[50] They took over the building, seized the arsenal and two or three cannons, rang the tocsin continuously, and spent several hours organizing a real fighting force as reinforcements streamed in. That afternoon the ormistes marched out behind their artillery and launched a two-pronged military attack on the

---

[48] This account of the uprising of 24 June is mostly from Lenet's descriptions in Ms. fr. 6707, fols. 229–36, reproduced in Cosnac, *Souvenirs*, vol. III, pp. 331–42 (24 June) and pp. 344–61 (subsequent days). See also the "Extrait de tout ce qui s'est fait et passé à Bordeaux depuis le 29 juin 1652" quoted in Jouhaud, "Idées et mentalités," pp. 42–3; Cayrac, "Récit," p. 235 has a brief account; and there is a brief description in the AM Bordeaux ms. 1501, Registres secrets. Extracts from other accounts are in AM Bordeaux ms. 437, fol. 565.   [49] Quoted by Westrich, *The Ormée*, p. 36, from a Mazarinade.
[50] Lenet to Condé, 24 June 1652: Ms. fr. 6707, fol. 236r.

Chapeau Rouge quarter. By this time preparations had been made. President Pichon and Councillor LaRoque across the street from him were barricaded in and guarded by two hundred bourgeois, as were other dignitaries. The ormistes deployed their cannons and prepared tarred bundles of wood to set fire to the houses systematically. The defenders, who had the advantage of shelter, fired back with small artillery pieces from the windows. Another battle ensued, "cannon to cannon," until a truce was declared when the princess paraded a priest carrying the holy sacrament through the battle lines. There had been at least nine houses put to the torch and casualties on both sides – perhaps ten defenders and sixty ormistes. President Pichon's house was "pillaged and cannonaded." A despondent President Daffis found only the walls of his house standing.

A year of Ormée domination

The uprising of 25 June 1652 demonstrated that for the moment force was on the side of the Ormée. In the next months the movement would set up regular committees of its own and infiltrate the centers of power. But it continued to see itself largely as a pressure group that influenced consti- tuted authorities without taking them over. This was strikingly different from the factional struggles that split other cities because one faction was not merely elevated at the expense of another; and it differed from the power plays of charismatic patrons in that the Ormée advocated a new way of looking at power instead of promoting unquestioning support for a particular leader. In the next days the ormistes established a Committee of Thirty that met daily within the hôtel de ville to "advise" the jurats when need arose and whose membership changed periodically.[51] They regularly sent envoys to Conti to demand that the suspects be expelled and that widows and orphans of those killed in the recent confrontation be compensated. They continued to project a relatively faceless collective power and never put forth their own leaders – not even Condé – as heros.

It is hard to get a clear picture of who the ormistes represented in the decisive year from June 1652 to August 1653 because we see them mostly through the eyes of their enemies. On the one hand they spoke for a broad segment of the population, with wide support from respectable citizens of modest to prosperous means – people who endorsed their goals of support for the Fronde and suspicion towards traditional leaders; on the other they were increasingly dominated by activists who met in restricted planning sessions and demanded strict conformity to their directives. Although the princes did everything they could to buy off the Ormée and

[51] Cosnac, *Souvenirs*, vol. III, pp. 359–60; vol. IV, pp. 308–9.

subordinate its leaders to their purposes, the movement was always a "third force" and never a mere instrument of the princely party.[52]

As time went on, the activists created their own parallel command structure consisting of a large Chamber of the Ormée, successor to the meetings at the platform, and the Chamber of Thirty that apparently became the real decision-making force. There was talk of a Chamber of Expulsions consisting of the Thirty, plus representatives from other municipal bodies; a Council of War; and a Chamber of Twelve that adjudicated private suits; and there were military forces that were used for intimidation and to guard gates and public places, no doubt parallel to the militia companies. But it is not always possible to distinguish between Ormée committees, the extraordinary committees set up by the Parlement and the princes, and regular institutions merely dominated by ormistes. Thus it is not entirely clear to what degree the ormistes instituted a separate government.

Condé, in Paris, still wanted a rebellion led by regularly constituted authorities. He indicated to Villars in no uncertain terms that his particular friends in the Parlement were not to be insulted, and he tried to keep the Ormée in its place: "they are to accord the Parlement all the respect it deserves; they are to refrain from undertaking anything against the authority of such an august company . . . and above all no one should be so bold as to propose any assembly without the express order of Monsieur le Prince to Conti my brother." On the other hand he had no scruples about conciliating the Ormée when necessary, as he indicated to Lenet: "If you cannot satisfy the Ormée by negotiation or finesse or any other means, it would be better to take its side than to see it chased out of Bordeaux. Nevertheless, this is only a last resort."[53]

The Ormée had a different point of view. In June the movement had apparently drawn up its own, more radical, oath on behalf of its demands. Isaac Descombes, city locksmith, later testified that various members of the Ormée had asked him to sign a "book of the Ormière," as distinguished from the city-wide "union," which he said he had already signed.[54] This book might have been the same notarized act signed by a large number of inhabitants that was presented to Avocat-Général Dussault by three men dressed in black on 20 June and which declared that all cases of bourgeois of Bordeaux were evoked out of the jurisdiction of the Parlement. It was probably also the document that Lenet described

[52] On 20 June Lenet had described to Condé how he made a point of regularly distributing alms and pensions to a wide variety of persons in the name of the princes to promote popularity. Lenet, 20 June 1652: Cosnac, *Souvenirs*, vol. III, p. 325.

[53] Condé to Villars, no date: Ms. fr. 6707, fol. 159; Condé to Lenet, 3 July 1652: Lenet, *Mémoires*, XXVI, 556.   [54] Registre secret, 26 October 1652: AM Bordeaux ms 1501.

on 24 May as "the most offensive [statement] that ever existed against the Parlement and even against Your Highness [Condé]; it is signed by almost five hundred persons, but three fourths of them disallow it." Another letter, dated 23 May, sarcastically describes the ormistes' program as entailing the abolition of venality, a rendering of accounts for the immense sums spent during the first wars, and a general evocation for all the bourgeois of Bordeaux out of the jurisdiction of the Parlement.[55] These objectives seem to have been widely publicized in May and June 1652. Thus the officially sponsored "union" of princes, Parlement, and city was now paralleled by a more critical Ormée "union" of citizens, the thrust of which was a liberation from the jurisdiction of the Parlement.

During the crisis of 25 June Lenet describes how the princes mobilized their allies to go out into the community and oppose the "extraordinary" propositions of the ormistes, which were evidently a variation on the same demands put forth in May. They were demanding the arrest of the jurats who had led the attack on them, the exile of the fourteen suspects who had returned to the city, that justice be done in the case of Monleau who had been killed in the 9 June attack, that there be a complete auditing of accounts, that the Ormée be allowed to occupy the hôtel de ville, and that ormistes be given entrance to all the councils of the princes.[56]

On 14 July the Ormée's Council of Thirty adopted a new credo, the "Articles of the Union of the Ormée," which is one of the most curious documents they left behind.[57] They began by acknowledging God's assistance in the "troubles that are not yet finished" and promising to "love our neighbor," especially "those who are of the same conviction." They promised to obey the king and serve their governor (Condé), be loyal to their "patrie" (Bordeaux) and risk their lives and property to defend its "privileges and franchises," notably the principle that "as titled bourgeois we have not just a consultative but a deliberative voice in the general assemblies of the city hall." They also promised to force those who had handled public monies to render a full account. The rest of the document echoes the mutual assistance provisions of a guild or a religious confraternity. The adherants promised to love and protect one another, to allow the "company" to arrange arbiters to settle differences among them and to accept the arbiters' decisions, to protect members of the company who were harassed "by law suits or otherwise," lending them money without interest if necessary, to help members who were sick, or their widows and

[55] Registre secret, 21 June 1652: AM Bordeaux ms. 1501. Lenet's letter of 24 June, Ms. fr. 6707, fol. 229v, alludes to the evocation; see also the anonymous letter of 23 May cited in note 43.   [56] Lenet to Condé 25 June 1652: Ms. fr. 6707, fol. 236r.
[57] Reprinted in Birnstiel, Die Fronde, pp. 262–4 and Bercé, Histoire des Croquants, vol. II, pp. 819–20.

orphans if they died, and to find employment for them if they fall into poverty.

These simple statements suggest the strengths and weaknesses of the Ormée at its height. The ormistes were proud of their city and ready to defend its constitution as they understood it, but they intended to demand their own input into decision-making and an accounting from those who had mismanaged public funds. They stressed these two simple aims, participation and accountability, because this was what their movement was really all about. To solidify their pact, especially after being attacked by all of the traditional leaders, they swore to protect one another from reprisals. But they perceived only their city, which they planned to reform, without fundamentally criticizing its civic institutions, and they had no critique of the connections between the king, whose authority they accepted, and his officers, whose authority they rejected.

It is also worth noting that they consistently identified themselves as "bourgeois" of Bordeaux. This was not a generic category, but rather a particular status that was granted to citizens by the jurade. It required five years of residence and possession of a house worth at least 1,500 livres. Once admitted, a bourgeois was registered in the *livre des bourgeois* and granted various privileges such as tax exemptions, freedom from troop lodgings, and preferential ability to sell one's own wine. Thus the "deliberative voice" was for established property holders, not for everyone, and the relationship of the bourgeois to the broader population which provided their support was never clearly defined.[58]

This "bourgeois" status was taken very seriously. On 27 July at a meeting of the one hundred and thirty called by the Parlement to arrange for the traditional election of jurats on 1 August, Ormée leaders announced that they had been charged by "their company" to admit parlementaires only as "bourgeois" of the city, an interesting attempt to redefine the nature of representation. Conti had the meeting annulled but the ormistes persisted. Like good lawyers they mustered legal precedents and brought them to show Conti, who refused to look at them. Sure enough, on election day the Parlement's deputies were challenged by a goldsmith, Guiraud, who claimed to be a representative of the "bourgeois," and charged that they could not be admitted as officers of the Parlement but only as bourgeois of the city. The parlementaires' rejoinder was that "the bourgeois did not form a separate corps in the jurades and could only act through the jurats." This was the real constitutional issue: who represented the city – the Parlement, the jurats, or the self-constituting Ormée

---

[58] *Livre des bourgeois de Bordeaux (XVIIe siècle)*, supplement to *Archives historiques de la Gironde*, vol. XXXIII, pp. i–x.

"company" which claimed to represent the collectivity of the bourgeois. Lenet's comment was that "we have allowed authority to become so debased, we have become so used to demanding their permission for everything and treated them so familiarly that they believe they are the masters of everything."[59]

During August the "so-called Bourgeois de l'Ormière" made frequent attacks on the authority of the Parlement.[60] On 3 September it became clear that the ormistes were making independent military decisions, introducing troops into Bordeaux and taking measures to guard La Bastide.[61] The Ormée also expanded its vigilance concerning loyalty and indulged in much crude threatening, though there was relatively little serious punishment. Isaac Descombes, the city locksmith mentioned above, was thrown in a dungeon in October for allegedly speaking ill of the princes and asserting "that all those of the Ormée should be hanged." He informed the Parlement that he had been forced to do amends for his statement before "their assembly of thirty" held in the house of Jean Coderc, merchant, a man "who had spoken of messieurs from the Parlement and of the jurats as if he were talking about demons." On the 25th this group made Descombes kneel and ask the pardon of Monsieur le Prince and the Ormée, but he was otherwise unharmed.[62]

These rigors were a reflection of the fact that royal troops were approaching from Catalonia and the king had offered amnesty to any Bordelais who would capitulate, stimulating fears of treachery. Around 28 October processions of five hundred to six hundred armed ormistes marched through the city and stopped at every corner threatening to drown anyone who advocated a separate peace and to burn his house down. At this point they begin to sound like the Paris Sixteen during the League. On 2 December rumors spread of a plan by parlementaires to capitulate to the king, and crowds of people accompanied Conti and many nobles to the Palais for a showdown in which the crowd arrested Councillor Massiot, the ringleader of a conspiracy to expel the Ormée from the hôtel de ville.[63] On 11 December Conti took the further step of going to the hôtel de ville and signing a "union" with the Ormée as a way

[59] Registre secret, 29–30 July 1652: AM Bordeaux ms. 1501; Lenet to Condé, 29 July 1652: Cosnac, *Souvenirs*, vol. IV, p. 338; Lenet to Condé, 8 August 1652: Lenet, *Mémoires*, vol. XXVI, p. 560.

[60] This important fact is noted by Westrich, *The Fronde*, p. 62 on the basis of the registers of the Chambre de Direction.

[61] Registre secret, 13, 17, 23 August, 4 September 1652: AM Bordeaux ms. 1501.

[62] Registre secret, 24–6 October 1652: AM Bordeaux ms. 1501.

[63] Lenet to Condé, 28 October and 5 December 1652, cited by Westrich, *The Fronde*, pp. 79, 81. The assassination plot is from a letter in *Archives historiques de la Gironde*, vol. VIII, pp. 423–4, as cited by Westrich, *The Fronde*, p. 81.

of keeping the opposition in check.[64] By this time the Parlement had officially been transferred to Agen, and even Condé was happy to see potential parlementaire troublemakers removed from the city.

Throughout the desperate spring of 1653 the ormistes explored the logical consequences of their position. One imperative was the need for foreign aid to counteract the power of a resurging royal army. The party of Condé became increasingly dependent on Spanish support, while the Ormée began to think about English connections. In early April when an embassy was dispatched to England, the signatures on its instructions are revealing. It was signed by Conti and Lenet for the princes; Marchin their military commander; the four jurats; Truchon, "juge de la bourse"; three "gentlemen"; and ten "bourgeois." All of these except Conti, Lenet and Marchin, were qualified as "bourgeois delegated by the *ville filleule et commune de Bordeaux* by virtue of the union which we have declared with His Highness [Conti] and under their authority" – in other words ormistes.[65] Here under the auspices of the princely party we see Bordeaux's new political order. What other seventeenth-century diplomatic document would have been signed by ten "bourgeois," consisting of two merchants, three avocats, a master jeweler, a master pewterer, and a musician?[66] Nothing came of the mission or of several other attempts which quite logically involved the assistance of Protestants and included allusions to republican tendencies. "Everyone has a republican spirit," wrote Lenet in January, "for there is so much fear of the future that these people will turn to anything." In March Condé alluded to a "second cabale of Huguenots" to establish a republic.[67]

But the ormistes did not forget their primary concern which was governance within the city. When a procession was organized on 18 February to celebrate the baptism of Condé's young son, the Ormée sent word that they could not permit lawyers and bourgeois to march *en corps* because

they [the Ormée] constituted the only legitimate body in the city inasmuch as their members came from all of the orders; that even if the Parlementaires were there they would not allow them to march except as private persons indistinct from anyone else; that they [the Ormée] were the sole rulers of the city and controlled all matters as in a republic; and to enforce their will, they had placed a large number of armed men in the vicinity of the hôtel de ville.[68]

[64] Lenet to Condé, 12 December 1652, Lenet, *Mémoires*, vol. XXVI, p. 586.
[65] Instructions dated 8 April 1653: ibid., pp. 602–6.
[66] These occupations are based on the list in Westrich, *The Fronde*, pp. 142–7; they are not definitive.
[67] Lenet to Condé, 13 January 1653: Cosnac, *Souvenirs*, vol. VI, p. 18; Condé to Lenet, 10 March 1653, Lenet, *Mémoires*, vol. XXVI, p. 599.
[68] Letter 20 February 1653 from *Archives historiques de la Gironde*, vol. VII, pp. 266–8, translated by Westrich, *La Fronde*, p. 86.

Here was the same insistence on primacy of the associated citizenry over any other corporate group, along with the determination to defend this hegemony by force.

Westrich has uncovered evidence of the spirit of the "Articles of Union" in notarial records, where specific individuals recorded treatment they had received during the period of Ormée control.[69] The ormistes redirected the channels of local justice. For one thing, they insisted that those they dealt with be willing to accept their authority. For example, a rich merchant, Pierre Manpetit, was summoned before the Ormée court because he was trying to make good on a sentence in his favor issued by the Parlement, and before they would hear him the judges asked whether he had signed their two registers, "the covenant and the general evocation." They also heard cases involving persons trying to evade parlementary arrêts. By denying the jurisdiction of the sovereign court the Ormée had opened a Pandora's box for appeals and created new business for the sénéchaussée, home of a number of prominent ormistes, and for their own Chamber of Twelve. In November when the Parlement left the city, the Twelve moved into the Palais, and Dureteste presided where royal judges had previously sat.[70] Like all seventeenth-century institutions, Ormée courts often favored their allies and made trouble for their enemies. There is evidence that they used their influence to impose arbitration – exactly as they had stated in their "Articles of Union." They also enforced wartime relief measures like a reduction in lodging rents issued by Conti to recompense artisans and other tenants for the time they lost doing guard duty. They may have liberalized admission to the bourgeoisie, or at least bent the rules to favor their friends, as the jurats had always done. In all these ways they were working out the consequences of their rejection of the authority of the Parlement and their assertion that people like themselves should be better served by the city.

The most salient consequence of rebellion against the crown was repression of political traitors. Father Berthod's account of the arrest of his co-conspirator Father Ithier, curé of Saint Pierre, is likely to have exaggerated the brutality of the proceedings, but it may convey some of the flavor of ormiste government. According to Berthod, the "procureur-général" of the Ormée court, who was an apothecary, sentenced Ithier to be drawn and quartered and his members hung at the gates of the city. A pastrycook wanted him broken on the wheel, and other artisans gave their "capricious" advice. He was then dragged through the streets, by five or six "rascals," followed by five hundred ormistes armed with guns and

---

[69] These discoveries are a major contribution. However Westrich emphasizes the class identity of the confrontations rather than the governmental logic of the measures taken. Westrich, *The Ormée*, pp. 101–15.   [70] Bercé, *Histoire des Croquants*, vol. I, p. 500.

halberds, and by "an infinity of orange sellers, fruitwomen, servants and small children who all cried out 'he must die.'" Finally he was delivered to the Council of War where he was sentenced to be shaved, defrocked, and driven through the streets on a cart with a rope around his neck carrying a torch, the hangman behind him, and imprisoned "for life."[71] We should note the carnivalesque quality of this account (especially the proverbial market women) and the fact that the official sentence was much more reasonable than the alleged popular hyperbole would have suggested.

A similar impression is derived from the description of the arrest of Jacques de Filhot in June. "Some immediately held a pistol to my head, others threatened to stab me with their swords, calling me a traitor of a Mazarin and an Epernoniste. Others beat me with the end of their muskets." Filhot was taken to a hearing before the Ormée in the presence of Conti and forty judges whom he describes with the same disdain as Berthod: they were "people of all conditions including captains of the ormistes Dureteste, Pontellier, Janet, Dupuy, Masurier, Tustal, Guirault, Crozillat, leather worker Le Rousseau, some fish merchants, some pewterers and the like." These inquisitors talked tough: Dureteste said they should cut off the nose of Filhot's wife; Janet added that they should hang everyone on Filhot's street and pillage and burn Filhot's houses in Bordeaux and in the countryside.[72] But we have learned not to take such statements literally, and Filhot lived to tell the tale. Berthod, Ithier, and Filhot were all, in fact, genuine spies for Mazarin.

As the royal army closed in during June and July 1653, Bordeaux experienced the fate of every other city in similar circumstances. On the one hand there were increasingly desperate efforts to arrest traitors; on the other a growing interior movement advocating capitulation. Bands of youths started roaming the streets and attacking ormistes. On 10 July when a merchant was arrested for saying that it was high time peace came, the people from the la Rousselle quarter and the rue Neuve rose up and demanded his liberation. La Rousselle was the quarter that had feted the princes in 1651. Now Conti and his guards found their way blocked by the corporation of butchers, armed and threatening, who demanded peace with loud cries.[73]

On 19 July a meeting of two hundred to three hundred "youths," bons bourgeois, parlementaires, avocats, and procureurs urged Conti to

[71] Père Berthod, *Mémoires du Père Berthod* [*Collection des mémoires relatifs à l'histoire de France*, ed. by M. Petitot, vol. XLVIII], pp. 407–8. The text of Ithier's confession is in Lenet, *Mémoires*, vol. XXVI, pp. 600–2.
[72] Communay, *L'Ormée*, pp. 102, 109, 119. Most of these names appear in Westrich's list of Ormée members, where they are identified as a lawyer, an avocat au Parlement, a hermit, a goldsmith, and two "écuyers."   [73] Communay, *L'Ormée*, pp. 150–1.

abolish the Ormée, replace the captains of the militia, withdraw soldiers from the city, and sue for peace.[74] In the future their "only party" would be "notable bourgeois and gens de bien who would join a union without reproach." At 7 or 8 p.m. that evening a large crowd of people appeared in the quartier Saint Michel of all ages and conditions wearing swords at their sides and white ribbons or handkerchiefs and marched through the principal streets crying "Long live the king, peace, and no more Ormée." They got popular leaders and bailiffs of trades to swear allegiance, and offered to receive former ormistes into this new "union."[75] Ironically their stated goals were not that different from the original goals of the Ormée. The impulse to form "unions" of citizens, by now a Bordeaux tradition, was being repeated yet again. But the tide had turned. Conti had long since made overtures to the Mazarin camp, and Villars had gone over to the other side. On 29 July, after many comings and goings, a peace was signed. Three hundred ormistes were expelled from the city, and Dureteste was executed a year later.

The significance of the Ormée

The Ormée was a step beyond any of the other movements we have studied. It involved crowds pillaging and demonstrating, but for a coordinated purpose that transcended immediate scapegoats. It included taking over of municipal power, but not merely to replace one faction of oligarchs with another. It embraced princely leadership without capitulating to the dictates of external authority. Most of all, it maintained continuity of existence for a year and a half while developing a rudimentary ideology and some institutions to sustain itself. It was a movement that improvised, that grew over time out of local experiences and eventually felt its way towards a dimly perceived vision of the way things ought to work. In a sense it tried to answer the question of what the honorable people of a city could do to improve their lot beyond denouncing the duplicity of authorities and mobilizing to attack immediate targets.

The ormistes were prepared for their role by the prior rebellions. It was the Parlement that had initiated the first "union" of citizens, right down to oaths in local assemblies, and it was the Parlement that had arranged the first expulsion of suspects and at least acquiesced in the march on Libourne, which had produced the first martyrs. The citizens threw

---

[74] Westrich, *The Ormée*, p. 123; more details cited in Communay, *L'Ormée*, pp. 225–34; Berthod, *Mémoires*, pp. 423–4.

[75] This account is far removed from events, since it is drawn from the "Journal de ce qui s'est passé de plus remarquable en la ville de Bordeaux depuis le 17 juillet 1653," as reported in the *Gazette de France* and reproduced in Communay, *L'Ormée*, pp. 225–34.

themselves enthusiastically into the struggle against Epernon, which seemed to represent for them a municipal liberation of almost mythical proportions. But the parlementaires did not really have their hearts in that kind of struggle. They were playing elitist games in a competition for power among top authorities, with no intention of calling into being a popular monster that took on a life of its own. When they started redirecting municipal finances and dictating to the committees that ran the city, they aroused the ire of respectable people and pushed them into alliance with the groups that normally expressed their anger in crowd actions. The Ormée was the result. It combined the anger and desire for retribution that we have seen in so many crowds with the broader opportunity provided by the rebellions of the Fronde, and it produced a curious ideological blend of civic patriotism, vindictive rage, and loyalty to princely leaders.

The persons involved were citizens respectable enough to feel slighted when important decisions were made without them, but insignificant enough to be normally excluded from power. In the list of 124 ormiste leaders identified by Westrich we see exactly this sort of individual: 28 legal practitioners and clerks, 45 merchants of various sorts, 30 master artisans from a variety of occupations, 8 nobles, a smattering of militia officers and financial receivers, 3 priests, 1 president from the Cour des Aides (the rival court to the Parlement), 1 teacher, 1 physician.[76] The leadership of these people must have emerged through popularity in neighborhoods, militia service, and professional contacts, especially through ties among lawyers, who frequented the chambers of power without ever sharing in the decision-making. Indeed, the Ormée list contains hardly anybody who had the chance to exercise real authority under the seventeenth-century system of tutelage by royal officers and titled commanders. The allies of these ormistes were the wider circles of persons, many of them more humble, who heard in Ormée protests the same messages of betrayal, bad management, popular suffering, and the need for retribution that regularly animated popular crowds.

There is no evidence that the ormistes were republicans in any sustained way. As Jouhaud has demonstrated, the chief mazarinades that make this claim were written by outside parties promoting their own agenda.[77] The concept of a republic did have meaning. It was natural for persons with classical educations to admire city-states like Rome or Athens, whose "republican" experience had resonance in a city where the "bourgeois" were demanding greater say in government. Mazarin heard

---

[76] My classifications do not correspond to those employed by Westrich, who approaches the subject differently. Westrich, *The Fronde*, pp. 41–9, 142–7.

[77] Jouhaud, *Mazarinades*, pp. 185–208.

reports as early as 1650 of a preacher who advocated a republic, probably in this sense of an independent city-state ("a free and independent government that would even be respected and sought out by all the other princes and potentates of Europe"); and one ormiste, Prades, professor in the Collège de Guyenne, was quoted by Lenet in 1652 as having said "that he saw in the stars that Bordeaux must become a powerful republic."[78]

Bordeaux was also a cosmopolitan port with access to more radical opinions. But the primitive nature of any "republican" impulse is highlighted by a comparison with truly progressive ideas arriving from England in the desperate spring of 1653. A tract called "Les Principes et fondement d'une république" which was based on the Leveller "Agreement of the People" was turned over by English agents in Bordeaux to the princes for political reasons.[79] It called for an elected parliament of freemen, freedom of conscience, freedom from illicit seizure, abolition of imprisonment for debts, and trial by jury – the sort of constitutional thinking that was completely absent in Bordeaux. Such demands fell on deaf ears. In fact, the ideas from England were never part of the ormiste program, and republicanism does not appear to have had anything more than separatist implications.

The real purpose of the ormistes emerges from their actions. They were a group of citizens who saw themselves as loyal bordelais out to take back control of their own hôtel de ville from the governor and the Parlement. They met openly in public, got a sense of the "people" being behind them, and experienced the almost spiritual camaraderie of living through the ups and downs of Condé's fortunes. They had already made military sacrifices, mocked Mazarin and Epernon joyfully, and feasted together. These experiences created an extraordinary patriotic bond between bourgeois leaders and popular crowds. But when they drew up practical measures to protect the city from treason and demanded an accounting of the sums used, they found themselves insulted and isolated by a Parlement whose arrogation of authority was hardly less infuriating than its apparently treasonous behavior. The result was that they turned against the very idea of rule by officers and set out to run their own city.

The best expression of this message emerges from the "Apologie pour

---

[78] Mazarin's letter of 25 August 1650 cited by Kossmann, *La Fronde*, p. 246 from Pierre-Adolphe Chéruel (ed.), *Lettres du Cardinal Mazarin pendant son ministère*, 9 vols. (Paris, 1872–1906), vol. III, pp. 741–2; Lenet to Condé, 30 June 1652: Cosnac *Souvenirs*, vol. IV, pp. 290–1.

[79] The text is in Cosnac, *Souvenirs*, vol. V, pp. 256–77; for an analysis, see Knachel, *England and the Fronde*, pp. 198–200. See also G. E. Aylmer, "The 'Ormée' and the Popular Movement in the English Revolution," in *Sociétés et groupes sociaux en Aquitaine et en Angleterre* [*Actes du Colloque franco-britannique 1976; Fédération historique du Sud-Ouest*] (Bordeaux, 1979), pp. 95–103.

l'Ormée," a mazarinade commissioned by the movement itself and written by a local man named Lartigue sometime in 1652.[80] Lartigue's argument is relatively simple, though it is embellished with pretentious language and crammed with classical erudition. The "plus apparens," he says, started meeting at the Ormée to discuss the corruption of the government during the second war and the resulting high taxes. They proposed reforms, but the Parlement insulted them and attacked their legitimacy: "they are answered with bloody, outrageous reproaches, they are loaded with insults, they are characterized as ignorant, unworthy persons incapable of having any knowledge of affairs." The group therefore formed a "corps regulier" bound by vows of mutual aid. Their purpose was to "maintain the public liberty, to conserve their privileges [i.e. those of the 'bourgeois'] and their ability to discuss affairs, to obtain an accounting of the public funds, to protect each other reciprocally and to settle their differences by arbitration" – a list that describes quite well what we have seen them doing. The chief issue was accountability: "this is the point where our Ormée began; it was this refusal to acknowledge reason, to *render accounts*, which gave it birth." The centerpiece of his argument is a denunciation of the Parlement:

> I speak against the petty ambitions, the shame and disgrace of this corps, the plague of its judgments which have burst forth in this time of public disorder like evil humors in the body when an accident occurs; [these are persons who] after a thousand injustices, a thousand corruptions in the judgments of private cases and in the exercise of posts which they only hold by virtue of fortune and wealth, have coveted absolute dominion in the management of public affairs; [persons] who, after a thousand brigandages and acts of piracy in the province under pretext of various commissions, would like to continue the same in this city.

Lartigue also projects something of the way the ormistes viewed themselves. "This name Ormée that you utter with such contempt will be the glory of this city that you have effaced, will forever be held in veneration" and he goes on to compare the bourgeois of Bordeaux with Socrates and Diogenes, "those kings of the wise . . . who were neither councillors nor conquerors but private persons and simple bourgeois." In fact, the merit of the Ormée for Lartigue is that it has not held onto power, but instead its members have returned power to its legitimate possessors and resumed the lives of private citizens.[81]

The Ormée pushed the outer limits of popular politics. It showed that popular crowds could advance beyond improvised mayhem if they had

---

[80] Jouhaud has discovered Lartigue's reimbursement in the municipal accounts: Jouhaud, *Mazarinades*, p. 203; "Apologie," in Birnstiel, *Die Fronde*, pp. 275–7.

[81] "Apologie," in Birnstiel, *Die Fronde*, pp. 269–98.

leaders who spoke the same language of indignation and retribution. The
way to achieve a lasting impact was to form an organized pressure group
to serve as a counterweight to vested interests. Such an effort required
more than an alternative faction to endorse. It called for collaboration
between informed leaders with broad perspectives and access to the
organs of government, on the one hand, and the local communities that
rallied to demonstrate and intimidate, on the other. And it required a
program based on goals accepted by all.

But such a common purpose could only be provided by an enemy like
Mazarin universal enough to enable people from different trades and
neighborhoods to feel a similar indignation. Lacking such a bond, conflicts were inevitable because the membership of the Ormée ranged from
lawyers aspiring after offices and merchants interested in free trade to
artisans, apprentices, laborers, women, and priests, all of whom had con-
flicting interests. The retribution demanded by ordinary crowds involved
issues of subsistence, tariffs, employment, taxes, and more generally the
mishandling of basic services. But such issues set one group against
another; there could never be a common position concerning export or
retention of grain, taxing of commodities, materials, or wine, regulating of
trades and apprentices. Issues of representation would be even more divi-
sive: who could be received as "bourgeois," how were militia officers
selected; who named the jurats? Thus a single city could not successfully
oppose the crown, but crowds would continue to demonstrate, and the
authorities they attacked would continue to need the royal government to
protect their interests.

The culture of retribution was a central phenomenon in the history of popular protest. It was a flexible, easily communicable form because it borrowed gestures used in private quarrels and spoke to popular conceptions of honor. It had a long history, but in the seventeenth century it became prominent enough to constitute a distinct phase in the annals of crowds. Although it could occur anywhere, it was a distinctively urban phenomenon, inasmuch as the abuses of governance and the affected subcommunities were most likely to coexist in cities.

Full-blown, community-based uprisings unfolded in stages, creating an improvised dialogue between protesters and authorities which went something like this. First there would be talk about an anticipated threat to necessities of life such as subsistence, work, children, sociability. Usually people started talking over a period of days or weeks in response to particular incidents, and during this same period elite or popular agitators had the opportunity to establish the identity of opponents by posting bills or denouncing enemies. This information was further disseminated in gossip which linked actual facts to preexisting assumptions. The threat was invariably construed as something offensive and outrageous: not just a rise in taxes but another example of what "they" are doing to "us" – a gabelle, the élus, the stamped paper, a tobacco shortage, a tax on our eating utensils. The fear, though possibly exaggerated, was always real. There might be popular planning in the form of meetings in markets and taverns or in cemeteries and on ramparts; or there might just be grumbling. The targeted agents might generate animosity by visibly sequestering goods, marking merchandise, or serving warrants. During this preparatory phase we are likely to hear about mounting tension in the form of verbal threats, posted exhortations, mobilizations of "children," sarcastic mockery, and attempts to make respectful appeals to the authorities. In the course of this period a consensus would emerge as to who was responsible. The targets would be persons, not institutions, because it was individuals who performed the offensive acts in front of people's eyes and because abstract forces were always personified in the seventeenth century.

At some point an incident, usually the beginning of the collection of the tax, would trigger phase two, the uprising itself. People would gather informally, egg each other on, rally an impromptu group by beating the drum, or set out in armed units organized in advance. They would act with singular purpose, heading straight for the chosen targets. If nothing stopped them they were likely to pillage the targeted houses, one after another, chasing away individuals and scattering offensive documents until the movement petered out – usually at nightfall. The idea was to insult and frighten the perpetrators or to register outrage at the way things were being handled, not to inflict pain. Physical attacks on persons were usually a response to provocation. The victim would have scolded the crowd, offered resistance, or been caught in flight. This second phase – what might be called the "pure revolt" – often ended of its own accord once the deed had been done. The danger was over; the gabeleurs were expelled; the crowd was happy.

Phase three would be set off by the response of those targeted. The most likely scenario was the capture of prisoners who would then need to be rescued. Another possibility was the intensification of the conflict when authorities fought back, diverting anger from the original targets towards the officials who were shielding the evil or the parties who were firing on the crowd. Now the collective conception of the problem would be expanded from "a few *partisans* to be expelled" to "our leaders who have failed us," and a fundamental belief in betrayal by the authorities would emerge which confirmed long-held suspicions. The new targets were selected by the course of events. Crowds might go after financial backers or rich residents, storm the hôtel de ville, threaten the Parlement, or besiege the governor and his troops. The demonstrators were usually quite discriminating in their choices.

Once the broader combat against authorities had been engaged, there was bound to be exhilaration. Criticism would expand from "we always knew someone would try to oppress us this way" to "this confirms our suspicions that our leaders themselves are profiteering and selling us out." Hyperbole would enter the rebel discourse in threats to "burn everything down" or "murder the rich." This was the moment when desperate combatants uttered curses against their leaders, tore off roofs, led assaults on houses and carriages, ripped apart fleeing suspects. It was also the time when basic military instincts, often borrowed from militia duty, came into play: seizure of belfries, ringing of the alarm, occupation of gates, patrolling of streets. From the rebels' perspective this was the high point of the uprising. The die was cast; the people were speaking; everyone should join in to protect gains and fend off military repression. It was also the time when the authorities played their two strongest cards:

...ey could restore order by caving in to the rebels' demands, or they could organize appeals to the crowd by respected leaders or through deployment of sacred images like favored relics from local churches.

The final phase was one of watchful waiting. It was time to return to shops and families. After the excesses that had occurred, everybody would know that repression was coming. Vigilance, introspection, and private exchanges of condolences would be the order of the day. If the movement still had life, there might be more flareups when new alarms were sounded. If not, resignation would greet the arrival of troops and inquisitors. This phase was always the beginning of the end because of the essential weakness of popular strategy. The crowd had no thought of instituting a different kind of regime and very little idea how to hold the current authorities to their promises.

The people involved in these community protests were a fluctuating group drawn from the masses of ordinary citizens. Prominent in one movement or another were shopkeepers, textile workers, leather workers, workers in the building trades, street vendors, butchers, bakers, peasants, boatmen, craftsmen of various sorts, that is, the entire range of humbler occupations, although not all at the same time. Women played a varied and creative role, although they tended to stay away from military operations. They ventured well beyond subsistence riots, and it would be misleading to attribute their predominence even there to "the almost biological nature of this kind of episode" or to assert that "they plunged into the riots over the bread price without having any other programme than anguish at what the future might hold and the basic rights of the starving."[1] The protesters drew on solidarities with people who felt the same way. They relied first on their parish, street, or neighborhood (the rue Haute in Rennes), or alternatively on their trade (the pewterers of Bordeaux, the silkweavers of Lyon); then on broader solidarities like those within the three popular quarters of Bordeaux. Inside such communities patrons from a few rungs up the social ladder – persons such as innkeepers, master craftsmen, procureurs and notaries – might nudge the activists towards particular targets. In some cases (Rennes) a larger civic patriotism ("defend our city against occupying troops") was in evidence.

These people saw themselves as sharply opposed to the persons with influence who ran their city. The goals and values of the majority differed markedly from the goals of the oligarchs, to the extent that crowds felt the need to punish the excesses of their purported leaders. The populations of cities had almost no legal way to affect the decisions that really mattered in their lives. No protest beyond humble supplication was legiti-

[1] Bercé, *History of Peasant Revolts*, pp. 174–5.

mate; no unauthorized assemblage was legal; no bargaining was permissible. But as we have seen, the populace was not relegated to employing the "weapons of the weak," because the system gave them a certain room to maneuver.[2] The menu peuple had influence because of their numbers, because of the échevins' need for their acquiescence in the normal functioning of government, and because their ranks included persons with standing in the various sub-communities that made up urban society. They talked back to authorities and chastised not only persons perceived as interlopers but also their own magistrates and occasionally even the agents of the king.

[This culture of retribution was the distinguishing feature of early modern French crowds. Urban demonstrators rejected practices threatening their essential well-being and asserted their right to better treatment, demanding not a return to a golden age but the implementation of practical measures to resolve immediate problems: maintenance of minimal levels of subsistence, rejection of an intruder introducing a threat, protection of fellow demonstrators from arrest and sentencing, outrage at treatment that fell below standards of minimal decency, opposition to new burdens that appeared unduly oppressive, defense of one's street or city from attack, and so forth. The common thread was the assertion of a set of values about acceptable government behavior. Crowds were saying to the responsible parties that they would have to do better, and they were punishing them on the spot for their lapses.]

This phenomenon has not been widely recognized by those who analyze collective protest. The tendency has been to focus on religious antagonisms in the sixteenth century and then move on to the subsistence crises of the eighteenth century, noting in passing that the seventeenth century was a time of tax revolts. Religious struggles can be connected to deeper mental structures and subsistence riots are seen as an expression of "moral economy." But the "tax" riots of the seventeenth century have little identity other than being viewed as a mechanical reaction to the fiscal demands of the state. In Sidney Tarrow's recent summary of pre-modern collective action, for example, the four types of popular revolt become "conflicts over bread, belief, land and death," with only a brief nod to the form that dominated the landscape for more than a hundred years.[3] Tarrow has interesting ideas about the rise of social movements, but his analysis joins those who draw a line between "modern" politics,

---

[2] Reference is to the analysis of James C. Scott in *Weapons of the Weak: Everyday Forms of Peasant Resistance* (New Haven, 1985) and *Domination and the Arts of Resistance: Hidden Transcripts* (New Haven, 1990).

[3] Sidney Tarrow, *Power in Movement: Social Movements, Collective Action and Politics* (Cambridge, 1994), p. 36.

revolving around national political issues, and "traditional" protest which relegates crowd actions to a folkloric pre-history. For many analysts looking back from the eighteenth century or beyond, early modern riots become timeless, repetitive rituals that replicated a certain kind of culture without contributing to real politics. Thus Perez Zagorin builds his argument around the distinction between "riots" which were short, spontaneous, and non-political, and "revolts" which were political, and notes that "the expressive function" in riots "tends to predominate over any instrumental purpose."[4] According to Bercé, "a riot, in the last analysis, was a performance in which the actors played their parts on every occasion in the same unchanging and time-honored ways, and in this performance the haling of the exciseman was an indispensable scene." Bercé's rioters followed routines which he perceives as recreational: "Outbreaks of jubilant rioting were a festival in themselves. They were a chance for the taxpayers to take their revenge by playing jokes, and people flocked to them." Success was crowned with celebration: "in the country and in the towns alike, barrels of wine were rolled into the squares and opened up once an uprising had been successful . . . the rebels got drunk and spent the nights drinking to their victory."[5]

Such statements make the demonstrators sound childlike and irresponsible. There were festive moments in revolts, to be sure, but the major uprisings represented frightening and serious experiences for the participants. We should focus on the anger, the existential risk, and the uncertainty involved in such enterprises. It is striking how little there was of ritual and mockery in genuine revolts, compared to the more colorful charivari and other forms of festive mockery described so well by Natalie Davis and by Bercé himself.[6] Indeed, the playful tone of those sorts of rituals in which loud noise and insulting pantomime were supposed to chastise an offender created a mood diametrically opposed to the intense search for retribution that characterized seventeenth-century revolts.[7] In charivari-style rituals the goal was to reintegrate the offender into the community by making him distribute coins or buy rounds of drinks as an acknowledgment of his obligations. In popular riots the goal was to punish wrong-doing and see that it never happened again. In fact, the

---

[4] Perez Zagorin, *Rebels and Rulers 1500–1660*, 2 vols. (Cambridge, 1982), vol. I, p. 20.

[5] Bercé, *History of Peasant Revolts*, pp. 219, 325.

[6] Natalie Davis, "The Reasons of Misrule," in *Society and Culture*, pp. 97–123; Natalie Davis, "Charivari, honneur et communauté à Lyon et à Genève au XVIIe siècle," in Jacques Le Goff and Jean-Claude Schmitt (eds.), *Le Charivari [Actes de la table ronde organisée à Paris, 25–27 avril 1977]* (Paris, 1981); Yves-Marie Bercé, *Fête et révolte: des mentalités populaires du XVIe au XVIIIe siècles* (Paris, 1976).

[7] An extremely helpful analysis is John Cashmere, "The Social Uses of Violence in Ritual: Charivari or Religious Persecution?," *European History Quarterly* 21 (1991), 291–319.

place where festive mockery appeared most prominently was in factional quarrels when rival factions insulted one another wittily and used banquet revelry to create an atmosphere of solidarity, as we saw in Béziers and in Aix.⁾

It is also misleading to categorize popular ideology as a list of recurring myths: that the king was not to blame; that the goal was a return to a past golden age; that the problem was the greed of financiers; that the community was rising up united to expel the outsider who had brought disaster.[8] Thoughts like these were often expressed, but to catalog them as myths suggests that the participants were incapable of rethinking and applying them and that their options were limited to choosing from a list of customary explanations in order to cope with things otherwise beyond their understanding. In fact, many of these beliefs were not myths at all, but popular memories of past complicities and intuitive insights into the deeper class interests of the authorities, expressed in simple language.

The culture of retribution also differed from the concept of "moral economy" so often attributed to early modern crowds.[9] To be sure, these crowds acted with moral purpose to correct an indignity viewed as upsetting the proper order of things. But E. P. Thompson's concept of moral economy referred to a set of commonly held values about the functioning of marketplace provisioning which were derived from the official practice of an earlier age and which confronted a set of competing values related to the emerging capitalist marketplace.[10] Those crowds' actions were defensive, bent on restoring traditional practices and forcing suppliers and sellers to do likewise, and their protest was relatively orderly because it set out to regulate not to destroy, and it was bolstered by the existence of a general consensus within the community, even among the magistrates.

By contrast, the seventeenth-century French urban crowd was angrier, more concerned with punishment, more determined to nullify bad decisions and punish known enemies. This anger focused initially on specific intrusions, but broadened to more general complaints about governance, invoking forms of retribution that derived from ritual humiliation and private defense of honor. This form of protest was political as well as

[8] Bercé, *History of Peasant Revolts*, pp. 244–76.

[9] Thus Natalie Davis invents a religious moral economy in "The Rites of Violence: Religious Riot in Sixteenth-Century France," in *Society and Culture*, pp. 152–87; Carlo Ginzburg studies "Ritual Pillages" in Edward Muir and Guido Ruggiero (eds.), *Microhistory and the Lost Peoples of Europe* (Baltimore, 1991), pp. 20–41; James C. Scott discusses *The Moral Economy of the Peasant: Rebellion and Subsistence in Southeast Asia* (New Haven, 1976), and so forth.

[10] E. P. Thompson, "The Moral Economy of the English Crowd in the Eighteenth Century," *Past and Present* 50 (Feb. 1971), 76–136; reprinted, with new commentary, in Thompson, *Customs in Common*, pp. 185–351.

social in that it was part of a dialogue about urban governance. To be sure, the demonstrators sometimes rejected novelties which might be construed as violations of ancient exemptions. But their emphasis was more on the outrageousness of the demand than on its historical illegality.[11] French crowds were setting the protesters' basic pride and right to a decent life up against the enemy's alleged malfeasance and corruption. As Bercé put it eloquently, these people "were fighting for the freedom to eat and drink, to be born, to get married, and to be given a Christian burial without being subject to the attentions of the taxman . . . These rebels were rising up in defense of their basic human dignity."[12] And the thrust of their protest was punitive as well as corrective. Instead of intervening benevolently to impose an adjustment which would restore a prior practice understood by all, as in the classic case of selling goods at a lower price in the market, French rioters were challenging their magistrates, telling them they were wrong, demanding more influence.[13]

This distinctive form of resistance had a long history. It can certainly be seen in earlier rebellions like the Grande Rebeine of 1529 in Lyon and the 1580 "Carnival" in Romans, and it continued to exist in the eighteenth century. As we have seen, it was not limited to a particular kind of abuse, since it might concern provisioning, taxes, or even defense. The connection between the culture of retribution and earlier religious conflicts is especially intriguing. Consider the actions of Catholic crowds in Paris during the religious wars, as reported by Diefendorf. Protestants being taken to prison for an illegal worship service were attacked by bystanders along the way and had their clothes torn and their faces smeared with mud. A house used for worship in Popincourt was torn to pieces by the crowd and its rubble was brought to the place de Grève and burned in a bonfire. In 1563 a crowd seized a woman being escorted to the conciergerie by a militia captain, killed her, stripped her naked, and dragged her body through the streets from the Porte Saint Denis to Les Halles in a manner reminiscent of the treatment of Madame de Falgairolles in Montpellier in 1645. Unruly mobs tore the bodies of exe-

[11] Roland Mousnier and Yves-Marie Bercé would argue that the centralizing tendencies of the absolutist state represented a revolutionary force against which local communities were fighting. To make this case they would have to show that the new administrative procedures were replacing the ideologies of deference, hierarchy, and privilege, and not just intensifying the effectiveness of state collections.

[12] Bercé, *History of Peasant Revolts*, p. 263.

[13] Cynthia Bouton's excellent analysis of the French Flour War of 1775 demonstrates that French rural communities did intervene in the eighteenth century against modernization in ways comparable to Thompson's crowds, but their motivation and behavior were different from that of the urban crowds in the previous century. Cynthia A. Bouton, *The Flour War: Gender, Class and Community in Late Ancien Regime French Society* (University Park, PA, 1993).

cuted heretics from the gallows to mutilate them, dragged them through the streets, or subjected them to other post-mortem atrocities.[14] According to Sir Thomas Smith the English ambassador, "it is enough if a boy, when he sees a man in the street, but cries 'voyla ung Huguenot,' and straight the idle vagabonds, and such as cry things to sell, and crocheters, set upon him with stones; and then come out the handicraftsmen and idle apprentices with swords, and thrust him through with a thousand wounds."[15] Substitute "gabeleur" for "Huguenot" here, and you have a description of a seventeenth-century riot. Thus the same sorts of ritual humiliations that we have encountered in the seventeenth century appear in the religious wars, the same expressions of the desire to humiliate and reject, though with entirely different principles for selecting the targets. It is possible that the crowd violence of the religious wars was carried over to the largely secular rebellions we have been studying, but it seems more likely that both were expressions of the same pre-existing popular language.

Consider also the ways the community had of defending itself from a threat of invasion or subversion. The measures taken would be echoes of official routines, but undertaken spontaneously without official sanction, as in 1625 in Bordeaux when false rumors set the whole city in motion. In Angers in 1627 during a Te Deum service to celebrate the capture of the Island of Ré, a loud dispute over precedence in the cathedral caused a rumor to spread through town that the Huguenots were massacring the Catholics, and people came running up with swords to join in the fray.[16] In a more prolonged crisis the community was likely to adopt "neighborhood watch" procedures. We have seen these carried out in the pennonages of Lyon. Again turning to Diefendorf, we find that in the Paris of the 1560s people were encouraged to report questionable activities by their neighbors, and special assemblies were organized in each quarter to denounce suspicious persons. The persons targeted were asked to sign a special confession of faith or else to leave the city immediately – a striking parallel to the "unions" of Bordeaux and the expulsions carried out by the Ormée. The fact that this repertory of defensive impulses also appeared in Paris in the 1560s and in a variety of other times and places once again suggests that these stonings, draggings, and watch procedures were not a function of religious strife or novel taxation, but rather a reflection of ways

---

[14] Diefendorf, *Beneath the Cross*, pp. 50, 53, 58–9, 63–7, 71. Henry Heller discusses similar conflicts in *Iron and Blood: Civil Wars in Sixteenth-Century France* (Montreal and Kingston, 1991), pp. 86–104. Although his argument is different, he reminds us that there was more to the religious wars than religious conflict. In *Les guerriers de Dieu* Denis Crouzet interprets many of these same actions as religiously motivated.
[15] Diefendorf, *Beneath the Cross*, p. 69.   [16] Jousselin, "Journal," p. 425.

of thinking and acting which were deeply ingrained in the consciousness of the city.[17]

It appears then that the culture of retribution was a form of popular involvement which emerged forcefully in the seventeenth century in the context of a set of distinctive urban conditions. The cities were places where the ideology of citizen participation, the lingering myth of the "bonnes villes," was strong. Still, it was becoming harder to believe in the benevolence of the échevins. City governments were increasingly dominated by narrow oligarchies with outside ties to power, whose authority in turn was being sabotaged by the decisions of distant royal councillors and undermined by rivalries with resident royal officers. Thus closer integration into the royal state was creating a gap between those with connections and those without them, and the new barrage of invasive taxes just called attention to the situation. Absolutism meant favored status for a few and reduced influence for the many, but the majority could still draw on powerful traditions of collective self-protection that lived on in urban sub-communities where potentially angry and largely disenfranchised neighborhood leaders maintained contact with poorer, more vulnerable groups.

But how general was this situation? The number of full-scale, genuinely popular uprisings in all of France in the course of the seventeenth century probably reached thirty or forty instances. With the known lesser episodes added in, the total would rise to at least several thousand.[18] But revolts were neither ubiquitous nor continuous. Big uprisings were concentrated in the 1620s, 1640s and the 1670s, all periods when the royal government was distracted. Their greatest incidence came in the second third of the century, the period when tax innovations were most noticeable and the central government was most divided. They tended to take place in peripheral provinces, in cities with long traditions concerning

[17] Civic and league identity are discussed in Elie Barnavi, *Le parti de Dieu: étude sociale et politique des chefs de la Ligue parisienne (1585–1594)* (Brussels, 1980) and Robert Descimon, "La Ligue à Paris (1585–1594): une révision" [followed by debate with Elie Barnavi], *Annales ESC* 37 (1982), 72–128; see also their joint book *La Sainte Ligue, le juge et la potence* (Paris, 1985); and Descimon, "Milice bourgeoise et identité citadine."

[18] These figures are just guesses. The only precise figures we have are Pillorget's 374 revolts between 1596 and 1715 in Provence and Bercé's 500 revolts between 1590 and 1715 in Guyenne (see chapter 7, note 4). If these two provinces had 874 revolts, surely the rest of France had at least a thousand more. But many of these were minor incidents. There is little value in cataloguing revolts without exploring the nature of each one: the classic case of misleading documentation is the "chronology of insurrections" given in the French edition of Porchnev's *Soulèvements populaires*, pp. 661–76, along with a sequence of impressive maps that have been widely reproduced in textbooks. This chronology was drawn up on the basis of mere citations in Porchnev's text, many of which were based on simple mentions in a single letter. Some of these revolts never existed while many other real revolts were unknown to Porchnev. Yet these lists continue to be used.

local immunities. These trends help pinpoint the optimal conditions which allowed major disturbances to emerge and develop, but the social antagonisms and political demands expressed in the favored instances were not distinctive to those communities. There is every reason to think that more revolts could be uncovered in the archives and that urban populations had similar reactions on a smaller scale even when their protests did not develop into a major revolt. The culture of retribution represented a phase in urban social relations, not an exceptional expression of unusual animosity.

The response of the authorities

The position of the magistrates who had to keep order and protect property also requires reexamination. Contrary to some accounts, they were not sympathetic to popular protest, which threatened their authority and their standing and – even worse perhaps – presented them with the necessity of making dangerous, personally humiliating, efforts to control the uncontrollable.[19] But they faced a dilemma. There was no happy outcome for them, no good way to "stop" a revolt. With hindsight it is easy to question the sincerity of their efforts but for them it was not so clear what to do. First, they had no way of telling that a given instance was going to turn into a crisis, since many times the preliminary stirrings did not lead to a full-scale revolt and routine containment measures such as patrolling did sometimes work. Second, once things got rolling, French cities had no effective form of crisis management, which would have required collaboration of a variety of unequal authorities. Third, municipal councils had no incentive to carry their repression to the limit, not because they sympathized with the rebels but because there was no advantage in doing so. There was much danger and little reward in fighting, since success would probably be limited and blame would be laid on the city regardless of the outcome. Beyond protecting property and authority, their interest lay in maintaining face and demonstrating for the record that they had courageously done their duty on behalf of the king. They needed to make an appearance, to take the appropriate steps, to display personal courage, and to rescue tax farmers from ultimate conse-

---

[19] Thus it is not possible to accept Roland Mousnier's assertion that "in the cities it was often the royal officers, the municipal magistrates, the rich bourgeois who fomented the revolts, took up their leadership, and openly directed them when the privileges of the province or the city were in jeopardy or simply when the taxes seemed too heavy." This view is based on a failure to appreciate the complexity of the magistrates' situation and a refusal to recognize the distinction between factional maneuvers and popular protests. Roland Mousnier, *La plume, la faucille et le marteau: institutions et société en France du Moyen Age à la Révolution* (Paris, 1970), p. 355.

...ut appropriate gestures would usually be sufficient to achieve
...and if the demonstrators forced them to retreat after that, so
...better.

Before the age of Louis XIV a repressive solution was ruled out by circumstances. Crowds at their peak were likely to turn on anyone who
opposed them directly. Vigorous intervention was likely to enflame the
situation and spawn new, more radical phases of conflict. Short of an
army occupation, the only thing that really worked was for armed soldiers
on horseback to intervene directly by firing on the crowd, killing as many
as possible. But this unpleasant task would shift responsibility to charismatic figures who were not part of the regular administration, or to a military governor whose intervention was not entirely welcome to either
échevins or parlementaires. Even the much-vaunted citadels, so highly
desired by royal ministers, proved largely useless in crowd control. They
had very small garrisons and their commanders were just as reluctant as
city officers to launch a bloodbath. The ultimate solution to law and
order, the occupation of the city by a sizeable number of royal troops, was
expensive and damaging, but it was the only way taxes and authority ever
really got going again. That this option was always necessary demonstrates the weakness of the urban oligarchies and their ultimate depen-
dence on the crown.

For these reasons all urban authorities – even intendants, even the
Keeper of the Seals in Lyon in 1630 – concluded that popular crowds
were best left to "burn themselves out," provided that property and
persons were not too seriously threatened. Bourgeois shut their doors and
refused to serve in the militia; échevins holed up in the hôtel de ville; notables hid in their hôtels; and the most vulnerable leaders hastened to join
the *partisans* holed up in the local fortress, where they stayed for the dura-
tion. It was best to lie low, to get through the crisis. It is in this context that
prisoners were released, edicts suspended, and parleys initiated with the
rebels, who generally remained unnamed and unpunished. This defensive impulse on the part of the authorities had nothing to do with sympathy for the protesters. The problem was not that they were protecting the
rebels, but rather that their authority would only become effective again if
things could be calmed down and people returned to their normal routines.

Sovereign courts, the ultimate authorities in certain cities, were similarly unsympathetic to revolt from below, although as a large company
with a variety of officers a Parlement had diverse tendencies within its
ranks, and in places like Aix parlementaires sometimes incited crowds to
support their own factional struggles. As a rule, parlementaires cultivated
an attitude of aloofness towards routine municipal affairs, believing that

their role was to oversee, not to manage. We have noted in Bordeaux how crippling this dual authority could be. Because a parlement had no immediate responsibility, it could sometimes curry favor with the public and spar with the king by suspending edicts and decreeing against tax collectors. There could also be divisions within the court between high officers representing the crown, lesser officers in subordinate chambers, and procureurs and avocats whose sympathies were more likely to lie with middling citizens than with the aloof oligarchs.

But when crisis erupted, the leading councillors, at least, found themselves in a position similar to that of the échevins: however distasteful it was for them, they would have to demonstrate their own loyalty by descending into the streets, trying to mobilize the militia, chastising the crowds, and with equally humiliating results. When the chips were down the sovereign court found itself besieged and threatened just like the hôtel de ville, and when the crowd turned on the propertied, it was sovereign court judges who were often threatened. Although the parlements of Bordeaux and Rennes in 1675 and the Cour des Comptes of Montpellier in 1645 were accused of complicity and exiled, they were being punished for having ultimate responsibility, not for leading or promoting the disturbance.

Did the situation change by the end of the century? We have seen a very different setup, even in 1675. By then royal authorities were better integrated into the national command structure orchestrated by the royal ministers at court, and the perils of insubordination were more palpable for échevins, officers, and royal agents. At the same time authorities were better supported when they acted, and their relationship to each other was better regulated. Popular groups were still demanding retribution, but the punishments were more immediate, better coordinated, and more severe. In short, the integration of the municipal governments into the national structure of policing institutions – the very same developments that sapped municipal autonomy in other ways – provided welcome reinforcement for beleaguered échevins.

In 1713 the consuls of Agen reported to the intendant of Guyenne about a riot of women against a tax on apprenticeship which the syndic of the innkeepers was refusing to pay. "Please permit me to inform you," the intendant replied, "that if you had not tried to appease all these people the tax would already be paid. Since one must disabuse the people of the idea that riots like this will keep them from having to pay the taxes demanded of them, you will please not fail to put this syndic in prison until the entire tax has been paid."[20] We can sense a different tone here. The consuls are

[20] AM Agen FF 234: 7 March 1713.

to arrest troublemakers directly and the royal authorities will back them up. They are becoming agents of the government, but their authority is enhanced.

Factions, parties, and the future

Municipal politics entailed much more than just containing indigenous community protests. We have seen that a second, fundamentally different kind of urban disturbance was the conflict in the streets between factions, and that taking account of such distinctions is essential in indentifying and understanding genuine popular protests. Factional conflicts were another consequence of the ambiguities in evolving local power structures and the rivalries between different kinds of authorities. When such groups competed for popular support to reinforce their claims to legitimacy they may have appeared to be fomenting popular rebellions, but the process was fundamentally different. Here the rhetoric involved promotion of charismatic leaders, humiliation of rival factions, and, in the realm of popular culture, the invocation of civic patriotism and the ideology of leadership by princely heroes who represented protection and valor. Or, conversely, enemies might be denigrated for the lack of these virtues, as in the case of Epernon in Bordeaux. Here too there was participation by men and women in the streets, but with a difference. Instead of plunging in to punish a wrong, onlookers pondered, stood back, weighed their options, consciously chose sides. When factions represented two segments of the elite with slightly different programs, as in Béziers and Albi, the majority would generally flock to the side reputed to represent reform, and the rival faction would be booed and scorned. When parties represented nothing more than factions, the crowd might well stay aloof, or join in selectively, as we saw in Marseille and Aix. Sometimes factional leaders had to fight quite consciously for the allegiance of the people in the streets, and their success was far from assured.

We are confronted, then, by two fundamentally different forms of action which represented two very different kinds of processes. The first form, protests originating in the popular community, spoke of the fundamental split between the oligarchs and the masses of the population. These actions demonstrated that urban communities were not an organic whole; that the theory of a society of orders was not universally accepted; that popular groups had a distinct conception of their own dignity; that they could and did organize protests against the perceived injustices in their lives; and that all authorities feared and opposed them, except perhaps in their most benign manifestations.

The second form, conflicts between factions, spoke of the divided nature of authority and the complex, ambiguous way that royal power had infiltrated the cities. These conflicts suggested that control was awk-wardly shared by diverse elites, that municipal constitutions were not well constructed, and that powerful client networks could still successfully hold their own against official procedures and royal agents. Culturally they demonstrated the broader appeals used to draw popular followings along into municipal power struggles. These conflicts tell us much about vertical ties and power conflicts, but not about the aspirations of the majority, which in these cases were clearly secondary.

What about those aspirations? Did it make any difference that for several generations groups of men and women decided one day, perhaps impulsively, to throw off fear, abandon deference, and join friends and neighbors in a courageous attempt to show interlopers and selfish officials a thing or two? The importance of such movements lay in redressing the local balance of power, in reminding those in charge that the common cit-izens could intervene; that they were not going to be passive victims or dupes of leaders, and that there was a price to pay for giving insufficient attention to the needs of the population. Within the community these lessons were remembered for generations and may have given heart to future protesters. On the governmental level they were recorded, studied, and feared. Agents of municipal governments compared notes with one another, and ministers acted more cautiously when imposing new burdens. For us the lesson is that popular protest was an essential feature of absolute monarchy.

But there was another lesson too. If the popular impulse to intervene energetically in protecting community values and attacking oppressors could be combined with the ongoing identity of a faction or a princely party, and if the leadership could be taken over by reformers from below with ideas about genuine constitutional reform, then a new, more pro-gressive movement could emerge, a party with a program and the exper-tise to carry it out. We saw glimmers of this in Angers and a partial realization in the Ormée of Bordeaux, a movement to democratize the city government led by bourgeois figures who provided the bridge between a traditional popular movement demanding retribution and the party of the princes. Such leaders could formulate new goals, even as they continued to speak the familiar language of denouncing injustices and humiliating perpetrators. They are already emerging in seventeenth-century French cities as the groups jealous of the absolutist takeover of local institutions. They were lawyers and notaries, master artisans, city functionaries, petty judges, middling merchants, innkeepers, professors, minor clerics who thought they should have more of a say in municipal affairs. They were a bourgeoisie of sorts, but not usually a capitalist bourgeoisie – the sort of people who would support the radical republic after 1789.

Thus the French Revolution was preceded by a long tradition of urban protest that contained many of its familiar elements and that links the seventeenth century to earlier and later popular traditions.[21] Even the Ormée had not expanded its sights beyond a single city or broadened its criticism beyond antagonisms towards specific local policies, nor had the ormistes thought through their loyalty to the monarch. Dissidents in other cities were equally particularistic. Still, this long tradition of civic defensiveness and interventionism provides a connection between the league revolts of the sixteenth century and the sans-culottes of the Revolution by highlighting an ongoing culture of urban popular protest which combined the defensive strategies of a beleaguered community with the offensive retribution of angry crowds.

This citizen party was just a possibility for the future. Even the most radical of seventeenth-century uprisings took place within the context of traditional power relations. The typical seventeenth-century crowd was intervening in urban politics by demanding respect from existing leaders, not by planning their overthrow, and the originality of urban uprisings as a distinctive phase in the history of popular movements lay in precisely this point, in the way they challenged social relationships on the local level. They permitted groups of relatively disenfranchised citizens to interact deliberately and consciously with every kind of authority figure, openly criticizing the social organization of their society while straining to imagine a better one. They did not change their world, but they left behind proof that they had struggled valiantly and successfully to influence it.

---

[21] Roger Chartier, "Culture populaire et culture politique dans l'ancien régime: quelques réflexions," in Keith Michael Baker, *The Political Culture of the Old Regime* [vol. 1 of *The French Revolution and the Creation of Modern Political Culture*] (Oxford, 1987), pp. 243–58; Colin Lucas, "The Crowd and Politics between Ancien Regime and Revolution in France," *Journal of Modern History* 60 (1988), pp. 421–57.

Appendix   Chronology of revolts and incidents mentioned

1636	CHALONS	Butchers agitate	96
1637	TOULOUSE	Quarrel with gabelle guard outside gate	76
1637	BORDEAUX	Precautions against an uprising	81
1638	AGEN	Tailor confronts tax collector	34
1638	AGEN	Merchant confronts tax collector	34
1639	DIJON	Cobblers discuss politics	38
1639	DIJON	Disturbance at gate by vinegrowers	47
1639	BORDEAUX	Precautions against seditious bills	81
1640	LYON	Protest by leather workers	43–5
1640	SOISSONS	Butchers riot against process-server	45–6
1641	CHALONS	Uprising against *subvention* tax	95–8
1641	TROYES	Riot over *subvention*	200–4
1642	DIJON	Agitation against wine tax	42–3
1642	BORDEAUX	Threats over *sol pour livre* tax	78
1643	AGEN	Altercation between consuls and notary	32–3
1643	DIJON	Innkeeper and wife throw dishes at échevin	37
1643	BORDEAUX	Women's bread riot	37
1643	VANNES	Grain riot turns against magistrates	52–4
1644	DIJON	Innkeeper and wife confront échevin	36
1644	BEZIERS	Conflict of factions over election	175–8
1644	MARSEILLE	Popular rioting assisted by faction	187–9
1644	ARGENTEUIL	Riot against process-server	2–6
1644	MARSEILLE	Valbelle faction rebels against consuls	186
1645	MONTPELLIER	Uprising against joyeux avènement tax	117–26
1646	ALBI	Factional conflict over consulate	178–83
1649–52	ANGERS	Loricard movement	207–18
1649	AIX	Battles of Sabreurs versus Semester	192–4
1649	BORDEAUX	First war of the Fronde	220–5
1650	BORDEAUX	Second war of the Fronde	225–8
1651–3	BORDEAUX	The Ormée movement	228–49
1651	MARSEILLE	Street battles by factions	186
1652	CARCASSONNE	First consul challenged over quarantine	31
1652	AGEN	Barricades against Condé's army	204–7
1653	LYON	Grain hoarder beaten in market by crowd	40
1656	MONTPELLIER	Armed protesters against Protestants	174
1656	ANGERS	Attack collectors, invade hôtel de ville	217
1657	CHALONS	Uprising against tax on serge	98–100
1659	AIX	Saint Valentine's Day Revolt	194–6
1661	ISLAND OF RÉ	Murder of royal sergeant over wine tax	59–61
1661	MENDE	Uprising against new tax	72
1668	DIJON	Attempt to raise a "lanturelu"	72
1672	DIJON	Insult over troop lodgings	33
1672	AGEN	Crowd looks at placard	62
1674	BORDEAUX	Seditious bills prosecuted	146
1675	GRENOBLE	Notary agitates during grain crisis	41
1675	BORDEAUX	Uprising against pewter and stamp tax	146–57
1675	RENNES	Tax uprising and mutiny against troops	159–70
1675	WEST COAST	Various stamped paper riots	158

Select bibliography

Focus is on urban forms of protest, not on urban institutions or political culture. For histories of individual towns, see footnotes.

METHODOLOGY, GENERAL SYNTHESIS, CLASSIC WORKS

Bercé, Yves-Marie, "Les femmes dans les révoltes populaires," in *La femme à l'époque moderne: Colloque 1984, Bulletin de l'Association des historiens modernistes des universités* (Paris, 1985), pp. 57–64.

Fête et révolte: des mentalités populaires du XVIe au XVIIIe siècle. Paris, 1976.

Histoire des Croquants: étude des soulèvements populaires au XVIIe siècle dans le sud-ouest de la France. 2 vols. Geneva, 1974.

History of Peasant Revolts: the Social Origins of Rebellion in Early Modern France, tr. Amanda Whitmore. Ithaca, NY, 1990 [abridgment of *Histoire des Croquants*].

"La mobilité sociale, argument de révolte," *XVIIe siècle* 122 (1979), 61–71.

"Signification politique des révoltes populaires du XVIIe siècle," in *Les révolutions françaises,* ed. by Frédéric Bluche and Stéphane Rials. Paris, 1989.

Bernard, Leon, "French Society and Popular Uprisings under Louis XIV," *French Historical Studies* 3 (1963–4), 454–74.

Bouton, Cynthia A., *The Flour War: Gender, Class and Community in Late Ancien Regime French Society.* University Park, PA, 1993.

Briggs, Robin, "Popular Revolt in its Social Context," in *Communities of Belief: Cultural and Social Tension in Early Modern France.* (Oxford, 1989), pp. 106–77.

Chartier, Roger, "Culture populaire et culture politique dans l'ancien régime: quelques réflexions," in Keith Michael Baker (ed.), *The Political Culture of the Old Regime* [vol. I of *The French Revolution and the Creation of Modern Political Culture*] (Oxford, 1987), pp. 243–58.

Chevalier, Bernard, *Les bonnes villes de France du XIVe au XVIe siècle.* Paris, 1982.

Cobb, Richard, *The Police and the People: French Popular Protest 1789–1820.* Oxford, 1970.

Coveney, P. J. (ed.), *France in Crisis 1620–1675.* Totowa, NJ, 1977 [translations of basic essays from the Mousnier–Porchnev debate].

Davis, Natalie Zemon, *Society and Culture in Early Modern France.* Stanford, 1975.

Foisil, Madeleine, *La révolte des Nu-pieds et les révoltes normandes de 1639.* Paris, 1970.

Gately, Michael O., A. Lloyd Moote, and J. Wills, "Seventeenth-Century Peasant 'Furies': Some Problems of Comparative History," *Past and Present* 51 (1971), 63–80.

Hincker, François, *Les français devant l'impôt sous l'ancien régime*. Paris, 1971.

Jouanna, Arlette, *Le devoir de révolte: la noblesse française et la gestation de l'état moderne, 1559–1661*. Paris, 1989.

Jouhaud, Christian, "Révoltes et contestations d'ancien régime," in André Burguière and Jacques Revel (eds.), *L'état et les conflits* [vol. III of *Histoire de la France*] (Paris, 1990), pp. 21–99.

Kettering, Sharon, *Judicial Politics and Urban Revolt in Seventeenth-Century France: the Parlement of Aix, 1629–1659*. Princeton, 1978.

Kierstead, Raymond F. (ed.), *State and Society in Seventeenth-Century France*. New York, 1975 [contains translations of leading French articles on revolts].

Lefebvre, Georges, *The Great Fear of 1789: Rural Panic in Revolutionary France*, tr. Joan White. Princeton, 1973.

Lemarchand, Guy, "Les soulèvements populaires en France au XVIIe siècle," *La pensée*, nouv. série 121 (1965), 109–19.

Le Roy Ladurie, Emmanuel, *Carnival in Romans*, tr. Mary Feeney. New York, 1979.

"Révoltes et contestations rurales en France de 1675 à 1788," *Annales ESC* 29 (1974), 6–22.

Ligou, Daniel, "Les soulèvements populaires en France de 1623 a 1648," *Revue d'histoire économique et sociale* 42 (1964), 378–85.

Mandrou, Robert, *Classes et luttes de classes en France au début du XVIIe siècle*. Messina-Florence, 1965.

"Vingt ans après, ou une direction de recherches fécondes: les révoltes populaires en France au XVIIe siècle," *Revue historique* 242 (1969), 29–40.

McClelland, J. S., *The Crowd and the Mob from Plato to Canetti*. London, 1989.

McPhail, Clark, *The Myth of the Madding Crowd*. New York, 1991.

Moscovici, Serge, *The Age of the Crowd: a Historical Treatise on Crowd Psychology*. Cambridge, 1985.

Mousnier, Roland, "Les mouvements populaires en France au XVIIe siècle," *Revue des travaux de l'Académie des sciences morales et politiques* (1962), 28–43.

Peasant Uprisings in Seventeenth-Century France, Russia, and China, tr. Brian Pearce. New York, 1970.

"Recherches sur les soulèvements populaires en France avant la Fronde," *Revue d'histoire moderne et contemporaine* 5 (1958), 81–113.

Nicolas, Jean (ed.), *Mouvements populaires et conscience sociale, XVIe–XIXe siècles* [*Actes du colloque de Paris 2–26 mai 1984*]. Paris, 1985 [a major collection of essays].

Pillorget, René, *Les mouvements insurrectionnels de Provence entre 1596 et 1715*. Paris, 1975.

Porchnev, Boris, *Les soulèvements populaires en France de 1623 a 1648*. Paris, 1963 [translation of a work published in Russian in 1948 and in German in 1954].

Ranum, Orest, "Revolts and community in 17th-century Provence and Périgord," [review of Pillorget and Bercé] *Journal of Interdisciplinary History* 8 (1977), 329–41.

Révolte et société [*Actes du IVe colloque d'histoire au présent, Paris, mai 1988*], 2 vols. Paris, 1989.

Rudé, George, *The Crowd in the French Revolution*. Oxford, 1959.

Ideology and Popular Protest. New York, 1980.

Salmon, J. H. M., "Venality of Office and Popular Sedition in Seventeenth-Century France: a Review of a Controversy," *Past and Present* 37 (1967), 21–43.

Scott, James C., *Domination and the Arts of Resistance: Hidden Transcripts*. New Haven, 1990.

The Moral Economy of the Peasant: Rebellion and Subsistence in Southeast Asia. New Haven, 1976.

Weapons of the Weak: Everyday Forms of Peasant Resistance. New Haven, 1985.

Soboul, Albert, *The Sans-Culottes: the Popular Movement and Revolutionary Government, 1793–1794*, tr. Remy Inglis Hall. Princeton, 1980.

Tarrow, Sidney, *Power in Movement: Social Movements, Collective Action and Politics*. Cambridge, 1994.

Thompson, E. P., *Customs in Common: Studies in Traditional Popular Culture*. New York, 1993.

Tilly, Charles, *The Contentious French: Four Centuries of Popular Struggle*. Cambridge, MA, 1986.

Tilly, Louise, "The Food Riot as a Form of Political Conflict in France," *Journal of Interdisciplinary History* 2 (1971), 23–57.

Vivanti, C, "Le rivolte populari in Francia prima della Fronda e la crisi del secolo XVIIe," *Rivista storica italiana* 4 (1964), 957–81.

Westrich, Sal Alexander, *The Ormée of Bordeaux: a Revolution during the Fronde*. Baltimore, 1972.

VIOLENCE, GESTURE, MENTALITIES

Audisio, Gabriel, *Procès-verbal d'un massacre: les Vaudois du Luberon (avril 1645)*. Aix-en-Provence, 1992.

Bremmer, Jan and Herman Roodenburg (eds.), *A Cultural History of Gesture*. Ithaca, NY, 1991.

Cashmere, John, "The Social Uses of Violence in Ritual: Charivari or Religious Persecution?," *European History Quarterly* 21 (1991), 291–319.

Castan, Yves, *Honnêteté et relations sociales en Languedoc à l'époque des Lumières*. Paris, 1980.

Crouzet, Denis, *Les guerriers de Dieu: la violence au temps des troubles de religion (vers 1525–vers 1610)*, 2 vols. Seyssel, 1990.

Eleuche-Santini, Viviane, "Violence dans le comté de Nice au XVIIIe siècle," *Provence historique* 28 (1978), 359–68.

"Paroles d'outrage," special issue of *Ethnologie française* 22 (July-Sept 1992).

Farge, Arlette, *Subversive Words: Public Opinion in Eighteenth-Century France*, tr. Rosemary Harris. University Park, PA, 1994.

Farge, Arlette and André Zysberg, "Les théâtres de la violence à Paris au XVIIIe siècle," *Annales ESC* 34 (1979), 984–1015.

Gauvard, Claude, *"De grace especial": crime, état et société en France à la fin du Moyen Age*, 2 vols. Paris, 1991.

Gilmore, David D., *Aggression and Community: Paradoxes of Andalusian Culture*. New Haven, 1987.

Goffman, Irving, *Interaction Ritual: Essays on Face-to-Face Behavior*. Garden City, NY, 1967.

Gonthier, Nicole, *Cris de haine et rites d'unité: la violence dans les villes, XIIIe-XVIe siècles*. Paris, 1992.

Greengrass, Mark, "The Psychology of Religious Violence," *French History* 5 (1991), 467–74.

Greenshields, Malcolm, *An Economy of Violence in Early Modern France: Crime and Justice in the Haute Auvergne, 1587–1664*. University Park, PA, 1994.

Hanlon, Gregory, "Les rituels de l'aggression en Aquitaine au XVIIe siècle," *Annales ESC* 40 (1985), 244–86.

Hufton, Olwen H., "Attitudes towards Authority in Eighteenth-Century Languedoc," *Social History* 3 (1978), 281–302.

Muchembled, Robert, *L'invention de l'homme moderne*. Paris, 1988.

"Pour une histoire des gestes (XVe-XVIIIe siècle)," *Revue d'histoire moderne et contemporaine* 34 (1987), 87–101.

La violence au village: sociétés et mentalités dans la France moderne, 16e-18e siècle. Paris, 1989.

Murguet, Elise, "Violences Beaucairoises au XVIIe siècle," *Bulletin de la Société historique et archéologique de Beaucaire* 24 (1984), 7–10.

Nicolas, Jean, "Une jeunesse montée sur le plus grand ton d'insolence: les tumultes juvéniles en France au XVIIIe siècle," in *Colloque Vizille 1988* (Grenoble, 1990), pp. 137–56.

Parrow, Kathleen A., *From Defense to Resistance: Justification of Violence during the French Wars of Religion* [*Transactions of the American Philosophical Society* no. 83, pt 6]. Philadelphia, 1993.

Peristiany, J. G. (ed.), *Honor and Shame: the Values of Mediterranean Society*. London, 1965.

Pradines-Veys, Anne-Marie, "Violence et comportements populaires à Annappes, Ascq et Flers, 1500–1570," *Bulletin de la Société historique de Villeneuve d'Ascq* (1980), 3–13.

Ramsay, Clay, *The Ideology of the Great Fear: the Soissonnais in 1789*. Baltimore, 1992.

Ranum, Orest, "The French Ritual of Tyrannicide in the Late Sixteenth Century," *Sixteenth Century Journal* 9 (1980), 63–81.

Raynaud, Christiane, "Le langage de la violence dans les enluminures des 'Grandes Chroniques de France' dites de Charles V," *Journal of Medieval History* 17 (1991), 149–71.

Reinhardt, Steven G., *Justice in the Sarladais 1770–1790*. Baton Rouge, LA, 1991.

Verdon, Jean, "La femme et la violence en Poitou pendant la guerre de cent ans, d'après les lettres de rémission," *Annales du Midi* 102 (1990), 367–74.

FOURTEENTH–FIFTEENTH CENTURIES

Avout, Jacques d', *Le meurtre d'Etienne Marcel*. Paris, 1960.

Boudet, Marcelin, *La jacquerie des Tuchins 1368–1384*. Riom, 1895.

Cazelles, R., "Les mouvements révolutionnaires du milieu du XIVe siècle et le cycle de l'action politique," *Revue historique* 228 (1962), 279–312.

Combes, Jean, "Finances municipales et oppositions sociales à Montpellier au commencement du XIVe siècle," *44e Congrès de la Fédération historique du Languedoc méditerranéen et du Roussillon, Privas, 1971* (Montpellier, 1972), pp. 99–120.

Fédou, René, "Le cycle médiéval des révoltes lyonnaises," *Cahiers d'histoire* 18 (1973), 233–47.

"Une révolte populaire à Lyon au XVe siècle, la Rebeyne de 1436," *Cahiers d'histoire* 3 (1958), 129–49.

Lecarpentier, G., "La Harelle, révolte rouennaise de 1382," *Le moyen âge* 2e série 7 (1903), 12–32, 89–109.

Leguai, André, "Emeutes et troubles d'origine fiscale pendant le règne de Louis XI," *Le moyen âge* (1967), 447–87.

"Les oppositions urbaines à Louis XI en Bourgogne et en Franche-Comté," *Annales de Bourgogne* 53 (1981), 31–7.

"Troubles et révoltes sous le règne de Louis XI: les résistances des particularismes," *Revue historique* 506 (1973), 285–324.

Martin, Henri, "Recherches sur le tuchinat," *44e Congrès de la Fédération historique du Languedoc méditerranéen et du Roussillon, Privas, 1971* (Montpellier, 1972), pp. 121–30.

Mollat, Michel and Philippe Wolff, *Popular Revolutions of the Late Middle Ages*, tr. A. Lytton-Sells. London, 1973.

Portal, Charles, "Les insurrections de Tuchins dans les pays de Langue d'oc vers 1382–1384," *Annales du Midi* 4 (1892), 433–74.

Rogozinski, Jan, *Power, Caste and Law: Social Conflict in Fourteenth-Century Montpellier*. Cambridge, MA, 1982.

Thomas, Louis-J., "La sédition du 8 septembre 1381 à Béziers et la légende de Bernard Pourquier," *Bulletin de la Société archéologique de Béziers* 47 (1930), 5–40.

Violence et contestation au Moyen Age [*Actes du 114e Congrès national des sociétés savantes, Paris, 1989; Section d'histoire médiévale et de philologie*], 2 vols. Paris, 1990.

Wolff, Philippe, "Les luttes sociales dans les villes du Midi français XIIIe-XVe siècle," *Annales ESC* 2 (1947), 443–54.

SIXTEENTH CENTURY

Barnavi, Elie, *Le Parti de Dieu: étude sociale et politique des chefs de la Ligue parisienne 1585–1594*. Paris, 1980.

Barnavi, Elie and Robert Descimon, *La sainte Ligue, le juge et la potence: l'assassinat du Président Brisson*. Paris, 1985.

Benedict, Philip, "The Saint Bartholomew's Massacres in the Provinces," *Historical Journal* 21 (1978), 205–25.

Bourgeon, Jean-Louis, "Pour une histoire, enfin, de la Saint-Barthélemy," *Revue historique* 282 (1989), 83–142.

Connac, E., "Troubles de mai 1562 à Toulouse," *Annales du Midi* 3 (1891), 310–39.

Crouzet, Denis, *La nuit de la Saint-Barthélemy: un rêve perdu de la Renaissance.* Paris, 1994.

"La représentation du temps à l'époque de la Ligue," *Revue historique* 548 (1983), 297–388.

Descimon, Robert, "La Ligue à Paris (1585–1594): une révision" [followed by debate with Barnavi], *Annales ESC* 37 (1982), 72–128.

Qui étaient les Seize? Mythes et réalités de la Ligue parisienne, 1585–1594 [Mémoires de la Fédération des sociétés historiques et archéologiques de Paris et de l'Ile-de-France 34]. Paris, 1983.

Deyon, Solange and Alain Lottin, *Les casseurs de l'été 1566: l'iconoclasme dans le Nord.* Paris, 1981.

Diefendorf, Barbara B., *Beneath the Cross: Catholics and Huguenots in Sixteenth-Century Paris.* New York, 1991.

Garrisson, Janine, *La Saint-Barthélemy.* Paris, 1987.

Gigon, J.-L., *La révolte de la Gabelle en Guyenne (1548–1549).* Paris, 1906.

Greengrass, Mark, "The Anatomy of a Religious Riot in Toulouse in May 1562," *Journal of Ecclesiastical History* 34 (1983), 367–91.

"The Sainte Union in the Provinces: the Case of Toulouse," *Sixteenth Century Journal* 14 (1983), 469–96.

Guigue, M.-C. and Georges, "La grande Rebeyne de Lyon, 1529," in *Bibliothèque historique du Lyonnais, mémoires, notes et documents*, vol. 1 (Lyon, 1886), pp. 233–96, 358–83, 417–39.

Heller, Henry, *The Conquest of Poverty: the Calvinist Revolt in Sixteenth-Century France.* Leiden, 1986.

Iron and Blood: Civil Wars in Sixteenth-Century France. Montreal and Kingston, 1991.

Kaiser, Wolfgang, *Marseille au temps des troubles 1559–1596: morphologie sociale et luttes de factions.* Paris, 1992.

Mousnier, Roland, "Structures sociales, révolutionnaires de Paris (1585–1594)," in *Les cités du temps de la Renaissance* (Paris, 1977), pp. 153–73.

Mouton, Léo, "L'affaire de la croix de Gastines," *Bulletin de la Société de l'histoire de Paris et de l'Ile de France* 56 (1929), 102–13.

Powis, Jonathan, "Guyenne 1548: the Crown, the Province and Social Order," *European Studies Review* 12 (1982), 1–16.

Raytses, Vladimir, "Le programme de l'insurrection d'Agen en 1514," *Annales du Midi* 93 (1981), 255–77.

Richet, Denis, "Les Barricades à Paris, le 12 mai 1588," *Annales ESC* 45 (1990), 383–95.

Salmon, J. H. M., "The Paris Sixteen 1584–94: the Social Analysis of a Revolutionary Movement," *Journal of Modern History* 44 (1972), 540–76.

Soman, Alfred, *The Massacres of St. Bartholomew: Reappraisals and Documents.* The Hague, 1974.

Van Doren, Liewain Scott, "Revolt and Reaction in the City of Romans, Dauphiné, 1579–1580," *Sixteenth Century Journal* 5 (1974), 71–100.

Venault, Philippe, Philippe Blon, Joël Farges, *Un soulèvement populaire (Romans 1580).* Paris, 1979.

Weiss, Nathaniel, "L'assemblée de la rue Saint-Jacques, 4–5 septembre 1557," *Bulletin de la Société de l'histoire du protestantisme français* 65 (1916), 195–235.

SEVENTEENTH CENTURY

Ancourt, André, "Nouvelle contribution à une étude sur la révolte des croquants villefranchois en 1643," *Société de lettres et sciences de l'Aveyron* 40 (1972), 411–21.

Aylmer, G. E., "The Ormée and the Popular Movement in the English Revolution," in *Sociétés et groups sociaux en Aquitaine et en Angleterre [Actes du Colloque franco-britannique 1976; Fédération historique du sud-ouest, Bordeaux, 1976]* (Bordeaux, 1979), pp. 95–103.

Bayard, Françoise, "Unité ou pluralité des lieux: la place Bellecour dans la révolte lyonnaise des 17 et 18 mai 1693," *Actes du 114e Congrès national des sociétés savantes, Paris, 1989; Section d'histoire moderne et contemporaine* (Paris, 1990), pp. 71–9.

Beaune, Joseph, "La fin de la Fronde à Villeneuve-d'Agenais," *Revue de l'Agenais* 16 (1889), 511–17.

Beik, William, "The Culture of Protest in Seventeenth-Century French Towns," *Social History* 15 (1990), 1–23.

"Magistrates and Popular Uprisings in France before the Fronde: the Case of Toulouse," *Journal of Modern History* 46 (1974), 585–608.

"Two Intendants Face a Popular Revolt: Social Unrest and the Structure of Absolutism in 1645," *Canadian Journal of History* 9 (1974), 243–62.

"Urban Factions and the Social Order during the Minority of Louis XIV," *French Historical Studies* 15 (1987), 36–67.

Benazet, J., "Le syndic du peuple," [concerns the croquants of 1643] *Mémoires de la Société des amis de Villefranche* 11 (1976), 134–41.

Bercé, Françoise, "L'émeute de 1627," *Bulletin historique et scientifique de la Société académique du Puy* 41 (1963), 185–90.

Bercé, Yves-Marie, *Croquants et Nu-pieds: les soulèvements paysans en France au XVIIe siècle*. Paris, 1974.

Birnstiel, Eckart, *Die Fronde in Bordeaux 1648–1653 [Schriften zur europäischen Sozial-und-Verfassungsgeschichte*, vol. III]. Frankfurt, 1985.

Bonnet, Jacques, "Les émotions populaires en Orléanais au XVIIe siècle," *Bulletin de la Société archéologique et historique de l'Orléanais*," nouv. série 5 (1969), 365–8.

Bousquet, Jacques, "Les troubles de la gabelle en Rouergue au XVIIe siècle et les difficultés municipales à Espalion (1660–1668)," *Actes du 32e et 34e Congrès de la Fédération des sociétés académiques et savantes Languedoc-Pyrénées-Gascogne* (Rodez, 1958), pp. 271–96.

Bouvier, Jean-Claude, "La nouvelle relation de la révolte du Roure," *Revue du Vivarais* 87 (1983), 180–2.

Caillard, Michel, "Recherches sur les soulèvements populaires en Basse Normandie (1620–1640) et spécialement sur la révolte des Nu-pieds," in *A travers la Normandie des XVIIe et XVIIIe siècles [Cahiers des Annales de Normandie*, no. 3] (Caen, 1963), pp. 23–152.

Charay, Jean, "Insurrection du Bas-Vivarais au temps de Louis XIV: une version de la révolte de Roure," *Revue de la Société des enfants et amis de Villeneuve-de-Berg*, nouv. série 42 (1986), 107–51.

Chartier, Roger, "L'Ormée de Bordeaux," *Revue d'histoire moderne et contemporaine* 21 (1974), 279–83.

Chaumie, E., "La misère du Port-Sainte-Marie et la sédition de 1635," *Revue de l'Agenais* 52 (1925), 355–77.

Communay, A., *Audijos (la gabelle en Gascogne)* [*Archives historiques de la Gascogne*, nos. 24–5]. Paris-Auch, 1893.

Coquelle, P., "La sédition de Montpellier en 1645 d'après des documents inédits," *Annales du Midi* 20 (1908), 66–78.

Couyba, Louis, *Etude sur la Fronde en Agenais et ses origines*, 2 vols. in 3 parts. Villeneuve-sur-Lot, 1899–1901.

De Bacourt, "Une émeute à Ligny-en-Barrois en 1618," *Mémoires de la Société des lettres, sciences et arts de Bar-le-Duc* 3e série 2 (1893).

Debidour, A., *La Fronde angevine: tableau de la vie municipale au XVIIe siècle*. Paris, 1877.

Degarne, Monique, "Etudes sur les soulèvements provinciaux en France avant la Fronde: la révolte du Rouergue en 1643," *XVIIe siècle* 56 (1962), 3–18.

Descimon, Robert, "Les barricades de la Fronde parisienne: une lecture sociologique," *Annales ESC* 45 (1990), 397–422.

"Les barricades frondeuses (26–28 août 1648)," in *La Fronde en question* [*Actes du XVIIIe colloque du Centre méridional de rencontres sur le XVIIe siècle, 1988*] (Aix, 1989), pp. 245–61.

Descimon, Robert and Christian Jouhaud, "De Paris à Bordeaux: pour qui court le peuple pendant la Fronde (1652)?," in Jean Nicolas (ed.), *Mouvements populaires et conscience sociale* [*Actes du colloque de Paris 1984*] (Paris, 1985), pp. 31–42.

Dubourg, Jacques, *Histoire des grandes révoltes aquitaines: XVIe-XVIIe siècle*. Bordeaux, 1994.

Foisil, Madeleine, "Un témoignage de 1663 sur la révolte des Nu-pieds: arrêt du conseil du 11 janvier 1663," *Annales de Normandie* 24 (1974), 247–56.

Gallet, Jean, "Recherches sur les mouvements populaires à Amiens en 1635 et 1636," *Revue d'histoire moderne et contemporaine* 14 (1967), 193–216.

Garlan, Yvon and Claude Nières (eds.), *Les révoltes bretonnes de 1675*. Paris, 1975.

Germain, Alexandre, "Les commencements du règne de Louis XIV et la Fronde à Montpellier," *Mémoires de l'Académie des sciences de Montpellier* 3 (1859–63), 579–602.

Goger, Jean-Marcel, "De l'émotion à la révolte: le cas de Rouen à la fin du règne de Louis XIV," in *Révolte et Société: Actes du IVe colloque d'histoire au présent*. Paris, 1988.

"Localisation des troubles rouennais à la fin du grand règne, 1690–1715," *Actes du 114e Congrès national des sociétés savantes, Paris, 1989; Section d'histoire moderne et contemporaine* (Paris, 1990), pp. 105–16.

Gresset, Maurice, "Louis XIV et le soulèvement à Listenois en 1673," *Travaux de la Société d'émulation du Jura* (1981), 181–98.

Groupe ESB (ed.), *Les Bonnets Rouges*. Paris, 1975.

Gutton, Jean-Pierre, "La sédition de Lyon en 1632," in *Mélanges offerts à Georges Couton* (Lyon, 1981), pp. 261–70.

Jolibois, Emile, "Troubles dans la ville d'Albi pendant l'épiscopat de Gaspard de Daillon du Lude," *Revue du Tarn* 9 (1892), 49–61, 135–45.

Jouhaud, Christian, "Geoffroy Gay: une lecture de la Fronde Bordelaise," *Annales du Midi* 91 (1979), 273–95.

"Idées et mentalités d'opposants ormistes (Bordeaux 1651–1653)," TER, Université de Bordeaux III, June 1973.

Knachel, Philip A., *England and the Fronde: the Impact of the English Civil War and Revolution on France*. Ithaca, NY, 1967.

Kossman, Ernst H., *La Fronde*. Leiden, 1954.

Kötting, Helmut, *Die Ormée (1651–1653): Gestaltende Kräfte und Personenverbindungen der Bordelaiser Fronde*. Munster, 1983.

La Borderie, Arthur de, *La révolte du papier timbré advenue en Bretagne en 1675*. Saint-Brieuc, 1884.

Lamarche, Louis, "L'émotion des femmes (Valence, 1644)," *Bulletin de la Société archéologique et statistique du Drôme* 75 (1962), 219–24.

Lavergne, Géraud, "Le capitaine Grellety et la révolte du pariage d'après des documents inédits (1637–1642)," *Bulletin de la Société historique et archéologique du Périgord* 58 (1931), 165–77, 206–17.

Lebrun, François, "Les soulèvements populaires à Angers aux XVIIe et XVIIIe siècles," *Actes du 90e Congrès national des sociétés savantes, Nice, 1965; Section d'histoire moderne et contemporaine*, vol. I (Paris, 1966), pp. 119–40.

Leguai, André, "Les 'émotions' et séditions populaires dans la généralité de Moulins aux XVIIe et XVIIIe siècles," *Revue d'histoire économique et sociale* 43 (1965), 45–64.

Lemarchand, Guy, "Crises économiques et atmosphère sociale en milieu urbain sous Louis XIV," *Revue d'histoire moderne et contemporaine* 14 (1967), 244–65.

Lemoine, Jean, "La révolte dite du papier timbré ou des bonnets rouges en Bretagne en 1675," *Annales de Bretagne* 12 (1896–7), 317–59, 523–50; 13 (1897–8), 180–259, 347–409, 524–59; 14 (1899–1900), 109–40, 189–223, 435–71.

Loirette, Francis, "La révolte des marins du Labourd contre le système de classes (janvier-avril 1671)," in *De l'Adour au Pays Basque [21e Congrès de la Fédération historique du Sud-Ouest, Bayonne, 1968]* (1971), 31–52.

"La sédition bordelaise de 1675, dernière grande révolte urbaine de l'ancien régime," *Actes du 102e Congrès national des sociétés savantes, Limoges, 1977; Section d'histoire moderne et contemporaine*, vol. II (Paris, 1978), pp. 237–60.

Machordeau, L., *Les troubles de Bretagne et l'exil du Parlement à Vannes*. 1897.

Magen, A., "Une émeute à Agen en 1635," *Recueil des travaux de la Société d'agriculture, sciences et arts d'Agen* 7 (1854–5), 196–224.

Marcet, Alice, "Une révolte antifiscale ou nationale: les Angelets du Vallespir, 1663–1672," *Actes du 102e Congrès nationale des sociétés savantes, Limoges, 1977; Section d'histoire moderne*, vol. I (Paris, 1978), pp. 35–48.

Marzaux, Serge, "La révolte des femmes en 1709 à Vaison-la-Romaine: crime, punition, pardon," *Actes du 107e Congrès nationale des sociétés savantes, Brest, 1982; Section d'histoire moderne*, vol. II (Paris, 1984), pp. 305–11.

Mateu, André, " 'Esmotion populaire' de Laplume le 6 juillet 1635," *Revue de l'Agenais* 118 (1991), 211–31.

"Les 'esmotions' populaires au temps d'Henri IV, un exemple: Layrac, 1609,"
   Revue de l'Agenais 108 (1981), 87–104, 255–68.
"Fête et révolte pendant la Fronde à Agen," *Revue de l'Agenais* 105 (1979),
   293–311.
"Les révoltes populaires de la juridiction d'Agen dans leur contexte socio-
   économique." Thèse de doctorat de 3e cycle, Université de Toulouse,
   1980.
Métrich, Jacques, "L'émeute de Chéniers: un exemple de résistance à la fiscalité
   au XVIIe siècle," *Mémoires de la Société des sciences Naturelles et d'archéologie de
   la Creuse* 42 (1985), 310–28.
"Une 'émotion' antifiscale à La Souterraine en 1689," in *Glanes d'archéologie
   d'histoire et de littératures creusoises offertes à Amédée Carriat et à Andrée
   Louradour* (Guéret, 1987), pp. 45–8.
Monsembernard, Guy de, "Une journée d'émeute en 1642 à Aix en Pardiac,"
   Bulletin de la Société archéologique du Gers 90 (1989), 184–99.
Montbas, H. de, *Episodes de la guerre de trente ans: une émeute gréviste des sayeteurs
   d'Amiens*. Paris, 1914.
Moulinet, Daniel, "Les troubles de 1640 à Moulins, d'après la correspondance du
   Chancelier Séguier," *Notre Bourbonnais*, série 10 no. 227 (1984), 285–93.
Mousnier, Roland, "La révolte dite du papier timbré en Basse-Bretagne en 1675,"
   *Actes du 92e Congrès national des sociétés savantes, Strasbourg-Colmar, 1967;
   Section d'histoire moderne*, vol. 1 (Paris, 1970), pp. 325–57.
Niderst, Alain, "Tragédie et conflits sociaux au XVIIe siècle: Corneille et la sédi-
   tion des Nu-Pieds (1639)", in *Mélanges offerts à Georges Couton* (Lyon, 1981),
   pp. 289–97.
Nières, Claude, "Boris Porchnev et les révoltes bretonnes de 1675," *Annales de
   Bretagne* 82 (1975), 459–75.
Patouillet, Xavière, "L'émeute des Lanturelus à Dijon en 1630," mémoire de
   maîtrise, UER, Sciences humaines, Université de Dijon, 1971.
Piasenza, Paolo, *Polizia e citta: Strategie d'ordine, conflitti, e rivolte à Parigi tra Sei et
   Settecento*. Bologna, 1990.
Pierre, Roger, "Une 'émotion de femmes' à Valence en 1644," *Association uni-
   versitaire d'études drômoises* no. 17 (1969), 6–7.
Pillorget, René, "Luttes de factions et intérêts économiques à Marseille de 1598 à
   1618," *Annales ESC* 27 (1972), 705–30.
"Réforme monastique et conflits de rupture dans quelques localités de la
   France méridionale au XVIIe siècle," *Revue historique* 253 (1975), 77–106.
"Vente d'office et journée des barricades du 20 janvier 1649 à Aix-en-
   Provence," *Provence historique* 15 (1965), 25–63.
Poetschke, Robert W. and George A. Rothrock, "The Chalosse Rebellion: a Case
   Study in Seventeenth-Century France," *Canadian Journal of History* 5
   (1970), 1–11.
Porchnev, Boris, " Le soulèvement de Bayonne en 1641," *Bulletin du Musée basque*
   (1974), 1–54.
Pournot, Patrice, "Troubles et révoltes dans la population maritime du Labourd
   au début du XVIIe siècle," *107e Congrès nationale des sociétés savantes, Brest,
   1982; Section philologique et historique*, vol. 1 (Paris, 1984), pp. 125–34.
Rabinel, Aimé-Daniel, "Le mouvement protestant contre l'impôt à Nîmes en

1653: Jean Roux, consul, frère aîné de Roux de Marcilly," *Bulletin de la Société de l'histoire du protestantisme français* 114 (1969), 33–65.

Ranum, Orest, "L'argent du roi; pillage populaire et recherches parlementaires pendant la Fronde parisienne," in *La Fronde en question* [*Actes du XVIIIe colloque du Centre méridional de rencontres sur le XVIIe siècle, 1988*] (Aix, 1989), pp. 287–96.

The Fronde: a French Revolution 1648–1652. New York, 1993.

Rigal, L., "Une sédition à Rodez en 1602," *Procès-verbaux de la Société des lettres et sciences de l'Aveyron* 37 (1954–58), 344–7.

Saint-Eloy, Madeleine, "Une émotion populaire à Nevers causée par la disette, août 1647," *Bulletin de la Société d'émulation du Bourbonnais* 53 (1967), 413–9.

Salmon, J. H. M., "The Audijos Revolt: Provincial Liberties and Institutional Rivalries under Louis XIV," *European History Quarterly* 14 (1984), 119–49.

Sede, Gérard de, *700 ans de révoltes occitanes*. Paris, 1982.

"Une sédition à Rennes sous Louis XIII," *Annales de Bretagne* 85 (1978), 141–4.

Sibassie, D., "Une petite émeute contre le fisc à Gaillan-en-Médoc en 1659," *Revue historique de Bordeaux* 13 (1964), 133–5.

Simon, Gérard, *La révolte du Boulonnais devant la violation de ses privilèges: 1662, Louis le Quatorzième, guerre dite de Lustucru*, ed. by Simon Bouly. Boulogne-sur-Mer, 1983.

Toujas, René, "Les mésaventures d'un intendant à Villefranche-de-Rouergue en 1643," *Actes du 32e et 34e Congrès de la Fédération des sociétés académiques et savantes Languedoc-Pyrénées-Gascogne, Rodez, 1958*, pp. 265–70.

"Une rébellion fiscale des habitants d'Ax-les-Thermes en 1667," *Société ariégeoise des sciences, lettres, et arts* 26 (1970–1), 27–33.

"Troubles à Moulins en 1640," *Notre Bourbonnais* 39 (1963), *Textes et Documents*.

Vasseur, Gaston, "Opposition et contestation à Valines (1684–1701)," *Bulletin de la Société d'émulation historique et littéraire d'Abbeville* (1971), 612–23.

Viard, Georges, "Catholiques et protestants à Langres au début du XVIIe siècle: l'émotion du 21 janvier 1613," *Bulletin de la Société d'histoire et d'archéologie de Langres* 17 (1977), 27–45.

Zeller, Olivier, "Géographie des troubles de découpage urbain à Lyon (XVIe-XVIIIe siècles)," *Actes du 114e Congrès national des sociétés savantes, Paris, 1989; Section d'histoire moderne et contemporaine* (Paris, 1990), pp. 43–59.

Ziegler, Charles, "La révolte des tanneurs de Rouen, 1634," *La science historique* 35 (1956), 47–55.

EIGHTEENTH CENTURY

Barros, Jean, "Une émeute à Carteret (4 juin 1764)," *Revue du Département de la Manche* 8 (1966), 87–90.

Barruol, Agnes and Valérie Sottocasa, "Contestation et vie sociale en Basse-Provence au XVIIIe siècle," *Actes du 107e Congrès des sociétés savantes, Brest, 1982; Section philologique et historique, 1984*, vol. I (Paris, 1984), pp. 125–34.

Bernard, R., "Une émeute dans le Valois en 1775," *Mémoires de la Société Historique et archéologique de Senlis* (1930), 35–148.

Boulanger, Pierre, "Une émeute frumentaire à Châlons-sur-Marne en 1768,"

Mémoires de la Société d'agriculture, commerce, sciences et arts de la Marne 103 (1988), 245–56.

Bourderon, H., "Recherches sur les mouvements populaires dans la généralité de Languedoc au XVIIIe siècle," *Actes du 78e Congrès national des sociétés savantes, Toulouse, 1953; Section d'histoire moderne et contemporaine* (Paris, 1954), pp. 103–18.

Bouton, Cynthia, "Gendered Behavior in Subsistence Riots: the French Flour War of 1775," *Journal of Social History* 23 (1990), 735–54.

Caraman, P., "La disette des grains et les émeutes populaires en 1773 dans la généralité de Bordeaux," *Revue historique de Bordeaux* 3 (1910), 297–319.

Castan, Nicole, "Emotions populaires en Languedoc au XVIII siècle," *Actes du 96e Congrès national des sociétés savantes, Toulouse, 1971; Section d'histoire moderne et contemporaine*, vol. II (Paris, 1976), pp. 223–36.

Cavignac, Jean, "Un épisode de la crise de 1773: l'émeute de Casteljaloux," *Revue de l'Agenais* 99 (1973), 63–70.

Desplat, Christian, "Fiscalité et sédition à Bayonne et en Labourd au XVIIIe siècle," *Société des sciences et lettres de Bayonne*, nouv. série no. 132, 137–53.

Engrand, C., "Mendier sa vie au XVIIIe siècle: de la résignation à la révolte (Amiens, 1764–1789)," *Revue du Nord* 66 (1984), 515–29.

Farge, Arlette, *Fragile Lives: Violence, Power and Solidarity in Eighteenth-Century Paris*, tr. Carol Shelton. Cambridge, MA, 1993.

Farge, Arlette and Jacques Revel, *The Vanishing Children of Paris: Rumor and Politics before the French Revolution*, tr. Claudia Mieville. Cambridge, MA, 1991.

Kaplan, Steven L., "The Paris Bread Riot of 1725," *French Historical Studies* 14 (1985), 23–56.

Lamarre, Christine, "Réticences, refus et révoltes devant l'imposition municipale durant le second XVIIIe siècle: l'exemple bourguignon," *Colloque Vizille*, 1988.

Lapied, Martine, "Les mouvements populaires à Avignon et dans le Contat Venaissin au XVIIIe siècle," *Provence historique* 36 (1986), 325–38.

Lemarchand, Guy, "Les troubles de subsistance dans la généralité de Rouen aux XVIIIe siècle," *Annales historiques de la Révolution française* 35 (1963), 401–27.

Lucas, Colin, "The Crowd and Politics between Ancien Regime and Revolution in France," *Journal of Modern History* 60 (1988), 421–57.

Maillard, Brigitte, "Une émeute de subsistances à Tours au XVIIIe siècle," *Annales de Bretagne* 92 (1985), 27–44.

Nicolas, Jean, "Ephémérides du refus: pour une enquête sur les émotions populaires au XVIIIe siècle, le cas de la Savoie," *Annales historiques de la Révolution Française* 45 (1973), 593–607; 46 (1974), 111–53.

Pillorget-Rouanet, Suzanne, "Une crise de colère des paysans d'Arles: les émeutes frumentaires des 2 et 3 janvier 1752," *Actes du 92e Congrès national des sociétés savantes, Strasbourg-Colmar, 1967; Section d'histoire moderne*, vol. I (Paris 1970), pp. 383–91.

Reddy, William, "The Textile Trade and the Language of the Crowd at Rouen, 1752–1781," *Past and Present* 74 (1977), 62–89.

Rudé, George, "The Bread Riots of May 1775 in Paris and the Paris Region," *Annales historiques de la Révolution française* (1956), 139–79.

Sgard, Jean, *Les trentes récits de la journée des Tuiles*. Grenoble, 1988.

Index